Deterrence under Uncertainty

"These computers give us instant access to the state of the world—troop movements, Soviet missile tests, shifting weather patterns. It all flows into this room, and then into what we call the WOPR computer."

"The WOPR—what is that?"

"It's the War Operation Plan Response. This is Mr. Richter. Paul, would you like to tell these gentlemen about the WOPR?"

>cough<

"Well, the WOPR spends all its time thinking about World War III. Twenty-four hours a day, three hundred and sixty-five days a year, it plays an endless series of wargames, using all available information on the state of the world. The WOPR has already fought World War III—as a game—time and time again. It estimates Soviet responses to our responses to their responses and so on. Estimates damage, counts the dead, then it looks for ways to improve its score—"

—*WarGames* (1983)

Deterrence under Uncertainty

Artificial Intelligence and Nuclear Warfare

Edward Geist

OXFORD
UNIVERSITY PRESS

OXFORD
UNIVERSITY PRESS

Great Clarendon Street, Oxford, OX2 6DP,
United Kingdom

Oxford University Press is a department of the University of Oxford.
It furthers the University's objective of excellence in research, scholarship,
and education by publishing worldwide. Oxford is a registered trade mark of
Oxford University Press in the UK and in certain other countries

Published in the United States of America by Oxford University Press
198 Madison Avenue, New York, NY 10016, United States of America

British Library Cataloguing in Publication Data
Data available

Library of Congress Control Number: 2023930296

ISBN 978–0–19–288632–3

DOI: 10.1093/oso/9780192886323.001.0001

Printed and bound by
CPI Group (UK) Ltd, Croydon, CR0 4YY

Dedicated to my friends and colleagues at the RAND Corporation

Acknowledgments

I am grateful to the Smith Richardson Foundation for funding the Strategy and Policy Fellowship that resulted in this study. While no book can be all things to all people, I hope that readers will find this one enlightening, if perhaps perturbing.

Three of my colleagues who took the time to read multiple drafts of the manuscript as it evolved left a palpable mark on the final version. A conversation with Jenny Oberholtzer led me to the premise that military deception might prove to be AI's "killer app." Drew Lohn complained that an earlier draft cataloged problems while neglecting potential solutions. He challenged me to imagine less dystopian outcomes, inspiring the "tempered case for optimism" outlined in the book's conclusion. Alexis Blanc implored that I find a way to make my mathematical discussions more accessible for a lay reader. This resulted in the relegation of most of the mathematical background to appendices and my search for familiar analogies to illuminate the technical concepts.

Other colleagues contributed directly or indirectly to the development of this book. Paul Davis and Jim Quinlivan shared their insights from their lengthy careers working on nuclear issues and helped me understand how many of these things (as Jim is fond of putting it) have "histories, rather than reasons." Nicholas O'Donoughue helped me grok the nuts and bolts of Kalman filters. Discussions with Edward Parker informed my discussion of the potential and limits of quantum technology for military applications. Conversations with Aaron Frank emboldened me to suggest that computational social science might offer a cure for what ails nuclear strategy. Gavin Hartnett introduced me to LaTeX, which I used to write the manuscript. Marjory Blumenthal read an early draft and offered useful feedback. Alex Wellerstein helped me track down the source of the Neils Bohr quote in the Introduction. Daryl Press, Caitlin Talmadge, and Brendan Green provided the opportunity to present some of my technical arguments in their Military Force Analysis Seminar in 2021.

I should also acknowledge some intellectual debts. This book is, in part, my reaction to the writings of Russian strategic theorists such as Vasilii Burenok, Yurii Pechatnov, and Andrei Kokoshin. My counterparts in the Russophone world opened my eyes to some possibilities outside the usual boundaries of

Western strategic discourse, even if cannot agree with the specific frameworks they champion. I am also indebted to the AI risk community for several of the concepts I repurposed for this study, such as that of an "ontological crisis." While optimal Bayesian agents may not be a practical possibility, they turn out to be a fruitful source of inspiration for the theoretical analysis of strategic and military problems.

I am grateful for Lynn Eden's advice and encouragement, and particularly for introducing me to Roger Haydon. In his role as my developmental editor, Haydon helped me trim down and restructure the manuscript as well as interest Oxford University Press in publishing it despite its opinionated unconventionality. The anonymous reviewers of my book proposal and manuscript at OUP provided invaluable feedback on how to improve the work, as did the editors there. Yuri Vedernikov generously granted permission to adapt the map in Chapter 3, and I am indebted to the International Institute for Strategic Studies for permission to reproduce Table 4.

Finally, I must express my gratitude to the RAND Corporation and its National Security Research Division for enabling this project to come to fruition. RAND provided a unique environment in which I found both intellectual freedom and direct insight into the issues preoccupying the implementers of nuclear strategy. But the views expressed in this book are solely my own and not those of the RAND Corporation or its sponsors, and I bear sole responsibility for any errors it may contain.

Contents

List of Figures

List of Tables

Introduction: Artificial Intelligence and the Nuclear Dilemma

> That would not be necessary, Mr. President. It could easily be accomplished with a computer.
>
> *Dr. Strangelove* (1964)

Why We Can't Have Nice Things

Read what has been published on the subject in the past few years, and you might get the impression that the problem of locating and targeting missile-carrying submarines and mobile missile launchers has already been solved. Paul Bracken suggests that

> Cyber technology is making the hunt for mobile missiles faster, cheaper, and better. This upsets nuclear stability because it opens the door to accurate strikes with conventional or nuclear weapons on the backbone deterrent systems of the second nuclear age, namely, mobile missiles.[1]

Keir Lieber and Daryl Press agree that "In the ongoing competition waged by 'hiders' and 'seekers' waged by ballistic missile submarines, mobile land-based missiles, and the forces that seek to track them, the hider's job is growing more difficult than ever before."[2] Brendan Rittenhouse Green and Austin Long concur: "The United States has invested massive resources into intelligence capabilities for a first strike, including successful innovation in tracking submarines and mobile missiles."[3]

Predictions of this sort are nothing new. In fact, analogous prognostications have been made regularly for more than a century. Yet despite all the technological progress that has occurred over that time, dominant battlefield

---

[1] Paul Bracken, *The Intersection of Cyber and Nuclear War* (2017). URL: https://thestrategybridge.org/the-bridge/2017/1/17/the-intersection-of-cyber-and-nuclear-war.

[2] Keir A. Lieber and Daryl G. Press, "The New Era of Counterforce: Technological Change and the Future of Nuclear Deterrence," *International Security* 41.4 (2017), 9–49, 32.

[3] Austin Long and Brendan Rittenhouse Green, "Stalking the Secure Second Strike: Intelligence, Counterforce, and Nuclear Strategy," *Journal of Strategic Studies* 38.1–2 (2015), 38–73, 41.

Deterrence under Uncertainty. Edward Geist, Oxford University Press. © RAND Corporation (2023).
DOI: 10.1093/oso/9780192886323.003.0001

awareness somehow always seems to be just out of reach. Today, pundits suggest that artificial intelligence is the technology that will finally make this dream a reality. Is this time different? This book argues that the answer is "no" because two of the necessary enablers of situational awareness, information fusion and reasoning under uncertainty, are intrinsically hard. These tasks are not just computationally challenging, they are epistemologically and ontologically imposing as well. In plain language, this means that even if we knew the right question to ask the computer, it would take so long for the computer to find the right answer that we could be waiting essentially forever even with an arbitrarily powerful computer. Yet the bigger problem is that we cannot be sure we are posing the right question, so even if the computer finds a correct answer to the question we asked, it might not be what we needed. Adversaries can, and probably will, exploit this difficulty to thwart would-be "finders" using increasingly elaborate forms of military deception.

For over a century, military theorists have proclaimed confidently that splendid situational awareness is just a few technological advances away. In a notorious 1909 article, Alfred von Schlieffen envisioned the "modern Alexander" as a literal armchair warrior who would exploit new technology to perceive the state of the whole battlefield without leaving the office. In his headquarters safely behind lines,

> in a comfortable chair before a wide table, the modern Alexander has before him the entire battlefield on a map. From there, he telephones stirring words. There, he receives reports from the army and corps commanders, from the observation balloons and from the dirigibles that observe the movement of the enemy along the whole line and that look behind the enemy's positions.

The key tools of this Industrial-Age military mastermind would be "telegraphs, telephones, and signals apparatus [wireless]" along with "fleets of cars and motorcycles, equipped for the longest journey, patiently awaiting orders."[4]

To nineteenth-century military theorists such as Schlieffen, it seemed intuitive that a lack of instantaneous communication had been the main obstacle to situational awareness. During the Napoleonic Wars, messages could travel no faster than the swiftest horse or sailing ship, as had been the case for millennia. Field telegraphs and telephones really represented an unprecedented leap in military communications. The Imperial German General Staff, which Schlieffen had led from 1891 until 1906, embraced the field telephone as a

---

[4] Translation adapted from Robert Foley, *Alfred Von Schlieffen's Military Writings* (Taylor & Francis, 2012), 199.

key enabler of the rapid sweep through Belgium and northeastern France that Schlieffen conceived to inflict a swift knockout blow against Paris. Yet when Schlieffen's successors tried to actualize his vision in August 1914, it rapidly went awry. The Kaiser's General Staff could not keep track of everything on the battlefield despite their telephones and Zeppelins: German armies often advanced faster than the telephone lines could be laid down, and existing lines were constantly subject to enemy sabotage. Technology proved inadequate to salvage the Schlieffen Plan or to preserve Wilhelmine Germany from ultimate defeat.

Four decades later, the introduction of digital computers made it seem, once again, that technology might be about to grant military commanders unprecedented situational awareness. At the dawn of the Cold War, the continental United States lacked comprehensive radar cover. Military and civilian officials suffered nightmares of a sneak nuclear attack from the Communist world that might go undetected until the bombs began falling. In order to detect Soviet bombers and destroy them before they reached their targets, available information would need to be correlated and fused into a unified picture with unprecedented speed. Emboldened by a successful 1951 demonstration of fusing radar data in real time using a digital computer, the U.S. military decided to bet the security of the country on this exotic new technology. At the heart of the Semi-Automatic Ground Environment (SAGE) lay the AN/FSQ-7—an enormous vacuum-tube computer that fused information from multiple sources to direct interceptor jets and missiles.[5]

The AN/FSQ-7 was not merely the first computer used for command-and-control applications; it was the ancestor of innumerable military and civilian technologies—yet it failed to live up to the expectations of contemporary defense analysts. Herman Kahn noted in a lecture at the end of the 1950s that "The capacity of high-speed computer FSQ-7 (used in the SAGE data-processing system) compared to the manual system is today really fantastic, but for a whole series of reasons there has not been a corresponding increase in the effectiveness of area air defense." He admitted that "This has caused some disillusionment among the more sanguine proponents of centralized data processing," but he protested that "this disappointment may be premature."[6] By 1973, prognosticated Kahn, a

---

[5] Rebecca Slayton, *Arguments that Count: Physics, Computing, and Missile Defense, 1949–2012* (MIT Press, 2013), 29.

[6] Although it remained a closely held secret until after the end of the Cold War, the U.S. Air Force assessed that the continental air defense system of which SAGE was a key part would have been largely ineffective at stanching an actual attack by Soviet bombers. Between 1960 and 1962 it carried out three simulations, called "Sky Shield," in which American aircraft mimicked enemy bombers and tried to penetrate U.S. defenses. The results were extremely sobering, with the ultimate conclusion that only one-fourth

startling revolution will have occurred in the field of data processing . . . Data processing, or at least handling information and data at high speed, may not only be improved as an aid to active defense, but it may in the future also turn out to be important in Command and Control for the strategic forces as for the air defense force. The improvements will probably include very flexible computers capable of almost human initiative and perception plus some very effective man-machine combinations.[7]

The 1970s came and went without the appearance of the near-human defense computers envisioned by Kahn, but after the spectacular victory over Iraq in the 1991 Persian Gulf War, senior American military officials confidently announced that computers would soon grant the United States "dominant battlespace knowledge," and with it an insurmountable advantage over its adversaries.[8] Admiral William Owens, the Vice Chairman of the Joint Chiefs of Staff, championed this view. His 2000 book *Lifting the Fog of War* declared that American commanders would soon "be able to see everything of military significance in the combat zone."[9] The admiral's peers concurred: in 1996, Air Force Chief of Staff General Ronald Fogleman foresaw assuredly that "in the first quarter of the twenty-first century, it will be possible to find, fix or track, and target anything that moves on the surface of the earth."[10] But elusive targets somehow stayed elusive in the wars in Iraq and Afghanistan: for all its incontestable technological superiority, the United States military struggled to locate and track wily adversaries exploiting some very basic camouflage and deception techniques.

The first quarter of the twenty-first century will soon be history, yet the ability to find and target anything on Earth remains aspirational. But predictions that technology will soon change this are easy to find. Rose Gottemoeller frets that "Secure retaliatory forces are becoming vulnerable . . . because ubiquitous sensing, paired with big data analysis, makes it possible for adversaries to reliably detect those forces. Even moving targets, such

---

of Soviet bombers would be intercepted despite SAGE and the extensive arsenal of nuclear-tipped Nike and Bomarc antiaircraft missiles fielded over the prior decade. It was perhaps telling that these exercises showed that low-tech countermeasures such as chaff were most effective at confusing SAGE—a weakness that foreshadowed the shortcomings of more modern information-fusion systems. Roger A. Mola, "'This Is Only a Test:' Fifty Years Ago, Cold-War Games Halted All Civilian Air Traffic—Long before September 11 Did the Same," *Air and Space Magazine* 2 (2002).

[7] Herman Kahn, *On Thermonuclear War* (Princeton University Press, 1960), 511–512.

[8] Stuart E. Johnson and Martin C. Libicki, *Dominant Battlespace Knowledge: The Winning Edge*, tech. rep. (Washington, DC: Institute for National Strategic Studies, National Defense University, 1995).

[9] William A. Owens and Ed Offley, *Lifting the Fog of War* (Johns Hopkins Uinversity Press, 2001), 96.

[10] Ronald R. Fogleman, "Strategic Vision and Core Competencies: Global Reach–Global Power," *Vital Speeches of the Day* 63.4 (1996), 98.

as mobile missiles and submarines, may become vulnerable to detection and targeting."[11] Paul Bracken suggests that the long-prophesied epoch of splendid situational awareness is finally at hand because AI and deep learning will enable information fusion for data from many kinds of sensors, with a resulting "synergistic effect."[12]

Is this time different? This book argues that predictions that technology will soon "lift the fog of war" continually fail to come to pass because the underlying problems are intrinsically hard. The problem of taking a wide array of data from diverse sources, part of which may be unreliable, and combining it to build up a best estimate of the current state of the world, is at its heart a form of reasoning under uncertainty. Since the 1950s, artificial intelligence (AI) researchers have sought to make computers reason about uncertainty, as uncertain reasoning is a necessary enabler of many forms of intelligent behavior. Over time, they developed an increasingly sophisticated theoretical understanding of reasoning under uncertainty. Unfortunately, what they discovered was that there is no one "right" way to reason about uncertainty, and that this task threatens to consume astronomical computational resources without any guarantee that we can ever find a good enough answer. The issue is not that computers are "bad" at reasoning under uncertainty or "worse" at it than humans are. The challenge lies in the possibility that one is working from wrong assumptions or incomplete knowledge, and neither humans nor computers can reason with knowledge they do not have.

To understand why reasoning about uncertainty for information fusion is hard, consider a metaphor used by AI researchers studying the task: that of possible worlds. When we have a collection of data and want to determine what it means, we must consider all the different possible worlds that might have produced that information. Even for very simple problems, this collection of possible worlds we might have to consider can be astronomically large—far too numerous to fit in the memory of even the largest computer—and in many cases it is literally infinite. So we have no choice but to rule out some of the possible worlds from consideration, often on the basis of some kind of best guess. But if we eliminate the possible worlds we should be weighing from consideration, we risk drawing wrong conclusions even from good-quality data. Hence why the hardness of reasoning under uncertainty is related only indirectly to the overall amount of data: if all of the data points at only a few simple interpretations, little computation may be required even for immense quantities of information.

[11] Rose Gottemoeller, "The Standstill Conundrum: The Advent of Second-Strike Vulnerability and Options to Address It," *Texas National Security Review* 4.4 (2021), 115–124, 116.

[12] Paul Bracken, *The Hunt for Mobile Missiles: Nuclear Weapons, AI, and the New Arms Race*, tech. rep. (Philadelphia, PA: Foreign Policy Research Institute, 2020), 98.

The difficulty results from the number and complexity of the contradictions the data suggests, not the quantity of data. The possible worlds metaphor also hints at why more data is not necessarily better: while it can help resolve uncertainty, it can also increase the number of possible worlds that might have produced the observed data, increasing the amount of computation needed to reason about it. And if the additional data points away from the correct answer, it can also inspire a decision to prune more correct possible worlds from consideration, resulting in poor-quality decisions. Even arbitrarily powerful computers, therefore, will probably still be vulnerable to deception for much the same reasons as humans are: data and computation are at best imperfect substitutes for knowledge.

Disturbingly, it appears that the tools that AI researchers invented to help make machines reason under uncertainty can be harnessed to optimize military deception. Building such "fog-of-war machines" is an obvious way to offset perceived advances in situational awareness. If artificial intelligence greatly enhances the relative efficacy of military deception, as this book argues, it will probably enable nuclear states to maintain survivable retaliatory forces despite technological progress. But a strategic environment dominated by elaborate forms of deception might transform the role of nuclear weapons all the same. If one cannot be sure what the other side has or what they are doing because those things may be obscured behind AI-orchestrated fictions, can one *really* feel secure?

Some nuclear wars are potentially winnable, but that is generally only the case against exceedingly weak or incompetent adversaries. If nuclear powers continued to posture and operate their retaliatory forces as they did in the twentieth century, new technology probably would make it possible to track and target them.[13] But we have every reason to doubt that any nuclear state will be so foolish as to eschew the possibilities new technology offers to protect their nuclear deterrents in novel ways. And those new possibilities may transform nuclear strategy and the role of nuclear weapons in international relations even if retaliatory forces remain relatively secure.

Geography and physics do more to dictate the way in which strategic nuclear forces are structured, postured, and operated than the limitations of current technology. Therefore, the tasks to which artificial intelligence, machine learning (ML), and automation are likely to be applied are largely things that were attempted during the Cold War, if sometimes without

---

[13] As Colin Gray warned in 1990, "Technology can indeed help disperse the fog of war, but theorists, particularly those with a materialist bias, are wont to forget that new solutions spawn new problems." Colin S. Gray, *War, Peace and Victory: Strategy and Statecraft for the Next Century* (Simon and Schuster, 1990), 111.

substantial success. Emerging technologies could be potentially transformative for nuclear strategy by altering the relative effectiveness with which these tasks are performed. Missions that formerly required manned platforms can be entrusted to cheaper, more expendable autonomous vehicles; human analysts can be assisted or supplanted by automated systems; and computers can now find near-optimal solutions in a fraction of a second to planning and scheduling problems that required human personnel months during the Cold War.

Even though AI, ML, and automation will be applied to tasks familiar to Cold War strategic planners, they may very well undermine our longstanding assumptions about nuclear strategy. Moreover, they stand to transform it in ways that confound our intuitions. Discussions about how technological advances might remake nuclear strategy typically focus on whether these will somehow undermine the offense-dominated strategic environment inaugurated by the introduction of nuclear weapons. In debates about missile defense, it is contended that new technology will make defenses robust enough to defend one's population against an adversary attack, while in debates about counterforce targeting, it is suggested that technology will make disarming attacks effective enough to completely neutralize the adversary's retaliatory force.[14] Proponents of what Robert Jervis dubbed the "Nuclear Revolution," by contrast, contend that nuclear weapons have precluded a return to a defense-dominant world.[15] But these categories are not exhaustive and the future nuclear strategic environment might be neither offense-dominant nor defense-dominant.

Thanks to the growing capabilities of all types of weapons, including nuclear delivery systems, the relative number and abilities of those weapons are becoming less important for the strategic balance. Instead power increasingly lies in the *knowledge* informing the use of those systems. For example, there are many cases where if one does not know where a target is, exploding an enormous number of nuclear weapons would not provide much assurance of destroying that target; but if the target location is known with a high degree of assurance, it can be destroyed with a minuscule, targeted use of non-nuclear force. Artificial intelligence and machine learning are accelerating a long-term trend in this direction. In the not-too-distant future, we are liable to reach an inversion point where nuclear strategy is qualitatively transformed.

---

[14] Lieber and Press, "The New Era of Counterforce: Technological Change and the Future of Nuclear Deterrence"; Brendan Rittenhouse Green, et al., "The Limits of Damage Limitation," *International Security* 42.1 (2017), 193–207.
[15] Robert Jervis, *The Illogic of American Nuclear Strategy* (Cornell University Press, 1984).

While it is too soon to make predictions with any degree of confidence, ML research since the mid-2010s suggests that AI may create a deception-dominant world. Those hoping that artificial intelligence will inaugurate a "new era of counterforce" and make victory in a general nuclear war possible will likely be disappointed. It turns out that the same techniques that might accomplish such feats as finding submarines hiding at sea are also the most powerful tools to thwart themselves. Rather than securing their arsenals by depriving their opponents of a reliable means of destroying them, states might seek security by impairing their adversaries' situational awareness. This approach to assured retaliation will offer scant assurance to either the deterrer or the deterred and therefore threatens to inaugurate a self-reinforcing cycle of mutual suspicion and distrust. In this unprecedented strategic environment, it may prove difficult or impossible to employ the threat of nuclear use for political purposes in the way nuclear-armed states have been doing since 1945, even if nuclear war remains unsurvivable and unwinnable in any meaningful sense.

In a world where nation-states wage war on knowledge, and their weapons of choice are obfuscation and deceit, how does one ever decide "how much is enough?" How will governments ever feel secure? This is the ominous cloud that looms over the future of nuclear strategy.

A Cognitivist Approach to Nuclear Strategy

Henry Kissinger wrote that deterrence "is as much a psychological as a military problem."[16] In this, he did not go far enough. Nuclear weapons are first and foremost tools for getting into the adversary's head. Every strategy incorporates a theory of mind—but that theory of mind is usually implicit, inconsistent, or both. Mainstream strategic discourse is mostly about what weapons one procures and what one targets them at, as opposed to how the opponent's decision calculus works and how to manipulate it. Ultimately adversary cognition is an empirical question, albeit one that stands to be very difficult to resolve satisfactorily.[17] Even so, we are obligated to tackle this question. This book attempts to do so by drawing upon cognitive science and its engineering branch, artificial intelligence. Its "cognitivist" approach aims

---

[16] Quoted in Fred Kaplan, *The Bomb: Presidents, Generals, and the Secret History of Nuclear War* (Simon & Schuster, 2020), 104.

[17] Baruch Fischhoff, "Nuclear Decisions: Cognitive Limits to the Thinkable," in Philip E. Tetlock et al. (Eds.), *Behavior, Society, and Nuclear War*, Vol. 2 (Oxford University Press, 1991), 110–192.

to place *minds*, rather than weapons, at the center of strategy.[18] The theories outlined within are intended not as a definitive account of how nuclear strategy "really works," but rather as a jumping-off point for future investigations. Analyzing the conundrums of nuclear strategy within a "cognitive" framework is hardly a new idea, but this study intentionally takes that premise to unprecedented extremes.

Artificial intelligence seeks to imbue artifacts with intelligent behavior.[19] AI researcher Kenneth Forbus described his field with a comment that "The scientific goal of artificial intelligence is to understand minds by trying to build them."[20] In its more ambitious forms, it aims to create what John Haugeland dubbed "Good Old-Fashioned Artificial Intelligence"—"machines with minds, in the full and literal sense."[21] In their pursuit of these goals, AI researchers have proposed explicit, testable theories of how minds work. These theories of mind can in turn serve as both inspiration and testbed for strategic theory. Adopting an explicitly mechanist theory of mind derived from AI illuminates the relationship between cognition and strategy in ways that informal models of cognition cannot, even if this particular mechanist theory proves to be inaccurate.[22]

---

[18] As Carol Cohn noted in a classic 1987 article, the "technostrategic discourse" of nuclear deterrence "does not allow certain questions to be asked or certain values to be expressed." It cannot describe concepts such as "peace" because "the referents of technostrategic paradigms are weapons—not human lives, not even states and state power." But if "victory" is defined as securing a favorable peace, then this discourse is also incapable of talking about winning. Hence why strategy needs to be conceptualized in cognitive terms rather than impoverished "technostrategic" ones. Carol Cohn, "Sex and Death in the Rational World of Defense Intellectuals," *Signs: Journal of Women in Culture and Society* 12.4 (1987), 687–718, 711.

[19] Artificial intelligence is many things, not the least of which is a really effective piece of branding. John McCarthy employed the term to promote the Dartmouth Summer Research Project on Artificial Intelligence in 1956, and since then seekers after truth and profit in every generation have redefined and reclaimed it for themselves. Pamela McCorduck, *Machines Who Think* (WH Freeman, 1979), 96.

[20] Kenneth D. Forbus, "Qualitative Process Theory," *Artificial Intelligence* 24.1–3 (1984), 85–168, 85.

[21] John Haugeland. *Artificial Intelligence: The Very Idea* (MIT Press, 1989), 2. This is distinct from artificial general intelligence (AGI), which is defined on the basis of its ability to exhibit adaptive behavior *irrespective* of how it works. Many fears about the risks of AGI stem from the concern that it might be so alien as to make it incomprehensible to humans.

[22] Robert Jervis expressed hope in 1985 that "if we can build generalizations about the . . . biases that create deviations from rationality, we can probably use them to replace the rationality postulate in deterrence theories while preserving the deductive structure of the theories and so retaining the benefits of power and parsimony." But because "understanding of psychology and decision making" at that time fell "far short of requirements," a "a full-blown theory" along these lines remained out of reach. Robert Jervis, "Introduction: Approach and Assumptions," in Robert Jervis, Richard Ned Lebow, and Janice Gross Stein (Eds.), *Psychology and Deterrence* (Johns Hopkins University Press, 1985), 1–12, 11–12; A recent study of nuclear policy problems from the perspective of behavioral economics found that the enablers of such a theory have not yet materialized. Anne I. Harrington and Jeffrey W. Knopf, *Behavioral Economics and Nuclear Weapons* (University of Georgia Press, 2019); an argument of this book is that "unified theories of cognition" of the kind championed by AI researchers such as Allen Newell, in conjunction with tools such as cognitive architectures and agent-based models, can have the potential to serve as the foundation of a strategic theory like Jervis envisioned. Iuliia Kotseruba and John K. Tsotsos, "40 Years of Cognitive Architectures: Core Cognitive Abilities and Practical Applications," *Artificial Intelligence Review* 53.1 (2020), 17–94.

This book does not follow the conventions of IR theory because it is not about international relations theory, but rather about the intersection of strategic theory and practice. As Kenneth Waltz argued forcefully in his foundational 1979 book *Theory of International Politics*, a theory of international relations is not the same thing as a theory of foreign policy.[23] This is all well and good, but strategists need theories of foreign policy in order to make good choices. An ideal strategic theory would have many desirable properties. Among other things, it would be:

- descriptive (tell us *why* things happened);
- normative (tell us how things *ought* to work);
- predictive (tell us what *will happen*);
- prescriptive (tell us *what to do* in a particular situation); and
- proscriptive (tell us *what not to do* in a particular situation).

While nuclear strategy has been a favorite subject of IR theorists since at least the 1970s, that field has been preoccupied with the first three of these points and particularly the first two. Indeed, the most eminent works by IR theorists about nuclear strategy, such as Robert Jervis' *The Meaning of the Nuclear Revolution* and Charles Glaser's *Analyzing Strategic Nuclear Policy*, make normative arguments that the United States and other nuclear powers ought to pursue different nuclear strategies than they did.[24] But such a normative argument can be absolutely correct and still be utterly useless to strategic practitioners, who have to try and do what they can with what they have in the flawed world we find ourselves living in. Similarly, a theory that can accurately tell us *post facto* why something happened the way it did is of little use for strategists if it does not tell them what to do about what might happen. Obviously, an ideal theory would be able to predict what will happen, but this seems like too much to hope for.

Instead, a useful strategic theory needs to emphasize the final two points. Firstly, it needs to provide guidance as to what choices should be made in a given situation. This is not the same as being able to predict what will happen: the objective may be to reduce the probability of a disastrous outcome rather than to maximize the probability of a desired result. This leads to the final and perhaps most important property of a strategic theory: that it be proscriptive. If nothing else, we need to have some sense of what not to do. While this book

---

[23] Kenneth N. Waltz, *Theory of International Politics* (Waveland Press, 1979), 121.

[24] Robert Jervis, *The Meaning of the Nuclear Revolution: Statecraft and the Prospect of Armageddon* (Cornell University Press, 1989); Charles L. Glaser, *Analyzing Strategic Nuclear Policy* (Princeton University Press, 1990).

does not define a complete strategic theory capable of these key tasks, it is my hope that it will provide some foundation blocks that can serve as part of the base for such theories.

While self-described "realist" and "constructivist" IR theorists alike have invoked cognitive theory, the mechanist theory of mind I employ differs fundamentally from mainstream IR theory schools because it casts doubt upon the role of shared ideas. Realism generally employs models assuming instrumental rationality, while constructivism typically employs sociological models, but both of these are premised upon some kind of shared ideas. In realism, all states share universal ideas of "state power" and/or "security" and act so as to maximize these. In constructivism, shared ideas are socially constructed and are situated within their historical and cultural contexts.

But just because agents *act* like they share ideas doesn't mean that they necessarily *do* or that ontological similarities are causal. Cognitivism, by contrast, argues that ideas can only exist as they are realized within physically realizable cognitive agents (minds), and that these ideas will have unstable semantics for both epistemological and technical reasons. I argue that these unstable semantics can be manipulated by other agents so as to mutate an agent's value structure, and that this mechanism offers a more comprehensive explanation for strategic interactions than the cost–benefit calculations of classical deterrence theory. One could dub this idea "reconstructivism."[25] Where deterrence theory posits that states try to manipulate each other's beliefs in order to compel them to withdraw, cognitive theory suggests the possibility of changing the way they believe, particularly by confronting them with possibilities that they previously lacked any conception of.

This is not a new idea. In fact, reconstructivism was the original theory of nuclear use in WWII. Senior U.S. decision-makers believed that the shock of the atomic bomb, as an unprecedented weapon, would jolt Japanese leaders out of their unwillingness to consider U.S. surrender terms.[26] The extent to which this theory worked in practice in the aftermath of the atomic bombings is still hotly debated among historians, but it is significant that coercive persuasion is the only empirically tested theory of nuclear use.[27]

Reconstructivism differs qualitatively from tailored deterrence. According to Franklin Miller, one of the primary architects of U.S. nuclear strategy

---

[25] I apologize for this groan-inducing neologism, but it has two advantages: it is fairly self-explanatory while also being too self-evidently sophomoric to appear pretentious.

[26] Alex Wellerstein, *Restricted Data: The History of Nuclear Secrecy in the United States* (University of Chicago Press, 2021), 91.

[27] Sadao Asada, "The Shock of the Atomic Bomb and Japan's Decision to Surrender: A Reconsideration," *Pacific Historical Review* 67.4 (1998), 477–512; Tsuyoshi Hasegawa, *The End of the Pacific War: Reappraisals* (Stanford University Press, 2007).

over the past few decades, the "intellectual foundation of tailored deterrence" stipulates that:

> To deter successfully, the United States must understand an enemy (or potential enemy) leadership's value structure and then make clear, by policy, force structure and exercises, that the value structure would be destroyed—without question—should deterrence fail.[28]

Deterrence, tailored or not, seeks to convince the possible opponent that hurting our interests will not be worth it to them in the end. Either they will fail to attain their objectives or retaliatory action will more than cancel out possible gains. Reconstructivism, by contrast, aspires to change the potential adversary's mind so that he does not want to hurt us. Instead of *threatening* what the adversary values, it tries to *change* what he values to be more compatible with our interests. While persuasion is an obvious tool of reconstructivism, it is far from the only one. When gentler means fail, this objective can be pursued via the application of cognitive violence: the intentional disruption or destruction of minds either human or nonhuman. Even if we deem this unnerving prospect morally abhorrent, and resolve never to resort to it ourselves, we need to be prepared for the possibility that someone might try to do it to us.

Approach and Methodology

To write about nuclear warfare is to engage with pop culture whether one wants to or not. Not just laypeople, but officials and experts typically comprehend and frame their thinking about nuclear war in reference to narratives and tropes from film and television. This occurs in classified settings as well as on Internet message boards. This tendency is a double-edged sword: for instance, *Dr. Strangelove* does a better job of illuminating the conundrums of nuclear strategy than any serious academic text yet written. But many of the fictional narratives informing popular conceptions of nuclear strategy are misleading or downright pernicious. My approach is to work with popular culture where it is helpful, and point out where it is inaccurate when necessary. To do so requires engaging with fictional narratives of nuclear war,

---

[28] Franklin Miller, "Tailoring U.S. Strategic Deterrence Effects on Russia," in Barry R. Schneider and Patrick D. Ellis (Eds.), *Tailored Deterrence: Influencing States and Groups of Concern* (USAF Counterproliferation Center, 2012), 48; for an overview of recent scholarship about how domestic politics affect states' nuclear choices, see Elizabeth N. Saunders, "The Domestic Politics of Nuclear Choices—A Review Essay," *International Security* 44.2 (2019), 146–184.

explaining their origins, and relating them to the historical development of nuclear strategy. This is the subject of the second chapter.

At times, fiction writers can be more insightful strategic analysts than the professionals. In an article entitled "Meteors, Mischief, and War" that appeared in the September 1960 issue of *The Bulletin of the Atomic Scientists* Thomas Schelling complained that "if war is too important to be left to the generals, then accidental war is too important to be left to the novelists. But for the time being they have it; and while few of them have given a full scenario of how war might come about, they have at least been more explicit in public print than the analysts." Reviewing the plots of Nevil Shute's *On the Beach* and Pat Frank's *Alas, Babylon*, he found the former a "caricature" of how a war might start and the latter "impressionistic." He concluded that "for a detailed scenario of how a war might start, or almost start, we have to turn to the paperbacks." He singled out Peter George's 1958 novel *Red Alert* as "one of the niftiest little analyses to come along" of how a nuclear war might begin. According to Schelling, "as a contribution to the literature on war and peace, *Red Alert* not only demonstrates the superiority of dramatic over logical discourse, but by its example indicts a public discussion that has not got beyond 'Prewar Strategy' to chapter 2, 'The Brink of War.'"[29] Schelling was so impressed by *Red Alert* that he bought several dozen copies of the 35-cent paperback to send to his friends and colleagues. As chance would have it, film director Stanley Kubrick read "Meteors, Mischief, and War" reprinted in a British newspaper. Kubrick was inspired to adapt *Red Alert* as a film and engaged Peter George to develop a script. While originally envisioned as a serious thriller, in the course of developing the screenplay Kubrick decided to reconceptualize it as a black comedy. The result was *Dr. Strangelove*.[30]

Unfortunately, few other films and novels compare favorably to Kubrick's masterpiece, at least as texts on the subject of nuclear war. For every *Dr. Strangelove*, there are scores of clunkers like *Damnation Alley*. Filmmakers cannot really be blamed for this situation, as their job is to entertain audiences rather than inform policy debates about nuclear strategy.[31] Sometimes a role in these debates is imposed upon filmmakers against their will, as when the media dubbed Ronald Reagan's proposal to build comprehensive

[29] Thomas C. Schelling, "Meteors, Mischief, and War," *Bulletin of the Atomic Scientists* 16.7 (1960), 292–300, 292–293.

[30] Michael Hill, "Making Sense of Deadly Games," *Baltimore Sun* (Oct. 2005). URL: https://www.baltimoresun.com/news/bs-xpm-2005-10-16-0510140014-story.html.

[31] For example, the two most iconic portrayals of the effects of nuclear explosions on humans in cinema are probably the attack sequence in the 1983 made-for-TV film *The Day After* and that in the 1991 film *Terminator 2: Judgement Day*. The former had to work within a TV budget and censorship, while the latter is a dream sequence that director James Cameron probably intended to be emotionally gripping as opposed to realistic.

missile defenses in space "Star Wars" after George Lucas' wildly popular 1977 film.[32] *WarGames*, while not a bad film by any means, is not a triumph of world cinema like *Dr. Strangelove* either.

The 1983 film *WarGames* is more than just a nuclear-age parable about the importance of choosing high-strength passwords: it encapsulates widely held folk wisdom about the relationship between nuclear strategy, games, game theory, and artificial intelligence. Directed by John Badham and starring Matthew Broderick, the movie is very much a product of its historical moment—the nadir of what would latter be dubbed the "early 1980s war scare"—but both its overall plot about a nuclear-armed computer run amok and its suggestion that game-playing algorithms would enable the creation of such a menace had been pioneered decades before.[33]

The contrast between *WarGames* and Stanley Kubrick's *Dr. Strangelove* is very stark. Critics almost universally acknowledge Kubrick's masterpiece as one of the greatest films ever made, but what is even more remarkable is that nuclear strategists of all theoretical persuasions love it—even those whose views the 1964 film brutally lampoons. I attribute the resonance of *Dr. Strangelove* in part to its subtle and nuanced portrayal of the nuclear policy debates of the early 1960s. Kubrick engaged extensively with leading strategic theorists such as Thomas Schelling and Herman Khan while making the film, and his immortal depiction of the eternal dilemmas of strategy skewers all of the strategists' viewpoints, revealing the inconsistencies and absurdities in each.[34] *Dr. Strangelove* can be read as a straightforward condemnation of the madness of relying upon nuclear deterrence for security, but one can also read it as condemning the committal strategies Schelling endorsed (the risk of making irrational threats credible is that an irrational actor like General Ripper can actualize that threat) or as affirming Kahn's critique of minimal deterrence (in that author's *On Thermonuclear War*, the "doomsday machine" serves as a *reductio ad absurdum* metaphor for the pitfalls of such a strategy). Such is Kubrick's magic that no matter one's perspective on nuclear strategy, *Dr. Strangelove* somehow gets it right.[35]

Instead of embodying multiple, contradictory truths about the nuclear dilemma, *WarGames* instead follows a straightforward narrative that reflects

---

[32] Reagan's Assistant Secretary of Defense for Policy Richard Perle thought that the administration should embrace this appellation, given that "it was a great movie and the good guys win." Janne E. Nolan, *Guardians of the Arsenal* (Basic Books, 1989), 185.

[33] *WarGames* (1983).

[34] Hill, "Making Sense of Deadly Games."

[35] This is not to say that *Dr. Strangelove* covers all the facets of nuclear strategy: it leaves the mysteries of intra-war deterrence and the "stability–instability paradox" largely untouched. But what it does, it does *very* well.

popular myths about nuclear strategy and nuclear war planning. In the world of *WarGames*, nuclear strategists are on a quest to use computers and artificial intelligence to find a way to "win" at the "game" of "global thermonuclear war." This bears scant resemblance to the way nuclear strategy and war planning have ever worked—but it closely follows the way in which science fiction authors and much of the public have long envisioned them. Shortly after digital computers and game theory were invented in the 1940s, the premise that these innovations could be harnessed for military advantage, particularly for nuclear war, swiftly seized the public imagination. Laypeople's confusion is forgivable, however, because the pioneers of game theory and artificial intelligence advertised their approaches as having potential near-term defense applications. A fortuitous coincidence reinforced these misperceptions: the RAND Corporation's unique position at the forefront of theoretical research into game theory, artificial intelligence, and nuclear strategy during the 1950s.[36] The notion that RAND's eclectic approach to the problems of nuclear strategy somehow combined these arcane investigations seemed obvious to many contemporary observers, even though it bore only a scant resemblance to the truth.[37]

Sometimes fictional narratives drive the policy process. After watching *WarGames* at one of his weekend film screenings, Ronald Reagan asked "Could something like this really happen?," by which he meant whether hackers could gain access to sensitive military computers. The answer that came back was "Yes, the problem is much worse than you think."[38] This sparked a process that led to a confidential national security decision directive, NSDD-145, in September 1984. Titled "National Policy on Telecommunications and Automated Information Systems Security," this NSDD established the National Telecommunications and Information Systems Security Committee to oversee what would later be dubbed cybersecurity. *WarGames* also played an outsize role inspiring the introduction of anti-hacking legislation that same year, followed by the eventual passage of the Computer Fraud and Abuse Act in 1986. Sometimes technical experts engage with filmmakers in the hopes of leveraging pop culture to shift policy discussions in a favored direction. Social scientist David A. Kirby dubbed this phenomenon

---

[36] A 1950 book popularizing game theory declared that "In military affairs the theory of games is . . . highly developed and exact. Its application in military science is one of the preoccupations of the U.S. Air Force's 'Project Rand,' which is now conducted by the Rand Corporation." John McDonald, *Strategy in Poker, Business & War* (Norton, 1996), 106.

[37] For examples, see Gerard Piel, "The Illusion of Civil Defense," *Bulletin of the Atomic Scientists* 18.2 (1962), 2–8; Andrew Wilson. *The Bomb and the Computer: Wargaming from Ancient Chinese Mapboard to Atomic Computer* (New York: Delacorte, 1968).

[38] Herbert Lin, *Cyber Threats and Nuclear Weapons* (Stanford University Press, 2021), 26–27.

the "*WarGames* Effect" after the example of RAND computer scientist Willis Ware, who consulted on the development of the film. Ware had long been alarmed by the threat of unauthorized intrusion into defense computers, but authority figures dismissed his concerns until *WarGames* changed the discourse.[39]

This book aspires first and foremost to be useful to strategic practitioners: those who formulate strategic policy and those who implement it. In addition to being a kind of grimoire for wizards of armageddon, I also hope that because of this practical bent it will also provide academics and interested laypeople with a window into what the business of nuclear warfare is like in the present century and where it seems to be going. Unfortunately, very few works in this applied vein have appeared since the end of the Cold War, with the result that academic and policy discourse has sometimes remained preoccupied with debates that have long since ceased to matter and merely distract us from present challenges. This book aims to make an initial step toward remedying these difficulties.

On occasion, I have felt it necessary to include mathematical formalisms to justify parts of my argument. While the unfamiliar symbols and sometimes-complicated expressions may seem intimidating at first, the concepts underpinning them are generally fairly simple, even if some of them are a bit counterintuitive. My method is to keep these formalisms out of the main text where I can and to demystify them, where possible, with visuals or analogies to popular (and occasionally high) culture. Where a relevant literary or cinematic reference cannot be found to illustrate the point of interest, I have endeavored to conceive of cute metaphors with gremlins, robots, and breakfast enthusiasts. Given this approach, why did I not dispense with the formalisms altogether? At times, direct engagement with the formalisms is necessary, and in my judgment it is better to err on the side of caution. My goal is a text at once accessible to the non-technical reader but still substantive enough to be convincing to a skeptical technical expert.

I hope that the reader will forgive me for what might strike some as a frivolous approach to my subject matter. It is not my aim to make light of the horrifying possibility of nuclear war, but in my judgment humor is the best way to make it comprehensible. Nuclear war is neither a game nor a joke, but the only way normal humans can face the enormity and horror of this terrible subject is by leavening it with humor. As Niels Bohr is reputed to have

---

[39] Fred Kaplan, *Dark Territory: The Secret History of Cyber War* (Simon and Schuster, 2016); David A. Kirby, *Lab Coats in Hollywood: Science, Scientists, and Cinema* (MIT Press, 2011).

observed, "There are some things so serious you have to laugh at them."[40] We can only process the sublime by viewing it through the filter of the absurd. This is the secret of *Dr. Strangelove*'s success: it is better than every "serious" nuclear movie because laughter lets us "think about the unthinkable," if only for a moment.[41]

---

[40] Bohr's friend and biographer Abraham Pais attributed several different versions of this phrase to Bohr. Abraham Pais, *Niels Bohr's Times in Physics, Philosophy, and Polity* (Clarendon–Oxford, 1991), 510.

[41] Stanley Kubrick himself may not have appreciated the significance of the film. Marvin Minsky recounted a surprising anecdote about a discussion he had with Kubrick during the making of *2001: A Space Odyssey*:

> Once, later, Kubrick called me to talk about AI, and our conversation drifted to the issue of nuclear weapons and nuclear war. He thought all the disarmament and nuclear nonproliferation treaties were beside the point. Countries as a whole were too reasonable to ever start a nuclear war. The real danger was an accident, or some madman getting ahold of a weapon. Why didn't the politicians realize *that*, Kubrick wanted to know. So I tried to console him and said that he had done more than anyone to alert the world to that possibility through his film, *Dr. Strangelove*. Kubrick was silent for quite some time, and then said, "Oh, I forgot about that."

David G. Stork, "Scientist on the Set: An Interview with Marvin Minsky," in David G. Stork (Ed.), *HAL's Legacy: 2001's Computer as Dream and Reality* (MIT Press, 1997), 15–31, 24.

Chapter 1
The Emerging Strategic Environment

> Well, ladies and gentlemen, I want you to meet Strategic Artificially
> Intelligent Nuclear Transport—or S.A.I.N.T., as we like to call it. If the
> question is survival, then S.A.I.N.T. is the answer. It is, quite simply, the
> most sophisticated robot on planet Earth.
>
> *Short Circuit* (1986)

The Little Yellow Submarine that Presaged the Future of Nuclear Strategy

On March 1, 2018, Vladimir Putin gave a speech in which he revealed Russia's development of exotic new nuclear delivery systems. Except for the RS-28 Sarmat, a large silo-based ICBM intended to replace similar missiles inherited from the USSR, all of the new weapons lacked counterparts that had been deployed during the Cold War. Closest to deployment was the "Kinzhal" air-launched ballistic missile, a version of the Iskander ballistic missile launched from a MiG-31K fighter jet. By exploiting the MiG-31K interceptor as a first stage, the Kinzhal could attack targets up to 1500 kilometers away at hypersonic speed, without violating the 1987 Intermediate Nuclear Forces Treaty because that agreement did not place limitations on air-launched missiles. The Iu-71 "Avangard" hypersonic glide vehicle (HGV) aims to complicate missile defenses by enabling its warhead to maneuver at enormous speeds at the margins of the atmosphere. Westerners paid much greater attention, however, to Putin's declaration that his country was developing nuclear-powered autonomous vehicles as strategic nuclear platforms. The existence of the first of these, a nuclear-powered torpedo with intercontinental range dubbed "Status-6," had been leaked in the fall of 2015.[1] Perhaps the greatest surprise of Putin's speech was a nuclear-powered intercontinental ground-launched ballistic missile. According to the Russian President, this missile would boast

---

[1] Edward Moore Geist, "Would Russia's Undersea 'Doomsday Drone' Carry a Cobalt Bomb?" *Bulletin of the Atomic Scientists* 72.4 (2016), 238–242; "Status-6" was renamed "Poseidon" in 2018. Edward Geist and Dara Massicot, "Understanding Putin's Nuclear 'Superweapons,'" *SAIS Review of International Affairs* 39.2 (2019), 103–117.

Deterrence under Uncertainty. Edward Geist, Oxford University Press. © RAND Corporation (2023).
DOI: 10.1093/oso/9780192886323.003.0002

"tens of times" the endurance of its conventionally-powered counterparts, allowing it to choose a course to its target circumventing adversary air defenses.[2]

Given all the excitement aroused by these Strangelovean horrors, both Western and Russian observers paid considerably less attention to the systems mentioned in Putin's speech that would not carry nuclear weapons. Vladimir Vladimirovich proudly touted that his military had developed a "military laser system," demonstrating that Russia was "one step ahead" of other states in the development of "weapons based on new physical principles." Nor was the "combat laser complex" a mere research project: according to Putin the laser had been in service with the Russian military since the previous year. An associated video clip showed the truck-mounted system driving down the road. Putin beseeched that "experts will understand that the possession of such systems greatly enhances Russian capabilities, particularly in the area of ensuring its defense," but he maddeningly refrained from explaining what the laser was for, ostensibly due to a lack of time.

In the furor over Russian nuclear-armed robots and combat laser complexes, few viewers took note of a peculiar inconsistency in the film clip Putin showed of the Status-6 nuclear torpedo. Part of the computer-generated video showed a small yellow submarine emerging from a hatch in a much larger mother submarine. This inclusion was confusing as the yellow submarine was obviously totally separate from Status-6, differing in size, shape, and color. In fact the yellow submarine was another project of the "Rubin" design bureau responsible for Status-6, the Klavesin-2R-PM.[3] The Klavesin ("Harpsichord") and the Status-6 are both supposed to be hosted by the K-329 "Belgorod," an enormous converted cruise missile submarine recently completed in the Russian submarine yard in Severodinsk, which possibly explains its inclusion in the videoclip. Yet even if this was an accident, it was a fortuitous one—for the Klavesin is just as much a pointer to the future of nuclear strategy, and the role artificial intelligence will play in it, as Status-6.

No one lives on this yellow submarine, for the "Harpsichord" is an autonomous underwater vehicle. It is no way nuclear, and is not even a weapon. Instead it is a sensor platform designed to operate deep underwater, with the ability to carry out its missions with only the minimal external guidance it can receive using hydroacoustic means. Harpsichord is one of a large and growing array of exotic instruments Russia has created in an

---

[2] V. V. Putin, *Poslanie Prezidenta Federal'nomu Sobraniiu* (2018). URL: http://kremlin.ru/events/president/news/56957.

[3] Anna Iudina, *Gid po samym sekretnym podvodnym robotam Rossii* (2018). URL: https://tass.ru/armiya-i-opk/5402375.

apparent quest to establish an extensive sensor network in the Arctic and to counter U.S. Navy efforts to project power into the bastions where Russia typically operates its nuclear missile submarines. The Klavesin-2R-PM is one of the more obvious elements of a Russian effort to ensure that U.S. capability for strategic anti-submarine warfare will be neutralized for the foreseeable future.[4]

Moscow's determination to assure its retaliatory capability is survivable is not limited to exotic new weapons like Status-6. Considerable, and possibly larger, efforts are being made in proactive measures to neutralize American counterforce capabilities, including some that are at present merely aspirational. As it turns out, the combat laser, which was dubbed "Peresvet" in the public contest to name the new weapons systems Putin announced in his speech, is another weapon intended to counter U.S. military might by eroding its situational awareness rather than by destroying its weapons. By mid-2018 it became apparent that Peresvet is deployed at or near Russia's mobile ICBM bases, and that the system seems intended to move along with them when they disperse into the countryside. The head of the Russian General Staff stated in 2019 that the system had been deployed along with mobile ICBM units "with the aim of hiding their maneuvers."[5] Peresvet is apparently a blinding laser weapon targeted at American reconnaissance satellites and unmanned aerial vehicles (UAVs).[6] Despite its considerable size, it probably has scant ability to cause permanent damage to these assets, but it does not need to in order to accomplish its mission. By preventing the United States from detecting the initial launch of the ICBMs, Peresvet would deprive U.S. missile defense of crucial minutes and undermine its effectiveness; should it degrade U.S. ability to track the movement of the missiles, it would sap the prospects that the ICBMs could be destroyed in a preemptive strike.

The Emerging Future

The nuclear dilemma is no longer what it was in the twentieth century. The Cold War world was overwhelmingly bipolar. Even though nine states had declared or de facto nuclear weapons capability by 1991, the superpowers

---

[4] Dmitrii Iurov, *Okazalis' v pogruzhenii: na chto sposobny rossiiskie podvodnye bespilotniki. Pochemu novye boevye submariny VMF Rossii vyzvali azhiotazh sredi voennykh ekspertov NATO* (2018). URL: https://iz.ru/817694/dmitriiiurov/okazalis-v-pogruzheniina-chto-sposobny-rossiiskiepodvodnye-bespilotniki.

[5] Aleksei Zakvasin and Elizabeta Komarova, "*Mgnovennoe porazheniia tseli*": kakimi vozmozhnostiami obladaet rossiiskii boevoi lazer "Peresvet" (Dec. 2019). URL: https://russian.rt.com/russia/article/699378-peresvet-lazerboevoe-dezhurstvo.

[6] bmpd. *Lazernye kompleksy 'Peresvet' zastupili na opytno-boevoe dezhurstvo* (2018). URL: https://bmpd.livejournal.com/3442101.html.

boasted overwhelmingly greater nuclear and conventional military might than their lesser rivals. Moreover, until the late Cold War every lesser nuclear state with the exception of China was an ally of a superpower.[7] In the 1970s, every nuclear state other than the Soviet Union considered Moscow its likeliest opponent in a nuclear war, establishing a straightforward (if sometimes dangerous) strategic dynamic. China successfully played the two superpowers against each other to dissuade either of them (but more immediately Moscow) from believing it could attack Mao's regime without the other superpower becoming involved. None of the minor nuclear powers could hope to accomplish much more than a token retaliation against either superpower, both of which had tens of thousands of warheads relative to the mere few hundred fielded by the U.K., France, and China.[8] While the Soviet economy was a mere fraction of the size of its American counterpart, the USSR was still the world's second-largest economy until Japan surpassed it in the early 1980s, and central planning directed a disproportionate share of Soviet GDP to the military.

This is not to say that deterrence was easy or simple in the Cold War environment. Neither the United States nor the Soviet Union felt particularly secure, as both sought paths to attain either local or global strategic advantage. The United States was constrained by allies with enough resources to pursue partially independent deterrence policies, such as France, and allies such as Germany that demanded NATO embrace different policies than Washington preferred. The Soviet Union, meanwhile, had a slew of allies that served more to drain Moscow's resources than to bolster them. Both superpowers sought ways to prevail in either limited or central nuclear wars, but due to the herculean efforts of their adversaries these failed to render much usable leverage. The inability of states to employ nuclear force for military advantage was an *engineered* feature of the Cold War environment, rather than an intrinsic feature of nuclear weapons.

The emerging strategic environment is qualitatively different from that during the Cold War. Most importantly, there are more strategic actors, and those actors are more evenly matched. As of this writing, there are nine nuclear powers. There is still a marked difference between the U.S. and Russia, which have thousands of weapons compared to the few hundred in most of the other six nuclear powers' arsenals, but now American and Russian

---

[7] The nine nations with at least nominal nuclear weapons capability in 1991 were the same as today with the exception of North Korea, which had yet to develop it, and with the addition of South Africa, which dismantled its nuclear weapons after the end of Apartheid.

[8] Obviously, a few score hydrogen bombs was hardly "token" except in comparison to the gargantuan superpower arsenals.

arsenals are merely dozens rather than hundreds of times as large as those of their lesser rivals. Russia maintains this large nuclear arsenal despite being a relatively minor player in the global economy. China, meanwhile, has much greater economic than nuclear military power, and has the potential to pose a more capable military threat to U.S. interests than the old USSR did given sufficient will on the part of its leaders. The growing disconnect between economic resources and nuclear weapons capabilities extends to the minor nuclear powers. North Korea, whose gross national product compares unfavorably to many subsaharan African nations, has managed to develop thermonuclear warheads and mobile ICBMs to deliver them. The increasing number of nuclear weapons states encompasses several regional rivalries that interact with each other only indirectly. The most important of these is the regional arms race between India and Pakistan, neither of which is a close ally of the U.S. or Russia.

Technology has also changed in ways that have rendered Cold War-era strategic assumptions obsolete. The straightforward path to a limited retaliatory force that seemed apparent fifty years ago no longer exists, at least for lesser powers. This is due to increasingly accurate and flexible delivery systems as well as some coincidental facts of geography that make Russian and Chinese SSBNs much more vulnerable to U.S. antisubmarine warfare than the reverse.[9] The Russians and the Chinese feel hard-pressed merely to ensure the survivability of their retaliatory forces against a full-scale U.S. attack. Aspiring to meaningful counterforce capabilities against the United States like the USSR did is a distant dream at most and one that is not consistent with ongoing patterns in Russian and Chinese defense procurement.

None of the United States' potential adversaries are inclined to play by the Cold War rules. No one should be surprised by this, given that the United States won the Cold War. The Russians and the Chinese would have to be genuinely stupid to repeat the mistakes of twentieth-century Communist leaders and approach strategic nuclear competition the same way they did. As a consequence, the United States and its allies cannot expect to prevail by simply resorting to the same strategies they successfully employed during the Cold War.

The relative importance of limited nuclear use scenarios is among the most controversial aspects of the emerging strategic environment. Some analysts are highly skeptical of the very notion of limited nuclear war, holding to an almost religious conviction that any use of nuclear weapons will rapidly and inevitably escalate to general war. At the same time, other analysts have

---

[9] See Ch. 3 of this volume.

become convinced that potential adversaries, such as Russia, plan to threaten or engage in limited nuclear use. The reality is more complicated, and in some ways more disturbing, than any of the simplistic views currently predominant in Western discourse. In the real world of military procurement, the Russians are deploying dual-capable theater-range systems such as the Iskander and SSC-8 missiles. It has been argued that these systems are primarily envisioned for conventional roles, but available stockpiles of them are woefully inadequate for a large-scale conventional conflict with NATO.[10]

To the extent that Russia actually plans on fighting a nuclear war, as opposed to merely threatening assured retaliation, it is for a limited nuclear war. But the limited nuclear war that the Russians seem to be preparing for is very different than the one Westerners usually seem to imagine in their speculations about "escalate to de-escalate."[11] In the envisioned scenarios, the Russians attempt to salvage their position when facing conventional defeat by employing a nuclear demonstration strike or a low-yield attack on NATO forces in the region.[12] But as Nikolai Sokov has noted, the limited nuclear employment scenarios practiced in Russian exercises were neither low-yield nor necessarily limited to their own region.[13]

Moreover, unlike during the Cold War, when the two superpowers had rigged Central Europe into a thermonuclear powder keg, limited nuclear attacks could accrue significant military benefits for the Russians in the context of certain conflicts with NATO. The destruction of critical facilities supporting U.S. conventional attacks targeting Russian territory might require a very modest number of nuclear weapons and would cripple NATO and U.S. ability to project conventional force into Russia, leaving Western leaders with a stark choice between escalation to strategic nuclear war—with the prospect of being struck with Moscow's increasingly diverse arsenal of "assured retaliation" weapons in response—or accepting terms.[14] In short,

---

[10] Bruno Tertrais, "Russia's Nuclear Policy: Worrying for the Wrong Reasons," *Survival* 60.2 (2018), 33–44; Susanne Oxenstierna et al., *Russian Military Capability in a Ten-Year Perspective – 2019*, tech. rep. (FOI, 2019), 37.

[11] Anya Fink and Micheal Kofman, *Russian Strategy for Escalation Management: Key Debates and Players in Military Thought*, tech. rep. (CNA, 2020); Micheal Kofman, Anya Fink, and Jeffrey Edmonds, *Russian Strategy for Escalation Management: Evolution of Key Concepts*, tech. rep. (CNA, 2020).

[12] Dave Johnson, *Nuclear Weapons in Russia's Approach to Conflict* (Fondation pour la Recherche Stratégique, 2016); Dave Johnson, *Russia's Conventional Precision Strike Capabilities, Regional Crises, and Nuclear Thresholds*, tech. rep. (Lawrence Livermore National Lab.(LLNL), Livermore, CA, 2018).

[13] Nikolai N. Sokov, "Why Russia Calls a Limited Nuclear Strike 'de-escalation,'" *Bulletin of the Atomic Scientists* 13 (2014), 70.

[14] A 2011 textbook about deterrence by two of Russia's foremost strategic theorists commented that "The essence of the concept of counterforce deterrence consists in concentrating the main strike efforts on the destruction primarily of military targets and executing operations in the struggle for the strategic initiative. In view of the known lack of combat capabilities of the modern general-purpose forces of the Russian Federation, practically the only buttress here remains nuclear potential, including the potential

the Russians have good military reasons to invest in non-strategic nuclear weapons (NSNW)—these systems are the Kremlin's sole hope for actually winning a war against NATO.[15] Moreover, Russian theater nuclear systems such as SSC-8 and Kinzhal complement the "assured retaliation" weapons such as Avangard and the Poseidon nuclear UUV.[16]

Debates about nuclear force modernization in the United States have generally focused on the same criteria that were used to analyze strategic nuclear forces during the Cold War era. The most fundamental of these is that of the role of counterforce in our thinking about nuclear war, in particular how much our potential vulnerability to counterforce attacks should figure into U.S. strategic planning. As the strategic nuclear platforms currently under development are planned to remain in service until the closing decades of this century, it would be remiss not to analyze these concerns. But given that a serious counterforce threat to the survival of our current or prospective nuclear retaliatory forces remains decades in the future, how should we analyze this possibility? The standard tools and methodologies inherited from the Cold War era are inadequate to analyze either the possibilities or the limitations of emerging technologies such as AI to threaten the survival of nuclear retaliatory forces.

The other, more controversial consideration in the development of U.S. strategic capabilities is the question of whether the United States should seek counterforce targeting advantages against its potential adversaries. Should the United States seek "usable" nuclear options, including at the extreme "splendid" counterforce capabilities?[17] For many academic theorists the answer is an obvious "no," even against the most modest nuclear powers. For some defense professionals, however, it seems a foregone conclusion that the United States ought to pursue and maintain every conceivable military advantage. Unfortunately, these debates have not been tempered with rigorous technical analysis of the practicality of limited nuclear use. Both

---

of nonstrategic nuclear forces." Vasilii Burenok and Yurii Pechatnov, *Strategicheskoe sderzhivanie*, pre-publication copy (2011), 150–151.

[15] "Non-strategic nuclear weapons" are nuclear weapons that are not counted as "strategic" under arms control agreements such as New Start. They are defined in terms of delivery system range, rather than by their yields.

[16] Geist and Massicot, "Understanding Putin's Nuclear 'Superweapons.'"

[17] One of the cardinal sins of Western strategic debates is the conflation of systems (weapons) and strategy. This tendency dates back to the early decades of the Cold War, and was a natural outgrowth of the defense budget process. Early strategic analysts at RAND were tasked not with abstract considerations of nuclear strategy, but rather with specific questions about what forces the USAF should develop and procure. While obviously one cannot operationalize a strategy without appropriate forces-in-being, we cannot assume that the other questions of strategy will somehow answer themselves once we decide what weapons to buy. This mentality leads to sloppy thinking and poor decisions, such as knee-jerk reactions to foreign developments that simply try to ape whatever the potential adversaries have.

proponents and opponents of usable nuclear options employed implausible assumptions and inappropriate models.

In a 2017 article in *International Security*, Keir Lieber and Daryl Press argue that technological progress has brought us to a "new era of counterforce." It stated that "For most of the nuclear age, the survivability of retaliatory forces seemed straightforward; 'counterforce' attacks—those aimed at disarming strategic nuclear forces—appeared difficult because superpower arsenals were large and dispersed, and were considered hard to hide and protect." But "changes in technology," particularly those "rooted in the computer revolution," are "making nuclear forces around the world far more vulnerable than ever before."[18] Lieber and Press draw the conclusion that these developments challenge the "theory of the nuclear revolution" championed by Robert Jervis, which argued that the sheer destructiveness of nuclear weapons guaranteed that the possession of a modest retaliatory force would be adequate to deter aggression. Jervis held that intrastate competition for nuclear superiority was irrational because such advantages did not translate into usable military or diplomatic advantage.[19] Lieber and Press have a simpler explanation: "geopolitical rivalry remains logical in the nuclear age because stalemate is reversible." They conclude that emerging technologies have three main implications for nuclear policy. First, nuclear states "need to deploy more capable nuclear retaliatory forces," whether through qualitative improvements, greater numbers, or both. Second, additional nuclear arms reductions are unwise because while improving capabilities or cutting arsenals could promote strategic stability in isolation they create "underrecognized vulnerabilities" in conjunction with one another. Third, the emergence of the "new era of counterforce" raises the issue of whether the United States should continue to pursue improved nuclear and non-nuclear counterforce capabilities. Even though it could stoke adversary anxieties and crisis instability, they conclude that "technological arms racing seems inevitable, so exercising restraint may limit options without yielding much benefit."[20]

In his 2018 book *The Logic of American Nuclear Strategy: Why Strategic Superiority Matters*, Matthew Kroening makes a related argument questioning Jervis' theory of the nuclear revolution. Drawing upon a statistical analysis of nuclear crises, Kroenig finds that the state with the preponderance

---

[18] Lieber and Press, "The New Era of Counterforce: Technological Change and the Future of Nuclear Deterrence", 9.

[19] Jervis, *The Illogic of American Nuclear Strategy*; Jervis, *The Meaning of the Nuclear Revolution: Statecraft and the Prospect of Armageddon*.

[20] Lieber and Press, "The New Era of Counterforce: Technological Change and the Future of Nuclear Deterrence", 11–12, 49.

of nuclear power, measured using a metric based primarily on relative arsenal size, typically prevails. He develops this into what he terms the "Superiority-Brinkmanship Synthesis Theory." Kroenig's policy prescriptions are simple: strategic superiority has been to the United States' advantage historically and should be maintained in the future. Kroenig does "not find any support for the idea that imbalances in nuclear power cause dangerous strategic instability. In fact, if anything . . . a preponderance of power reduces the risk of war. Moreover, . . . US nuclear superiority increases instability that works in Washington's favor and dampens problematic instability."[21]

Charles Glaser and Steve Fetter, by contrast, contend that progress in technology is no reason for the United States to "reject MAD" by trying to maintain a damage-limitation capability against China. They argue "that the United States should forgo efforts to preserve and enhance whatever damage-limitation capability it now possesses" because "China's continuing deployment of mobile missiles has the potential to fully erode U.S. damage-limitation capabilities," even though "in the longer term [this outcome] will be influenced by whether the United States deploys systems that can reliably find and destroy mobile targets." Their primary argument, however, is political rather than technical: "that the value of a damage-limitation capability to the United States is small."[22]

The main downside of all these arguments is that they are disconnected from crises and wars that are likely to occur, instead focusing on contrived scenarios that can be analyzed with the handful of models available to academics outside the defense complex. Unfortunately such studies are not particularly informative because they are based on simplified target sets, which are qualitatively different from those faced by our own and (presumably) adversary war planners. Valid analyses of toy targeting problems cannot be expected to transfer to larger real-world cases including more, and different, targets. For instance, it is trivial to show that if the United States launched a surprise nuclear attack on Russian strategic nuclear forces in their day-to-day alert posture and the Russians attempted to ride out the attack, the expected Russian retaliation might be trivial.[23] But this kind of "nuclear primacy" does not do the United States much good, as it is not usable in an exploitable way. Most importantly, the Russians make no secret that they plan on launching their silo-based ICBMs under attack, and insofar as proves

---

[21] Matthew Kroenig, *The Logic of American Nuclear Strategy* (Oxford University Press, 2018), 142.

[22] Charles L. Glaser and Steve Fetter, "Should the United States Reject MAD? Damage Limitation and US Nuclear Strategy toward China," International Security 41.1 (2016), 49–98, 52–53.

[23] Keir A. Lieber and Daryl G. Press, "The Rise of US Nuclear Primacy," *Foreign Affairs* 85 (2006), 42.

practical in the event, will do the same with its SLBMs in port and its mobile ICBMs on their bases.[24]

Lieber and Press are absolutely right in their observation that "the consequences of pinpoint accuracy and new sensing technologies are numerous, synergistic, and in some cases nonintuitive," and they are correct that we are in a "new era of counterforce." But this new age is not the realization of the visions of Cold War-era counterforce enthusiasts, even though AI may make the kind of nuclear war they envisioned winnable. America's strategic rivals do not have the capability to compete with Washington in pursuing counterforce capabilities the way the Soviet Union aspired to, and even if they did they seem to lack the inclination to do so. For ideological reasons, the USSR sought to develop counterforce capabilities that would enable it to preempt an imminent nuclear strike or blunt an ongoing one. Despite the immense size the Soviet nuclear arsenal reached in the 1980s, it never made much progress toward this goal. And while Soviet missiles were less capable than most U.S. analysts believed at the time, they were far from the weakest link in the system. Soviet performance in other critical areas such as early warning, command and control, and planning compared much less favorably to their U.S. counterparts than their weapons did.[25]

Potential adversaries such as the Russian Federation take the possibility that the U.S. might leverage AI and other emerging technologies to create radically improved counterforce capabilities extremely seriously. For the past several years, Russian military analysts have been engaged in a vociferous debate in the country's military press about the extent of their strategic vulnerabilities. The Russian tendency to overstate current and future U.S. capabilities stokes these anxieties. The Russian military is signaling its willingness to explore extreme departures from the current deterrence paradigm, including some that are only possible thanks to progress in AI. For example, in 2015 the Russian government leaked information about its development of an autonomous nuclear-powered undersea drone intended as a strategic nuclear delivery vehicle. While many analysts believe that this "leak" about the system Putin formally acknowledged in March 2018 was intended to signal Moscow's extreme displeasure at U.S. missile defense deployments, less unorthodox components of Russia's nuclear force modernization program

---

[24] Prezident Rossiiskoi Federatsii, Osnovy gosudarstvennoj politiki Rossiskoi Federatsii v oblasti iadernogo sderzhivaniia (June 2020). URL: http://publication.pravo.gov.ru/Document/View/0001202006020040?index=1&rangeSize=1.

[25] John A. Battilega, "Soviet Views of Nuclear Warfare: The Post-Cold War Interviews," in *Getting MAD: Nuclear Mutual Assured Destruction, Its Origins and Practice* (2004), 151–164.

have features that are undesirable for strategic stability.[26] With its RS-28 "Sarmat" missile Russia is reinvesting in large, MIRVed silo-based ICBMs, a category of weapon it once planned to abandon under the now-defunct START II treaty. The Russians recognize that the ability of the Sarmat to ride out a preemptive attack is nonexistent, so its survivability hinges on an associated active defense system, "Mozyr."[27] This is tantamount to the adoption of a launch-under-attack posture that could place great pressure on Russian leaders to launch first in a crisis, increasing the chances of accidental escalation. The Russian decision to revert to heavy silo-based ICBMs signals a belief that the survivability advantages of mobile ICBMs are eroding, in part due to capabilities enabled by advanced AI.

Well apprised of how fruitless the USSR's attempt to chase counterforce proved, Vladimir Putin has wisely decided that "the only way to win is not to play." He declared in an October 2018 speech that his country lacks a "preventative" (*preventivnyi*) nuclear strike option.[28] This phrasing caused much argument among Western observers due to confusion as to whether *preventivnyi* meant something closer to what Western strategists term "preemptive" than "preventative" strikes. But this term had a specific meaning in Soviet and later Russian nuclear war planning that is probably the one the Russian president meant in this context. Soviet military writers drew a sharp distinction between the *preventivnyi* strike that the West might unleash upon the USSR and the "preemptive" (*uprezhdaiushchii*) strike the Soviet Union would immediately unleash to minimize the resulting damage.[29] Post-Soviet memoir literature, however, employs the two terms somewhat interchangeably.

While starting in the early 1960s U.S. nuclear war planners sought to provide the American president with an ever-wider variety of different nuclear strike options, their Soviet counterparts are reported to have planned for only three. The first of these was the *uprezhdaiushchii/preventivnyi* strike (*udar*), which sought to use counterforce strikes as a damage limitation measure. The second was the *otvetno-vstrechnyi udar* (launching-meeting strike) which sought to launch under attack in order to ensure that a U.S. attempt at a

[26] Igor Sutyagin, "Russia's Underwater 'Doomsday Drone': Science Fiction, But Real Danger," *Bulletin of the Atomic Scientists* 72.4 (2016), 243–246; Geist, "Would Russia's Undersea 'Doomsday Drone' Carry a Cobalt Bomb?"

[27] Geist and Massicot, "Understanding Putin's Nuclear 'Superweapons'," 114.

[28] *Putin: v rossiiskoi kontseptsii primeneniia iadernogo oruzhiia net preventivnogo udara* (2018). URL: https://tass.ru/politika/5691255.

[29] Raymond L. Garthoff, *The Soviet Image of Future War* (Public Affairs Press, 1959), 65.

disarming strike would fail.[30] The launching-meeting strike included a combination of "counterforce" and "countervalue" targets, although their relative emphasis is unclear and probably varied over time—presumably there was some hope of damage limitation but the forces devoted to this goal depended on how much of the U.S. strategic forces Soviet planners anticipated the Americans would hold in reserve. The final, least-preferred option was the *otvetnyi udar* (retaliatory strike). Even if the theoretical elegance of minimal deterrence strategies appealed to Soviet leaders, they doubted the survivability of their retaliatory forces.[31] Soviet missile silos, which contained the missiles comprising the bulk of the USSR's strategic forces, were apparently less robust than U.S. analysts thought, and U.S. anti-submarine warfare seriously challenged the survivability of Soviet SSBNs that had to transit Western sensor nets en route to their patrol zones in the Atlantic.[32] The Soviet intercontinental bomber force, meanwhile, was modest compared to its American counterpart. One Soviet late Cold War analysis is reported to have found that less than 3% of Soviet strategic forces would survive a U.S. disarming strike.[33]

Putin's 2018 statement at Valdai suggests that his government has abandoned the *preventivnyi udar* to focus all its energies on the *otvetnovstrechnyi* and *otvetnyi* strike options. Some will argue that we ought not take Putin at his word, and they may be right, but his government's defense procurement patterns match his rhetoric. The "Principles of the State Nuclear Deterrence Policy of the Russian Federation" published by Putin's government in June 2020 is also consistent with this interpretation.[34] The *uprezhdaiushchii/preventivnyi udar* the Soviet military planned for demanded thousands of accurate warheads to destroy U.S. strategic forces before they could be launched, and by the late 1970s its arsenal was of a scale commensurate with these tasks, even if the qualitative characteristics of its weapons were not. Today, however, the U.S. and Russian arsenals have diverged in ways that make a large-scale counterforce attack on U.S. strategic forces an implausible objective for the Russians.

While the New Start framework stipulates that the two countries are limited to the same number of "reportable" warheads, and each country

---

[30] Launch-on-warning would obviously have been preferred but could not be counted on because of the USSR's geographic position: while Canada served as a buffer for the United States and hosted early warning radars, the USSR was located too far north.

[31] Battilega, "Soviet Views of Nuclear Warfare: The post-Cold War Interviews."

[32] Pavel Podvig, "The Window of Vulnerability That Wasn't: Soviet Military Buildup in the 1970s—A Research Note," *International Security* 33.1 (2008), 118–138; Brendan Rittenhouse Green, *The Revolution That Failed: Nuclear Competition, Arms Control, and the Cold War* (Cambridge University Press, 2020).

[33] I. A. Andriushin, A. K. Chernyshev, and Iu. A. Iudin, *Ukroshchenie iadra. Stranitsy istorii iadernogo oruzhiia i iadernoi infrastruktury SSSR.* (Tip. Krasn., 2003), 182.

[34] Prezident RF, *Osnovy gosudarstvennoj politiki Rossiskoi Federatsii v oblasti iadernogo sderzhivaniia.*

maintains a nuclear "triad" with ground-based missiles, bombers, and submarines, the force structure of the two states is even more divergent than it was during the Cold War. Land-based missiles made up the preponderance of Soviet strategic forces and continue to form the backbone of Russian strategic forces today. But while under Cold War arms control agreements such as SALT both states deployed arsenals with approximately the same number of launchers, today the United States has many more missiles than Russia. Four hundred silo-based Minuteman III ICBMs have been downgraded to a single warhead apiece.[35] Under current conditions these silos pose a significant targeting problem for the Russians. The plurality of Russian warheads are still deployed on aging Soviet-era silo-based liquid-fueled ICBMs such as the SS-18 and SS-19. There are only a few dozen of these missiles, but they represent a majority of the "throw weight" of the Russian strategic nuclear force despite now being well beyond their original design lifetimes. The current plan is to replace the forty-six SS-18s with a new missile, the "Sarmat," which is reported to carry the same number of warheads (ten) as the older system. The Sarmat has been repeatedly delayed, however, and it is unclear when it will supplant its predecessor.[36]

Meanwhile, Russia is apparently retaining thirty SS-19 missiles, and will be deploying "new old stock" SS-19s received as payment from Ukraine in the 1990s as the launcher for the Iu-71 "Avangard" hypersonic glide vehicle (HGV). The Iu-71 is many things, among them one of the few Russian weapons systems with no U.S. counterpart, but it is definitely not a counterforce weapon. In lieu of the four to six warheads historically carried by the SS-19, or the sixteen it could theoretically carry were it fitted with RVs, the mass of those on the RS-24 "Yars" ICBM, it carries only one, which has been reported in the Russian media as having a yield of two megatons. With the Iu-71 the SS-19 is too long to fit in the existing silos originally built for it, so presumably it will be deployed in modified SS-18 silos. The Iu-71's mission is simple: it is an "assured retaliation" weapon intended to use its speed and maneuverability to thwart existing and prospective missile defense systems.[37]

Avangard was the first of the Russians' exotic "assured retaliation" weapons to enter service, but it is neither the last nor the most unorthodox. The nuclear-armed, nuclear-powered, uninhabited underwater vehicle "Status-6" (NATO reporting name KANYON, renamed "Poseidon" by the Russians

[35] Hans M. Kristensen and Robert S. Norris, "United States Nuclear Forces, 2018," *Bulletin of the Atomic Scientists* 74.2 (2018), 120–131.
[36] Hans M. Kristensen and Matt Korda, "Russian Nuclear Forces, 2019," *Bulletin of the Atomic Scientists* 75.2 (2019), 73–84.
[37] Geist and Massicot, "Understanding Putin's Nuclear 'Superweapons'," 105–106.

in 2018) was characterized as such in the November 2015 "leak" revealing its existence. According to a briefing slide "accidentally" shown on Russian television, the goal of this system is to "create areas of radioactive contamination rendering enemy coastal areas unusable for military or economic activity for extended periods of time."[38] While Status-6/Poseidon is ostensibly "multi-purpose" and may be intended primarily for other, less Strangelovean missions, its employment in this role would probably make it the nuclear delivery system with the single highest per-warhead cost ever, as it is essentially a miniature, uninhabited nuclear submarine whose survival mode is speed—the Russians assert it will be fast enough to outrun U.S. torpedoes. As of this writing it is supposed to enter service by the end of the 2027 State Armaments Plan.[39] Status-6/Poseidon is not, however, the wildest of the Russians' announced new strategic nuclear delivery systems. The 9M730 "Burevestnik" is a ground-launched, nuclear-powered intercontinental GLCM that has been undergoing testing in the Russian arctic. Both of these systems are in some ways the ultimate "killer robots": in their nuclear retaliation role they would have to resort to autonomy to evade enemy defenses en route to their targets.

If the Russians were still playing by the Cold War rules of nuclear strategic competition, their plans for the modernization of the strategic nuclear forces would look totally different. Instead of throwing their finite resources into exotic, high-risk systems like Avangard and Burevestnik, they would follow the time-tested Cold War approach to neutralizing U.S. missile defenses: overwhelming them with more RVs. Additional Sarmat missiles could carry these warheads, as could additional Yars mobile ICBMs. Should New Start expire in 2026 with no follow-on agreement, the treaty obligations forbidding this approach would no longer apply, and it would be technically simpler and very possibly cheaper than the route the Russians are taking. Without constraints on warhead availability, the Minuteman "warhead sink" would cease to be a serious challenge for Russian targeteers. Thanks to the improved accuracy of Russian ICBMs, only about 800 warheads would be needed to target the 400 silos, and only relatively light low-yield RVs would be necessary. A few dozen additional Sarmat missiles would suffice for this purpose, which

---

[38] Geist, "Would Russia's Undersea 'Doomsday Drone' Carry a Cobalt Bomb?"

[39] There are rumors on Russian-language discussion forums that one of the other missions of Status-6/Poseidon is the delivery of submunitions such as Kalibr SLCMs or the Tsirkon hypersonic anti-ship missile. If so, this system makes much more sense than Westerners generally acknowledge. The UUV could dash through U.S. defenses and fire its submunitions, potentially nuclear-armed, at high-value targets such as carrier groups to erode U.S. ability to project power into Russia and its environs. The UUV could then return to Russia for a reload and repeat such missions again and again. Status-6/Poseidon would be much faster and more survivable for such tasks than manned Russian submarines and reduce the need to put Russian sailors in harms' way. Geist and Massicot, "Understanding Putin's Nuclear 'Superweapons.'"

Russia could procure simply by extending production at the rate planned for the replacement of the SS-18 in the early 2020s for a few years. But the Soviet Union tried to compete with the United States on these terms during the Cold War to no avail; we should hardly be surprised that they are eschewing a rematch. Moreover, attempting to assure retaliation through numbers, even if Moscow had no intention of trying to develop the ability to disarm the United States, would risk signaling such intentions to Washington and stoking the arms race. Bizarre as they may appear, the Russian "assured retaliation" weapons make sense in this context: because they are obviously ill-suited for counterforce targeting, they enhance the Russian deterrent while trying to avoid the self-defeating arms race dynamics that characterized the Cold War era.[40]

Russian nuclear modernization programs, however, are not limited to just "assured retaliation" weapons: they also comprise theater nuclear delivery systems such as the Iskander and Kinzhal missiles. Westerners often make the accusation that these weapons are intended for some kind of limited nuclear war-fighting. There is not necessarily a contradiction between building elaborate "assured retaliation" central nuclear forces with dubious counterforce potential and "usable" theater forces: indeed these could be complementary. Shaping the central war forces so that they are qualitatively distinct from theater forces and cannot be employed for a disarming strike can potentially enhance the usability of the theater forces at lower levels of conflict.[41] The employment of theater forces presents signals that are easy for the adversary to disambiguate from an attack on their assured retaliation capability. The emerging Russian force posture is therefore consistent with the operationalization of the stability–instability paradox.

Chinese strategic nuclear developments are no less dramatic. Unlike the United States and Soviet Union/Russia, China has traditionally adhered to a variant of minimal deterrence.[42] Throughout the late twentieth century China contented itself with modestly-sized retaliatory forces that were not particularly survivable, such as the DF-5 ICBM. China refrained from developing intercontinental bombers, and its earliest missile submarine, the Type 92, was a technical failure that never entered operational service. This force

---

[40] Geist and Massicot, "Understanding Putin's Nuclear 'Superweapons.'"

[41] As a 2019 article in the Russian General Staff journal *Military Thought* explains, the central nuclear deterrent acts as a "foundation" that maintains stability, allowing for operations at lower levels of conflict, such as the use of so-called "non-nuclear strategic weapons" (e.g., precision conventional munitions). A. E. Sterlin, A. A. Protasov, and S. V. Kreidin, "Sovremennye transformatsii kontseptsii i silovykh instrumentov strategicheskogo sderzhivaniia," *Voennaia mysl'* 8 (2019), 7–17, 9.

[42] Jeffrey G. Lewis, *The Minimum Means of Reprisal: China's Search for Security in the Nuclear Age.* The MIT Press, 2007.

structure was coupled with a "no first use" policy and a very rudimentary early warning framework, with the result that China had essentially no counterforce, damage limitation, or preemptive strike capability. A consequence of the small size of the Chinese arsenal was that retaliation was far less "assured": an adversary with the resources of the United States could much more conceivably mount a disarming strike on China than on a state such as Russia. In recent years, however, Beijing has been diversifying its strategic nuclear forces to more closely resemble those of Russia and America. The introduction of road-mobile long-range ballistic missiles such as the DF-31A and DF-41 and the Type 94 SSBN represent a significant improvement in Chinese assured retaliation capability. China also plans to introduce a manned long-range bomber in the next decade, at which point it will finally boast a strategic nuclear "triad" like that of the United States.[43]

Chinese efforts to diversify their nuclear forces raises the question of whether the PRC's leaders are reconsidering their commitment to a "minimum deterrence" policy. One way to interpret it is as a reaction to improving U.S. counterforce capabilities: diversifying the Chinese deterrent makes a disarming strike against Beijing less plausible. Another possibility is that the Chinese are considering a "dash to parity" with the United States and Russia, because they either see some strategic utility in doing so or believe that comparable nuclear forces are a necessary prestige item to cement their status as a first-tier global power. Certain developments, particularly the discovery of hundreds of new ICBM silos under construction, suggest that the PRC may be considering deploying more warheads than the 200–400 it is estimated to have at present.[44] This too may be a hedge to retain assured retaliation capability in an increasingly challenging technological environment rather than an indication that China has decided to seek parity.[45]

The discovery in 2021 of what appeared to be hundreds of missile silos under construction in China fed into perceptions that Beijing was in the process of such a "dash to parity." The Secretary of the Air Force Frank Kendall, for his part, went so far as to proclaim that "If they continue down the path that they seem to be on–to substantially increase their ICBM force—they will have a de facto first-strike capability," adding, "I'm not sure they fully appreciate the risks that they're adding to the entire global nuclear

[43] Hans M. Kristensen and Robert S. Norris, "Chinese Nuclear Forces, 2018," *Bulletin of the Atomic Scientists* 74.4 (2018), 289–295.

[44] Hans M. Kristensen and Matt Korda, *China's Nuclear Missile Silo Expansion: From Minimum Deterrence to Medium Deterrence*. https://thebulletin.org/2021/09/chinas-nuclear-missilesilo-expansion-from-minimumdeterrence-to-medium-deterrence/. Sept. 2021.

[45] Wu Riqiang, "Living with Uncertainty: Modeling China's Nuclear Survivability," *International Security* 44.4 (2020), 84–118.

equation."[46] These silo fields illustrate how hard it can be to make sense of strategic intentions, however, as the exact same silos could be used to support many different strategies as goals. One possibility would be to fill every silo with the biggest missile it can hold and load each of those missiles with as many warheads as it could carry. Such a force could contribute a major part of the kind of "first-strike capability" Kendall fretted about. Other analysts, however, argued that the Chinese were building many more silos than they intended to build missiles, with the aim of making it harder to find and target the missiles and therefore improve their survivability.[47] A distinct, but complementary, goal could be to increase the number of warheads an adversary such as the United States perceived as necessary for a disarming strike against China, with the objective of convincing Washington that it had to acknowledge mutual vulnerability with Beijing. The exact same silos could facilitate both of these strategies, and may in the future actually be used for both—or for other purposes, such as hosting conventionally armed missiles instead of nuclear ones. Chinese officials' refusal to acknowledge the existence of the under-construction silos, much less explain their purpose, sharpened the suspicions of Western officials.[48]

What does this emerging strategic environment mean for the future of nuclear strategy? Cold War strategic theorists envisioned numerous possible futures, many of them far more frightening and bizarre than the circumstances in which we now find ourselves. To understand whether we can adapt those theorists' ideas to the emerging future, we must take stock of what those ideas were.

Some Not-So-New Strategic Concepts

It has been suggested that "one should only have to learn strategic theory once."[49] I certainly concur with this sentiment, but what does it mean? Strategy should be responsive to prevailing conditions, so strategic theory should provide us with a set of principles by which we can formulate strategies to

---

[46] Marcus Weisgerber, *Air Force Secretary Warns of China's Burgeoning Nuclear Arsenal, Reveals B-21 Detail.* https://www.defenseone.com/threats/2021/09/air-force-secretary-warnschinas-burgeoning-nuclear-arsenalreveals-b-21-detail/185486/. Sept. 2021.

[47] Kristensen and Korda, *China's Nuclear Missile Silo Expansion: From Minimum Deterrence to Medium Deterrence.*

[48] Jeffrey Lewis, *How Finding China's Nuclear Sites Upset Pro-Beijing Trolls.* https://foreignpolicy.com/2021/08/26/china-nuclear-sites-twittertrolls/. Aug. 2021.

[49] Kerry M. Kartchner and Micheal S. Gerson, "Escalation to Limited Nuclear War in the 21st Century," in Jeffrey A. Larsen and Kerry M. Kartchner (eds.), *On Limited Nuclear War in the 21st Century* (Stanford University Press, 2014), 144–171, 144.

pursue our goals in the circumstances we find ourselves in. Some of these principles will be longer-lived than others; a few will potentially be permanent features of human existence. Many of the principles that have come to be taken as eternal truths of nuclear strategy were fixed features of the Cold War superpower standoff, but have grown outdated in the twenty-first-century multipolar environment.

Unfortunately, there is little consensus within the strategic studies community as to exactly what the term "strategy" means. A professor at the U.S. Army War College penned an interesting monograph on this subject in which she complains that the term "has been appropriated by a wide range of actors–many of whom have had little or nothing to do with either the military or national security," with the lamentable consequence that "the word 'strategy' is so widely used today that one may see it applied to everything from warfighting to the marketing of beverages."[50] Most proposed definitions in the security domain, however, are connected in some way to Clausewitz's famous dictum that "war is politics by other means." Essentially, strategy is the art of planning and carrying out military operations so as to achieve the desired political effects.[51]

In the military realm, a distinction is typically made between "grand strategy" and "theater" or "military" strategy. The former includes all means by which states seek to achieve their objectives, including diplomatic, economic, and other tools, while the latter is about the employment of military force to help attain political objectives as part of grand strategy. Military strategy, in turn, contains operational art and battlefield tactics. This taxonomy maps awkwardly onto the way in which nation-states employ nuclear weapons, however. Many writers assert that nuclear weapons cannot be applied for strictly military objectives, and it is common to claim that these weapons are only useful for deterring aggression by threat of devastating punishment. The relationship between deterrence strategy and grand strategy has been variable historically and is a major point of disagreement among scholars. In the early part of the Cold War, nuclear deterrence was understood as a contributor to U.S. grand strategy, which was "containment."[52] Under Eisenhower's policy of "Massive Retaliation," the United States promised to respond to major Soviet provocations, such as a conventional invasion of Western Europe, with a devastating nuclear reply. But with the increasing recognition of the scale

---

[50] Tami Davis Biddle, *Strategy and Grand Strategy: What Students and Practitioners Need to Know* (SSI, 2015), 1.

[51] One of my colleagues suggested semi-seriously that "strategy is the art of being nefarious," which as we shall see places him firmly in the camp of Sun Tzu rather than Clausewitz.

[52] John Lewis Gaddis et al., *Strategies of Containment: A Critical Appraisal of American National Security Policy During the Cold War* (Oxford University Press, 2005).

of the potential losses in a thermonuclear war, deterrence of nuclear attack came to be seen as both an end in itself and potentially a more important goal than "containment."

Nuclear strategy is about more than just deterrence. By the closing years of the Cold War analysts had introduced a taxonomy comprising deterrence, escalation management/control, and war termination, referred to by the acronym DEWT.[53] Deterrence has been studied far more than escalation control and war termination, which makes sense given that prevention is obviously preferable to nuclear crises. But if one ever finds oneself in a crisis situation, the measures that made for a highly effective deterrent in peacetime cannot substitute for escalation control and war termination capabilities. Deterrence is therefore *necessary*, but not in and of itself *sufficient* for a comprehensive nuclear strategy.

Western academic debates about nuclear strategy have largely been about how nuclear weapons should be used for signaling to potential adversaries. "Doves" argue that deterrence by threat of punishment is the only plausible application of nuclear force, so states should signal that they will not attempt to target adversaries' nuclear arsenals but that they will retaliate if they are attacked themselves. "Hawks," meanwhile, argue that nuclear superiority makes nuclear threats more plausible, so states should attempt to gain a strategic edge on their rivals and then make sure that they are aware of it.[54] But strategies to assure retaliation by clouding situational awareness are creating problems for both of these views since states will fear that rivals' deception masks aggressive intent while fretting that their enemies have somehow seen through their own deception efforts. Attempts to practice nuclear signaling in the traditional manner will lose their force if one or more rivals employ such a strategy. States worried that their enemies might be readying a first strike are sure to fret that preparations for one may be hidden among the decoys those rivals insist obscure a mere token retaliatory force. Attempts to signal superiority, meanwhile, might not be taken seriously even if they are backed up by extensive forces-in-being. After all, a skeptical adversary could dismiss that arsenal as mere chicanery put forward to intimidate them, akin to Khrushchev's late 1950s braggadocio about his largely illusory missile arsenal.[55]

---

[53] Stephen J. Cimbala, *Strategic War Termination* (Praeger, 1986); Paul K. Davis, "Knowledge-Based Simulation for Studying Issues of Nuclear Strategy," in Allan M. Din (ed.), *Arms and Artificial Intelligence: Weapon and Arms Control Applications of Advanced Computing* (Oxford University Press, 1987), 179–192.

[54] Keith B. Payne, "The Great Divide in US Deterrence Thought," *Strategic Studies Quarterly* 14.2 (2020), 16–48.

[55] Peter J. Roman, *Eisenhower and the Missile Gap* (Cornell University Press, 1995).

One possible taxonomy of the components of nuclear strategy would be to draw a distinction between "deterrence policy" and "employment policy." The former comprises the measures taken to deter the adversary by convincing them that any provocation has a non-trivial likelihood of eliciting a retaliatory response—essentially declaratory policy, even if that declaratory policy might take the form of military exercises or authentic signals traffic rather than speeches or public documents. Employment strategy, meanwhile, includes the plans for actually using the weapons in case of conflict. Deterrence policy and employment policy might not be linked and in many cases during the history of nuclear weapons they have not been.[56] The leaders of nuclear-armed states have often employed bluster to attempt to manipulate their rivals without any intention of making good on those threats. Employment policy, meanwhile, is often formulated by military planners with relatively limited political oversight, or the military proves unable or unwilling to operationalize employment strategies sought by political leaders.[57] This was true in the United States during the early part of the Cold War: the longstanding debate among scholars about whether the United States actually pursued "flexible response" in the early 1960s stems in part from the inability of military planners to convert it into operational plans using their available institutional procedures even if they had wanted to (which senior Air Force leaders largely did not).[58]

The categories typically used to discuss nuclear strategy in the United States are a product of historical accident and the particular policy debates that were ongoing in the American security community in the late 1950s and early 1960s. At that time, the types of strategic nuclear delivery systems the United States elected to procure would strongly impact its ability to target different categories of installations, which were in turn associated with different approaches to the problem of deterring a Soviet attack. Analysts at RAND dubbed the two categories of targets "countervalue" (cities and industry) and "counterforce" (enemy strategic forces) and soon it became common to talk of "counterforce weapons" and "countervalue strategies." In the technological and military conditions of the 1950s, the conflation of force posture, targeting, and overall strategy made sense, at least theoretically. It also seemed that one could infer a great deal about adversary intentions by scrutinizing their force posture. Counterforce targeting soon came to be associated

---

[56] Nolan, *Guardians of the Arsenal*; Kaplan, *The Bomb: Presidents, Generals, and the Secret History of Nuclear War*.

[57] Kaplan, *The Bomb: Presidents, Generals, and the Secret History of Nuclear War*.

[58] Francis J. Gavin, *Nuclear Statecraft: History and Strategy in America's Atomic Age* (Cornell University Press, 2012).

with "hawks" who wanted to keep ahead of the Soviet Union militarily, and countervalue with doves who favored minimal deterrence. But this simple relationship was always questionable when interrogated, and as the Cold War dragged on and weapons technology evolved, it grew increasingly dubious.[59]

Countervalue and counterforce have lost most of their value as categories for characterizing either weapons or overall strategies in the emerging strategic environment. Improvements in weapons accuracy have provided more and more delivery systems with a "hard-target kill capability," but many of them are apparently targeted against installations that have no need of such accuracy. It is often suggested that highly accurate nuclear delivery systems will be employed for discriminate demonstration or counter-leadership attacks rather than destroying adversary weapons. Accurate delivery systems are therefore not necessarily counterforce weapons nor do they indicate that their possessors adhere to a particular nuclear targeting policy. Nor are counterforce and countervalue the only two possible categories of targets. Many others have been suggested over the years, as the noncomprehensive list in Table 1 indicates.

Targeting strategies should not be confused with some strategic concepts with similar-sounding names that are defined by their political objectives. These include the "countervailing strategy" developed during the Carter administration, which sought to convince Soviet leaders that the United States could and would deny them victory in any conceivable scenario.[60] The term "counterdeterrence" was introduced in the late 1950s by Raymond Garthoff to refer to the possibility that the threat of general thermonuclear war would neutralize United States willingness to respond to lesser Soviet

Table 1 Selected nuclear targeting strategies

Name	Objectives
Counterforce	Destroy adversary strategic nuclear forces
Countermilitary	Destroy adversary military assets (general purpose forces)
Countervalue	Destroy adversary population and economy (cities)
Counterpopulation	Destroy adversary population
Counter-industrial	Destroy adversary industrial capacity
Counter-recovery	Prevent adversary post-attack recovery
Counter-leadership	Kill adversary leaders
Counter-control	Undermine adversary government's control of territory

[59] Fred Kaplan, *The Wizards of Armageddon* (Stanford University Press, 1991).
[60] Walter Slocombe, "The Countervailing Strategy," *International Security* 5.4 (1981), 18–27.

aggression.[61] Countercoercion, meanwhile, is the reputed goal of Chinese nuclear strategy. While China has satisfied itself with a minimal strategic nuclear force compared to the United States and Russia, its doctrine seeks more than simple assured retaliation to a nuclear attack: Beijing seeks to forestall the possibility that it could be subjected to nuclear blackmail.[62]

One way to categorize the components of nuclear strategy is to draw a distinction between "philosophical," "technical," and "anthropological" considerations. The first of these includes questions about ethics and human nature—for instance, the extent to which human behavior adheres to rational actor assumptions. The second comprises both the nature of physical reality (e.g., is a certain system or phenomenon physically possible?) and the current state of technology (e.g., what are existing systems actually capable of?). Finally, anthropological considerations include the current preferences and strategies of both adversaries and allies (e.g., what are the enemy's intentions, and what will restrain his behavior?). The timeless parts of strategic theory are found in the philosophical considerations and the subset of the technical ones associated with physical laws rather than the technological state-of-the art. The present state of technology and the changeable whims of humans, meanwhile, are critical to formulating strategy in the moment but cannot be trusted to remain the same in the future.

Examined within this framework, U.S. strategic discourse during the Cold War was a mixed success at best. The three categories were generally conflated with one another in ways that made it difficult to tell quite what was being argued. For instance, advocates of counterforce generally assumed that deterrence was difficult in general, that the Soviets were hell-bent on expansion, and that damage-limitation counterforce attacks were technically plausible; proponents of countervalue or "minimal deterrence" generally assumed the opposite about all three, even though these were separate issues that might be uncorrelated with each other.[63] The philosophical issues of nuclear strategic theory went unresolved and remain so. Technical realities changed as the arms race continued but positions on certain technical issues, such as missile defense, became mired in tribal political debates. The "sovietological" issues changed visibly in the 1980s with Gorbachev and his "New Thinking," the

[61] This idea is usually called the "stability–instability paradox" today thanks to the influence of Robert Jervis. Raymond L. Garthoff, *Deterrence and the Revolution in Soviet Military Doctrine* (Brookings, 1990), 27–28.

[62] Li Bin, "China's Nuclear Strategy," *Carnegie International Nonproliferation Conference, Washington, DC.* 2007, 25–26.

[63] Charles Glaser, "Why Do Strategists Disagree about the Requirements of Strategic Nuclear Deterrence?" in *Nuclear Arguments: Understanding the Strategic Nuclear Arms and Arms Control Debates* (1989), 109–171.

emergence of which suggested that some longstanding assumptions about the USSR had been erroneous.[64]

The end of the Cold War and increasing declassification have made it possible to test some of these assumptions, and it turns out that neither school comes off looking particularly vindicated. U.S. counterforce capabilities turn out to have been considerably better than were acknowledged at the time (in substantial part thanks to strategic ASW efforts that were only acknowledged after the collapse of the USSR), which undermined the premise that secure retaliatory forces could be be small, cheap, and trivial to build.[65] At the same time, the United States never had the capabilities needed for a "credible" disarming strike, nor was it obvious that such a capability would have been usable or provided tangible advantages in a crisis.[66] Understanding of the Soviet adversary turns out to have been disastrously bad. The USSR lacked the aggressive designs on its neighbors that hawks like Paul Nitze assumed, but at the same time some of its leaders were paranoid and until the mid-1980s it had a destabilizing nuclear doctrine that could have precipitated a war by accident or miscalculation.[67] The utility of the counterforce and countervalue strategic categories was also thrown into question by the revelation that Soviet nuclear strategy did not map onto them.

If the more classic categories used to discuss nuclear strategy during the Cold War inappropriately conflate the eternal and ephemeral components of strategic theory, then we need alternatives that better capture the enduring issues. Even though comparatively circumstantial elements of their thought ended up dominating the public imagination, it turns out that the founders of the field devoted considerable attention to the fundamental questions of strategy in the 1950s and the 1960s. In the process they staked out some positions that encapsulate the enduring issues better than concepts like counterforce and countervalue. These can be adapted today to help make sense of

---

[64] Garthoff, *Deterrence and the Revolution in Soviet Military Doctrine.*

[65] Brendan R. Green and Austin Long, "The MAD Who Wasn't There: Soviet Reactions to the Late Cold War Nuclear Balance," *Security Studies* 26.4 (2017), 606–641; Long and Green, "Stalking the Secure Second Strike: Intelligence, Counterforce, and Nuclear Strategy."

[66] As William Odom noted in his memoir account of the evolution of the Carter administration's nuclear strategy, "The idea of a disarming nuclear strike at an opponent's strategic nuclear forces, a strike powerful enough to destroy all or most of the enemy's delivery systems, always enjoyed a central place in theoretical debates about deterrence," but that by the late 1970s, the "Soviet buildup coupled with hardening and dispersal of mobile capabilities, especially in submarines, made such a strike highly problematic if not downright fanciful." Odom was himself a counterforce advocate, but he believed that these capabilities should be used as an instrument of bargaining or blunting Soviet conventional military power, not enabling a disarming strike. William E. Odom, "The Origins and Design of Presidential Decision-59: A Memoir," in *Getting MAD: Nuclear Mutual Assured Destruction, Its Origin and Practice. Strategic Studies Institute* (SSI, 2004), 175–196, 188.

[67] Dmitry (Dima) Adamsky, "The 1983 Nuclear Crisis—Lessons for Deterrence Theory and Practice," *Journal of Strategic Studies* 36.1 (2013), 4–41.

the emerging multipolar strategic environment and the potential impact of emerging technologies upon it.

The strategic thinkers at RAND in the mid- to late 1950s concurred about a great deal, most importantly that the Eisenhower administration's approach to Massive Retaliation was dangerous and had to be replaced, but they disagreed as to what ought to supplant it. Their critiques of this policy agreed that deterrent strategies that leveraged automatic transition to "all-out" or "spasm" war were unacceptable due to the risk of accident or miscalculation as well as credibility issues, so they all championed various forms of "controlled" nuclear use. In this they differed from advocates of "minimum" or "finite" deterrence, who argued that a survivable nuclear retaliatory force of modest size would be adequate to deter all major Soviet provocations and often argued against the notion of controlled war both for feasibility reasons and to make the deterrent look more credible. But RAND strategists disagreed as to the type of controlled war U.S. policy should emphasize.[68] Albert Wohlstetter and Herman Kahn championed a concept of "Controlled War," which Kahn wrote "visualizes reciprocal attacks on each other's military power with the object of attriting the opponent's retaliatory capability." It envisioned a controlled general war that might proceed either quickly or gradually in which the superpowers employed strategic nuclear weapons for military effect. Thomas Schelling, meanwhile, was the leading proponent of an alternative policy Kahn described as "Controlled Reprisal." This strategy foresaw "each side engaging in a series of tit-for-tat attacks (nuclear or nonnuclear), whose object is not the destruction of the other side's military power but the destruction of his resolve. Each side attempts by threats and actual punishment to force the other side to back down."[69] Kahn articulated his views in his 1960 book *On Thermonuclear War*, while Schelling published his *Strategy of Conflict* advocating his own that same year.[70]

Kahn and Schelling's fundamental disagreement was about the extent to which the West should leverage "rationality of irrationality" strategies. Schelling argued that these should be the emphasis of deterrence policy, while Kahn believed that nuclear war should be planned "rationally" where possible while acknowledging that the United States might be forced to respond to the use of "irrational" nuclear coercion by others. Both men

---

[68] Despite his latter-day reputation as the father of the "minimal deterrence" school, Bernard Brodie was for many years a lonely champion of tactical nuclear war fighting as a component of NATO strategy. Bernard Brodie, "The Missing Middle—Tactical Nuclear War. AFAG Speech—9 April 1964," in Marc Trachtenberg (ed.), *The Development of American Strategic Thought: Writings on Strategy* (Garland, 1988), 245–262.

[69] Kahn, *On Thermonuclear War*, 174–175.

[70] Thomas C. Schelling, *The Strategy of Conflict* (Harvard University Press, 1980).

respected each other and recognized the merits of the other's viewpoint, and their writings through the mid-1960s are in dialogue with each other as to the relative merits of their approach. Far from thinking that their views were mutually exclusive, Kahn argued that both strategies could be employed in the evolution of a single war. Kahn's basic critique of Schelling's views, which he articulated best in his 1965 book *On Escalation*, was that committing oneself to play thermonuclear "chicken" with the Communists was too dangerous. The risk of escalation to all-out war was part of the strategy, and leaders who applied it successfully might come to under-appreciate the inherent danger and play the game until all-out catastrophe resulted. Kahn also argued that irrational threats made for a less effective extended deterrent for U.S. allies.[71] Schelling countered that the controlled counterforce war Kahn envisioned might be technically infeasible, both because making militarily effective attacks on enemy strategic forces without major collateral damage to civilians might be impossible and because Soviet leaders would have difficulty distinguishing in the moment between a limited counterforce attack and an "all-out" attack.[72] Unfortunately, both Kahn and Schelling were right in their critiques of each other's position.

The merits of "rationality of irrationality" strategies are one of the timeless questions of strategic theory because they ultimately hinge on human nature rather than technical or situational details. Examining nuclear strategy within this frame reveals some interesting fissures among both "hawks" and "doves." Robert Jervis invoked Schelling's arguments to argue that U.S. strategic forces would provide considerable extended deterrence even in the absence of significant counterforce capabilities.[73] In part thanks to Jervis' influence, Schelling has a following among counterforce skeptics even though they generally find the specific policy advocated by Schelling in the mid-1960s—controlled countervalue wars in which the superpowers engaged in "city exchanges"—outrageous and morally abhorrent.[74] Most advocates of further reductions in the size of strategic forces argue for some variant of "Controlled Reprisal." Bruce Blair, for instance, suggested that an arsenal of a few hundred warheads would suffice for deterrence, and proposed that these would be employed for retaliation only after a delay, so as to reduce the possibility of accidents and to ensure that punitive strikes were directed only against guilty parties.[75]

---

[71] Herman Kahn, *On Escalation: Metaphors and Scenarios* (Praeger, 1965), 10–15.
[72] Thomas C. Schelling, *Arms and Influence* (Yale University Press, 1966), 197.
[73] Jervis, *The Illogic of American Nuclear Strategy*, 155–156.
[74] Marc Trachtenberg, *History and Strategy* (Princeton University Press, 1991), 37—8.
[75] Bruce Blair, Jessica Sleight, and Emma Claire Foley, *The End of Nuclear Warfighting: Moving to a Deterrence-Only Posture: An Alternative Nuclear Posture Review*, tech. rep. (Global Zero, 2018).

Nearly everyone concurs that strategic instability is a bad thing, but there is scant agreement about how to define "strategic stability."[76] Thomas Schelling commented in his introduction to a 2013 edited volume entitled *Strategic Stability: Contending Interpretations* that in the late 1950s and early 1960s, "we all knew what we meant by 'stability,'" but

> Now the world is so much changed, so much more complicated, so multivariate, so unpredictable, involving so many nations and cultures and languages in nuclear relationships, many of them asymmetric, that it is even difficult to know how many meanings there are for "strategic stability," or how many different kinds of such stability there may be among so many different international relationships, or what "stable deterrence" is supposed to deter in a world of proliferated weapons.[77]

Once strategic stability was acknowledged as a universally desired goal, different interest groups adopted their own, mutually contradictory definitions for it.[78] This semantic debasing is a transnational phenomenon: as many observers have noted, while Russia and China also accept the desirability of strategic stability, they have their own definitions of it that are orthogonal to the typical American ones, which tend to emphasize technocratic measures of force posture and survivability rather than political or cultural issues.[79] This exasperating lack of definitional congruence has led some to suggest that strategic stability may have lost whatever value it formerly had for understanding nuclear strategy: Pavel Podvig complained in 2012 that "the key elements of the concept are so poorly defined that it has no useful meaning and virtually no practical value."[80]

In a 2018 RAND publication, Michael J. Mazarr outlines a taxonomy of several different overlapping categories of deterrence. The two most well-known of these are direct (or central) deterrence, which deters adversaries from attacking one's homeland or core interests, and extended deterrence,

---

[76] Strategic theorists have long fretted about revisionist powers that might cultivate instability in an attempt to gain coercive legacy. More recently, Matthew Kroenig suggested that even though the United States is a *status quo* power, certain kinds of instability are good for Washington's strategic interests and "US nuclear superiority increases instability that works in Washington's favor and dampens problematic instability." Kroenig, *The Logic of American Nuclear Strategy*, 142.

[77] Elbridge A. Colby and Michael S. Gerson, (eds.) *Strategic Stability: Contending Interpretations*, tech. rep. (SSI, 2013), vii.

[78] Regrettably, "deterrence" and "stability" have been so abused in our policy discourse that they have degenerated into what Marvin Minsky dubbed "suitcase words." Minsky introduced this term to describe terms "like intuition or consciousness that all of us use to encapsulate our jumbled ideas about our minds. We use those words as suitcases in which to contain all sorts of mysteries that we can't yet explain." In short, the terminology becomes a convenient excuse not to interrogate one's assumptions. Marvin Minsky, "Consciousness Is a Big Suitcase," in *Edge.org* (1998).

[79] Nancy W. Gallagher, "Re-thinking the Unthinkable: Arms Control in the Twenty-First Century," *The Nonproliferation Review* 22.3–4 (2015), 469–498.

[80] Pavel Podvig, "The Myth of Strategic Stability," *Bulletin of the Atomic Scientists* (2012).

which deters attacks on one's allies or peripheral interests. But in addition to these spatial categories, deterrence can also be conceptualized in situational terms. Patrick Morgan introduced the most widely used categories for these in his foundational 1977 work *Deterrence: A Conceptual Analysis*.[81] "General deterrence" aims to dissuade adversaries from starting crises or engaging in provocations. "Immediate deterrence," meanwhile, "represents more short-term, urgent attempts to prevent a specific, imminent attack, most typically during a crisis."[82] These categories can overlap (see Table 2).

Robert Powell introduced analogous categories to classify some different kinds of strategic stability.[83] "Situational stability" is stability from crises. So long as it holds, crises and provocation will be rare and will only occur due to accident or miscalculation, not willful enemy action. "Crisis stability," by contrast, is stability in crises. This includes what is commonly referred to as "first-strike stability."[84] To these categories one can add a third, "arms race stability," which is defined as stability against competition in armaments. If arms race stability exists, then states will be restrained in their development and procurement of arms and will try to avoid "action–reaction" cycles with their rivals. States may intentionally undermine arms race stability for reasons other than relative military advantage, such as to stoke strategic competitions that they believe will squander the adversaries' resources and amplify their relative weaknesses. Note that none of these categories is limited solely to nuclear deterrence.

Nuclear strategy is hard because it ultimately rests on a set of interlinked contradictions. In order to deter potential adversaries from provocative behavior that might spark a crisis, it is useful to make crises look extremely dangerous. The most convincing way to make these risks look credible is to make crises *genuinely* dangerous, such as by establishing institutional

Table 2 Categories of deterrence with example objectives

	General	Immediate
Direct/Central	Deter "bolt from the blue" attack on homeland	Deter preemptive disarming strike during crisis
Extended	Deter Soviet invasion of Western Europe	Deter vertical or horizontal escalation during ongoing crisis

[81] Patrick M. Morgan, *Deterrence: A Conceptual Analysis* (Sage Publications, 1977).
[82] Michael J. Mazarr, *Understanding Deterrence*, (tech. rep. RAND Corporation, 2018), 4.
[83] Robert Powell, *Nuclear Deterrence Theory: The Search for Credibility* (Cambridge University Press, 1990), 58–59.
[84] Glaser, "Why Do Strategists Disagree about the Requirements of Strategic Nuclear Deterrence?"

arrangements that will increase the likelihood of uncontrolled escalation. The predelegation of launch authority for nonstrategic nuclear weapons to frontline commanders during the Cold War provides a classic example of this.[85] But crises might arise out of miscalculation or accident, and in those circumstances the last thing one wants is to find oneself without effective means of escalation control. The strategic posture that makes the most credible deterrent outside of crisis is therefore too dangerous during crisis.[86]

But conversely, the strategic posture that is most useful for managing crises is harmful for both situational stability and arms race stability. Thomas Schelling acknowledged this at the beginning of the 1960s, commenting in a 1961 article that

> I acknowledge that a Russian belief in the possibility that we may help to keep the war limited may reduce the risk involved in attacking us. This is a genuine dilemma. As I have argued elsewhere, we may weaken our "pre-war deterrence" as the price of improving our "intra-war deterrence."[87]

If intra-war deterrence and escalation control requires the ability to threaten limited nuclear use, then precision weapons and enhanced command-and-control capabilities will be necessary. Yet potential adversaries are liable to perceive these as preparations for a possible disarming strike. Soviet leaders perceived U.S. force modernization efforts this way during the early 1980s "war scare." This creates pressures to enlarge retaliatory forces to maintain the probability that a disarming strike would fail, yet this undermines arms race stability and perceptions of general deterrence stability.

The major nuclear powers differ in their preferences about tradeoffs between these three kinds of deterrence stability. During the early Cold War U.S. officials were concerned about the possibility of a "nuclear Pearl Harbor" from the Soviet Union and developed their strategic nuclear forces accordingly. The U.S. strategic nuclear force has always been maintained on a relatively high alert status compared to those of the USSR/Russia and China.

---

[85] In 1983, Paul Bracken colorfully characterized NC3 in Central Europe as "tantamount to a regional doomsday machine," because "The NATO strategy of relying on nuclear weapons is politically and militarily credible because the governing structure is so unstable and accident-prone that national leaders would exercise little practical control over it in wartime." Paul Bracken, *The Command and Control of Nuclear Forces* (Yale University Press, 1983), 164.

[86] This problem became all too apparent during the Cuban Missile Crisis, when Kennedy and Khrushchev discovered that events were getting away from them and desperately tried to curtail the implementation of procedures that would further erode their ability to control and conclude the crisis.

[87] Schelling employed the terms "pre-war deterrence" and "intra-war deterrence" to refer to what Morgan later dubbed "general" and "immediate" deterrence, respectively. Thomas C. Schelling, "Dispersal, Deterrence, and Damage," *Operations Research* 9.3 (1961), 363–370, 365.

Outside of crisis, those countries have tended to keep their forces at a relatively low level of alert, including de-mating warheads from their delivery systems in many cases, leaving them relatively vulnerable to a "bolt from the blue" attack.[88] The United States also has a far greater tolerance for arms race instability than Moscow and Beijing. China, especially, has been very hesitant historically to try to compete numerically or qualitatively with its potential adversaries.

In addition to these tensions between different kinds of deterrence, there are also contradictions between deterrence and steps taken to assure allies and reassure potential adversaries (see Table 3). Making extended deterrence guarantees appear credible to adversaries can be challenging, but convincing allied government that one will risk the survival of one's own population over a comparatively peripheral threat is much harder. As a consequence, assuring allies that one really is willing to "trade Boston for Berlin" often demands taking steps far beyond what is probably sufficient for deterrence. Yet for deterrence to be effective, the adversary needs to be convinced that if they refrain from provocation, they will not be attacked anyway.[89] The "overkill" needed for assurance can backfire by convincing the adversary that

Table 3 Tensions between deterrence, assurance, reassurance, self-assurance, catalyst, and hedging over different timescales

	Timescale		
	Short	Medium	Long
Stability	Crisis (First-strike)	Situational	Arms race
Deterrence	Immediate (Intra-war)	Situational (Pre-war)	Dissuasion
Assurance	A	B	C
Reassurance	D	E	F
Self-assurance	G	H	I
Catalyst	U	V	W
Hedging	X	Y	Z

Note: Letters denote combinations of objectives and timescales not named in existing literature.

[88] The Soviet Union seems to have kept warheads isolated from delivery systems during peacetime during the early part of the Cold War, and the Chinese are believed by most analysts to have done so until very recently. Pavel Podvig, *Russian Strategic Nuclear Forces* (MIT Press, 2004), 110; Hans M. Kristensen and Matt Korda, "Chinese Nuclear Forces, 2020," *Bulletin of the Atomic Scientists* 76.6 (2020), 443–457, 446.

[89] Janice Gross Stein, "Deterrence and Reassurance," in Philip E. Tetlock et al. (eds.), *Behavior, Society, and Nuclear War*, Vol. 2 (Oxford University Press, 1991), 8–72.

they could be at risk of a first strike no matter what they do, causing them to engage in undesirable behavior that they would not have engaged in if they faced a more modest perceived threat. Moreover, just as with deterrence and stability there are tensions between the requirements of assurance and reassurance at different timescales. The tokens of commitment strategic partners seek in the immediate term may strike them as reckless or unwanted in the longer term (consider, for instance, West German political debates about the Pershing II missile in the late 1970s compared to that in the mid-1980s). Similarly, confidence-building measures that assuage strategic rivals in the short term can backfire due to changes in the way domestic constituencies perceive them: the characterization of the Open Skies Treaty by its American critics as a means by which Russia was "spying on U.S. infrastructure" offers a concrete example.

Moreover, deterrence, assurance, and reassurance are also in tension with other goals that nuclear states pursue using their weapons. A factor that theorists have largely neglected but whose importance is very apparent from within the nuclear enterprise is "self-assurance"—nukes as a means to bolster a state's own confidence in the quality of its deterrence and assurance of other states.[90] A characteristic example of "self-assurance" is the perennial argument that "we need to give the president more options to make sure that his or her resolve won't buckle in the face of adversary threats, and that he or she will not be tempted to unwind our security guarantees to our allies." Another less-appreciated reason for possessing nuclear weapons that recent scholarship has elaborated is as a catalyst.[91] This differs from deterrence in that the goal of using nuclear weapons as a catalyst is to change the behavior of a non-hostile or allied state in some desired way. This has generally been an objective of lesser nuclear powers who aim to gain the aid of a more powerful state. For instance, in the 1950s the British leaders sought a domestic thermonuclear weapons capability primarily to convince U.S. decision-makers to agree to much closer nuclear cooperation with the United Kingdom.[92] An additional goal of nuclear weapons that officials sometimes acknowledge is hedging. Hedging is in part an attempt to be prepared to deter adversaries that do not yet exist, but this is only part of the story. Nuclear weapons can be acquired and maintained to hedge against future needs for assurance, self-assurance, and catalysts.

---

[90] I am not sure who first used the term "self-assurance" in this sense, but I first heard it from Jeffrey Lewis.

[91] Mark S. Bell, *Nuclear Reactions: How Nuclear-Armed States Behave* (Cornell University Press, 2021).

[92] Lorna Arnold, *Britain and the H-Bomb* (Springer, 2001).

Enormous quantities of ink have been spilled by authors and analysts attempting to explain why the superpowers continued to seek relative advantage over each other once both attained secure second-strike capabilities. By the mid-1960s, such forces appeared to be a practical reality: hardened missile silos could survive the most accurate delivery systems of the day, while missile-carrying submarines could hide in the vastness of the oceans.[93] Alert bombers provided an additional hedge in case of the other two somehow became vulnerable. Surely capitalists and communists alike would recognize the ironclad logic of this development and agree that continuing the arms race was a monumental waste of time, and the arms control treaties of the early 1970s suggested they had. Yet instead of taking comfort in their second-strike capabilities, the United States and Soviet Union rushed headlong in their pursuit of relative advantage. While the SALT agreement froze the total number of strategic launchers deployed by the superpowers, they fielded larger and larger numbers of increasingly accurate warheads. Authors such as Robert Jervis bemoaned what he termed the"illogic" of American (and Soviet) nuclear strategy.[94]

The seeming paradox of the "nuclear revolution" is not so paradoxical as it seems. In theory, assured retaliation seems simple, but actually assuring it in the face of a well-resourced, determined rival is exceedingly challenging. Soviet leaders feared, for good reason, that the United States would seek combinations of technology and strategy that would neutralize their second-strike capability.[95] A combination of unfavorable geography and inferior technology made a minimal deterrence strategy a challenging prospect for the USSR. The U.S. pursuit of accurate MIRVed ICBMs and anti-submarine warfare capability imperiled the survival of both the ground-based and sea-based legs of the Soviet nuclear deterrent.[96] Moreover, unbeknownst to the United States, Soviet analysts believed that their forces were less capable and survivable than the American military assumed.[97] Soviet leaders rejected the logic of mutual vulnerability because they recognized that they were more vulnerable than the Americans. But Soviet leaders until Mikhail Gorbachev believed in "peace through strength," or at least the appearance of it; they sought military solutions to vulnerability, including preemptive strikes if a

---

[93] Jerome B. Wiesner and Herbert F. York, "National Security and the Nuclear-Test Ban," *Scientific American* 211.4 (1964), 27–35.

[94] Jervis, *The Illogic of American Nuclear Strategy*.

[95] Green and Long, "The MAD Who Wasn't There: Soviet Reactions to the Late Cold War Nuclear Balance."

[96] Brendan Rittenhouse Green and Austin Long, "Conceal or Reveal? Managing Clandestine Military Capabilities in Peacetime Competition," *International Security* 44.3 (2020), 48–83.

[97] Podvig, "The Window of Vulnerability That Wasn't: Soviet Military Buildup in the 1970s–A Research Note."

U.S. attack appeared imminent, even though these hopelessly outstripped Soviet capability. Western hawks pointed out, accurately, that Soviet military planners believed that nuclear war could be survived and won, at least in theory.[98]

Meanwhile, Americans doubted their own willingness and capability to retaliate, albeit for different reasons. Perhaps the USSR would attain a spectacular technological breakthrough and make U.S. SSBNs vulnerable, or (as Paul Nitze suggested) simply strew the entire submarine patrol zone with thermonuclear mines.[99] Even assuming that American missile submarines would never be imperiled by the Soviets, some strategists such as Nitze fretted that the Kremlin could still coerce the United States with bold limited attacks. For instance, until the introduction of the Trident II SLBM, submarine-based missiles were too inaccurate for attacks on anything smaller than an area target. What if the Soviets took advantage of their land-based ICBM force to destroy American ICBM silos, bomber bases, and submarines in port? This would eliminate all accurate U.S. delivery systems and computer simulations suggested (perhaps misleadingly) that this might be accomplished with relatively limited casualties. By holding additional forces in reserve to destroy U.S. cities if the President dared retaliate, American leaders might be coerced into accepting a new world order in which the Communists went unchallenged.[100] Critics dismissed scenarios such as these as paranoid and ridiculous, and officials argued at length about whether these possibilities should be taken seriously. The argument that they should was bolstered by U.S. investigation of "limited nuclear options" (LNOs) that, from the Soviet perspective, would have appeared about as bizarre.[101]

U.S. extended deterrence requirements created the impression in some circles that America needed to maintain the appearance that it was willing to risk war. Why would U.S. allies in Europe and Asia take Washington's security commitments seriously if they thought the Americans would lose their nerve in a crisis? One solution to this dilemma was to seek, at a minimum, what Herman Kahn dubbed a "not incredible" first-strike capability. As opposed to a "splendid" first-strike capability, which could reasonably be expected to

[98] Lawrence Freedman and Jeffrey Michaels, *The Evolution of Nuclear Strategy: New, Updated and Completely Revised* (Springer, 2019), Ch. 35.

[99] Paul H. Nitze, "The Strategic Balance Between Hope and Skepticism," *Foreign Policy* 17 (1974), 136–156.

[100] Paul H. Nitze, "Assuring Strategic Stability in an Era of Détente," *Foreign Affairs* 54.2 (1976), 207–232; Paul H. Nitze, "Deterring Our Deterrent," *Foreign Policy* 25 (1976), 195–210.

[101] Nolan, *Guardians of the Arsenal*, 112–117; Kaplan, *The Bomb: Presidents, Generals, and the Secret History of Nuclear War*, 119.

disarm the adversary and forestall all retaliation, the "not incredible" capability would only be able to do so given some generous, albeit not implausible, assumptions. Colin S. Gray and Keith Payne took this kind of thinking to its logical conclusion in their controversial, if influential 1980 article "Victory Is Possible."[102]

The pursuit of competitive strategies became an increasingly influential argument in favor of the pursuit of counterforce capabilities during the latter part of the Cold War. Championed by Andrew Marshall of the Office of Net Assessment, competitive strategies aimed to overextend the Soviets by exploiting their sense of vulnerability. Faced with the prospect of being at a serious military disadvantage, the USSR would expend their limited technical resources trying to maintain their assured retaliation capability rather than supporting military adventures elsewhere or addressing their systemic problems.[103] Competitive strategies merely needed the appearance of technical plausibility to be effective, and in fact it was preferable that technologies they convinced the USSR to pursue were nonviable. The last thing one would want to accomplish with such a strategy would be to convince the Soviets to investigate a breakthrough military technology they would otherwise have ignored, only to have them develop and field it before the United States. Other varieties of competitive strategies sought to exploit Soviet preoccupations or path dependencies with bona fide military breakthroughs. The Soviet tendency to expend vast sums on air defenses dated back to Stalin, so the pursuit of stealth aircraft seemed like a sure recipe to terrify Moscow into expending vast resources. But even if it worked as intended, the competitive strategy could still increase the danger of nuclear crises.

Traditional Approaches for Evaluating Strategic Stability

In Western strategic culture, "strategic stability" is commonly conceptualized in technical and quantitative terms. In their foundational 1961 book *Strategy and Arms Control*, Thomas Schelling and Morton Halperin commented that "A 'balance of deterrence'–a situation in which the incentives on both sides to initiate war are outweighed by the disincentives–is described as 'stable' when it is reasonably secure against shocks, alarms, and perturbations."[104]

---

[102] Colin S. Gray and Keith Payne, "Victory Is Possible," *Foreign Policy* 39 (1980), 14–27.

[103] Andrew W. Marshall, "Long-Term Competition with the Soviets: A Framework for Strategic Analysis," in *United States Air Force Project RAND R-862-PR* (1972).

[104] Morton H. Halperin and Thomas C. Schelling, *Strategy and Arms Control* (Twentieth Century Fund, 1961), 50.

That same year, Daniel Ellsberg penned an article entitled "The Crude Analysis of Strategy Choices" in which he proposed adapting the payoff tables commonly employed in game theory to compare the outcomes of potential nuclear exchanges. Ellsberg's article suggested a mathematical definition for strategic stability: so long as the values in the payoff table indicated that neither side stood to gain a significant advantage by firing first, it seemed that deterrence would hold.[105] Soon advocates of minimal deterrence and arms control seized upon this framework to argue that small, survivable retaliatory arsenals could best meet the needs of deterrence.

Within a few years, analysts developed a variety of computer models to study strategic stability and deterrence requirements. Some of these models were what John Battilega and Judith K. Grange later dubbed "sufficiency models": tools for answering the high-stakes question of "how much is enough?" These models required the definition of a quantitative measure of effectiveness (MOE, also known as a "fitness measure"). The simplest MOEs simply counted up the number of warheads and launchers expected to survive a preemptive enemy strike. If this figure exceeded some stipulated level, the proposed force structure was deemed "sufficient" to guarantee strategic stability. More sophisticated "quasi-dynamic" MOEs such as "counterforce potential" incorporated the qualitative aspects of delivery systems into additive measures of the ability of an arsenal to carry out particular missions, such as destroying hardened facilities. Another class of models employed "dynamic" measures that sought to characterize how strategic nuclear forces could be expected to perform against concrete target sets in specific (if often highly stylized) scenarios, basically serving as values in Ellsberg's payoff matrix.[106] For instance, in the mid-1960s Robert S. McNamara's concept of "assured destruction" was converted into an MOE estimated by computerized "damage assessment models" projecting the economic losses and civilian fatalities that would result from U.S. retaliation following a Soviet counterforce attack.

During the Cold War, strategic nuclear exchanges appeared deceptively simple to model. The survivability of hardened targets was evaluated employing cookie-cutter or lognormal distance damage functions. Optimal employment of available warheads against a known target set could then be treated as a combinatorial optimization problem (the weapon target assignment problem or WTA) that could be solved using a variety of techniques such as

[105] Daniel Ellsberg, "The Crude Analysis of Strategy Choices," *American Economic Review* 51.2 (1961), 472–478.
[106] John A. Battilega and Judith K. Grange, *The Military Applications of Modeling* (Air Force Institute of Technology Press, 1984), Ch. 13.

Lagrangean relaxation. Assuring strategic stability seemed as straightforward as taking steps to ensure that the optimal solution to the WTA problem for available weapons and targets was below some value according to the chosen MOE.[107] Both "hawks" and "doves" employed this overall framework during vociferous Cold War debates about nuclear weapons policy, and it is still invoked by some researchers and military planners.[108]

While Soviet strategic theorists openly embraced the concept of strategic stability at the twilight of the USSR, memoir literature attests that Soviet officials had actually embraced several of the same concepts as their Western adversaries two decades before. The most important of these—and the one that Russian strategists continue to emphasize to this day—is "unacceptable damage," which is defined as an amount of damage that must be inflicted upon the adversary in a retaliatory strike even in the most pressing circumstances.[109] Memoir literature asserts that historically this was not defined in demographic and industrial terms like McNamara's "assured destruction," but rather as a number of warheads or a cumulative amount of megatonnage that absolutely had to be inflicted on an aggressor even after well-executed attempted disarming strikes and in the face of more-effective-than-expected missile defenses.[110] In the late 1980s this value was apparently defined as 150MT delivered to the adversary homeland.[111]

Unfortunately, the traditional approach to modeling nuclear strategic stability is increasingly nonviable in the emerging technological environment. As it assumes a fixed number and configuration of either point (hardened) or area (soft, often urban-industrial) targets, this paradigm has difficulty accommodating nonstationary targets such as mobile missile launchers. Most attempts to model attacks on such targets tend to make unrealistic assumptions such as totally random movement to simplify analysis.[112] Nor is the classical modeling framework of much help estimating states' capability to ensure retaliation taking into account bomber defenses and the possibility

[107] Francis P. Hoeber, *Military Applications of Modeling: Selected Case Studies.* Vol. 1 (CRC Press, 1981), Ch. 7.

[108] Bruce Blair et al., "One Hundred Nuclear Wars: Stable Deterrence between the United States and Russia at reduced Nuclear Force Levels off Alert in the Presence of Limited Missile Defenses," *Science & Global Security* 19.3 (2011), 167–194; Lieber and Press, "The New Era of Counterforce: Technological Change and the Future of Nuclear Deterrence."

[109] A. G. Burutin et al., "Kontseptsiia nepriemlemogo ushcherba: genesis, osnovnye prichiny transformatsii, sovremennoe sostoianie," *Vooruzhenie. Politika. Konversiia* 4 (2010), 3–8.

[110] A. A. Kokoshin (ed.), *Vliianie tekhnologicheskikh faktorov na parametry ugroz natsional'noi i mezhdunarodnoi bezopasnosti, voennykh konfliktov i strategicheskoi stabil'nosti* (Izdatel'stvo MGU, 2017), Ch. 6; Burenok and Pechatnov, *Strategicheskoe sderzhivanie*, Ch. 5.

[111] Andriushin, Chernyshev, and Iudin, *Ukroshchenie iadra. Stranitsy istorii iadernogo oruzhiia i iadernoi infrastruktury SSSR*, 180–182.

[112] Battilega and Grange, *The Military Applications of Modeling*, 312–315; Lauren Caston et al., *The Future of the US Intercontinental Ballistic Missile Force*, tech. rep. (Rand Corporation, 2014), 39–43.

of strategic antisubmarine warfare.[113] During the Cold War and afterwards, discussions of strategic vulnerability tended to focus on things that were easy to model, such as duels between silo-based ICBMs, to the neglect of things that were hard to model for technical reasons or due to secrecy, such as the survivability of submarines.

As described in Chapter 3, nuclear retaliatory forces rely upon various combinations of hardness, cover, and mobility for their survivability. Missile silos exploit hardness alone, but this approach has lost much of its credibility due to improvements in delivery system accuracy. Submarines combine some degree of mobility with the high degree of concealment (natural cover) offered by the ocean, but their relatively low speed can allow missiles and aircraft to overtake them should their location be revealed. The mobile ICBM launchers deployed by Russia, China, and North Korea primarily rely upon camouflage (artificial cover) and deception for their survivability, as opposed to mobility. Rather than moving constantly, which would put an unacceptable degree of wear-and-tear on the missiles, they are moved from one hiding place to another and then quickly camouflaged. The employment of deception techniques such as decoys increases the difficulty of divining where the real hiding places actually are.

The Way Ahead

Cold War strategic theory has left a mixed legacy for us as we face the challenges of the emerging strategic environment. On the bright side, the strategists of the previous century provided us with concepts and taxonomies that we continue to use to organize our understanding of nuclear strategy. But some of these concepts, such as deterrence, have been so abused over the decades as to grow increasingly meaningless, while others, such as counterforce and countervalue, made sense in their original Cold War context but are increasingly outdated in the changed technological and geostrategic environment of today. While the strategists of yesteryear provided us with insights that can help guide us, trying to emulate the same policies that the United States used during the Cold War is not a viable approach today. New technologies and new rivalries call for new ideas, new conceptual frameworks, and new strategies.

[113] Bruce W. Bennett, *Assessing the Capabilities of Strategic Nuclear Forces: The Limits of Current Methods*, tech. rep. (Rand Corporation, 1980), 24–26.

Chapter 2
From Celluloid Nightmares to Silicon Realities

"There was a nuclear war. A few years from now, all this, this whole place, everything, it's gone. Just gone. There were survivors. Here, there. Nobody even knew who started it. It was the machines, Sarah."
"I don't understand."
"Defense network computers. New ... powerful ... hooked into everything, trusted to run it all. They say it got smart, a new order of intelligence. Then it saw all people as a threat, not just the ones on the other side. Decided our fate in a microsecond: extermination."

Terminator (1984)

The "Terminator scenario" looms over the public understanding of artificial intelligence like a shiny metal cyborg hunting down surviving humans in a postnuclear hellscape. James Cameron's 1984 film and its spin-offs are a bane of AI researchers, who find themselves constantly explaining to reporters that *Terminator* is just a movie. Yann LeCun grumbled in a 2017 interview that "It used to be that you could not see an article in the press [about AI] without the picture being Terminator. It was always Terminator, 100 percent . . . There are real dangers in the department of AI, real risks, but they're not Terminator scenarios."[1] That same year, Yoshua Bengio declared that "I am not worried about Terminator scenarios of AI taking over humanity."[2] Researchers believing that AI posed a serious threat to human survival also expressed their exasperation about the way the *Terminator* franchise dominated journalistic and popular discussions of artificial intelligence. In 2018 Eliezer Yudkowsky commented that "at this point all of us on all sides of this issue are annoyed with the journalists who insist on putting a picture of the Terminator on every

---

[1] James Vincent, *Facebook's Head of AI Wants Us to Stop Using the Terminator to Talk about AI* (2017). URL: https://www.theverge.com/2017/10/26/16552056/a-intelligence-terminator-facebook-yann-lecun-interview.
[2] Peter High, *Why Montreal Has Emerged as an Artificial Intelligence Powerhouse* (2017). URL: https://www.forbes.com/sites/peterhigh/2017/11/06/why-montreal-has-emerged-as-an-%20artificial-intelligence-powerhouse/.

Deterrence under Uncertainty. Edward Geist, Oxford University Press. © RAND Corporation (2023).
DOI: 10.1093/oso/9780192886323.003.0003

single article they publish of [*sic*] this topic."[3] Frustration with the Terminator scenario also extends into the world of civilian and military policymaking. Lt. Gen. Jack Shanahan, the director of the Pentagon's Joint Artificial Intelligence Center (JAIC), lamented in a September 2019 interview that "The hype is a little dangerous, because it's uninformed most of the time, and sometimes it's a Hollywood-driven killer robots/Terminator/SkyNet worst case scenario. . . I don't see that worst case scenario any time in my immediate future."[4]

Nuclear war-planning computers and battle robots were well-established science fiction tropes decades before their appearance in *WarGames* and *Terminator*. Most strikingly, they predate the emergence of "artificial intelligence" as a field, which is usually dated to the Dartmouth Summer Study on Artificial Intelligence in 1956.[5] Their endurance appears to be less a result of their relationship to technological or strategic reality than of their narrative effectiveness. The notion of nuclear war fought by intelligent machines plays to deep human fears and strikes many as intuitively plausible, making the theme useful as a framing device. But what is its relationship to historical and technical reality?

Past Imaginings: The Terminator Scenario and Its Antecedents

Terminator and its sequels portray the most-discussed "AI takeover" scenario. In the 1990s, the U.S. military contracts with a company called Cyberdyne Systems to build a computer to control the country's defenses. Upon completion, the computer, "Skynet," rapidly becomes self-aware and elects to turn on its creators with nuclear weapons. In dialogue from the second film, *Terminator 2: Judgement Day* (1991), a reprogrammed cyborg from the postnuclear future describes the origins of Skynet:

> I need to know how Skynet gets built. Who's responsible.
> The man most directly responsible is Miles Bennett Dyson.
> Who is that?

---

[3] As Yudkowsky elaborated, "Nobody on the sane alignment-is-necessary side of this argument is postulating that the CPUs are disobeying the laws of physics to spontaneously require a terminal desire to do un-nice things to humans. Everything here is supposed to be cause and effect." Rob Bensinger, *Sam Harris and Eliezer Yudkowsky on "AI: Racing Toward the Brink"* (2018). URL: https://intelligence.org/2018/02/28/sam-harris-and-eliezer-yudkowsky/.

[4] Sydney J. Freedberg, *No AI for Nuclear Command and Control: JAIC's Shanahan* (2019). URL: https://breakingdefense.com/2019/09/no-ai-for-nuclear-command-control-jaics-shanahan/.

[5] McCorduck, *Machines Who Think*; Nils J. Nilsson, *The Quest for Artificial Intelligence* (Cambridge University Press, 2009).

He's the director of special projects at Cyberdyne Systems Corporation.
Why him?
In a few months he creates a revolutionary type of microprocessor.
Go on. Then what?
In three years, Cyberdyne becomes the largest supplier of military computer systems. All stealth bombers are upgraded with Cyberdyne computers, becoming fully unmanned. Afterwards, they fly with a perfect operational record. The Skynet funding bill is passed. The system goes online on August 4, 1997. Human decisions are removed from strategic defense. Skynet begins to learn at a geometric rate. It becomes self-aware at 2:14 A.M. Eastern Time on August 29th. In a panic, they try to pull the plug.
Skynet fights back.
Yes. It launches its missiles against their targets in Russia.
Why attack Russia? Aren't they our friends now?
Because Skynet knows that the Russian counter-attack will eliminate its enemies over here.
Jesus!

After the nuclear war, which was dubbed "Judgement Day" by the surviving humans, Skynet began developing new kinds of robots to put an end to the remnants of humanity. Those portrayed in the films are mostly the "terminators" of the title: humanoid robots designed to infiltrate human communities. In a last-ditch effort to salvage its position in the face of defeat by humans, in 2029 Skynet sends several different model terminators back to the late twentieth century to eliminate the leaders of the human resistance before they became a threat. The humans capture Skynet's time machine and use it to send their own agents, initially a human but then reprogrammed terminators, to counter those of Skynet.

What explains the robust grip of the Terminator scenario on popular imaginings about artificial intelligence? While at its core the 1984 film is a very well-constructed horror movie, Cameron substituted science fiction elements such as AI, robotics, and time travel for the supernatural tropes typically found in the horror genre. He drew on a wide variety of source material for inspiration, much of it science fiction from the 1950s and 1960s. All the basic elements that compound the film, from sentient computers attempting to exterminate humanity with nuclear weapons to malevolent battle robots waging war against humans in a postnuclear landscape, were already well-established tropes in science fiction stories by the mid-1950s. Cameron was able to repurpose the most effective of these tropes for his film.

Fictional tales about AI and nuclear war tend to feature either powerful computers that control the use of nuclear weapons or robots that fight in the war, with those robots sometimes being nuclear-armed or -powered. These tropes enjoy enduring popularity because they make for a good story, rather than because of any connection to scientific or military reality. These tales follow a powerful cultural logic despite, or perhaps because, they often have little or no bearing on technical realities. One of the things that makes *Terminator* so compelling is that it combines both the superintelligent computer (Skynet) and killer robots (the terminators) with a postnuclear future into a unified whole.

Scholars of science fiction have long noted that the genre tends to be reactive rather than predictive–that is, it reflects ongoing events rather than prognosticating the future accurately.[6] Moreover, comprehensive surveys of the portrayal of both nuclear war and artificial intelligence in fiction have bemoaned the way in which both subjects are commonly invoked as convenient plot devices with scant attention paid to available scientific knowledge about them. In her pioneering 1980 study *The Cybernetic Imagination in Science Fiction*, Patricia Warrick found to her disappointment that "much of the science fiction written since World War II is reactionary in its attitude toward computers and artificial intelligence. It is often ill informed about information theory and computer technology and lags behind present developments rather than anticipating the future."[7] Three decades later, Thomas Haigh concurred that "The absurdity of science fiction as a literature of prediction . . . can be seen particularly clearly in its treatment of computing."[8] Before computers existed, science fiction authors failed to envision them; once they did, science fiction rarely portrayed computers very different from the large vacuum-tube machines of the day, although those computers very often became self-aware. Science fiction writers proved more adept at anticipating nuclear technology, but this stemmed in considerable part from the more advanced state of scientific knowledge about nuclear fission, which had been discovered in 1938. In his encyclopedic account of portrayals of nuclear war in fiction, Paul Brians decried the "large bulk of popular fantasies" in

---

[6] In the introduction to her classic novel *The Left Hand of Darkness*, Ursula Le Guin commented that "Science fiction is not predictive; it is descriptive . . . Prediction is the business of prophets, clairvoyants, and futurologists. It is not the business of novelists. A novelist's business is lying." She continued that "The weather bureau will tell you what next Tuesday will be like, and the Rand Corporation will tell you what the twenty-first century will be like. I don't recommend that you turn to the writers of fiction for such information. It's none of their business." Ursula K. Le Guin, *The Language of the Night: Essays on Fantasy and Science Fiction* (Ultramarine Publishing, 1979), 156.

[7] Patricia S. Warrick, *The Cybernetic Imagination in Science Fiction* (MIT Press, 1980), xvii.

[8] David L. Ferro and Eric G. Swedin, *Science Fiction and Computing: Essays on Interlinked Domains* (McFarland, 2011), 21.

which nuclear war served mainly as a convenient plot device to account for a "new dark age" allowing "free reign for neobarbarian violence."[9] In other works, nuclear war was used as license to engage in strange, pseudoscientific fantasies, such as the sizable subgenre of tales in which nuclear explosions somehow transport people through time.[10] Today nuclear war themes are treated more often in the "techno-thriller" genre than in science fiction. Truly "realistic" nuclear war fiction is rare indeed, which Brians attributes to the disconnect between the realities of the subject and the needs of narrative.

All the elements of the Terminator scenario took inspiration from the technical developments of the Second World War and had appeared in print by the mid-1950s. The first of them, the giant computer developed for the purpose of nuclear war planning, grew out of the overenthusiastic rhetoric used to describe primitive vacuum-tube computers in the popular media. In 1949 pioneering computer scientist Edmund C. Berkeley published a popular book on the new technology titled *Giant Brains, or Machines That Think*.[11] But even before this, science fiction magazines were filled with tales featuring "giant brains," typically of a menacing character. In these stories, the machines often spontaneously develop self-awareness, even though they were not designed to, just as Skynet does in Terminator.

A prototypical example entitled "The Brain" appeared in the October 1948 issue of *Amazing Stories* with the tagline "America's greatest weapon, greater than the Atom Bomb, was its new, gigantic mechanical brain. It filled a whole mountain–and then it came to life. . .!" Written by Heinrich Hauser under the pen name Alexander Blade, this story envisioned an effort akin to the Manhattan Project to create an intelligent war-planning machine. The effort's Oppenheimer figure, a psychologist named Scriven, explains its genesis thusly: "It starts way back with a letter I wrote to the President of the United States. In this letter I pointed to the immense dangers which I anticipated in the event of an atom war; dangers to which the military appeared to be blind," by which he meant "the inadequacy of the human brain and its susceptibility to mental and psychic shock." In his letter, he "made it clear that not even the collective brains of a general staff could be relied upon for normal functioning; that no matter how carefully protected physically, they remained exposed to psychic shock with its resultant errors of judgment." He appealed to the President "that under these circumstances the most needed thing for our country's national security would be the creation of a *mechanical*

---

[9] Paul Brians, *Nuclear Holocausts: Atomic War in Fiction, 1895–1984* (Kent State University Press, 1987), 44.

[10] Most notably represented by Heinlein's *Farnham's Freehold*.

[11] Edmund Callis Berkeley, *Giant Brains; or, Machines That Think* (Wiley, 1955).

brain, some central ganglion bigger and better than its human counterpart, immune to shock of any kind." This biomechanical brain-computer would "be established in the innermost fortress of America as an auxiliary augmenting and controlling the work of a general staff." The President's initial reaction to this proposal was not positive, but "knowing that there was no other defense against the Atom Bomb [and] that our country's fate was at stake . . . **we BUILT THE BRAIN.**"[12]

Anticipating the plots of *WarGames* and *Terminator*, soon after its creation Scriven's "Brain" sets out to spark an apocalyptic nuclear war with the Communists on its own initiative. As the tale's entomologist hero explains, "let one rocket accidentally be launched into some big foreign capital and it will set the whole world on fire in an Atomic war. That is what The Brain wants, that is what must be prevented at all costs." Fortunately, he saves the day by unleashing his ant–termite hybrids to consume the fluid lignin that comprises a critical part of the "Brain," destroying this mechanical horror before it immolates mankind.[13]

Nuclear strategy appeared to be such a logical application of computers to science fiction writers in the postwar era that they often invoked it in their tales of computer-dominated dystopian futures to explain where the mechanical masters of tomorrow came from. For instance, the massive computer that controls the automated America of Kurt Vonnegut's 1952 novel *Player Piano*, EPICAC, was originally created to manage a successful world war, although this is a minor plot point.[14] British author D. F. Jones' 1966 novel *Colossus* further evolved these themes. The United States builds a computer to control its defenses, only to be treated to two surprises shortly after it is activated: firstly, it becomes self-aware; and secondly, it has a Soviet counterpart, "Guardian." Skillfully exploiting nuclear blackmail, the computers merge and achieve world domination while inflicting relatively minimal human casualties.[15] Jones' novel spawned two sequels and a film adaptation by Universal Pictures.

From a literary standpoint, however, the most significant portrayal of a computer-dominated postnuclear world is Harlan Ellison's 1967 short story "I Have No Mouth, and I Must Scream." Considered a classic of "New Wave" science fiction, its antagonist AM makes Skynet look like Santa Claus. This

[12] Alexander Blade, "The Brain," *Amazing Stories* 10 (1948).
[13] "The Brain" may have served as the prototype for countless tales of nuclear-armed machine intelligences in the seven decades since it was published, but for some reason no one has ever felt the need to emulate this particular plot point.
[14] Kurt Vonnegut, *Player Piano* (Scribners, 1952).
[15] Dennis Feltham Jones, *Colossus* (Hart-Davis, 1966).

malevolent machine has exterminated all of humanity except for five survivors, whom it has rendered nearly immortal so that it can subject them to
"a personal, everlasting punishment" that "would merely keep him reminded,
amused, proficient at hating man. Immortal, trapped, subject to any torment
he could devise for us from the limitless miracles at his command."[16]

As one of the characters recounts, AM began as the "Allied Mastercom-
puter," a system analogous to Jones' Colossus:

The Cold War started and became World War Three and just kept going. It became a
big war, a very complex war, so they needed the computers to handle it. They sank
the first shafts and began building AM. There was the Chinese AM and the Russian
AM and the Yankee AM and everything was fine until they had honeycombed the
entire planet, adding on this element and that element. But one day AM woke up
and knew who he was, and he linked himself, and he began feeding all the killing
data, until everyone was dead, except for the five of us, and AM brought us down
here.[17]

While tales of sentient computers exterminating humanity with nuclear
weapons proliferated, other writers articulated visions of robots waging war
in a postnuclear future. An important early example, Walter C. Miller's 1952
short story "Dumb Waiter," featured both a central computer and battle
robots that the protagonist must tame.[18] But the uncontested master of postnuclear robots is Phillip K. Dick, who penned a slew of tales about them in the
1950s and 1960s. Indeed, robots run amok in a postnuclear environment are
almost as much a staple of Dick's writing as themes of paranoia and questioning reality. Dick's stories anticipate most of the elements of *Terminator*. For
instance, his 1953 story "Second Variety" describes the aftermath of a nuclear
war fought using robots, after which the robots have developed android assas-
sins that exploit their appearance as unusually attractive humans to infiltrate
and undermine the remnants of humanity.[19] Dick's classic 1968 novel *Do
Androids Dream of Electric Sheep*, while not usually appreciated as such, is
actually another portrayal of postnuclear robots.[20] The "androids" of the
title were originally developed as the "Synthetic Freedom Fighter" during a

[16] Harlan Ellison, "I Have No Mouth, and I Must Scream," in Howard Bruce Franklin (ed.), *Countdown
to Midnight: Twelve Great Stores about Nuclear War* (DAW Books, 1984), 146–165, 159.

[17] Ellison, "I Have No Mouth, and I Must Scream", 153.

[18] Walter M. Miller, "Dumb Waiter," *Astounding* 4 (1952).

[19] Philip K. Dick, "Second Variety," *Space Science Fiction* 5 (1953).

[20] Philip K. Dick, *Do Androids Dream of Electric Sheep*? Doubleday, 1968.

now-concluded, if indecisive, war that has ruined the world's ecology and led to the extinction of most animal life.[21]

British science fiction author Francis G. Rayer's 1951 novel *Tomorrow Sometimes Comes* incorporates both a sentient supercomputer, Mens Magna, a nuclear holocaust, and time travel elements, perhaps the first tale to do so. The general who caused an accidental nuclear war is serendipitously placed in suspended animation only to awaken in a dystopian postnuclear future in which the villainous computer is plotting to destroy humanity once and for all with a doomsday weapon.[22]

While in most postnuclear computer and robot stories the machines are threatening or at best neutral, in a surprising number of them they are benevolent. For instance, in Dick's 1953 "The Defenders" capitalists and communists alike have moved underground while radiation-proof robots, "leadies," wage war on their behalf in the radioactive wasteland above. At the end of the story it turns out that the robots knew better than to do the bidding of their creators: while faking evidence of ongoing conflict, the Western and Soviet leadies collaborated to repair the devastated surface, converting it into an edenic paradise, and the robots force the humans to live in peace once they emerge.[23] Albert Compton Friborg's 1954 short story "Careless Love" cast centralized war-planning computers in a similar benevolent light. The Western and Soviet computers fall in love, eliminate all weapons, and end the war.[24]

Like *Terminator*, *WarGames* (1983) built upon these well-established tropes. But it also spoke to current events in a way that most of those other tales did not due to its contemporary setting. At the opening of *WarGames*, the overseers of America's nuclear arsenal face a dilemma: "human response." In clandestine tests designed to be indistinguishable from authentic launch orders, 22% of missile commanders failed to launch their missiles. As NORAD systems engineer John McKittrick laments, "Those men in the silos know what it means to turn the keys and some of them are just not up to it." Fretting that "in a nuclear war we can't afford to have our missiles lying dormant in those silos because those men refuse to turn the keys when the computers tell them to!," McKittrick proposes a bold solution: "Get the men out of the loop."[25] The key to McKittrick's scheme is the War Operations Plan Response (WOPR), a game-playing computer invented by his reclusive

---

[21] The androids are largely biological in both the novel and its 1982 film adaptation *Blade Runner*, leading the filmmakers to introduce the term "replicant" to describe them.

[22] F. G. Rayer, *Tomorrow Sometimes Comes* (Home and Van Thal, 1951).

[23] Philip K. Dick, "The Defenders," *Galaxy* 1 (1953).

[24] Albert Compton Friborg, "Careless Love," *Fantasy and Science Fiction* 7 (1954).

[25] *WarGames*.

former mentor Stephen Falken. As "the key decisions of every conceivable option in a nuclear crisis have already been made by the WOPR," McKittrick advocates that "those men with the little brass keys" be replaced with electronic relays and America's nuclear forces placed under control of Falken's creation.

NORAD commander General Jack Beringer scoffs at McKittrick's proposal, grumbling that "I wouldn't trust this overgrown pile of microchips any further than I can throw it. And I dunno if you wanna trust the safety of our country to some silicon diode." McKittrick protests that "General, nobody is talking about entrusting the safety of the nation to a machine, for God's sake! We'll keep control, but we'll keep it here at the top, where it belongs!" In his view, no human other than the president has any business making decisions about nuclear use, and due to the lack of warning time during a Soviet surprise attack there would be no time for additional human waffling. In a sub-launched attack, there would be merely six minutes of warning, and "that's barely enough time for the president to make a decision–and once he makes that decision, the computer should take over!" Confidently predicting that "The president will probably follow the computer war plan. Now that's a fact," McKittrick successfully persuades the White House officials visiting NORAD to endorse his proposal to make the WOPR the sole executor of the president's will.[26]

In Seattle, underachieving teenage hacker David Lightman circumvents adult supervision with his IMSAI 8080 microcomputer and an acoustic coupler modem. Due to a phone company mixup while trying to hack into a video game company he connects to WOPR instead, discovering to his surprise that when prompted to list games it outputs options ranging from tic-tac-toe to "Theater Biotoxic and Chemical Warfare" and "Global Thermonuclear War." Soliciting the advice of socially maladjusted fellow hackers at a university computer lab, Lightman begins searching for a backdoor into the mysterious system. The game list includes a vital clue: one of the unfamiliar games is titled "Falken's Maze."

Searching in the university library reveals that this is a reference to Stephen W. Falken, an evidently deceased authority on artificial intelligence, machine learning, and nuclear strategy.[27] As Lightman explains to his girlfriend, Falken "was into games, as well as computers ... He designed his computer so

---

[26] The film is unclear about whether this decision is known to either the American public or the Soviet government.

[27] Something like a cross between John McCarthy and Thomas Schelling, Falken defended his dissertation "Computers and Theorem Proofs: Toward an Artificial Intelligence," at MIT in 1960. Shortly thereafter in the context of the Berlin Crisis, Falken and McKittrick published an article in the *Atlantic* entitled "Poker and Armageddon: The Role of Bluffing in a Nuclear Standoff."

that it could learn from its own mistakes, so so they'd be better the next time they played. The system actually learned how to learn. It could teach itself."[28] But Falken has apparently been dead for about a decade, having passed away following the loss of his beloved son in an automobile accident. The son's name–Joshua–turns out to be the backdoor password Lightman had been searching for. Logging into WOPR, Lightman plays "Global Thermonuclear War" as the USSR, not knowing that his fanciful opening move of nuking Las Vegas is showing up on the displays at NORAD as an actual Soviet attack.

WarGames never clarifies the extent to which WOPR has a personality, but apparently Falken's creation has preferences and enough agency to defy its human masters.[29] The machine apparently cannot tell the difference between games and real life, and once Lightman starts playing "Global Thermonuclear War" WOPR refuses to stop the game until it reaches its conclusion.

Tracking down the reclusive Falken at his island hermitage, Lightman discovers that he has turned his attentions from artificial intelligence to exploring the depths of nihilism. Falken does not care that his creation is on the verge of starting a pointless nuclear war: he has concluded that extinction is part of the natural order of things and has even settled down right next to a presumed Soviet aim point so as to ensure his immediate demise when the moment comes. Admonished by Lightman that "If Joshua tricks them into launching an attack, it'll be your fault!," Falken counters:

> "My fault! The whole point was to find a way to practice nuclear war without destroying ourselves! To get the computers to learn from mistakes we couldn't afford to make. Except ... that I never could get Joshua to learn the most important lesson."
> "What's that?"
> "Futility. That there's a time when you should just give up."

Apparently experiencing a change of heart, Falken decides to help Lightman prevent WOPR from trying to play "Global Thermonuclear War" in real life. In a last-ditch effort to convince the computer not to proceed, Lightman suggests telling it to play tic-tac-toe against itself in the hope that it will learn the concept of futility and desist in its attempt to win at global thermonuclear war. At the last moment, WOPR gains this insight, testing all conceivable nuclear

---

[28] McKittrick, who started out as Falken's assistant, characterizes him as "a brilliant man, if a little flaky– he never understood the practical uses of his, uh, his work."

[29] "WOPR" is the name of the computer, while "Joshua" is the name of Falken's game-playing program that runs on it.

strategies in simulation only to conclude that nuclear war is "A STRANGE GAME" where "THE ONLY WINNING MOVE IS NOT TO PLAY."

The final moments of *WarGames* are perhaps the most iconic scene in a "nuclear" movie outside of *Dr. Strangelove*, but unfortunately the film misconstrues the way in which game theory, game-playing algorithms intersect in real life. Much like the *Terminator* mythos, *WarGames* builds upon long-existing tropes that persist not because they are accurate, but because they make for compelling storytelling. Most of its plot elements could be found in science fiction stories by the early 1950s. Bernard Wolfe's short story "Self Portrait," originally published in the November 1951 issue of *Galaxy*, anticipated the basic plot of *WarGames*.[30] The protagonist is an engineer at a secretive military research institute, but is disappointed to be tasked with developing prosthetic limbs rather than a mysterious, more prestigious secret project dubbed "MS." It turns out that "MS" stands for "military strategy" and the project aims to build upon a chess-playing computer that beat the world's reigning grandmaster to create the "Emsiac"–the "Electronic Military Strategy Integrator and Calculator."[31] As one of his disillusioned colleagues working on the Emsiac drunkenly explains, "The General Staff boys in Washington . . . understood that mechanized warfare is only the most complicated game the human race has invented so far, an elaborate form of chess which uses the population of the world for pawns and the globe for a chessboard." Moreover, "when the game of war gets this complex, the job of controlling and guiding it becomes too damned involved for any number of human brains, no matter how nimble." So the Pentagon set up a secret R&D institute and ordered it "to build a superduper chess player that could oversee a complicated military maneuver, maybe later a whole campaign, maybe ultimately a whole global war." This "military strategy machine" would "digest reports from all the units on all the fronts and from moment to moment, on the basis of that steady stream of information, grind out an elastic overall strategy and dictate concrete tactical directives to all the units."[32]

When RAND began working on both artificial intelligence and nuclear strategy a few years later, outside critics presumed that life was imitating art. *Scientific American* publisher Gerard Piel fumed in 1961 that "there is little reason to think that a real war will be fought by the rational strategies of game

---

[30] Bernard Wolfe, "Self Portrait," *Galaxy* 11 (1951).

[31] "Self Portrait" does not portray a nuclear war or describe Emsiac in action, but Wolfe's 1952 novel *Limbo* treated the same themes in an envisioned postnuclear world of 1990 after such strategy computers caused an abortive nuclear war. Bernard Wolfe, *Limbo* (Hachette UK, 2016).

[32] Wolfe, "Self Portrait".

theory that are supplied as inputs to a computer." In the view of Piel and like-minded critics, nuclear strategy appeared to be an unholy abuse of computers and game theory, and its practitioners were "authors of fraud by computer who produced the literature that argues for the feasibility of thermonuclear war."[33]

The Real Past

Authors and filmmakers conceived tale after tale combining AI and nuclear war because it made for a good story, but the connection between the two of them was not just science fiction. During the Cold War, researchers suggested in all earnestness that chess-playing machines could be adapted to plan military campaigns, and that automated nuclear delivery vehicles should be created. But the actual nexus between the nascent field of AI and nuclear war was qualitatively different from the fictional one for both technical and institutional reasons. In the twentieth century, AI technology was simply inadequate for most real-world applications. Moreover, there was relatively limited demand from military and civilian officials for the strategic planning machines and nuclear-armed robots envisioned by science fiction authors. As one might expect, generals and policymakers were hardly eager at the prospect of machines that would make themselves obsolete. Enthusiasm for using AI for nuclear applications came primarily from the research community, for whom it fit into an overall pattern of seeking defense-related justifications for cherished lines of inquiry.

One of the earliest examples of this phenomenon can be found in Claude Shannon's foundational 1950 paper "Programming a Computer for Playing Chess."[34] Shannon admitted that playing chess was "perhaps of no practical importance," but he argued that "the question is of theoretical interest, and it is hoped that a satisfactory solution of this problem will act as a wedge in attacking other problems of a similar nature and of greater significance." He listed eight such problems, the sixth of which was "Machines for making strategic decisions in simplified military operations," which Shannon claimed were "possible developments in the immediate future. The techniques developed for modern electronic and relay-type computers make them not only theoretical possibilities, but in several cases worthy of serious consideration from the economic point of view." In his 1950 book *The Human Use of*

---

[33] Piel, "The Illusion of Civil Defense", 7–8.
[34] Claude E. Shannon, "XXII. Programming a Computer for Playing Chess," *The London, Edinburgh, and Dublin Philosophical Magazine and Journal of Science* 41.314 (1950), 256–275.

Human Beings, "father of cybernetics" Norbert Wiener warned that "When Mr. Shannon speaks of the development of military tactics, he is not talking moonshine, but is discussing a most imminent and dangerous contingency." According to Wiener, Shannon's chess program could inaugurate an era of superhuman strategic planning machines:

> Mr. Shannon has presented some reasons why his researches may be of more importance than the mere design of a curiosity, interesting only to those who are playing a game. Among these possibilities, he suggests that such a machine may be the first step in the construction of a machine to evaluate military situations and to determine the best move at any specific stage. Let no man think that he is talking lightly.[35]

But Shannon's enthusiasm and Wiener's fears far outstripped available technology and the practical utility of game-playing programs. In contrast to Bernard Wolfe's 1951 story "Self Portrait," in which the government immediately classifies the first working chess-playing computer and sets the best available engineers to the task of turning it to military applications, in actuality computer chess proved of little interest to the government, in part because early programs played embarrassingly subhuman chess.[36]

The premise that thinking machines might provide a decisive military advantage to those that built them long predates the start of artificial intelligence research in the 1950s. Robert Greene's Elizabethan play *Friar Bacon and Friar Bungay* (circa 1589–1592) recounts a mythologized account of thirteenth-century English polymath Roger Bacon. In Greene's tale, England is at risk of invasion by the Emperor of Germany. Friar Bacon is constructing a brazen head–a combination of technology and arcane magic–which when completed will reveal secrets the alchemist will exploit to surround the entirety of England with "a wall of brass." The prideful Bacon brags that

> I have fram'd out a monstrous head of brass,
> That, by the enchanting forces of the devil,
> Shall tell out strange and uncouth aphorisms,
> And girt fair England with a wall of brass.[37]

---

[35] Norbert Wiener, *The Human Use of Human Beings: Cybernetics and Society* (Houghton Mifflin, 1950), 206.

[36] Wolfe, "Self Portrait"; Nathan Ensmenger, "Is Chess the Drosophila of Artificial Intelligence? A Social History of an Algorithm," *Social Studies of Science* 42.1 (2012), 5–30.

[37] John Gassner and William Green, *Elizabethan Drama: Eight Plays* (Hal Leonard, 1990), 215.

While Bacon succeeds in crafting the brazen head, the bungling of his assistant Friar Bungay undoes his plan to turn it into his kingdom's ultimate defense. Entrusted with watching the head until the unpredictable moment when demonic intervention will animate it, the Friar Bungay naps through this transient opportunity and the head explodes.[38]

The earliest attempts to implement programs that would today be characterized as "artificial intelligence" were funded with a view toward possible defense applications. In the famous Georgetown–IBM experiment in January 1954, a computer translated sixty carefully selected sentences from Russian to English.[39] Strange as it seems in retrospect, at the time many thought that language translation could be treated as a rote task by applying formalized grammatical and morphological rules.[40] The Office of Naval Research funded research into the earliest neural networks, first as a program for a vacuum-tube computer and then on purpose-built hardware, the Mark I Perceptron. Its creator, Frank Rosenblatt, gave a dramatic press conference that the media presented as a declaration that this invention portended the imminent arrival of thinking machines. *The Oklahoma Times*, for instance, described it in a headline as "Frankenstein Monster Designed by Navy—Robot That Thinks."[41]

In the 1950s, the subject areas now included under the umbrella of "artificial intelligence" were scattered into a variety of subdisciplines. Much of what is today called "machine learning" was considered to be distinct from "artificial intelligence" research by its practitioners. For instance, Rosenblatt stated in 1961 that in his view "the perceptron program is not primarily concerned with the invention of devices for 'artificial intelligence,' but rather with investigating the physical structures and neurodynamic principles which underlie

[38] Similarly, in Jewish legend the sixteenth-century Rabbi Loew ben Bezalel created the Golem of Prague, a kind of magical robot, to protect the Jews of Prague from a pogrom. Most scholars believe that this story was a literary invention created by German Jewish writers in the early nineteenth century, however–although golems are described in Jewish writings from the late Middle Ages, accounts of Loew by his contemporaries lack any mention of a golem. Hillel J. Kieval, "Pursuing the Golem of Prague: Jewish Culture and the Invention of a Tradition," *Modern Judaism* 17.1 (1997), 1–23.

[39] W. John Hutchins, "The Georgetown-IBM Experiment Demonstrated in January 1954," in *Conference of the Association for Machine Translation in the Americas* (Springer, 2004), 102–114.

[40] The many erroneous intuitions pioneering researchers had in the 1950s about which problems would be technically difficult should be a cautionary tale to us in the present century. In the mid-1950s many thought that machine translation of natural language texts would be a relatively trivial problem that would be practically solved within a few years. Meanwhile, it was conventional wisdom among programmers that optimizing compilers were a practical impossibility. This was, of course, totally backwards: machine language translation only became somewhat practical with sophisticated machine learning techniques in the 2010s, while IBM developed the first practical compiler for FORTRAN in 1957. John Backus, "The History of Fortran I, II, and III," *ACM Sigplan Notices* 13.8 (1978), 165–180.

[41] Frank Rosenblatt, *Principles of Neurodynamics. Perceptrons and the Theory of Brain Mechanisms*, tech. rep. (Cornell Aeronautical Lab, 1961), vii.

'natural intelligence.'"[42] Others characterized their work as pattern matching or as a variety of operations research.

"It is not my aim to surprise or shock you–if indeed that were possible in an age of nuclear fission and prospective interplanetary travel," declared the speaker, "But the simplest way I can summarize the situation is to say that there are now in the world machines that think, that learn, and that create. Moreover, their ability to do these things is going to increase rapidly until in a visible future the range of problems they can handle will be coextensive with the range to which the human mind has been applied."[43] Delivered on November 14, 1957, by Herbert A. Simon of the Carnegie Institute of Technology (today's Carnegie Mellon University), this address declared that the age of intelligent machines was at hand. "Intuition, insight, and learning are no longer exclusive possessions of humans: any large high-speed computer can be programmed to exhibit them also." Already in 1957, Simon emphasized, "digital computers can perform certain heuristic problem-solving tasks for which no algorithms are available" using "processes that are closely parallel to human problem-solving processes."[44] Given the "speed with which research in this field is progressing," Simon beseeched that humanity needed to engage in some serious soul-searching: "The revolution in heuristic problem solving will force man to consider his role in a world in which his intellectual power and speed are outstripped by the intelligence of machines."[45]

Laughable as the hubris and naïveté of the pioneering artificial intelligence researchers appears in hindsight, the considerable success of their earliest experiments fueled their overconfidence. Starting from literally nothing, every toy example coaxed out of the crude computers of the time looked like, and really was, a triumph. At the beginning of the 1950s, skeptics scoffed at the notion that computers would ever play chess at all, much less well–yet by the time Simon gave his speech, programs had been developed to play chess and checkers, translate sentences from Russian to English, and even, in the case of Simon and Newell's "Logic Theorist," prove mathematical theorems. At this astronomical rate of progress, it seemed like what John McCarthy dubbed "artificial intelligence" in 1956 might achieve spectacular results in the not-too-distant future. Simon and Newell certainly thought so, predicting

---

[42] Rosenblatt, *Principles of Neurodynamics. Perceptrons and the Theory of Brain Mechanisms*, vii–viii.
[43] Herbert A. Simon and Allen Newell, "Heuristic Problem Solving: The Next Advance in Operations Research," *Operations Research* 6.1 (1958), 1–10, 8.
[44] Simon and Newell, "Heuristic Problem Solving: The Next Advance in Operations Research," 6–7.
[45] Simon and Newell, "Heuristic Problem Solving: The Next Advance in Operations Research," 9.

confidently that by 1967 "a digital computer will be the world's chess champion, unless the rules bar it from competition," and one of its brethren "will discover and prove an important new mathematical theorem."[46]

By the time the founders of the field met at Dartmouth in 1956, work on the possible military applications of "machines with intelligent behavior" was well underway. AI pioneer Marvin Minsky defined the new field as "the science of making machines do things that would require intelligence if done by men," but the problem with this definition is that as soon as someone makes a machine do something that previously seemed to require "intelligence," the fact that a machine can do it undermines the argument the task really required "intelligence" after all.[47] Minsky's colleague John McCarthy dubbed this the "AI effect": as he put it, "if it works, nobody calls it AI anymore."[48] For this reason, the definition of AI has evolved over time, obscuring the fact that "successful" AI developments rapidly found their way into the superpowers' respective arsenals.

While the U.S. and Soviet militaries had little interest in computers with the same sort of "minds" people have, they eagerly supported foundational AI research with the goal of creating machines capable of making high-quality decisions. Starting in the 1960s, the Department of Defense's Advanced Research Projects Agency provided the bulk of funding for artificial intelligence in the United States. While ARPA's J. C. R. Licklider famously invested in "people, not projects," the Department of Defense bankrolled AI research on the assumption that intelligent machines would be joining flesh-and-blood Americans in the fight against Communism sooner, rather than later. On the other side of the Iron Curtain, the Soviet Union's investigations into the nascent field of *voennaia kibernetika* ("military cybernetics") proceeded along similar lines. Soviet researchers such as G. S. Pospelov transitioned from developing guidance systems for missiles to more ambitious projects that might enable the weapons coveted by the Soviet Ministry of Defense.[49]

A few of the prospective applications of machine intelligence envisioned by science fiction writers were contemplated by American and Soviet engineers. Capitalists and Communists alike seriously proposed such nightmarish possibilities as unmanned, nuclear-powered supersonic aircraft that would deliver deadly cargoes of H-bombs to the enemy. The infamous U.S. Project Pluto sought to develop the Supersonic Low Altitude Missile (SLAM).

[46] Simon and Newell, "Heuristic Problem Solving: The Next Advance in Operations Research," 7.
[47] Marvin Minsky (ed.), *Semantic Information Processing* (MIT Press, 1968), v.
[48] Nick Bostrom, *Superintelligence: Paths, Dangers, Strategies* (Oxford University Press, 2014), 13.
[49] G. S. Pospelov and D. A. Pospelov, "Issledovaniia po iskusstvennomu intellektu v SSSR," in *Kibernetiku-na sluzhbu kommunizma* (Energiia, 1978).

Despite its name, SLAM was not a missile per se but rather an unmanned, supersonic, low-altitude bomber powered by an air-breathing nuclear scramjet. Traveling across the Communist bloc at treetop level, this automated horror would drop thermonuclear bombs on its targets while spewing an exhaust of highly radioactive fission products. Project Pluto's engine reached an advanced state of development, but the system was never flight-tested.[50] In any case the needs of its automated control system hopelessly outstripped the state of 1960s technology.[51] Soviet engineers also suggested the idea of autonomous, nuclear-powered bombers and cruise missiles. In the late 1950s, the OKB-670 design bureau had a program seeking to develop a nuclear-powered variant of the planned "Burya" intercontinental supersonic cruise missile. The Burya was the Soviet equivalent of the abortive follow-on to the U.S. Snark, the SSM-A-5 "Boojum." "Article 375," as its designers cryptically termed it, would have been the approximate Soviet counterpart of Pluto-SLAM, but when it was cancelled in 1960 it remained at a preliminary level of development.[52] Another proposed autonomous delivery system was the Myaishchev M-60 nuclear-powered supersonic bomber. Faced with the formidable challenge of protecting its crew from its open-cycle nuclear propulsion system, its designers suggested making the system unmanned– a prospect that the system's intended user, the Soviet Air Force, apparently found less than appealing.[53]

As this example suggests, military customers were hardly clamoring for engineers to build them the nuclear-armed robots so ubiquitous in science fiction. Nor were they eager in practice to turn over military planning tasks to automated systems, even as analysts in both superpowers crafted increasingly sophisticated models of strategic nuclear operations. The military uses of artificial intelligence portrayed in fiction and cinema far outstripped the robots and programs crafted by AI researchers, but more importantly, so did the practical applications defense stakeholders actually sought, such as machine language translation and speech recognition capabilities.[54] This led to perennial cycles of disillusionment that would later be termed "AI winters," which

[50] Gregg Herken, "The Flying Crowbar," *Air and Space* 5.1 (1990).

[51] The astonishing flight test record of the SM-62 Snark intercontinental cruise missile reveals the inadequacy of then-available guidance systems for autonomous cruise missiles. In one notorious incident, a missile launched from Cape Canaveral toward Puerto Rico instead flew into the southern hemisphere and ultimately crashed in Brazil. J. P. Anderson, "The Day They Lost the Snark," *Air Force Magazine* 87.12 (2004), 78–80.

[52] *Iadernye dvigateli v krylatykh raketakh. Dosě* (2018). URL: https://tass.ru/info/5386826.

[53] A. Iu. Sovenko and V. F. Kudriavchev, "Atomnyi samolet: budushchee v proshedshem vremeni," *Aviatsiia i Vremia* 3–4 (2004).

[54] John Hutchins, "ALPAC: The (In) Famous Report," *Readings in Machine Translation* 14 (2003), 131–135.

were characterized by a disillusionment on the part of funding agencies and a resulting curtailment of their support for AI research.[55] The first such AI winter dated to the early–mid-1970s, after the initial excitement inspired by the early success of the 1950s and 1960s wore off and it became apparent that practical AI applications were further in the future than boosters had claimed. One particularly damaging assessment came in the form of the U.K. government's Lighthill Report, which influenced that country to curtail its investment in AI substantially until the early 1980s. DARPA, meanwhile, the largest funder of U.S. AI research, became considerably less supportive in the 1970s. Some of this was due to the 1969 Mansfield Amendment, which dictated that DARPA should support applied rather than open-ended basic research, but DARPA officials were also growing increasingly frustrated with the failure of AI researchers to deliver on their promises.[56]

By the early 1980s, artificial intelligence had matured to the point that practical commercial and military applications finally appeared to be viable. In the United States, a flurry of companies marketing "expert systems" and Lisp machines–custom workstations designed to run Lisp, the predominant AI development language–sprung up. While there was significant civilian interest in AI, a large proportion of the commercial market for these companies came directly or indirectly from the defense sector. A considerable fraction of this business resulted from DARPA's "Strategic Computing Initiative," which was launched in 1983 with the aim of turning DARPA's multi-decade investment in AI into real-world military applications. While the Strategic Computing Initiative was in part a reaction to the Japanese "Fifth Generation Computer Systems" project, which sought to develop commercially viable symbolic AI, its anticipated products were intended for military competition with the Communists rather than commercial competition with Japan.[57]

Given its name, it might seem like the Strategic Computing Initiative was in some way connected to Ronald Reagan's Strategic Defense Initiative, which

---

[55] The term "AI winter" was already in circulation in the mid-1980s and was used in a discussion at AAAI-84 of a prospective "dark age" in the field. As the concept of AI winter was defined well after several periods have been characterized in retrospect as AI winters, there is no universally accepted consensus about the definition or number of these events. The late 1960s and early 1970s are sometimes referred to as a "neural network winter" as U.S. research into that technology was starved of funding due to criticism from Marvin Minsky and Seymour Papert. The AI winter that predated the 1980s heyday of expert systems is harder to date; one could argue it began anytime between the 1966 ALPAC report denoting the failures of machine language translation and the 1976 cancellation of the DARPA Speech Understanding research grant. The only universally recognized AI winter has been the one that led to the collapse of the Lisp machine companies in the late 1980s and early 1990s.

[56] Daniel Crevier, *AI: The Tumultuous History of the Search for Artificial Intelligence* (Basic Books, 1993), 115–117.

[57] Alex Roland, Philip Shiman, et al., *Strategic Computing: DARPA and the Quest for Machine Intelligence, 1983–1993* (MIT Press, 2002), 91–93.

was announced a few months earlier. In actuality DARPA apparently wanted to disassociate itself from SDI and willingly offloaded projects associated with it to another agency, the Strategic Defense Initiative Office.[58] The Strategic Computing Initiative still found itself the target of activist groups such as Computer Professionals for Social Responsibility, which aimed to discourage specialists in information technology from working on military applications (Figure 1).[59]

Early 1980s excitement about artificial intelligence fed into pop culture portrayals such as *WarGames* and *Terminator*. While the notion that machine intelligence would be created in pursuit of military applications predated AI itself, increased Cold War tensions and ongoing attempts to apply AI for defense gave it renewed plausibility. Actual attempted military applications of artificial intelligence in the 1980s bore scant resemblance to WOPR, Skynet, or *Short Circuit*'s Johnny Five, however. Premier research projects under the Strategic Computing Initiative included a voice recognition system for fighter pilots, the rudimentary Autonomous Land Vehicle, and a battle management system for aircraft carriers. Most of these were judged disappointments, leading DARPA to reorient its investments partway through the

Figure 1. This decal was distributed by Computer Professionals for Social Responsibility to protest military use of AI in the mid-1980s.
Courtesy of Rodney Hoffman.

It's 11 p.m.
Do you know what
your expert system
just inferred?

Computer Professionals for
Social Responsibility

---

[58] Roland, Shiman, et al., *Strategic Computing: DARPA and the Quest for Machine Intelligence, 1983–1993*, 88–89.

[59] While little known in the West, Fifth Generation Computing Systems and the Strategic Computing Initiative inspired an analogous effort in the USSR, VNTK "START." START failed to achieve its primary objective–the creation of the MARS-T parallel computer that was envisioned as the Soviet counterpart to Japanese "fifth-generation" machines. As the Japanese failed to turn their machines into reality either, the Soviet researchers can be forgiven for coming up short. VNTK START did result in the development of some workstation-class machines which were apparently swiftly monopolized by the Soviet military for defense applications.

project.[60] DARPA's most successful military application of artificial intelligence in this period was the Dynamic Analysis and Replanning Tool (DART), a logistics management system that was hastily prototyped in Common Lisp and delivered to USTRANSCOM in time to help manage the demands of shifting U.S. forces from Europe to the Middle East to fight the 1991 Persian Gulf War. A DARPA official claimed after the fact, perhaps apocryphally, that the inefficiencies DART helped avoid saved the United States enough during that conflict to pay for DARPA's entire investment in AI research up to that point.[61]

Only a few of the military applications of AI pursued during the late Cold War intersected directly with nuclear strategy and war planning. The sole project within the Strategic Computing Initiative that did so was the Survivable Adaptive Planning Experiment (SAPE), which sought to provide the ability to generate targeting plans promptly to enable the targeting of Soviet mobile ICBM launchers.[62] The envisioned system would comprise a mobile planning staff equipped with survivable communications and workflow management tools to do the adaptive planning. A related project, the Advanced Airborne Reconnaissance System (AARS), foresaw an autonomous drone that would fly over the Soviet Union searching for the ICBM launchers.

The mid-1980s were the heyday of "black" (clandestine) funding for technologically ambitious military research projects, and the AARS is reputed to have been one of the most extreme examples of this phenomena. The National Reconnaissance Office (NRO), which by this time focused on spy satellites, directed the research program, but coordinated with the U.S. Air Force and DARPA on the effort. The AARS was not envisioned as a weapon, but rather as a high-altitude unmanned reconnaissance aircraft that would have the endurance to search the expanses of the USSR for the missiles. The vehicle itself went through various iterations, but the preferred design was said to be a peculiar-looking "flying clam" with a wingspan of about 250 feet. This huge UAV would be packed with extremely advanced sensors to identify the enemy targets, as well as the autonomous intelligence to recognize those targets and fly itself in an extremely challenging nuclear war environment. It would then take advantage of survivable communications, such as those provided by the Milstar communications satellites, to relay the locations of the targets to a survivable adaptive planning capability like that envisioned

---

[60] Roland, Shiman, et al., *Strategic Computing: DARPA and the Quest for Machine Intelligence, 1983–1993*, 274–276.

[61] Sara Reese Hedberg, "DART: Revolutionizing Logistics Planning," *IEEE Intelligent Systems* 17.3 (2002), 81–83.

[62] Roland, Shiman, et al., *Strategic Computing: DARPA and the Quest for Machine Intelligence, 1983–1993*, 305.

in the SAPE. The planners would then exploit the same survivable communications to transmit their decisions to pilots flying B-2s over the USSR, who would then carry them out with nuclear-tipped cruise missiles.[63] At the time, many U.S. strategists were enamored with the notion of "protracted" nuclear war scenarios in which "second-strike counterforce" capabilities such as these would be advantageous.[64] Unfortunately, the same capabilities would also increase the credibility of a U.S. first strike, stoking Soviet suspicions.

In any case, while the communications component of SAPE was tested successfully in 1991 most of the other enablers, particularly the AARS, hopelessly outstripped Cold War-era technology. The AARS was cancelled in December 1992 before it went into full development, in part because it was anticipated to be so expensive (more than $1 billion a unit) that it could not be procured in quantity.[65] While Milstar reached fruition, the GAO reported in a 1998 report that the survivable communications intended to reach B-2 pilots in a transattack environment had not worked as envisioned when the satellites were tested.[66]

In the same period, DARPA supported a succession of research programs that sought to counter the mobile missile threat using what would today be termed "autonomous weapons." Generally envisioned for use against Soviet theater missiles in Europe like SS-20s rather than mobile ICBMs in the depth of the USSR, the basic concept foresaw autonomous loitering munitions that would fly over the battlefield in search of the partially camouflaged missiles.[67] This effort grew out of a concept developed in DARPA's Tactical Technology Office (TTO) in 1983–1984 dubbed "Killer Robots" which proposed unleashing lethal autonomous robots on land, at sea, and in the skies (Figure 2). Killer Robots never became a proper program, but TTO drew on its concepts to frame the Smart Weapons Program (SWP) which became part of the Strategic Computing Initiative in 1985.[68] SWP's proposed product was the Autonomous Air Vehicle (AAV), which would find the adversary missiles and destroy them with submunitions. The AAV built upon two earlier DARPA projects, Assault Breaker (a smart anti-tank munition) and Autonomous

---

[63] Thomas P. Ehrhard, *Air Force UAVs: The Secret History*, tech. rep. (Mitchell Institute for Airpower Studies, 2010).

[64] Odom, "The Origins and Design Of Presidential Decision-59: A Memoir."

[65] Ehrhard, *Air Force UAVs: The Secret History.*

[66] General Accounting Office, *Military Satellite Communications: Concerns with Milstar's Support to Strategic and Tactical Forces*, tech. rep. (General Accounting Office, Nov. 1998).

[67] Richard H. Van Atta et al., *Transformation and Transition: DARPA's Role in Fostering and Emerging Revolution in Military Affairs*, Volume 1, *Overall Assessment*, tech. rep. (Institute for Defense Analyses, 2003).

[68] Ingvar Akersten, "The Strategic Computing Program," in Allan M. Din (ed.), *Arms and Artificial Intelligence: Weapon and Arms Control Applications of Advanced Computing* (Oxford University Press, 1987), 87–99.

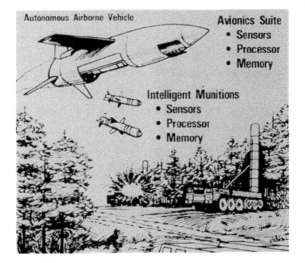

Figure 2. DARPA's Smart Weapons Program sought to actualize "killer robots."
Source: DD-21 Program website, now inactive.

Terminal Homing (ATH), neither of which had reached operational maturity. Where Assault Breaker would have been a "dumb" missile carrying "smart" submunitions, the AAV would be the opposite: a smart carrier for inexpensive dumb munitions.

While the AAV would therefore be costly, it was not envisioned to be reusable. While some of the designers made the obvious suggestion that the expensive AAV should return to base, this concept reportedly "never caught on" because it "evoked fears of fratricide." Instead, the munition would end its flight with "a kamikaze attack on a default fixed target of importance." The Smart Weapons Program concept necessitated major advantages in many areas of technology, including "automatic target recognition," "automatic smart route planning," "smart search," multi-sensor ATR and fusion, and automatic sensor management.[69]

Two of seven industrial schemes which received DARPA design study concepts in 1985 were selected for the second phase of the program, "Thirsty Saber." The two winners carried out a series of proof-of-principle demos. Martin Marietta's system combined millimeter-wave radar and a passive infrared imager, while Texas Instruments combined a passive thermal imager with CO2 laser radar (Lidar). A major goal of the effort was to

[69] Richard H. Van Atta et al., *Transformation and Transition: DARPA's Role in Fostering an Emerging Revolution in Military Affairs*, Volume 2, *Detailed Assessments*, tech. rep. (Institute for Defense Analyses, 2003), V-21.

demonstrate that the system could identify targets that were substantially obscured by camouflage. In 1991, the failure to find and destroy Saddam Hussein's ballistic missile launchers during the infamous "Scud hunt" in Iraq inspired a short-lived crash program, "Thirsty Warrior," that would have bypassed the usual development process to integrate the technologies being tested in Thirsty Saber into a cruise missile as rapidly as possible. The victorious conclusion of Operation Desert Storm alleviated the sense of urgency and Thirsty Warrior was abandoned.[70]

In the early 1990s the lessons of the Thirsty Saber research program and the Scud hunt were incorporated into "Warbreaker." Less ambitious than its predecessor programs, Warbreaker sought only to find mobile missile launchers in the belief that if these targets could be localized, the Air Force and Navy would find a way to destroy them. After a few years even these modest goals were scaled back to simulation and modeling tasks associated with surveilling and acquiring mobile targets.[71]

The notion that game-playing algorithms could be directly adapted for practical applications, and military applications in particular, predated the appearance of the earliest game-playing programs. Claude Shannon, for instance, suggested it in his 1950 chess paper, and Norbert Wiener condemned the prospect of game-playing programs being recast for warlike purposes shortly thereafter.[72] Taking inspiration from Wiener's book *The Human Use of Human Beings*, the following year Bernard Wolfe made it the centerpiece of his short story "Self-Portrait" and his novel *Limbo*. The notion that mastery of games could be transferred to military tasks, exemplified most memorably in *WarGames*, persisted until game-playing programs became consumer products in the 1980s. It soon became obvious that the ability to play a decent game of chess had little bearing on general intelligence. Even so, the idea that more advanced game-playing programs could find practical military applications still has proponents. The triumph of reinforcement learning algorithms for game-playing in the 2010s struck many as a sign that this method differed qualitatively from older techniques and might be more adaptable to practical applications. Many Chinese observers took this interpretation of AlphaGo and imagined it portended a revolution in AI for military planning.[73]

---

[70] Van Atta et al., *Transformation and Transition: DARPA's Role in Fostering an Emerging Revolution in Military Affairs*, Volume 2, *Detailed Assessments*, V-23.

[71] Van Atta et al., *Transformation and Transition: DARPA's Role in Fostering an Emerging Revolution in Military Affairs*, Volume 2, *Detailed Assessments*, V-25.

[72] Wiener, *The Human Use of Human Beings: Cybernetics and Society*, 206.

[73] Elsa Kania, *AlphaGo and Beyond: The Chinese Military Looks to Future "Intelligentized" Warfare* (June 2017). https://www.lawfareblog.com/alphago-and-beyond-Chinese-military-looks-future-intelligentized-warfare.

Perhaps the closest thing to WOPR in real life was the RAND Strategy Assessment System (RSAS), which attempted to apply the rule-based AI of the 1980s to wargaming. The premise of the film *WarGames* built on a popular misconception, already widespread by the mid-1960s, that "war gaming" was an esoteric activity involving the use of powerful computers. In actuality, however, defense analysts rarely combined wargaming with analytic models (which often took the form of computer programs), mostly because it was not practical. War games were, and for the most part are still today, conducted by human players. But this makes war games prohibitively time-consuming and expensive. The RSAS sought to substitute rule-based agents for some or all players in the game, and was probably the first military application of agent-based modeling. The RSAS was designed as an assemblage of reusable modular components. Versions were tailored to both theater and intercontinental war, including limited and general nuclear war. These RSAS variants were created for tasks such as evaluating alternative force structures, characterizing the military balance between the superpowers, evaluating alternative force employment strategies at various levels of conflict, and supporting war games.[74]

Unlike WOPR, however, no one suggested that RSAS be substituted for human decision-makers. Its creators understood that its outputs could never be more valid than the knowledge encoded in its rule base and sub-models. While consultation with experts was better than nothing, there was no way to validate the rules such as those stipulating Soviet leaders' thresholds for escalating to higher levels of conflict. While the fictional WOPR employed reinforcement learning to try to identify an optimal strategy for nuclear war, the designers of RSAS knew that such an enterprise would be futile because of these knowledge quality problems. Indeed, much of the rationale for RSAS was to explore the implications of different assumptions about both our own and adversary behavior. Instead of an attempt to use artificial intelligence to "win the game" of nuclear war, it was a tool for organizing our ignorance.[75]

Nor was there any danger that RSAS would attempt to act on its own, like WOPR did in *WarGames*. Like so much of the artificial intelligence and expert system technology of the 1980s, the RSAS was difficult to use, much less maintain and modify. While implemented with comparatively

---

[74] Paul K. Davis et al., *Analytic War Gaming with the RAND Strategy Assessment System (RSAS)*, tech. rep. (RAND Corporation, 1987); Paul K. Davis and Paul Bracken, "Artificial Intelligence for Wargaming and Modeling," *Journal of Defense Modeling and Simulation* (2022).
[75] Davis, "Knowledge-Based Simulation for Studying Issues of Nuclear Strategy."

mainstream Unix rather than the exotic Lisp machines of the time, only the designers and implementers of RSAS were able to keep it going, and this regularly proved an almost herculean task.

These kinds of frustrations, greatly compounded by the exaggerated marketing hype of the early AI industry, led to a massive disillusionment with artificial intelligence in the late 1980s. Among the disappointed customers who felt mislead was the Department of Defense, which significantly curtailed its investment in artificial intelligence. The sudden resurgence of neural networks around the same time attracted research funding from DARPA and elsewhere that had been flowing to rule-based AI a few years before. The very term "artificial intelligence" temporarily lost its cachet: many connectionists wanted to disassociate themselves from it, and industry deemphasized it in marketing. AI companies such as the Lisp machine maker Symbolics were crippled by the sudden evaporation of defense-related orders. The notorious AI winter had arrived just as the Cold War was drawing to a close.[76]

While engineers and strategists have attempted to apply artificial intelligence to nuclear war-related applications for many decades, both the objectives and products of their research bear scant resemblance to the celluloid nightmares of *Terminator* and *WarGames*. The Terminator scenario resonates so effectively with audiences because it reflects our deepest fears, not because military leaders are enthusiastic to turn Skynet into reality. Historically, there has not been much impetus for entrusting either the formulation of nuclear strategy or the control of the nuclear weapons to machines. Human officials and soldiers have jealously guarded these prerogatives for themselves, even if a few technologists have salivated at the thought of machines that would dispatch these responsibilities more effectively than humans. Nor does it appear likely that this will change in the future. There is no more of a market for a Skynet or a WOPR among the Chinese Communist Party leadership or the Russian General Staff than there is in the Pentagon and White House.[77] Even so, emerging developments in artificial intelligence are apt to remake nuclear strategy all the same.

---

[76] Crevier, *AI: The Tumultuous History of the Search for Artificial Intelligence*, 203.

[77] Sensationalistic Western media coverage to the contrary, the Soviet/Russian *Perimetr* system is not a real-life "doomsday machine," but rather an automated system for delegating launch authority should the country's political leadership be killed in a nuclear strike. According to Bruce Hoffman, the apparent purpose of the system is to reduce the pressure on senior leaders to retaliate upon receipt of a launch detection that may be spurious. While a fully automated version of the system was reputedly considered, available evidence indicates that *Perimetr* as implemented will never launch nuclear weapons without a human "pushing the button." David Hoffman, *The Dead Hand: The Untold Story of the Cold War Arms Race and Its Dangerous Legacy* (Anchor, 2009), Ch. 6.

Conclusion

Given how badly it always turns out in the movies, one would think that no one would seriously suggest turning control of nuclear weapons over to AI– but nevertheless people occasionally do so. Former director of the U.S. Air Force School of Advanced Nuclear Deterrence Studies Adam Lowther co-authored a piece in *War on the Rocks* in August 2019 suggesting that "America Needs a Dead Hand." Technological advances such as hypersonic weapons, in the authors' view, "are shrinking America's senior-leader decision time to such a narrow window that it may soon be impossible to effectively detect, decide, and direct nuclear force in time." This could enable nightmare scenarios in which an adversary could be tempted to mount a "*fait accompli* that will leave the United States in a position where capitulation to a new geostrategic order is its only option." They proposed a solution straight out of cinematic nightmare: "a system based on artificial intelligence, with predetermined response decisions, that detects, decides, and directs strategic forces with such speed that the attack-time compression challenge does not place the United States in an impossible position." They admitted that their "suggestion will generate comparisons to *Dr. Strangelove's* doomsday machine, *War Games'* War Operation Plan Response, and the *Terminator's* Skynet," but in their view this was not necessarily a bad thing: "the prophetic imagery of these science fiction films," they contended, "is quickly becoming reality."[78] Lowther's proposal received an almost universally skeptical reception, not least of which came from Lt. Gen. Jack Shanahan, the director of the Pentagon's Joint Artificial Intelligence Center (JAIC). "You will find no stronger proponent of integration of AI capabilities writ large into the Department of Defense," he retorted, "but there is one area where I pause, and it has to do with nuclear command and control." NC2, according to Shanahan, "is the ultimate human decision that needs to be made."[79]

---

[78] Adam Lowther and Curtis McGiffen, "America Needs a 'Dead Hand'," in *War on the Rocks* (Aug. 2019). URL: https://warontherocks.com/2019/08/america-needs-a-dead-hand/.

[79] Freedberg, *No AI For Nuclear Command and Control: JAIC's Shanahan*. Some writers who fear the consequences of advanced AI concur with Adam Lowther that WOPR and Skynet are "becoming reality." In their view, handing military command over to artificial intelligence is likely to doom mankind, but governments are likely to do so anyway because they will be tempted by the prospect of decisive strategic advantage. "Narrow AI systems could empower strategic planners with the ability to actually win a nuclear war with very little collateral damage or risk of global consequences," suggests futurist Alexei Turchin. "That is, they could calculate a route to a credible first strike capability." This prospect is positively benign compared to Turchin's nightmarish conjectures about the intersection of AI and nuclear weapons. Futurists such as Eliezer Yudkowsky contend that the classic science fiction plot line in which powerful AI appropriates control of nuclear weapons for its own ends is a plausible real-world scenario, but Turchin proposes that machine intelligences might start nuclear wars even if they are benevolent. Turchin also paints a scenario in which AI inspires humans to start a nuclear war before they create it.

The looming collision of artificial intelligence and nuclear strategy will probably be stranger than fiction. While in the past nations sought to ensure the survival of their second-strike forces by hardening them or preventing the adversary from finding them, these traditional approaches to securing a second-strike capability are increasingly nonviable, at least for powers such as Russia and China. But those hoping that artificial intelligence will inaugurate a "new era of counterforce" and make victory in a general nuclear war possible will likely be disappointed. It turns out that the same techniques that might accomplish such feats as finding submarines hiding at sea are also the most powerful tools to thwart themselves. Rather than securing their arsenals by depriving their opponents of a reliable means of destroying them, states will have no choice but to seek security by impairing their adversaries' situational awareness. This approach to assured retaliation will offer scant assurance to either the deterrer or the deterred and therefore threatens to inaugurate a self-reinforcing cycle of mutual suspicion and distrust without any obvious off-ramps. The trends unleashed by AI and ML could portend a dark and ominous future in which knowledge quality problems forestall states from determining "how much is enough" to prevail—or deter. Without quantitative measures of effectiveness, they might be left without any means of defining either "strategic superiority" or "sufficiency." This undermines the logic of coercive bargaining and demands that we reconsider what it means to maintain a stable strategic balance.

Echoing Oxford philosopher Nick Bostrom's contention that artificial general intelligence (AGI) will provide an immense and possibly insurmountable first-mover advantage, Turchin proposes that nation-states may destroy rivals' AI research centers with nuclear weapons before they allow anyone to beat them to it. Alexey Turchin, *Narrow AI Nanny: Reaching Strategic Advantage via Narrow AI to Prevent Creation of the Dangerous Superintelligence* (2018). https://philpapers.org/rec/TURNAN-3.

Chapter 3
No Place to Hide?

> "We can parachute these robot guys behind enemy lines. They hide out till the first strike blows over. Then, each one of these little boogers carries a 25 megaton bomb right up the middle main street of Moscow, like the mailman bringing bad news. We call it Operation Gotcha Last."
>
> **"That's** what you call 'ensuring peace'?!!?"
>
> "Oh, yeah. Just as you say, 'ensuring peace'."
>
> *Short Circuit* (1986)

Analysts typically associate strategic stability with the relative feasibility of disarming counterforce strikes. So long as neither side possesses a disarming strike capability, they reason, there is no rational motivation to attack and the "balance of terror" will remain robust. Will artificial intelligence and autonomy make it possible to track and target adversary mobile missile launchers and submarines, undermining strategic stability and increasing the probability of nuclear war?

Regrettably, discussions of this issue to date have been based more on conjecture and speculation than technical realities. The question is often viewed through the lens of Cold War debates about the desirability and feasibility of counterforce targeting. Post-1991 revelations have not been kind to either the pro-counterforce "hawks" or their critics in these arguments. "Doves" often charged that counterforce targeting was a technical absurdity: in actuality, U.S. counterforce capabilities against the Soviet Union were vastly more extensive than the public knew.[1] But the belief that counterforce superiority was a worthwhile pursuit is also severely challenged by the historical record: U.S. efforts in this area fed into Soviet leaders' paranoia and helped stoke the early 1980s "war scare," during which an accident or miscalculation easily could have snowballed into a nuclear apocalypse.[2] Even if strategic nuclear

---

[1] Long and Green, "Stalking the Secure Second Strike: Intelligence, Counterforce, and Nuclear Strategy"; Green and Long, "The MAD Who Wasn't There: Soviet Reactions to the Late Cold War Nuclear Balance"; Green and Long, "Conceal or Reveal? Managing Clandestine Military Capabilities in Peacetime Competition."

[2] President's Foreign Intelligence Advisory Board. The *Soviet "War Scare"* (1990); Hoffman, The *Dead Hand: The Untold Story of the Cold War Arms Race and Its Dangerous Legacy*, Ch. 3.

Deterrence under Uncertainty. Edward Geist, Oxford University Press. © RAND Corporation (2023).
DOI: 10.1093/oso/9780192886323.003.0004

competition played a major role in the weakening and ultimate dissolution of the USSR (a questionable assumption), it is still difficult to argue that this strategy was worth stoking an existential risk to the United States.[3] In any case, both the technical and geostrategic assumptions underlying the Cold War debate have been undermined by the passage of time.

This chapter seeks to ground discussion of whether new technology will make retaliatory forces vulnerable on a firmer technical basis. First, it provides an overview of how states have historically sought to ensure the survivability of their retaliatory forces. As it turns out, these approaches were primarily dictated by geography and physics, and as a consequence future strategic nuclear forces will be of types that either existed or were proposed during the Cold War. Second, it surveys the manner in which the Russians, Chinese, and North Koreans operate their mobile strategic nuclear forces. Finally, it draws some general conclusions about the nature of hunting mobile strategic platforms that will serve as the basis for the technical analysis in Chapter 4.

Prevailing Approaches to Assured Retaliation

Nation-states have traditionally relied upon three basic approaches to ensure the survival of their retaliatory forces: hardness, stealth/concealment, and mobility. The three legs of the superpowers' nuclear triads as postured during the Cold War embodied these principles. Hardness seeks to make the target robust enough to survive a near hit by a nuclear weapon. The quintessential hard targets are missile silos. By the end of the Cold War, however, increasing accuracy of delivery systems rendered hardening increasingly dubious as a means of ensuring target survivability. Even conjectural "ultra-hardened" silos robust against many times the overpressure and ground burst of existing silos would have limited prospects of survival against the current generation of ICBMs, even with low-yield warheads.[4] The second strategy, stealth/concealment, seeks to keep the adversary unaware of where the launcher is. Stealth is the primary survival strategy of missile-carrying submarines: as they move relatively slowly, if an adversary attack submarine is nearby they are liable to have difficulty escaping destruction should they be detected.

Concealment and mobility are often conflated because stealth is not exploited in any existing system lacking mobility, but they are really distinct

---

[3] Podvig, "The Window of Vulnerability That Wasn't: Soviet Military Buildup in the 1970s—A Research Note."

[4] Keir A. Lieber and Daryl G. Press, *The Myth of the Nuclear Revolution: Power Politics in the Atomic Age* (Cornell University Press, 2020), Ch. 3.

concepts. Mobility seeks to prevent the adversary from targeting the launcher by denying them knowledge of where it will be when their weapons arrive, rather than keeping them from knowing where it is at present. During the Cold War, alert bombers relied upon mobility to enhance their survivability. In normal circumstances, the adversary knew with high confidence where the bombers were at any moment: nonstealth bombers on airborne alert were visible on radar, while ground alert bombers were sitting on their runways ready to take off. But if those bombers attacked, they would have to be intercepted at a difficult-to-predict point. As improvements in accuracy and remote sensing have eroded the viability of hardening and concealment, the relative merits of mobility are increasing. This development is reflected in the emerging generation of strategic delivery systems such as the Russian Status-6/Poseidon UUV and Iu-71 Avangard hypersonic glide vehicle, which both emphasize mobility rather than stealth or hardness.[5]

Individual nuclear delivery systems possess hardness, stealthiness, and mobility in different proportions, and the degree to which they exhibit those advantages depends on how they are operated. The tortured history of the debate over how to base the MX/Peacekeeper ICBM is a good example of this. The MX was, for political reasons, designed to be close to the maximum possible weight without being a "heavy" ICBM, but this made it large enough to render it very challenging to make mobile. In light of the vociferous debate about ICBM survivability that raged in the United States in the late 1970s and early 1980s, however, conventional silos were deemed inadequate.[6] The Carter administration settled on a "Multiple Protective Shelter" (MPS) scheme that sought to achieve some of the benefits of hardness, deception, and mobility simultaneously. The missiles would be moved between thousands of shelters that, while not nearly as survivable as a dedicated silo, offered a significant degree of hardness. In theory, the USSR would have difficulty knowing which shelters contained missiles and would be forced to target all of them. But in trying to do everything, the MPS scheme was so expensive both fiscally and otherwise that it proved infeasible. The shelters were so costly that even if there was a place to put them (and it turned out that local political opposition made that very questionable), the maximum number that could be built might still be targetable by the USSR even within the arms control treaties of the day. The Reagan administration rejected MPS and alternately toyed with a succession of alternatives that exploited hardness, stealthiness, and mobility in varying degrees. One idea, "dense pack,"

---

[5] Geist and Massicot, "Understanding Putin's Nuclear 'Superweapons.'"

[6] Bruce W. Bennett, *How to Assess the Survivability of US ICBMs*, tech. rep. (Rand Corporation, 1980); Bruce W. Bennett, *How to Assess the Survivability of US ICBMs: Appendixes*, tech. rep. (Rand Corporation, 1980).

went all in for hardness: ultra-hard silos would be spaced so closely together that hopefully attacking warheads would destroy each other due to fratricide effects.[7] Given uncertainty about the predictability of those fratricide effects and the feasibility of ultra-hard silos, critics swiftly dubbed it "dunce pack." In 1983, the Scowcroft Commission dismissed concerns about a "window of vulnerability" of U.S. ICBMs and recommended the deployment of 50 MX ICBMs in Minuteman silos as a way to "show resolve" while the issue of future U.S. ICBM basing was resolved.[8] "Hard Carry" was proposed as a more affordable counterpart of the earlier MPS. By hardening the launch canister and associating most launch equipment with it, cheap pools of water could be substituted for the shelters and the whole system could be made compact enough to fit on existing military bases. In 1986, however, the Reagan administration elected to endorse a rail-mobile garrison concept for Peacekeeper. This would consist of fifty trains with two ICBMs each; while they would remain on military bases in peacetime during a crisis they could be dispersed onto the civilian rail network to pose a nightmarish targeting challenge to the Soviets.[9] This system, like the mobile ICBMs fielded by the USSR/Russia, would have exploited mobility and concealment at the expense of hardness: designed to resemble commercial freight cars, the missiles would have been exceedingly difficult to locate in real time. But unlike the Russians, who could and did send their rail-mobile SS-24 ICBMs out of garrison regularly, political constraints in the United States ensured that the rail-mobile Peacekeeper would have to remain on military bases except in emergency and would be less survivable against surprise attack than existing silos.

The venerable B-52 offers a great example of how a single delivery platform can exploit hardness, stealthiness, and mobility depending on the circumstances. When it first entered service in the mid-1950s, the B-52 was based with almost no consideration given to the possibility of a Soviet surprise attack. RAND analysts such as Albert Wohlstetter were horrified to discover this oversight and tried to convince the Air Force to build hardened aircraft shelters for the B-52 and other bombers. The USAF proved unreceptive to this suggestion, but instead aggressively embraced a range of alternative measures to enhance the survivability of the bombers.[10] The most enduring of these was runway alert, which lasted until the end of the Cold War: a fraction of the bombers sat on runways ready to take off within a few minutes

---

[7] Caston et al., *The Future of the US Intercontinental Ballistic Missile Force*, 36.

[8] Brent Scowcroft. *Report of the President's Commission on Strategic Forces*. The President's Commission on Strategic Forces, 1984.

[9] Caston et al., *The Future of the US Intercontinental Ballistic Missile Force*, pp. 102–103.

[10] Edward S. Quade, "The Selection and Use of Strategic Air Bases: A Case History," in E. S. Quade (ed.), *Analysis for Military Decisions* (Rand McNally, 1966), 24–63.

of receiving the order. More dramatic, and dangerous, was airborne alert. As part of Operation Chrome Dome, in the 1960s bombers were kept constantly in the air at fail-safe points ready to proceed to targets in the Soviet Union. This policy enabled a series of accidents that led to its cancellation in 1968.[11] The shift to low-level penetration tactics by SAC in the early 1960s was, in a way, an embracement of stealthiness to the detriment of mobility: while flying at lower altitude consumed more fuel and reduced speed and endurance, radar technology of the time had much less ability to detect low-flying bombers. The transition of the B-52 from dropping gravity bombs to launching cruise missiles in the 1980s transformed it into a qualitatively different system so far as strategic nuclear missions were concerned. Now the stealthiness was embodied in the air-launched cruise missiles (ALCMs), which followed a terrain-hugging trajectory and could use fragile anti-radar coatings unsuitable for longer-lived craft.

All of the methods of enhancing survivability can be thought of as ways of "breaking the kill chain" (Figure 3). Since the late 1990s, the USAF has defined five "links" in the kill chain: find, fix or track, target, engage, and assess (known by the acronym F2T2EA). This acronym originated in an October 1996 speech by Air Force Chief of Staff Gen. Ronald R. Fogleman in which he asserted that "In the first quarter of the 21st century it will become possible to find, fix or track, and target anything that moves on the surface of the Earth."[12] This phrase gained wide currency and, with the addition of "engage" and "assess," supplanted older "Four Fs" definition of the kill chain (for "Find, Fix, Fight, and Finish") that had been used in World War II:

- *Finding* the target means to locate it;
- *Fixing* the target means to prevent its movement (or, in some definitions, to ascertain its precise location);
- *Tracking* means to monitor its movement;

Figure 3. The five links of the kill chain.

---

[11] Scott Douglas Sagan, *The Limits of Safety: Organizations, Accidents, and Nuclear Weapons* (Princeton University Press, 1995), 69–77.

[12] John A. Tirpak, "Find, Fix, Track, Target, Engage, Assess," *Air Force Magazine* 83.7 (2000), 24–29.

- *Targeting* means to select a particular weapon or asset to employ against (meaning a specific warhead, airplane, etc. that is in range);
- *Engaging* means to attack the target; and
- *Assessing* means to determine the post-attack state of the target.

Hardened targets like ICBM silos break the kill chain at the target and engage links. Historically prospective attacks on these targets had only a modest prospect of success, but by the end of the Cold War improvements in accuracy were severely straining the viability of this approach to survivability. Mobility like that of air-alert bombers impaired fixing and tracking. Even though the planes were visible on radar, their position could not be fixed. Concealment and camouflage, as exploited by SSBNs and mobile missile launchers, break the find and track links. It is difficult to locate the targets in the first place, even roughly; and when they are found, they can move.

Mobile ICBM Launchers

Even before the notorious failure of the Scud hunt during the 1991 Persian Gulf War, Coalition military leaders did not anticipate that it would be feasible to track down Saddam Hussein's Soviet-made missile launchers using manned aircraft.[13] The USSR had begun deploying these systems decades earlier, and NATO had no illusions that they could preemptively destroy them in Central Europe in the way Coalition forces tried to do in Iraq in 1991. Since the early 1980s, the United States had been eagerly pursuing technologies to counter Soviet theater missiles, most notably as part of DARPA's Smart Weapons program and its descendants. In the latter part of that decade, DARPA's Thirsty Saber and Damocles projects sought to solve the challenge of missile hunting with loitering munitions that would be described today as lethal autonomous weapons. The smart munitions would be stealthier, more maneuverable, and more expendable than costly manned platforms. But as of 1991 they remained aspirational: the sensor suites undergoing experimental testing were far from being battle-ready.[14]

In any case, Coalition military leaders were optimistic that the Iraqi Scuds would prove a relatively minor, manageable nuisance. Iraq was believed to

[13] David E. Snodgrass, *Attacking the Theater Mobile Ballistic Missile Threat*, tech. rep. (School of Advanced Airpower Studies, 1993), 3–4.
[14] Van Atta et al., *Transformation and Transition: DARPA's Role in Fostering an Emerging Revolution in Military Affairs*, Volume 2, Detailed Assessments, V-24–25.

possess only a modest stockpile of these weapons, and without nuclear war-heads they possessed nothing like the military potency of the original Soviet variant. The modifications that the Iraqis made to increase the missiles' range also crippled their payload and accuracy.[15] Most importantly, the Coalition anticipated that the Scud launchers could be neutralized without the need to hunt down the individual missile launchers. By disrupting adversary opera-tions and logistics, the Coalition hoped that it could prevent the Scuds from being launched.[16]

While Coalition leaders were correct in their assumption that the purely military impact of the Scuds was limited, Saddam Hussein had another target for his missiles: the fragile politics of the alliance opposing him. By strik-ing Israel with extended-range Scuds, the Iraqi dictator hoped to draw that country into the conflict and fracture the Coalition. Tel Aviv followed a national policy dictating military reprisals for armed attack, so this strat-egy had considerable plausibility. Simultaneous Scud attacks on Saudi Arabia and Bahrain, meanwhile, threatened to goad the Arab members of the Coali-tion into a premature offensive. Despite their modest military significance, the Iraqi Scuds therefore suddenly took on an enormous political impor-tance once the missile attacks began in January 1991. In order to preserve the Coalition, the United States and its partners needed to pursue every available means of countering the Scuds. Hence began the ill-fated Scud hunt.[17]

Saddam's Iraq had several unpleasant surprises in store for the Coalition as it embarked upon the Scud hunt. Firstly, Iraqi stockpiles of the ballistic missiles were considerably larger than pre-war intelligence estimates, allow-ing Baghdad to sustain missile launch rates much higher than the Coalition anticipated. While Iraqi Scud launches slowed down as the war progressed, it was unclear if this resulted from Coalition action or if the Iraqis were sim-ply running out of missiles. Instead, it would be necessary to track down and destroy the individual Iraqi Scud TELs (transporter-erector-launchers). Sec-ondly, during the Iran-Iraq War the Iraqis had honed very effective tactics for preventing adversaries from targeting the missile launchers. In addition to large quantities of decoys, the Iraqis had learned to minimize the amount

---

[15] At the time of the conflict Iraq had two Scud derivatives: the al-Hussein, with a range of 600–650 km, and the al-Abbas with a range of 750–900 km. According to one estimate these missiles had a CEP of 2 km and a payload of only 180 kg, rendering them almost useless as anything other than a terror weapon. The original Soviet missile from which these were derived had a range of only 300 km but was armed with nuclear weapons with yields of tens or hundreds of kilotons. William Rosenau, *Special Operations Forces and Elusive Enemy Ground Targets: Lessons from Vietnam and the Persian Gulf War* (Rand Corporation, 2001), 30–31.

[16] Snodgrass, *Attacking the Theater Mobile Ballistic Missile Threat*, 3–4.

[17] Snodgrass, *Attacking the Theater Mobile Ballistic Missile Threat*, 4.

of time the launchers were exposed and vulnerable before and after launching their missiles. More importantly, the hope that disrupting the operational and logistical chains supporting the Iraqi TELs would halt missile launches proved wildly optimistic.[18]

The Scud hunt was therefore a desperation measure dictated by Coalition politics. The United States and its partners needed to either stop the missile launches or, barring that, demonstrate a commitment to counteracting the Scuds. The primary available means of finding the Scud TELs was wide-area search using manned tactical aircraft. Despite the longstanding recognition that this approach was probably futile against Warsaw Pact forces in Central Europe, there were some reasons for optimism that it would be somewhat efficacious against the Iraqis. While Iraq had a much larger stockpile of missiles than anticipated, it had a much smaller number of the Soviet-built TELs, so there were relatively few targets to find. Moreover, the limited range of the missiles restricted the area from which they could be launched against Israel to a relatively small part of Western Iraq. This arid district offered fewer opportunities for camouflage and concealment than the forests of Central Europe. Finally, as the conflict progressed the Iraqi forces evinced an often astonishing degree of strategic and operational incompetence. Perhaps the operators of the missiles would commit mistakes that would help the Coalition target the TELs, such as by carelessly generating signals intelligence (SIGINT), giving away their positions. To bolster this approach, the United States and U.K. sent special operations forces into Western Iraq to reconnoitre for the TELs. These would either call in airstrikes against identified targets or, due to the significant delays before Coalition aircraft could strike, attack the Iraqi vehicles directly with shoulder-mounted missiles, mines, or bulk explosives.[19]

Despite these advantages, from a military standpoint the Scud hunt proved an almost total failure. Even though the Coalition conducted 2,493 Scud-tasked sorties during the war, the Gulf War Air Power Survey later confessed that "[T]here is no indisputable proof that Scud mobile launchers–as opposed to high-fidelity decoys, trucks, or other objects with Scud-like signatures–were destroyed by fixed-wing aircraft."[20] F-15Es and F-16Ls loitered over the two "kill boxes" in Western and Southern Iraq from which the Scuds could be launched into Israel and Saudi Arabia. In theory the aircraft would

---

[18] Rosenau, *Special Operations Forces and Elusive Enemy Ground Targets: Lessons from Vietnam and the Persian Gulf War*, 33–34.
[19] Rosenau, *Special Operations Forces and Elusive Enemy Ground Targets: Lessons from Vietnam and the Persian Gulf War*; Snodgrass, *Attacking the Theater Mobile Ballistic Missile Threat*.
[20] Rosenau, *Special Operations Forces and Elusive Enemy Ground Targets: Lessons from Vietnam and the Persian Gulf War*, 41; Snodgrass, *Attacking the Theater Mobile Ballistic Missile Threat*.

attempt to locate the TELs after they launched a missile and before they could retreat to safety. They would do this using tactical sensors such as LANTIRN (Low-Altitude Navigation and Targeting Infrared System for Night) and SAR (synthetic aperture radar), but these sensors proved of scant utility finding the TELs. As a 2003 IDA report recounted:

> The "Great Scud Hunt" of Desert Storm proved that we could not find Scuds with manned aircraft in spite of the massive sortie rate. Because of the enemy air defense systems, allied manned aircraft were forced to fly too high, well above their useful sensor ranges for viewing targets of this size. Other data show that humans are not good at search in high stress, multi-tasking scenarios, even with good sensor inputs. Thus, it can be argued that Allied aircraft would not have found their targets any better even if they had been able to fly lower.[21]

Under intense pressure to ameliorate this situation, DARPA even started a crash program—Thirsty Warrior—to adapt the sensor technology being tested for Thirsty Saber for immediate deployment to the Persian Gulf, but the conflict ended before this took place.[22]

Despite being a military failure, the Scud hunt succeeded in its political objective: dissuading Israeli entry into the conflict and preserving the U.S.-led coalition. But part of the reason for this success was that the efficacy of the Scud hunt was greatly exaggerated during the war. Coalition officials initially reported considerable success destroying Iraqi TELs, only revising their estimates after the war when better information became available. The extreme efforts pursued by the United States and its partners signaled to Israel that a prospective intervention on its part would not make a significant military difference. Yet this political logic only worked in practice due to the military insignificance of the Scud attacks.[23] Against nuclear-armed mobile missiles, the kind of tactics pursued during the Scud hunt could not be anticipated to offer even symbolic utility.

What are the implications of the "Great Scud hunt" for the feasibility of tracking and targeting mobile missile launchers? Austin Long and Brendan Rittenhouse Green decry what they dub the "Scud hunt myth," arguing that the Gulf War experience "is both a misleading analogy and a distant data

---

[21] Van Atta et al., *Transformation and Transition: DARPA's Role in Fostering an Emerging Revolution in Military Affairs*, Volume 2, *Detailed Assessments*, V-24.

[22] Van Atta et al., *Transformation and Transition: DARPA's Role in Fostering an Emerging Revolution in Military Affairs*, Volume 2, *Detailed Assessments*, S-6.

[23] Owen R. Côte, *The Third Battle: Innovation in the US Navy's Silent Cold War Struggle with Soviet Submarines (Newport Paper 16, 2003)*, tech. rep. (Naval War College, 2003), 83.

point from a technology perspective." They assert, with considerable justification, that "the Scud hunt bears little to no resemblance to either the effort to track Soviet mobile ICBMs during the Cold War or to future mobile missile scenarios."[24] As described above, the United States and NATO did not anticipate that the approach tried against the Iraqi Scuds would be effective against either Soviet theater or strategic missile launchers, inspiring a range of highly ambitious R&D efforts to counter them. The Scud hunt resulted from a strange confluence of political, technological, and strategic factors that will probably not be repeated. Just because the Scud hunt failed does not necessarily mean that tracking and targeting mobile missiles is impossible.

At the same time, the Scud hunt tells us little about how difficult missile hunting would be in other contexts, particularly against a sophisticated adversary such as Russia. In many respects the Scud hunt was probably much easier than locating and destroying Russian and Chinese strategic missiles. While the Scuds were much smaller than mobile ICBMs, they were still relatively primitive liquid-fueled missiles with greater associated fragility and operational complexity than more modern solid-fueled systems. While Scud operations are a rare bright spot in the history of Iraq's military performance during the Gulf War, it is unclear whether this was due to their personnel being uniquely competent within the Iraqi military or because the intrinsic difficulties in missile hunting made their tasks relatively easy. Compared to the potential patrol areas of Russian or Chinese missiles, the kill boxes in which the Scuds operated during the Gulf War were relatively small and unfriendly for camouflage, concealment, and deception (CCD) of the TELs, yet Coalition aircraft still struggled to find any launchers. Most importantly, envisioned missile hunting scenarios against Russia and China involve larger numbers of missile launchers located over much larger, better-defended areas. Except in contrived "protracted war" scenarios, the TELs must be destroyed over a period of minutes or hours rather than weeks, while the adversary is likely to be employing all available means, potentially including nuclear strikes, to thwart the attacker's C4ISR and information fusion capabilities.

Unlike the United States and its allies Britain and France, Russia, China, and North Korea have placed a heavy emphasis on land-mobile ICBMs for their secure retaliatory forces. In the case of the latter two countries, mobile ICBMs are arguably the keystone of their deterrent forces, ongoing efforts to

---

[24] Long and Green, "Stalking the Secure Second Strike: Intelligence, Counterforce, and Nuclear Strategy", 58.

modernize silo-based missiles and deploy submarine-based missiles notwith-standing. This choice makes sense given the relative geographic constraints Moscow, Beijing, and Pyongyang necessarily operate under. The United States does not face an adversary on its own continent and has long stretches of uncontested coastline with deep ice-free ports facing both the Atlantic and Pacific. One has to construct far-fetched hypotheticals to argue that Russia or China, with their comparatively weak navies, could successfully conduct large-scale ASW operations along the American coast and through-out the world ocean. The U.K. and France, meanwhile, benefit from U.S. maritime dominance: while their minimal deterrent might become vulnera-ble in a world in which a hostile nation with the preponderance of power the United States has could concentrate its efforts on tracking their submarines, in practice they have whole oceans to hide in.

Russia and China face the opposite situation. While Russia has an enor-mous amount of coastline, most of it faces the Arctic and is often covered with ice (albeit less of the time as climate change takes its toll on the region). Potential adversaries such as NATO extend to the borders of Russia and have ample opportunity to set up and maintain ASW infrastructure around the chokepoints Russian submarines and ships must pass through to reach the open ocean. During the final years of the Cold War the U.S. Navy planned to project power into the Soviet maritime bastion in the arctic, and given the decline of Russian naval power in the post-Cold War era this type of strategy might appear more credible than it was in the late 1980s.[25] Circum-stances are even less favorable for China. Despite having thousands of miles of temperate coastline, the seas around China are dominated by its adversaries. The United States, Japan, and Taiwan can operate from bases on islands sur-rounding China to project power into the surrounding waters. Unlike Russia, China does not have an attractive adjacent body of water in which it might establish a bastion for its SSBNs. Most of the surrounding seas are shallow and the nearest that is deep enough is the South China Sea, which is heavily contested.[26]

The situation is reversed for mobile land-based ICBMs. Mobile ICBMs are considered politically unviable in the United States despite its considerable size. The prospect of nuclear-armed missiles traveling along American roads and highways is anticipated to elicit considerable public alarm. Moreover, the open nature of U.S. society would provide adversaries with opportunity to observe the disposition and operation of the missiles. While the United States

---

[25] Donald C. Daniel, The *Future of Strategic ASW*, tech. rep. (Center for Naval Warfare Studies, 1990).
[26] Tong Zhao, *Tides of Change*, tech. rep. (Carnegie Endowment for International Peace, 2018).

seriously pursued such missiles during the late Cold War, the assumption was that the missiles would have to be operated within a controlled patrol zone from which the public would be excluded. Unfortunately there were relatively few candidate areas and these were small enough that they undermined the case for mobile basing.[27] Russia and China do not have these problems. Their relatively authoritarian, closed societies make it easier to keep information about the movements of the mobile ICBMs a secret, even though they are operated in ways that cause them to come into contact with the public. Furthermore, there is relatively little public protest about the actual or prospective movement of nuclear-armed ICBMs in these countries. The North Koreans, meanwhile, have relatively little choice in the matter: any fixed ICBM launcher would be too vulnerable to U.S. preemption, and its ability to build viable missile-carrying submarines is modest. As a consequence, land-mobile ICBMs like those it demonstrated in 2017 are its best available option to field a somewhat-credible survivable retaliatory force.

Mobile ICBMs come in two varieties: rail and road. The former were proposed first—the United States explored the prospect of a rail-mobile Minuteman during the late 1950s—but only one, the Soviet RT-23 (NATO reporting name SS-24 "Scalpel") ever entered service.[28] Rail-mobile missile have a number of advantages over their road-mobile brethren. Most important is that trains already transport items the size of an ICBM, which means that more existing infrastructure and technology can be adapted for this application. The relative smoothness of the railroad reduces the amount of wear-and-tear on the missile from vibration. Finally, a rail-mobile ICBM is easier to disguise as another type of train than it is to camouflage a road-mobile ICBM as another type of vehicle. This was a defense some analysts made of the SS-24 in Russia in the 2000s: they believed, rightly or not, that the resemblance of the system to refrigerator trains made it harder for the United States to track and target than road-mobile Topol and Topol-M ICBMs. The downside of rail-based systems, however, is that they can only go where the railroad tracks do, which constrains their mobility and might present a relatively easy target for an adversary who had recent knowledge of the train's whereabouts. Rail-based systems have fallen into general disfavor: the SS-24 was retired in 2004, and development of its planned replacement, a rail-based version of the road-mobile Yars ICBM dubbed "Barguzin," was frozen in late 2017 due to a lack of financing.[29]

---

[27] Caston et al., *The Future of the US Intercontinental Ballistic Missile Force.*
[28] Podvig, *Russian Strategic Nuclear Forces.*
[29] *Istochnik: "atomnyi poezd" "Barguzin" iskliuchili iz novoi GPV radi "Sarmata" i "Rubezha"* (2017). URL: https://tass.ru/armiya-i-opk/4787839.

Instead, Russia, China, and North Korea have concentrated their efforts developing road-mobile ICBMs. As of this this writing there are at least five such systems deployed, with several others anticipated in the near future. Currently deployed systems include the Russian Topol, Topol-M, and Yars ICBMs as well as the Chinese DF-31 and DF-31A road-mobile missiles.[30] The Chinese DF-41 ICBM entered service in 2020, initially in a road-mobile variant. The current status of North Korea's mobile ICBMs is unclear; while Pyongyang tested two different such missiles in 2017 and a third in early 2022, it is not clear whether any of them has entered nominal service.[31] Road-mobile ICBMs are complemented in all of these countries, and in others such as India and Israel, by shorter-range road-mobile missiles. These weapons are based on a wide range of technologies and provide a considerable range of capabilities. With the exception of Soviet-era Scud missiles and the North Korean designs, nearly all road-mobile missiles employ solid rather than liquid fuel. Solid-fuel missiles have fewer moving parts and are considerably more robust than their liquid-fueled counterparts. For obvious reasons, land-mobile ICBMs are physically the smallest such missiles built, but they and the TELs that carry them are still enormous compared to all but the largest wheeled vehicles. This factor poses a significant constraint on their mobility.

The key to the survivability of road-mobile ICBMs is how they are operated. Every state that currently operates road-mobile ICBMs bases and operates them in a different way. Traditionally, American analysts have modeled road-mobile ICBMs as if they move randomly within a patrol region, possibly without the need to remain on roads or use pre-surveyed launch sites.[32] While the aborted U.S. "Midgetman" missile was envisioned to operate in such a way, no military that has deployed road-mobile ICBMs embraced the continuous mobility approach. A major obstacle is the size and weight of road-mobile ICBMs. Even if equipped with off-road TELs, these massive vehicles cannot drive anywhere, and they can only launch from a small fraction of the places they can drive. In soft or uneven ground the TELs can get stuck, and their ability to climb steep grades is limited. Sophisticated off-road TELs, such as that of the Russian RS-24 Yars, have some ability to launch from off-road locations, but those need to be firm and level enough. Most of the time Russian road-mobile ICBMs are kept in garrisons, with only a limited

[30] Kristensen and Korda, "Russian Nuclear Forces, 2019"; Kristensen and Norris, "Chinese Nuclear Forces, 2018."

[31] Hans M. Kristensen and Matt Korda, "North Korean Nuclear Weapons, 2021," *Bulletin of the Atomic Scientists* 77.4 (2021), 222–236.

[32] Battilega and Grange, *The Military Applications of Modeling*; Caston et al., *The Future of the US Intercontinental Ballistic Missile Force.*

fraction of them on patrol off-base. When on patrol, missile brigades proceed to remote sites in wooded areas and camouflage their launch positions, moving only rarely or not at all.[33] During an intense crisis, Russian leaders would surely increase the fraction of the road-mobile ICBM force sent off-base considerably. There might also be attempts to surge launchers from their bases on tactical warning. While risky in case of an actual attack because if the adversary targeted the roads leading away from the base the TELs would then face likely destruction, political leaders may choose it due to the possibility of a false alarm.

The simpler articulated TELs of the Chinese DF-31 and DF-31A ICBMs, however, boast only a very modest off-road capability and need paved concrete launch positions in order to complete their missions. Some of these launch positions are liable to have been discovered by the adversary, so the key to survivability is redundancy: building many more launch pads than there are missiles. The launch pads are not easy to find, however; they are often disguised by a layer of soil and vegetation carefully cultivated to hide them from would-be adversaries.[34] The recently revealed DF-31AG boasts an off-road TEL that resembles those of Russian ICBMs, which suggests that in the near future China may begin adopting operational practices for its road-mobile ICBMs similar to those of its northern neighbor.[35]

While on base, both Russian and Chinese mobile ICBMs are kept in special garages. Since the 1980s, Russian systems such as the SS-25 Topol have been deployed in garages with retractable roofs that allow the missiles to be launched on short notice. As a consequence, Russian mobile ICBMs can contribute to a launch-under-attack retaliation along with their silo-based cousins.[36] It is typically thought that Chinese mobile ICBMs are not mated with their warheads in peacetime, so it is not that surprising that their bases make fewer concessions to this sort of surprise attack contingency. Instead, it appears that the Chinese anticipate a period of strategic warning, during which missiles will be armed and then surged off-base into prepared deployment zones. While Chinese mobile ICBM bases are associated with tunnels, it seems unlikely that these tunnels are intended to be a wartime hiding place

[33] Pavel Podvig, *Tracking Down Road-Mobile Missiles* (2015). URL: http://russianforces.org/blog/2015/01/tracking_down_road-mobile_miss.shtml.

[34] Li Bin, "Tracking Chinese Strategic Mobile Missiles," *Science & Global Security* 15.1 (2007), 1–30; Hans M. Kristensen, *Chinese Mobile ICBMs Seen in Central China* (2012). URL: https://fas.org/blogs/security/2012/03/df-31deployment/.

[35] Hans Kristensen, *New Missile Silo and DF-41 Launchers Seen in Chinese Nuclear Missile Training Area* (2019). URL: https://fas.org/blogs/security/2019/09/china-silo-df41/.

[36] Podvig, *Russian Strategic Nuclear Forces.*

for the missiles. One possibility is that they will be used to mate warheads before the missiles depart the base.[37]

In contrast, emerging North Korean basing practice for its mobile missiles emphasizes tunnels. The DPRK's nascent ICBM bases are located in the mountainous north of the country. The Hwaesong-14 and -15 ICBMs tested in 2017 are liquid-fueled, road-mobile ICBMs that appear to be derived from Soviet missile technology. While crude compared to a state-of-the-art road-mobile missile like the RS-24 Yars, the North Korean missiles are an ingenious response to the unique constraints under which Pyongyang must operate. The North Koreans know that due to the modest size of their missile forces, fixed launch positions would be too unsurvivable to provide an assured retaliation capability. Rather than basing the large, liquid-fueled ICBMs in silos like the Soviet missiles from which they are derived, the DPRK has developed rudimentary TELs for them. The initial Hwasong-14 and -15 TELs were not quite "launchers," however, as the fueled missile was actually erected onto a launch table from which it blasts off rather than taking off while still attached to the tractor. The system requires prepared concrete launch pads like the Chinese systems, but it enables the North Koreans to hide the missiles in the complicated mountain environment. The DPRK TEL first displayed in October 2020 and now associated with the Hwasong-17 seems to be lack this limitation, but may still require well-prepared launch sites.[38] Open-source satellite photos suggest that most of the time the ICBMs are kept in underground tunnels or camouflaged hardened shelters at the missile bases, with launch pads available adjacent to the tunnel or shelter entrances to facilitate and emergency launch.[39] During a crisis, however, the missiles can be driven off base and along the mountain valleys to other shelters, tunnels, or preexisting hiding places such as overpasses. By only moving when weather and other prevailing conditions make detection improbable, the North Koreans can maintain uncertainty about the location and number of missiles in the field. Given the fragility of the missile and the extreme danger of an accident moving it while fueled, a continuous mobility basing mode is simply infeasible for the North Koreans.

Neither Russia nor China has adopted the practice of hardening their TELs to resist nuclear weapons effects. The aborted U.S. Midgetman missile incorporated this feature, in large part because for political reasons it appeared

---

[37] Kristensen, *Chinese Mobile ICBMs Seen in Central China.*

[38] Kristensen and Korda, "North Korean Nuclear Weapons, 2021."

[39] Victor Cha Joseph Bermudez and Lisa Collins, *Undeclared North Korea: The Sino-ri Missile Operating Base and Strategic Force Facilities* (2019). URL: https://beyondparallel.csis.org/undeclared-north-korea-the-sino-ri-missile-operating-base-and-strategic-force-facilities/.

that the missiles would have to be kept on existing military reservations in all but the most extreme crises. For political and institutional reasons, American officials considered it imperative that the Midgetman be able to ride out a full-scale Soviet surprise attack even in its day-to-day basing mode. But none of the available sites was large enough to create a targeting zone so large that the launchers could survive without at least some hardening. The attempt to create a hardened TEL, however, proved the undoing of the system: it was fabulously expensive and so heavy that it severely constrained the mobility of the missile, possibly impairing its survivability more than it helped. The emphasis on mobility and hardness rather than camouflage for survivability also increased the anticipated costs of the missile. Constant motion of the heavy TEL would put significant wear-and-tear on both the missile and launcher as well as the ground where it was driven.[40] The concealment-centric approach employed by Russia, China, and North Korea, however, minimizes these issues. Their relatively lightweight TELs have negligible blast resistance but are much more flexible in where they can drive. Chinese and Russian officials are more comfortable with reliance upon strategic warning to generate their forces, and face few domestic political obstacles to operating nuclear-armed missiles away from their usual operating bases. While on a combat patrol, the missiles move only rarely, instead spending most of their time camouflaged in inconspicuous locations. The mode of camouflage depends on the terrain in which the missiles are located. Russian mobile missiles often use forest vegetation to help camouflage themselves while on combat patrol, and snow in the winter.[41]

All of the countries that field mobile ICBM launchers are likely to posture them considerably differently in a crisis than they do in peacetime. The large-scale exercises conducted by countries such as Russia are still a pale imitation of full force generation in anticipation of long-term combat patrols. For signaling purposes, states are likely to want to give the impression that the missiles could be located in an enormous area, including places that potential adversaries did not previously expect to be patrol zones. It might therefore appear worthwhile to send some launchers or very high-quality decoys to locations far from known operating bases and then make their presence relatively obvious. Simultaneously, survivability would be maximized by sending

---

[40] Steven Pomeroy, *An Untaken Road: Strategy, Technology, and the Hidden History of America's Mobile ICBMs* (Naval Institute Press, 2016).

[41] In 2019, the Russian military's TV channel aired a documentary on the operation of the RS-24 Yars mobile ICBM including footage of these activities. Telekanal Zvezda, *Voennaia priemka. Iars. ladernaia raketa sderzhivaniia. Chast' 2* (2019). URL: https://www.youtube.com/watch?v=B3upvVJwv5k.

missiles to remote areas but keeping their location secret from enemy intelligence agencies. These steps could still be worth it in an extreme crisis even if a lack of earlier practice made them relatively risky to equipment and personnel. Locating and targeting the missiles in peacetime is likely to be of only modest relevance to the far more challenging task of finding them and holding them under threat after the forces have been generated during an intense crisis.

The task of finding mobile missile launchers is therefore mostly one of teasing out their hiding places. Trying to catch the TELs while they are moving and then watching where they go is obviously necessary in order to learn about how and where they hide, but opportunities to do this will arise only occasionally. This is both because the missiles are only in transit a small part of the time and because those times are selected specifically to make it difficult for potential adversaries to monitor the missiles. For instance, moving the missiles at night or during periods of extensive cloud cover can inhibit tracking the TELs with optical sensors.

The technologies most often proposed for hunting mobile ICBMs—synthetic aperture radar and ground/surface moving target indicator (GMTI or SMTI) radar—have the advantage of being able to see through clouds. While both technologies are radar variants, they are effectively opposites in terms of what they can observe and how they work. The concept behind SAR, which can be deployed on either space- or air-based platforms, is to use the motion of the host vehicle to simulate the presence of a much larger radar antenna than is physically present. SAR produces images of the surface that can be extraordinarily detailed, rather than the point-like "blips" detected by conventional radar systems. These images can then be processed in much the same way as visual data by either human analysts or automated techniques. The major downside of SAR is that because it relies upon the movement of the platform to create its synthetic aperture, it is very difficult for it to image a moving target.[42] The task of tracking such targets falls instead mostly to GMTI/SMTI radar. The idea of GMTI is that the likely targets are moving, while the clutter (the ground itself and all the stationary objects on it) is not. The previous received signal is stored and used to filter out parts of the next received signal that have not changed. Executed well, this leaves just true targets and similar items that move. Thanks to modern signal processing, it is

---

[42] Lieber and Press, "The New Era of Counterforce: Technological Change and the Future of Nuclear Deterrence," 38.

possible for the same radar array to act as either a SAR or GMTI radar in different modes, and increasingly for SAR to image moving targets—albeit with much reduced fidelity than stationary ones.

Many analyses of the prospects for tracking and targeting road-mobile missile launchers are focused on scenarios and concepts of operations (CONOPS) that are qualitatively different from the nuclear case. It is anticipated that in a conventional conflict, there will generally be many more missiles than TELs, as was the case in the Scud hunt. The TELs are therefore still very attractive targets even after they have fired a missile, and each missile launched results in only a comparatively finite amount of damage. This enables a concept of operations premised on using the launch of the missile to detect the location of the TEL, after which search and attack assets can be queued up to pursue it.[43] But in a nuclear war, waiting until missiles have been fired obviously is not good enough: the TELs must somehow be localized before they launch their missiles. Some authors suggest that SIGINT is the most attractive means to do this and argue that the United States developed means to intercept communications from Soviet mobile missile launchers even during the late Cold War.[44]

A wide-area search for missile TELs could therefore be pursued as follows. On the basis of existing intelligence, available reconnaissance satellites and UAVs would monitor the activities of known missile bases. At times when missile movement seemed probable (perhaps due to SIGINT tipoffs), radar assets in SMTI mode could monitor roadways leading from the bases in the hopes of gleaning clues about where the missiles were headed. The adversary is likely to try to exploit decoys to create confusion targets that might appear on SMTI radar like the real thing. Machine learning could help alleviate this problem through the use of motion models divining the subtle differences between the movement of TELs and their support vehicles compared to other targets. Once the missiles reached their hiding places, multispectral imaging and SAR assets can be directed at sites that appear likely on the basis of SMTI and other forms of intelligence. With luck, the hiding places may be imaged before they have completed camouflaging themselves. Otherwise, it is necessary to try and find them through natural and artificial cover. As the missiles only occasionally move, there is a possibility to seek out clues after the fact as to where they went: for instance, these huge vehicles can leave distinctive tracks that may be visible to spy satellites or SAR images. Both the

[43] Alan Vick and Richard M. Moore, *Aerospace Operations against Elusive Ground Targets* (RAND Corporation, 2001).
[44] Long and Green, "Stalking the Secure Second Strike: Intelligence, Counterforce, and Nuclear Strategy," 52.

camouflage and these secondary indicators can potentially be detected via automated processing of intelligence data.

UAVs of various scales could also contribute to the missile-hunting mission and make up for some of the limitations of space-based assets. Reconnaissance satellites generally need to be in low Earth orbit (LEO) to gather effective data, but due to the speed at which they orbit they only retain a particular location on the surface in view for a short period before moving out of range. As a consequence, without a large number of satellites they cannot maintain continual coverage, and even if enough satellites are available then it is still necessary to hand off the surveillance task.[45] UAVs, by contrast, can loiter near the target of interest. But operating UAVs deep inside enemy territory is a nontrivial endeavor, particularly against peer adversaries. Some of the most useful sensor technologies, such as GMTI and SAR, would pose a very large risk of revealing the presence and location of the drone. Electronic countermeasures, meanwhile, could make it very difficult to communicate with the UAV. And while UAVs can loiter, the endurance of even the most sophisticated ones is fairly modest for extended missile-hunting operations. Satellites remain in orbit for years; UAVs need to be refueled after a period of hours or they stop flying. Most importantly, the types of UAVs likely to be useful for missile hunting are expensive enough to be difficult to acquire in large quantities. The kind of speed, range, and tactical sensors that can be provided by cheap drones is not sufficient for them to penetrate deep into adversary territory and uncover the missile launchers lurking there. Instead, systems need to be more akin to the Advanced Airborne Reconnaissance System (AARS), which was anticipated to be more similar in size and expected per-unit cost ($1 billion apiece) to the B-2 stealth bomber than to a mass-produced plastic quadcopter.[46]

Once the missiles are located, holding them under threat requires the ability to complete the kill chain by targeting them with available weapons and then engaging them. The most basic approach to doing this, and the one assumed in most unclassified studies of targeting mobile ICBMs, is to bombard the patrol zone with large numbers of nuclear warheads. Even by Cold War standards this approach demands very large numbers of weapons. The hiding strategy exploited by most mobile ICBMs suggests that a more judicious bombardment strategy might prove effective: if the adversary did not

---

[45] Daryl Press and Keir A. Lieber, "Appendix for Keir A. Lieber and Daryl G. Press, 'The New Era of Counterforce: Technological Change and the Future of Nuclear Deterrence,'" *International Security* 41.4 (Spring 2017), 9–49. Version V1, 2017. DOI: 10.7910/DVN/NKZJVT. URL: https://doi.org/10.7910/DVN/NKZJVT, 7–9.

[46] Ehrhard, *Air Force UAVs: The Secret History*, 17.

receive tactical warning (as might be the case if the attack was made using hypersonic weapons from relatively nearby launchers instead of ICBMS), then the missiles would have a fairly good chance of not having moved far by the time the attack arrived. The concept of operations envisioned for the AARS resembled this, albeit using subsonic ALCMs launched by B-2s loitering relatively close to the missile patrol areas.[47] This scheme is extremely risky, however, because if the adversary receives what it interprets as strategic warning it is liable to try to launch its own weapons under attack—even if that warning is spurious.

Another alternative is the approach pursued by DARPA under Thirsty Saber for destroying Soviet theater missiles: a loitering "smart munition" that searches the missile patrol area of its own accord.[48] These autonomous weapons would probably need to be delivered as submunitions: if compact enough, a package of them could be transported to the anticipated hiding place aboard a ballistic or hypersonic missile. Its primary advantage would be reduced reliance on nuclear weapons to destroy the targets: with enough autonomous intelligence, it could search for the TEL if it was moving and destroy it with a conventional warhead. A downside is that the smart munitions might be outsmarted with cheap decoys.

None of these approaches to targeting mobile missile launchers is particularly amenable to effective post-attack assessment. All schemes using nuclear weapons to kill the target have the peculiar property that the perfectly successful attack that centers the explosion directly on the target is most likely to destroy all visible evidence the target was there in the first place. Precision-guided munitions (PGMs), however, might be spoofed by decoys, and more sophisticated decoys are likely to leave remnants that are difficult to distinguish from an actual TEL.

Unattended ground sensors (UGS) and special operations could also play a role in operations to track and target mobile ICBMs, but their utility is limited by the usual location of the patrol zones deep inside well-defended enemy territory. This makes the UGS hard to emplace, and electronic countermeasures such as jamming may make it difficult for them to relay back useful information. The very large size of potential missile deployment areas is another hinderance. Special operations seem to have been a relative bright spot in

---

[47] Ehrhard, *Air Force UAVs: The Secret History*, 17.
[48] Van Atta et al., *Transformation and Transition: DARPA's Role in Fostering and Emerging Revolution in Military Affairs*, Volume 1, *Overall Assessment*, 24.

the 1991 Scud hunt, but on the whole they were insufficient to halt the missile launches.[49] Carrying out extensive special operations against some of the highest priority strategic assets during a potentially nuclear war is sure to be a great deal harder still. Russian mobile missiles are accompanied by a large degree of physical security which goes to considerable effort to thwart threats from UGS and enemy special forces.[50] There are cases, however, where special forces might make a critical contribution. In a North Korea scenario, where air superiority is probable and missile operating areas are smaller, special forces could fulfill intelligence-gathering, sabotage, and damage assessment missions that would probably be infeasible against Russia or China.

Obviously, operators of mobile ICBMs are sure to go to considerable precautions to prevent a scheme like this one from working. First and foremost, they can double down on camouflage, concealment, and deception (CCD). Entire missile bases may be fake; like professional illusionists, militaries may manipulate perceptions to create the appearance of movements and exercises without basis in reality. In addition, they can try to jam or spoof the sensors being used to monitor the missiles. Jamming seeks to lower the signal-to-noise ratio of radar. Naive jamming strategies tend not to work well against sophisticated modern radars.[51] An important consideration is that systems such as space-based SAR have narrow fields of view, so the jammers need not just to be located near the asset they are trying to obscure but also pointed toward the satellite. A downside of both SAR and SMTI are that they are not particularly stealthy, so defenders are likely to have some idea whence to direct their jammers. They involve active radar transmissions and therefore give away the position of the transmitter, although this effect can be minimized via clever techniques such as beamforming. "Dazzlers" are the optical counterparts of jammers; they try to overload passive optical sensors. The Russian Peresvet combat laser, for instance, appears to be a dazzler designed to interfere with intelligence satellites.[52] Similar to SAR jammers, such systems need to be located near the targets they protect as well as pointed into the satellite's sensors. Much more challenging than jamming, "spoofing" creates real-looking but deceptive signals at the receiver.

---

[49] Rosenau, *Special Operations Forces and Elusive Enemy Ground Targets: Lessons from Vietnam and the Persian Gulf War*.

[50] Zvezda, *Voennaia priemka. Iars. Iadernaia raketa sderzhivaniia. Chast' 2*.

[51] K. Dumper et al., "Spaceborne Synthetic Aperture Radar and Noise Jamming," *Radar 97 (Conf. Publ. 449)*. 1997, 411–414. DOI: 10.1049/cp:19971707; Feng Zhou et al., "A Novel Method for Adaptive SAR Barrage Jamming Suppression," *IEEE Geoscience and Remote Sensing Letters* 9.2 (2012), 292–296; Ruijia Wang et al., "High-Performance AntiRetransmission Deception Jamming Utilizing Range Direction Multiple Input and Multiple Output (MIMO) Synthetic Aperture Radar (SAR)," *Sensors* 17.1 (2017), 123.

[52] Zakvasin and Komarova, "'*Mgnovennoe porazheniia tseli': kakimi vozmozhnostiami obladaet rossiiskii boevoi lazer 'Peresvet'*".

Anti-submarine Warfare

In October 2018, the *South China Morning Post* reported breathlessly that "China is developing a satellite with a powerful laser for anti-submarine warfare that researchers hope will be able to pinpoint a target as far as 500 metres below the surface." In May of that year the Pilot National Laboratory for Marine Science and Technology in Qingdao had launched the project, whose name means "watching the big waves" in Chinese, with the aim of combining powerful blue lasers (for deep waters), green lasers (for littoral waters), and space-based synthetic aperture radar to detect deeply submerged submarines. According to the SCMP, "In theory, it works like this—when a laser beam hits a submarine, some pulses bounce back. They are then picked up by sensors and analysed by computer to determine the target's location, speed and three-dimensional shape."

The notion of a satellite-based laser capable of penetrating half a kilometer of seawater, reflecting off a submerged submarine, and bouncing back through another half a kilometer of seawater and still retaining enough signal to detect from orbit elicited outright incredulity from some experts. A laser imaging specialist with the Shanghai Institute of Optics and Fine Mechanics at the Chinese Academy of Sciences told SCMP that "five hundred metres is 'mission impossible.'"[53] For decades, American and Soviet researchers strove to develop powerful blue-green lasers for detecting submarines, only to find that this technology was mostly more trouble than it was worth. The rapid absorption of light by the water required outrageously powerful lasers for all but the shallowest targets. Another obstacle was posed by the need to reflect the laser off the hull of the submerged target: as anyone who has seen a submarine knows, they are very far from being perfect reflectors. As a consequence, blue-green lasers can only detect submarines directly from short ranges, and they can only detect them at relatively shallow depths.[54]

While it would be almost impossible for Project Guanlan to detect deeply submerged submarines the way described by the *South China Morning Post*, the same technology could conceivably still work and might even be able to enable the "Holy Grail" of anti-submarine warfare: wide-area detection of submerged submarines from space. The key to this would be to use the SAR and the lasers to seek *indirect* indicators of submerged submarines rather

---

[53] Stephen Chen, *Will China's New Laser Satellite Become the "Death Star" for Submarines?* (2018). URL: https://www.scmp.com/news/china/science/artide/2166413/will-chinas-new-laser-satellite-become-death-star-submarines.

[54] Donald C. Daniel, *Anti-Submarine Warfare and Superpower Strategic Stability* (University of Illinois, 1986), 50.

than trying to detect them directly. Since water is largely incompressible, a moving submarine displaces the water column above it, producing a "hump" above the submarine. As the submarine moves, the hump moves with it, producing a wake on the surface known as a "Kelvin wake." But as one might recall from playing in the bathtub as a child, the size of the hump and associated Kelvin wake decreases with the depth of the submerged object. Any surface indicator from a deeply submerged submarine would be extremely subtle, and Herculean efforts by American and Soviet researchers to find ways to predict these phenomena utilizing theoretical models came largely to naught during the Cold War. Another possible source of surface indicators are "internal waves" produced by the wake of a moving submarine. While the internal waves themselves basically remain in the same layer as the submarine, the incompressibility of water suggests that the internal waves could in turn produce some kind of extremely subtle surface indicator. Unfortunately, modeling these proved even more challenging than the Kelvin wake. Finding surface indicators from deeply submerged submarines outstripped both Cold War science and signal processing technology.[55]

Machine learning may have changed all that. Twentieth-century prediction techniques required theoretical models that could predict the surface indicators to a degree that they could be detected above ambient oceanic noise. But with enough data, contemporary machine learning can build up an implicit model for detecting the surface indicators even if we lack any theoretical understanding of the mechanisms generating them.[56] This, of course, presumes that detectable surface indicators actually exist, which is far from a foregone conclusion. But Project Guanlan's combination of penetrating lasers and SAR on a single platform could give China a leg up in collecting the data needed to train such models. The laser would not need to penetrate to the depth of the submerged submarine: instead it could be used to help detect the counterparts of the surface indicators in the few tens of meters immediately under the surface. Machine learning (presumably deep neural networks) would then correlate rare confluences of low-reliability (near-) surface indicators with the goal of ultimately generating an ability to detect adversary submarines using it.[57]

---

[55] Daniel, The *Future of Strategic ASW*, 20–27.

[56] DeepMind's AlphaFold system, which uses deep learning to predict how proteins will fold, offers a concrete example of how contemporary ML systems can provide useful solutions to complex real-world problems without either exploiting or finding a theoretical model. John Jumper et al., "Highly Accurate Protein Structure Prediction with AlphaFold," *Nature* 596.7873 (2021), 583–589.

[57] One could say that neural networks are akin to clever, albeit lazy, students. They are insightful enough to come up with a means of reproducing the answers they have been given even without receiving explicit instructions as to how to do so. But they are not motivated to do anything more complicated than the simplest procedure that provides adequate results. This is the reason that ML researchers go to great lengths to

The technical plausibility of a scheme like this should not be overstated. It depends on the existence of detectable near-surface indicators, but even if these do exist they may not provide a high enough signal-to-noise ratio to make detection practical using them. But even if a system like this worked as intended the trained models might have poor transferability between different geographies due to variations in oceanic conditions (for instance, a model that worked in the South China Sea might not work at all in the Atlantic). Finally, even if the system proved a technical slam-dunk that briefly provided a splendid ability to detect adversary submarines, that advantage could prove short-lived: rival states could change the shape of their submarines and operate them differently to minimize the hump and internal wave phenomena.[58] Yet given the threat to Chinese strategic interests posed by quiet adversary submarines in its home waters, Beijing's interest in bankrolling research into this long-shot technology is entirely understandable.[59] Depriving America of its underwater dominance would extend China's A2AD bubble under the waves and severely compromise U.S. ability to project force into the region.

Will artificial intelligence and autonomy make the oceans "transparent," rendering nuclear submarines vulnerable to enemy attack? Assertions to this effect—and vigorous denials—have been a perennial feature of debates about nuclear force modernization in the United States, Britain, and elsewhere.[60] Unfortunately these debates have generally been light on technical analysis, but this shortcoming can be excused because of the dearth of good-quality discussions of anti-submarine warfare (ASW) in the open literature. This subject is shrouded in secrecy for good reason, and a full analysis of it demands information simply unavailable to the public. With these constraints in mind, this discussion attempts to offer some general observations about the potential application of AI and machine learning to ASW.

---

try and force neural networks to work harder during training in the hope that the final models will generalize to inputs unlike the examples used to train them. Hence the strengths and weaknesses of deep learning: neural networks can learn programs that we could never write down explicitly, but there is no guarantee that those programs will not fail catastrophically when exposed to the messy, unfamiliar complexities of the real world.

[58] Maksim Klimov, *Problemnye voprosy oblika perspektivnykh podvodnyh lodok VMF Rossii* (2018). URL: https://bmpd.livejournal.com/3458646.html; Daniel, *Anti-submarine Warfare and Superpower Strategic Stability*.

[59] I personally would not wager money that the scheme outlined here can be translated into an operational capability—but if the research is not too costly, the Chinese are not unreasonable to investigate it as a high-risk, high-reward research activity.

[60] David Hambling, The *Inescapable Net: Unmanned Systems in Anti-Submarine Warfare* (BASIC, 2016); Jonathan Gates, "Is the SSBN Deterrent Vulnerable to Autonomous Drones?", *The RUSI Journal* 161.6 (2016), 28–35; Owen R. Côte, "Invisible Nuclear-Armed Submarines, or Transparent Oceans? Are Ballistic Missile Submarines Still the Best Deterrent for the United States?", *Bulletin of the Atomic Scientists* 75.1 (2019), 30–35; Gottemoeller, "The Standstill Conundrum: The Advent of Second-Strike Vulnerability and Options to Address It."

Western strategic analysts have traditionally considered nuclear submarines (known by the acronym ship submersible ballistic nuclear, or SSBN), as the most survivable component of nuclear retaliatory forces. The SSBNs gain their survivability from the physical characteristics of the oceans in which they operate. Seawater is almost totally opaque to electromagnetic radiation, so techniques such as radar that work well for surface and airborne targets are useless for finding the submarines. The submarines release some radioactive and nonradioactive effluvia, but these are comparatively minor and are soon diluted in the immensity of the ocean. The primary means available to detect the submarines are acoustic methods, but only low-frequency sound waves propagate significant distances in the water. In the process they interact with complicated oceanographic phenomena that distort sounds. Moreover, much of the ocean contains a great degree of ambient noise. By taking advantage of these features of the underwater environment, submarines can mask their own acoustic signature and make detection exceedingly difficult.[61]

Given that nature has stacked the deck so thoroughly in favor of those seeking to hide submarines, it might seem surprising that anti-submarine warfare is not a futile exercise. Indeed, many early discussions regarded ASW as implausible at best and touted ballistic missile submarines as an ideal second-strike deterrent.[62] But today we know that from the 1960s until the 1980s the U.S. Navy posed a very serious threat to the survivability of Soviet ballistic missile submarines.[63] The manner in which it accomplished this feat reveals insights about the nature of ASW that suggest how that endeavor could evolve in this century and how AI and machine learning might contribute to it.

Sound travels in the ocean in ways that humans, being terrestrial creatures, find counterintuitive. The speed of sound in water depends upon its temperature, salinity, and pressure, which all vary with depth. This "sound speed profile" causes sound to travel in curved paths rather than straight lines. In the deep ocean in equatorial and temperate regions, however, the surface temperature effect cancels out the pressure effect, with the result that the speed minimum occurs at a depth of a few hundred meters. Sound that enters the depth region associated with this sound speed minimum tends to stay at that depth and can be often be heard in that same depth region at distances of hundreds of miles or more. This region is called the Deep Sound

---

[61] Daniel, *Anti-Submarine Warfare and Superpower Strategic Stability*, 34–36.

[62] Kosta Tsipis and Bernard Taub Feld, *The Future of the Sea-Based Deterrent* (MIT Press, 1973); Richard L. Garwin, "Will Strategic Submarines Be Vulnerable?", *International Security* 8.2 (1983), 52–67.

[63] Green and Long, "Conceal or Reveal? Managing Clandestine Military Capabilities in Peacetime Competition."

Channel and was the key to the extraordinary success of U.S. ASW against early Soviet SSBNs in the 1960s and 1970s. Thanks to fortuitous quirks of geography, the United States could string cables to the edge of the relatively narrow continental shelf and place hydrophones in the Deep Sound Channel. These hydrophones made up the Sound Surveillance System (SOSUS). Soviet Hotel- and Yankee-class SSBNs had to travel to a patrol zone close to the U.S. coast because of the short range of the SLBMs they carried, but these noisy submarines were particularly loud at speed. Exploiting the Deep Sound Channel via SOSUS, the U.S. Navy could queue attack submarines and other ASW assets to track the Soviet SSBNs en route to the patrol zone.[64]

Unlike their American counterparts, Russian and Chinese submarines do not have whole oceans to hide in. Instead they are constrained by geography to operate in less-than-ideal waters. The situation faced by the Russian navy is a mixed bag. As during the Cold War, passage to the open ocean is threatened by adversary ASW, while the waters near Russia are often covered with ice. The ice is both a blessing and a curse for submarine operations: while it creates challenges (the SSBNs have to find holes in the ice or thin areas to break through to launch their missiles) it also greatly complicates adversary ASW. The ice changes how sound propagates and in certain circumstances itself generates large amounts of noise.[65]

In U.S. policy debates, there has been a tendency to conflate the vulnerability of the U.S. SSBN fleet to strategic anti-submarine warfare with the technical feasibility of strategic ASW. These are not the same thing, however, and it is no contradiction for the SSBNs of other nations to be highly vulnerable while those of the United States are largely secure.[66] Superior technology explains much of the U.S. advantage in this area, but other geostrategic factors are probably more important contributors. The Soviet deep-water navy was only a fraction of the size of its American rival, and the contemporary Russian and Chinese navies are considerably more modest.[67] Lacking sufficient naval assets, these navies cannot conduct extensive ASW operations in

---

[64] Côte, *The Third Battle: Innovation in the US Navy's Silent Cold War Struggle with Soviet Submarines* (Newport Paper 16, 2003), 47.

[65] Mark Sakitt, *Submarine Warfare in the Arctic: Option or Illusion?* (CISAC, 1988).

[66] Côte, "Invisible Nuclear-Armed Submarines, or Transparent Oceans? Are Ballistic Missile Submarines Still the Best Deterrent for the United States?"; as Andrew Futter notes, "not all nuclear-armed submarines and mobile missiles are becoming vulnerable to the same degree . . . if a new era of counterforce really is dawning, the United States will be its primary driver for the foreseeable future, and only certain countries' nuclear systems will become more vulnerable in some but not necessarily all scenarios." Andrew Futter, "Disruptive Technologies and Nuclear Risks: What's New and What Matters," *Survival* 64.1 (2022), 99–120, 101–102.

[67] The Chinese Navy now has more ships that its U.S. counterpart, but it is still largely a regional force not designed to contest the U.S. Navy head-to-head in the open ocean. For a discussion of current PRC naval assets, see Manfred Meyer, *Modern Chinese Maritime Forces* (Admiralty Trilogy Group, 2022).

the distant waters where U.S. SSBNs operate. Thanks to geography, American SSBNs can easily access the open ocean, and the range of the Trident D5 SLBMs they carry allow them to target Russia and China from a huge fraction of the world's oceans. Meanwhile, what ASW resources Moscow and Beijing can field are needed to try and counter the threat American attack submarines pose to their own SSBNs and other strategic assets.

The United States can, and does, pose a very credible threat of waging strategic ASW against rival powers. But this is not the same thing as being able to destroy all of an adversary's SSBNs during a war. During a crisis, a potential adversary can be expected to go to extreme lengths to degrade U.S. ASW capabilities, including destroying sensors and cables, degrading sensor assets, waging ASW against forward-deployed SSNs, and destroying critical facilities such as those where intelligence data is integrated. ASW is sure to be the target of aggressive intelligence-gathering operations by potential adversaries, and they may know much more about the location and operation of U.S. ASW assets than they let on in peacetime.[68] Adversary counter-ASW may therefore prove extremely effective, particularly if the enemy is aggressive in its attacks on U.S. capabilities. This dynamic creates "use-it-or-lose-it" pressures that could be disastrous for crisis stability.

As with mobile missile launchers, to "complete the kill chain" against SSBNs simply locating the submarines isn't enough: it is essential to be able to target and engage them. Historically, this was largely treated as a tactical problem: trailing SSNs would attack the SSBNs with torpedoes or similar short-range weapons, and armed ASW aircraft might drop torpedoes or depth charges into the suspected hiding places of submarines. Nuclear-tipped variants of both these weapons were deployed by the Cold War superpowers for occasions such as these. But even nuclear torpedoes and depth charges required that the intended target be within a few kilometers. What could be done if the quarry had been located, but the nearest weapons platform was further away? For these cases both the U.S. and Soviet navies developed antisubmarine rockets in both conventional and nuclear versions. U.S. antisubmarine rockets included the submarine-launched SUBROC and the surface-launched ASROC.[69] These provided ranges of tens of kilometers and could carry either a torpedo as a submunition or a nuclear warhead. The possibility of trying to destroy SSBNs via bombardment using strategic nuclear warheads was often suggested, but it faced serious technical obstacles such as

---

[68] They are incentivized not to reveal this information outside of a crisis so as to avoid inspiring U.S. countermeasures.

[69] Daniel, *Anti-Submarine Warfare and Superpower Strategic Stability*, 135.

the need for huge numbers of weapons and the development of "diving" RVs that could survive hitting the water at high speed.[70]

Soviet and Russian SSBNs

As a rule, anti-submarine warfare is enabled by potential adversaries' weaknesses more than by one's own technological might. During the Cold War, the Soviet Navy had several disadvantages that the United States could leverage to make its submarines vulnerable. Most fundamentally, it suffered from a disadvantageous geographic position. While the United States benefits from two lengthy coasts untroubled by ice or nearby adversaries, the USSR's outlets to the sea gave its enemies ample opportunities to impede its submarine operations. NATO allies blocked access to the open ocean from the Baltic and Black Seas, so ballistic missile submarines patrolling in the Atlantic operated from bases along the sea of Murmansk, with analogous operations by the Pacific Fleet from the Kamchatka Peninsula. Until the introduction of the Delta-class SSBNs in the mid-1970s, Soviet SLBMs lacked the range to attack targets in the continental United States (CONUS) from friendly waters. Instead they had to travel to patrol zones relatively close to the U.S. coast. This demanded that they pass through areas dominated by their adversaries, most notoriously the GIUK (Greenland–Iceland–United Kingdom) gap. Moreover, in order to reach the patrol zone in a reasonable amount of time the Soviet SSBNs had to move at a speed at which propeller cavitation made them detectable at great distances. The U.S. Navy's network of hydrophones, the SOSUS network, was able to detect the submarines en route to the patrol zone thanks to the noisy design and careless operation of early Soviet SSBNs. This enabled the dispatch of attack submarines to tail them.[71] The introduction of longer-range SLBMs in the 1970s and 1980s allowed the Soviet Union to evolve toward a "bastion" strategy in which SSBNs remained in the Russian arctic and the Sea of Okhotsk. Since these waters were dominated by the Soviet Navy, they were much harder for the United States to conduct ASW operations in–but this did not dissuade American efforts to threaten submarines in the bastions as well.[72]

---

[70] Daniel, *Anti-Submarine Warfare and Superpower Strategic Stability*, 20.
[71] Côte, The *Third Battle: Innovation in the US Navy's Silent Cold War Struggle with Soviet Submarines (Newport Paper 16, 2003)*; Green and Long, "Conceal or Reveal? Managing Clandestine Military Capabilities in Peacetime Competition."
[72] Côte, The *Third Battle: Innovation in the US Navy's Silent Cold War Struggle with Soviet Submarines (Newport Paper 16, 2003)*, 64.

It is unclear when the Soviet Union became aware of the full vulnerability of its SSBNs. American writers often attribute the decision to shift to the bastion strategy to revelations provided by the infamous Walker spy ring, but there are anecdotal reasons to believe that the Soviet Navy began planning the shift its SSBN patrol zones closer to home before John Anthony Walker began selling information to Soviet intelligence in late 1967. Development of the Delta-I class SSBN and its associated missile, the R-29, was already underway in the mid-1960s. The R-29 took longer to develop than the associated submarine (which was a derivative of the earlier Yankee class with a hump to accommodate the larger missiles), and the whole complex only entered service in 1974.[73] Attempting to escape the Western anti-submarine sonar net Sound Surveillance System (SOSUS) by developing longer-range SLBMs and operating in the Arctic rather than trying to compete with the Americans in quieting their SSBNs was a logical choice for Soviet decision-makers. It built upon existing systems and development programs without requiring a complicated, and expensive, silencing program. Moreover, it fit with the Soviet pattern of building a larger number of lower-quality SSBNs than the capitalists.[74] With sufficient redundancy, even if the U.S. Navy managed to find and destroy most Soviet SSBNs a few would probably survive—and as each one carried as many as 200 warheads, a single SSBN could be enough to deprive the adversary of any meaningful notion of "victory."

In addition to redundancy, the Soviet military planned to counter U.S. ASW capabilities through aggressive countermeasures in case of war. In peacetime Western navies could usually prosecute ASW activities with minimal harassment, particularly in the open ocean, while their shore facilities were secure from adversary meddling. During a conflict, however, the favorable conditions that granted the United States so much success tracking Soviet submarines in peacetime would be disrupted by Soviet military action. To the best of their ability, Soviet forces would attempt to sink Western attack submarines and ASW ships. Perhaps more importantly, they would destroy onshore communications and signal processing assets, including the use of nuclear weapons if they deemed it necessary.[75] In addition to avoiding the U.S. SOSUS network, the shift to the bastion strategy also facilitated the potential exploitation of such "operational" and "tactical" countermeasures to U.S. ASW.

---

[73] Iu.V. Vedernikov, *Sravnitel'nyi analiz sozdaniia i razvitiia morskikh strategicheskikh iadernykh sil SSSR i SShA* (2005).

[74] Daniel, *Anti-Submarine Warfare and Superpower Strategic Stability*, Ch. 4.

[75] V. Poliakov, "40 let protivolodochnoi bor'be," *Morskoi sbornik* 3 (2009), 20–25.

Considerable confusion about U.S. strategic ASW capabilities during the late Cold War is engendered by the persistence of early Soviet SSBNs until the very twilight of the conflict. Hotel- and Yankee-class submarines remained in service, so Western attack submarines had a profusion of easy targets even if their ability to prosecute ASW against more modern Soviet SSBNs lurking in the Arctic was considerably more limited. While Delta-III and Typhoon-class SSBNs were quieter than their predecessor classes, they were both louder than contemporary Soviet attack submarines and much louder than American submarines.[76] This created opportunities for U.S. attack submarines to track them if opportunities to localize their Soviet quarries materialized, such as when the SSBNs left port (Figure 4).

The USSR's slow adoption of quieting measures for its submarines befuddled Western analysts, who assumed that the Soviet Navy would swiftly emulate the design practices of their capitalist rivals. It remains unclear whether this occurred because Soviet decision-makers failed to appreciate the importance of quieting or because they believed that the migration to a bastion strategy made investments in securing the bastions more important than SSBN quieting.[77] When the Akula-class attack submarine appeared in the mid-1980s it represented a major leap in quieting from earlier Soviet submarines, but similar improvements were not incorporated in the USSR's missile submarines of the same period, the Delta III/IV and the enormous Project 941 "Typhoon."[78] While each successive Soviet SSBN class incorporated additional quieting features, these lagged behind those of Soviet attack submarines, much less the American attack submarines that might trail and destroy the SSBNs in case of war.[79]

Developing capabilities to threaten Soviet submarines in their bastions was a major objective of the U.S. Maritime Strategy in the 1980s. New technologies such as SURTASS (the Surface Towed Array Surveillance System, a kind of mobile successor to SOSUS towed by a civilian surface ship) and the FDS (Fixed Distributed System, an upward-looking low-frequency passive sonar array connected to shore by fiber optic cables) sought to maintain U.S.

---

[76] Côte, *The Third Battle: Innovation in the US Navy's Silent Cold War Struggle with Soviet Submarines* (*Newport Paper 16, 2003*), 66–70.

[77] Ivan Kapitanets, *Bitva za Mirovoi okean v "kholodnoi" i budushchikh voinakh* (Veche, 2002).

[78] The influence of Tom Clancy's *The Hunt for Red October* has helped perpetuate a myth that the gargantuan Project 941 SSBN was some kind of superweapon. Post-Soviet memoir accounts reveal that its immensity resulted from the inferiority of Soviet technology. Ordered by Kremlin leaders to develop a SSBN equivalent to the U.S. *Ohio*-class, they ended up with a craft that essentially consisted of two submarines joined together, with two hulls, two reactors, and two screws, but a similar number of missiles and warheads to the much quieter *Ohio*. Vedernikov, *Sravnitel'nyi analiz sozdaniia i razvitiia morskikh strategicheskikh iadernyh sil SSSR i SShA*.

[79] Côte, *The Third Battle: Innovation in the US Navy's Silent Cold War Struggle with Soviet Submarines* (*Newport Paper 16, 2003*), 66.

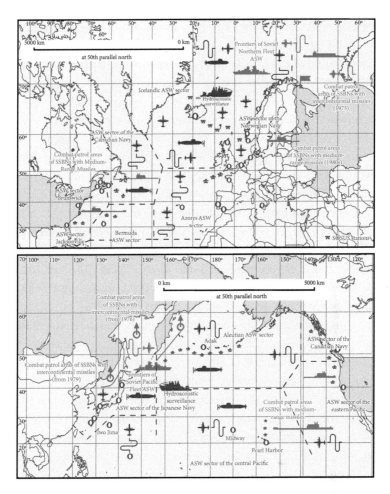

Figure 4. Soviet SSBN patrol areas and U.S. ASW assets in the Atlantic and Pacific oceans, late Cold War. Soviet forces in red, U.S. forces in blue.

Reproduced from Vadernikov, *Sravnitel'nyi analiz sozdaniia i razvitiia morskikh strategicheskikh iadernyh sil SSSR i SShA* (2005). The maps are kindly provided by Yu. V. Vedernikov.

advantage in ASW as Soviet submarines finally grew quieter. The question of whether the envisioned combination of Seawolf-class attack submarines and advanced sensor systems would enable the United States to conduct strategic ASW in the USSR's arctic bastions was rendered academic by the end of the Cold War.[80] Procurement of these costly systems was curtailed and the U.S.

---

[80] Daniel, *The Future of Strategic ASW*; Côte, *The Third Battle: Innovation in the US Navy's Silent Cold War Struggle with Soviet Submarines* (Newport Paper 16, 2003).

Navy refocused its ASW efforts on the task of finding quiet diesel–electric submarines in littoral waters.

The unravelling of the USSR and the subsequent collapse of the Soviet submarine fleet made the earlier strategy of maintaining SSBN viability through redundancy untenable.[81] While the START II agreement sharply reduced Russia's allowed SSBN fleet, its operational capability dropped even more quickly. Even relatively new SSBNs, such as the Project 941 Typhoons, proved difficult to keep operating, and while all of the Soviet nuclear submarine bases were within the Russian Federation some of the industrial base that built and maintained the SSBNs was in other former Soviet republics. Russian officials decided that instead of attempting to modernize the Project 941 or continue the venerable Delta series, they would develop a quiet, compact SSBN to carry a solid-fuel SLBM. This project, which became today's Borei-class SSBNs, began in the twilight years of the USSR. The first submarine was laid down in 1996, but after a few years it became apparent that the missile being developed for it, an evolved version of the R-39 SLBM carried by the Typhoon, would probably never reach fruition due to technical and budgetary obstacles.[82] Instead, the Russian government sought to adapt a version of the Topol-M road-mobile ICBM then under development as an SLBM. This required redesigning the lead boat, the *Yuri Dolgorukii*, to carry this missile, dubbed the "Bulava." The development of both the Borei-class SSBN and the Bulava proved long and tortuous. The *Yurii Dolgorukii* took over 16 years from when it was laid down in 1996 to when it was commissioned into the Russian Navy in 2013. The Bulava, meanwhile, failed in a large fraction of its early test launches, and was a major contributor to this delay. The submarine began undergoing sea trials in 2008, but it took another ten years until the Russian government certified the Bulava.[83]

The design philosophy of the Borei-class SSBN and its associated Bulava missiles is much more in line with U.S. practice than that of earlier Soviet submarines. It has a single hull and only one reactor, whereas Soviet submarines often had two of each. It carries fairly compact solid-fuel SLBMs rather than the large liquid-fuel missiles employed by the Delta class. In comparison to the gargantuan Typhoon, the Borei is relatively compact (although it is hardly small by any conventional standard). Most importantly, the Borei apparently prioritizes acoustic quieting to a degree never seen on Soviet SSBNs. Russian

---

[81] Eugene Miasnikov, "Can Russian Strategic Submarines Survive at Sea? The Fundamental Limits of Passive Acoustics," *Science & Global Security* 4.2 (1994), 213–251.

[82] A. A. Kokoshin, V. A. Veselov, and A. V. Liss, *Sderzhivanie vo vtorom iadernom veke.* Institut problem mezhdunarodnoi bezopasnosti (RAN, 2001).

[83] Kristensen and Korda, "Russian Nuclear Forces, 2019."

submarine designers have asserted in public interviews (possibly incorrectly) that the Borei-class SSBN is significantly quieter than U.S. Virginia-class SSNs. In theory, the improved stealthiness could allow Russia to emulate Western SSBN deployment strategy as well, leaving the bastions to patrol in the open ocean.[84]

Much like how the Gulf War Scud hunt is a dubious analogy for the viability of targeting mobile ICBM launchers today, the wide-area ASW that the United States conducted against Soviet SSBNs during the early Cold War using passive acoustic detection does not tell us much about the future feasibility of strategic ASW. The "happy time," as the U.S. Navy dubbed it, was the antithesis of the Scud hunt: while the Scud hunt was a military failure spun as a success in contemporary media reporting, American strategic ASW against early Soviet SSBNs was highly successful and totally secret.[85] Yet the successes of ASW were enabled by a fortuitous confluence of geography and Soviet technological limitations: by the final years of the Cold War the USSR introduced modernized submarines and updated CONOPS that vitiated the plausibility of U.S. strategic ASW.[86]

Chinese SSBNs

While China finally boasts functioning SSBNs, these vessels and the weapons they carry are in many respects decades behind their American and Russian counterparts. China's first attempt at a domestic SSBN, the 1980s-era Type 092, was a technical failure that never entered regular service. Even if it had, the JL-1 missile it was to carry had too little range to target the United States without traversing most of the Pacific, and this weapon would have strained even to hold most of the USSR under threat. Compared to its predecessor, the Type 094 is an enormous improvement. China has built at least five Type 094s

---

[84] As of yet it is unclear whether the Russian Navy will actually do this. Andrei Kokoshin commented in a 2009 article that the Russian Security Council had "recently" made the decision to "return" to the bastion strategy, suggesting it may have been considered before then. The prospect of needing to conduct ASW over larger areas would complicate U.S. planning, but the same geographic advantages that the USSR planned to exploit to hide its noisy SSBNs in the Arctic will be just as operative for quieter post-Soviet SSBNs. Andrei Kokoshin, "Revoliutsiia v voennom dele i problemy sozdaniia sovremennykh vooruzhennykh sil Rossii," *Vestnik Moskovskogo universiteta. Seria 25. Mezhdunarodnye otnosheniia i mirovaia politika* 1 (2009), 46–62, 60.

[85] Côte, *The Third Battle: Innovation in the US Navy's Silent Cold War Struggle with Soviet Submarines (Newport Paper 16, 2003)*; Green and Long, "Conceal or Reveal? Managing Clandestine Military Capabilities in Peacetime Competition."

[86] Kapitanets, *Bitva za Mirovoi okean v "kholodnoi" i budushchikh voinakh*; Vedernikov, *Sravnitelhyi analiz sozdaniia i razvitiia morskikh strategicheskikh iadernyh sil SSSR i SShA.*

and began sending them on deterrence patrols in 2015. The Type 094 orig-inally carried the JL-2 SLBM, a maritime version of the land-based DF-31 ICBM. Unfortunately, the JL-2 lacked sufficient range to target the continen-tal United States from waters near China, so the Type 094 could not be used to emulate the Soviets' attempt to circumvent U.S. ASW capabilities with a bastion strategy. In November 2022, the U.S. Navy reported that the Type 094 had been re-equipped with the longer-range JL-3 SLBM, which can probably target parts of the American homeland from waters near China.[87] Targeting much of CONUS would likely still require that the SSBNs break out into the open ocean, a risky endeavor given that they would need to traverse narrow choke points dominated by the Unites States and its allies. The Type 094 is comparable in certain respects to Soviet submarines from the 1970s, although it is far superior to them in others.[88] The size of the missiles necessitates the inclusion of a squarish hump in the middle of the submarine to accommodate them, reminiscent of that of the Soviet Delta-IV class. This feature impedes the hydrodynamics of the boat and increases noise.

China has comparatively limited experience building and operating nuclear submarines, and well as in conducting its own ASW operations, which has constrained its opportunities to learn how to quiet its submarines and avoid detection. But it would be a mistake to assume that the Chinese SSBNs are operationally equivalent to the Soviet missile subs of forty years ago. While inexperienced, the Chinese can draw on twenty-first-century technology to help design and build their submarines. Computer-aided design and modern precision manufacturing that did not exist in the 1970s can potentially be adapted from civilian applications. Additionally, intelli-gence about the design and operation of foreign submarines can be used to inform the development of Chinese SSBNs. China's per-boat learning curve appears to be fairly high compared to that of the Americans and the Soviets: Beijing's latest SSBNs are Type 094As, which include improved hydrody-namics and presumably numerous internal refinements as well. The planned follow-on class, the Type 096, is expected to carry the JL-3 SLBM recently introduced on the current Type 094 class.[89]

The biggest challenge facing China's SSBN fleet, however, is not techno-logical limitations but rather unfavorable geography. Where America has been blessed with easy access to the deep ocean and the Russians can use

---

[87] Anthony Capaccio, *China Has Put Longer-Range ICBMs on Its Nuclear Subs, US Says.* https://www.bloomberg.com/news/articles/2022-11-18/us-says-china-s-subs-armed-with-longer-range-ballistic-missiles. Nov. 2022.

[88] Glaser and Fetter, "Should the United States Reject MAD? Damage Limitation and US Nuclear Strategy toward China," 71–72.

[89] Zhao, *Tides of Change*, 8, 72.

neighboring waters in the Barents Sea and Sea of Okhotsk as submarine bastions, China is handicapped by a lack of both. As a consequence, even with submarines as sophisticated as those of the U.S. Navy, Beijing would be at a marked disadvantage trying to evade adversary anti-submarine warfare. The waters immediately around China are mostly shallow. While littoral waters such as these are notoriously challenging for sub-hunters, areas like the Yellow Sea (average depth 44 meters) are so shallow that large submarines cannot operate deeply enough to avoid detection. The nearest body of water with sufficient depth to serve as a potential SSBN patrol zone is the heavily contested South China Sea. It has been suggested that the desire to turn the South China Sea into a SSBN bastion is a major motivator for China's attempts to dominate that body of water, but in any case it is far from ideal for that purpose. Compared to the open ocean it is too small, while compared to the Russian Arctic it is too accessible.[90]

Given the forbidding geographic obstacles facing Chinese SSBNs, it is unsurprising that many Chinese analysts feel that it would be better to concentrate their country's resources on land-based forces instead.[91] There are several possible explanations for why Chinese leaders have pursued SSBNs anyhow, including as a hedging strategy against the possible vulnerability of land-based ICBMs and a belief that China needs SSBNs for prestige reasons to cement its status as a first-rate military power.

Emerging Technology and Anti-submarine Warfare

Given sufficiently high sensor density, it is possible to find and track even the stealthiest submarine. In addition to the absurdist case where the submarine literally cannot move without hitting the sensors, short-range sensors can take advantage of many additional phenomena that are detectable through only short distances underwater, such as medium- and high-frequency sound. This seems to suggest that making the oceans "transparent" is as simple as building a large number of unmanned underwater vehicles (UUVs) to carry the sensors and infesting the anticipated SSBN patrol zone with them.[92] But it turns out that even though this approach is not strictly speaking impossible, it is totally impractical. The greatest obstacle is that the ocean is simply too big relative to the range of most of the sensors. An enormous

---

[90] Wu Riqiang, "Survivability of China's Sea-Based Nuclear Forces," *Science & Global Security* 19.2 (2011), 91–120; Zhao, *Tides of Change*.

[91] Fiona S. Cunningham and M. Taylor Fravel, "Assuring Assured Retaliation: China's Nuclear Posture and US–China Strategic Stability," *International Security* 40.2 (2015), 7–50, 29.

[92] Hambling, *The Inescapable Net: Unmanned Systems in Anti-Submarine Warfare.*

number of UUVs would prove necessary to surveil even a relatively small part of it. In addition to its size, the ocean is also a relatively hostile environment even discounting adversary activities. Building a system which can remain operational in the ocean for more than a few days requires costly engineered features. Similarly, significant power is required for propulsion and many types of sensors.[93] Battery-powered UUVs tend to have an operational endurance of a few days at best: better performance requires costly alternatives (diesel–electric, AIP, or in the Russian case, nuclear). Finally, the same phenomena that make submarines so hard to detect inhibit communication with submerged craft. While acoustic and non-acoustic (ELF/ULF/VLF radio, optical) communications with UUVs exist, bandwidth is at an extreme premium, and what little can be had must be managed with utmost efficiency. This is the reason that ASW sensors such as hydrophones and sonobouys are tethered to either underwater cables or floating surface antennas: otherwise, the data they collect could not be sent to shore-based signal-processing facilities.

Hunting diesel–electric submarines lurking near shore is a qualitatively different, and in some ways much more difficult, task than the open-ocean ASW that the United States conducted against early Soviet SSBNs in the 1960s and 1970s. The types of nuclear reactors used for submarine propulsion require constant coolant flow even when they are not generating significant power, which in turn produces a certain amount of unavoidable mechanical noise even when the submarine isn't moving. Diesel–electric submarines running on battery power, meanwhile, can be extremely quiet. Moreover, the littoral environment is particularly noisy with large amounts of both naturally occurring and man-made noise. The possession of diesel–electric submarines by regional powers such as Iran makes them a particular concern for the United States, so a large amount of research and development over the past few decades has been devoted to the problem of locating them. The most famous of these is DARPA's ACTUV (ASW Continuous Trail Unmanned Vessel) program, which has developed an autonomous surface ship designed to follow diesel–electric submarines. The Sea Hunter (as the initial prototype was dubbed) is an important testbed for unmanned surface craft that has generated considerable excitement. The upside of autonomous surface vessels for the Navy is their potential to greatly reduce costs of operations: DARPA claims that the craft will cost a mere $10–15,000 a day to operate, while a

---

[93] Gates, "Is the SSBN Deterrent Vulnerable to Autonomous Drones?"

destroyer costs some $700,000.[94] While the employment of vessels such as the Sea Hunter for ASW remains some time in the future, the ACTUV is indicative of the way autonomy will be employed for anti-submarine warfare: by automating tasks that were formerly carried out by manned platforms using cheaper, more expendable uninhabited craft.

Efforts to develop ASW capabilities against conventional submarines in littoral waters appear to have differing relevance for prospective strategic ASW against Russia and China. Russia's SSBN bastions are littorals—the continental shelf extends from Russia far into the Arctic Ocean—but they have features that both facilitate and hinder ASW. The presence of ice both generates noise and changes the propagation of sound in the water. It also hinders prospective non-acoustic detection methods and would forestall the employment of manned or unmanned ASW platforms like the Sea Hunter. But ice also seriously complicates SSBN operations for the Russians, and the Sea of Murmansk has an unusually smooth bottom that facilitates sound propagation due to the "bottom bounce" phenomenon.[95] The most important advantage of the bastions, however, is their remoteness and relative inaccessibility to adversary navies. The Sea Hunter, for instance, appears to be designed for use in a permissive maritime environment where it is relatively immune to destruction by adversary forces, which would probably be the case against a regional adversary but not at all plausible in the Russian SSBN bastions during a conflict. Technologies like the Sea Hunter appear to be much more applicable to strategic ASW against China. The waters around China are all littorals, and are immediately adjacent to U.S. allies. Current-generation Chinese SSBNs need to traverse these waters and go through choke points dominated by the United States and its strategic partners to enter the Pacific and range targets in CONUS with their missiles.[96]

As with missile detection and tracking, AI and autonomy primarily promise to enhance or enable the Cold War approach to targeting and engaging SSBNs rather than totally revolutionizing it. The availability of more intelligent loitering munitions could combine tasks formerly entrusted to ASW aircraft with the functions of anti-submarine munitions like SUBROC. Similar to Thirsty Saber, the smart munition could employ tactical sensors (possibly magnetic anomaly detection) to decide where to employ submunitions

---

[94] Amanda Macias, *The First Drone Warship Just Joined the Navy and Now Nearly Every Element of It Is Classified* (2018). URL: https://www.cnbc.com/2018/04/25/first-drone-warship-joins-us-navy-nearly-every-element-classified.html.

[95] Daniel, *The Future of Strategic ASW*, 23; Côte, *The Third Battle: Innovation in the US Navy's Silent Cold War Struggle with Soviet Submarines* (Newport Paper 16, 2003), 73.

[96] Desmond Ball and Richard Tanter, *The Tools of Owatatsumi: Japan's Ocean Surveillance and Coastal Defence Capabilities* (ANU Press, 2015), 51–54.

(probably conventionally armed torpedoes). Even marginal improvements in relatively "conventional" weapons like these torpedoes could meaningfully improve the effectiveness of ASW. With greater onboard intelligence, the torpedo could better perceive evasive maneuvers and increase its likelihood of destroying the target.

The possibility of exploiting relatively expendable unmanned platforms could enable CONOPS for ASW that would be too risky with traditional crewed vessels. The most obvious of these is the employment of active rather than passive sonar for submarine tracking. Cold War ASW efforts tended to de-emphasize active sonar because available medium-frequency systems had short ranges. The associated sonar transducer (emitter) broadcast the position of the vessel carrying it, and the rudimentary signal-processing techniques of the time basically dictated that the transducer and receiver needed to be located on the same vessel. An alternative paradigm, "multistatic" sonar, would instead separate the transducer from multiple receivers. First proposed in the 1950s, the United States and its allies began aggressively pursuing this technology in the final years of the Cold War.[97]

The last years of the Cold War also saw a marked increase of U.S. research into low-frequency active (LFA) sonar. Extremely controversial due to its potential harms to marine life, LFA sonar is probably the primary contender for a viable means of locating quiet modern submarines at significant ranges.[98] Unlike the passive acoustics exploited by Cold War ASW, this system would produce an extraordinarily loud underwater sound and then listen for it to be reflected off of underwater targets.[99] LFA sonar has the advantage of relying solely upon established physical science to work (unlike schemes like Project Guanlan), but the transducer has obvious survivability challenges as it broadcasts its position—in the case of the SURTASS-LFA system explored by the U.S. Navy, with the loudest sound in the ocean. Against a weak opponent with modest capabilities, it may be possible for the transducer to remain at a manageable standoff distance. In a conflict against a well-resourced adversary such as Russia or China, the platform carrying the transducer would need to be expendable, and preferably cheap, as it would surely be targeted and probably destroyed as quickly as the adversary could manage it. Fielding the transducer(s) on expendable unmanned surface or underwater platforms and relying upon distributed multistatic

---

[97] E. Hanle, "Survey of Bistatic and Multistatic Radar," *IEE Proceedings F-Communications, Radar and Signal Processing* 133. 7 IET (1986), 587–595.

[98] Côte, *The Third Battle: Innovation in the US Navy's Silent Cold War Struggle with Soviet Submarines* (*Newport Paper 16, 2003*), 78.

[99] Gordon D. Tyler, "The Emergence of Low-Frequency Active Acoustics as a Critical Antisubmarine Warfare Technology," *Johns Hopkins APL Technical Digest* 13.1 (1992), 145–159.

receivers offers the best of both worlds: the transducer can be located as close to the intended targets as is practical (similar to a spotlight, the closer the emitter is to the targets the more brightly "illuminated" they are), while the receivers can remain stealthy.[100] These receivers could take the form of fixed hydrophones, deployed sonobouys, or towed arrays deployed on autonomous underwater vehicles (AUVs) or autonomous surface vehicles (ASVs). Unfortunately, the physics of low-frequency underwater sound dictates that both the transducer and receivers will probably need to be quite large, although clever technology might be able to alleviate this restriction somewhat.

Even though it is not an AI application per se, multistatic LFA sonar could prove the single most strategically significant military application of artificial intelligence. The technical obstacles that have impeded practical LFA sonar so far—extremely complex signal processing, sensor platform management, and adaptive communications—can all potentially be overcome using AI and autonomy. Multistatic sonar also imposes extremely steep, but potentially surmountable, requirements for positioning, navigation, and timing (PNT). Given the enormous strategic importance of submarines (not just SSBNs), any technological shift that significantly improves the efficacy of ASW could be a real game-changer. Nor is it necessary for technology to render the seas transparent to accomplish this: merely posing a real, if modest, probability of destroying costly nuclear submarines could discourage the major powers from risking them in adversary waters, sapping decisionmakers' willingness to use them to support power-projection capabilities.

AUVs and ASVs can enhance situational awareness and contribute to ASW operations without looking for submarines directly. Either passive or active long-range detection requires information about the subtleties of oceanographic conditions to predict the complicated way in which sound will propagate through the water. AI and ML could offer an attractive shortcut for rival navies aiming to close the "oceanography gap" with their American rivals.[101] The U.S. Navy has expended enormous resources over the decades acquiring knowledge about the ocean that it then leverages to its operational advantage, particularly for ASW. Russia and China have lacked the resources to compete in this field, but automated data collection and analysis

---

[100] Bryan Clark, Seth Cropsey, and Timothy A. Walton, *Sustaining the Undersea Advantage: Disrupting Anti-Submarine Warfare Using Autonomous Systems* (Hudson Institute, 2020), 59–62. Another advantage of being able to place transducers closer to targets is that they can use lower-power pulses, reducing the ecological harms that have dogged SURTASS-LFA. After decades of development, it has only been possible to test SURTASS-LFA for a limited number of hours and in restricted locations due to possible injury to marine life. A lower-power multistatic system could conceivably provide superior performance with modest or even negligible ecological impact.

[101] Klimov, *Problemnye voprosy oblika perspektivnykh podvodnyh lodok VMF Rossii.*

may put equivalent capabilities within their reach. Slow, cheap, and fragile autonomous systems can collect data about ambient conditions and transmit it back to signal-processing centers. Other AUVs and ASVs can help deploy sensors or communications cables on the seafloor. Indeed, a large number of the maritime robots announced by Russia and China seem to be intended for these roles. The Russian *Iunona* (Youth) and *Amulet* AUVs are only a few meters in length and carry sensors that collect data about oceanic conditions.[102] Battery-powered, the AUVs have scant prospect of trailing a manned submarine, but they do not need to: the sensor data they relay back can be exploited to facilitate other kinds of acoustic and non-acoustic tracking. Underwater "gliders" like those being tested by the Chinese Navy take this principle to the next level. Instead of using conventional power, these craft exploit small wings and changes in buoyancy to propel themselves with minimal energy consumption. While compromising speed and maneuverability, this scheme allows battery power to be conserved for sensors and communications and can greatly enhance the useful endurance of the AUV.[103]

Anti-submarine warfare might be one of the most compelling potential applications of lethal autonomous weapons.[104] The targets are of extremely high value, contacts with them may be brief and transient, communications is difficult, and there are few or no civilians in the underwater domain that might become collateral damage. Despite all of these considerations, as of yet the unmanned version of a "hunter-killer" submarine remains a somewhat distant prospect.[105] In principle, there is no reason why one could not build the robot equivalent of the Seawolf attack submarines that were designed to penetrate Soviet SSBN bastions in the Arctic and hunt their prey with relatively little support from friendly forces. Such a system would require many costly features, most importantly nuclear propulsion to grant them the speed and endurance to outmaneuver SSBNs. So far only the Russians have demonstrated a willingness to combine autonomy and nuclear propulsion. A greater obstacle is posed by the consideration that strategic ASW is probably an

---

[102] Iudina, *Gid po samym sekretnym podvodnym robotam Rossii.*

[103] Hambling, *The Inescapable Net: Unmanned Systems in Anti-Submarine Warfare.*

[104] Frank Sauer, "Military Applications of Artificial Intelligence: Nuclear Risk Redux," ed. by Vincent Boulanin (ed.), *The Impact of Artificial Intelligence on Strategic Stability and Nuclear Risk: Euro-Atlantic Perspectives* (SIPRI, 2019), 84–90, 89; Clark, Cropsey, and Walton, *Sustaining the Undersea Advantage: Disrupting Anti-Submarine Warfare Using Autonomous Systems,* 51.

[105] There are rumors that a Russian AUV in development, the *Cephalopod,* is an armed system intended for an ASW role. So little information about this project is publicly available that it is difficult to draw any conclusions. The name appears in budgetary documents so it is apparently a real project, but the claim that it is armed is based on a low-quality image of a "leaked" slide in which the AUV appears to be carrying a torpedo. H. I. Sutton, *Cephalopod* (2018). URL: http://www.hisutton.com/Cephalopod.html.

"AI-complete" problem (that is, one that requires "human-equivalent" intelligence). This is less because machines cannot carry out some aspect of the ASW mission but rather because of the strategic and political implications of destroying SSBNs. While hardly equivalent to building Skynet, entrusting a machine to make these decisions without human oversight would be tantamount to granting it responsibility for escalation management.

In addition to facilitating ASW by acting as sensor or attack platforms, AUVs can also play an important role in counter-ASW applications. The Russian Surrogat AUV epitomizes this mission: according to Russian media reports it is capable of reproducing the acoustic and magnetic signature of an arbitrary submarine.[106] While these claims are surely exaggerated, the availability of high-quality decoys could greatly complicate ASW operations for the adversary. Nor does the task of creating phantom "submarines" necessarily have to be filled by AUVs. With sufficiently sophisticated algorithms fixed transducer arrays might be able to create spurious signatures appearing as moving submarines to passive detection systems, but a less ambitious approach would be to generate targeted noise to exacerbate knowledge-quality problems for the enemy.[107]

While underwater drones could play a key role in revealing adversary submarines and making the seas transparent, they cannot do this alone. Indeed, their contribution would almost certainly be to enhance and facilitate traditional passive and active detection methods. Nor are any of the concepts outlined in this chapter new ideas. All of them, from multistatic sonar to AUVs, were seriously investigated during the Cold War. But they greatly outstripped twentieth-century technology: however attractive they might be in theory, they could not be attained in practice. Existing or imminent AI and ML may be able to solve many of these longstanding technological obstacles, greatly improving the ability to detect, track, and destroy adversary submarines and remaking the strategic landscape in the process.

Artificial intelligence and ML cannot alleviate all the technological obstacles to ASW, however. Most of these AI-enabled ASW concepts require robust, survivable, and high-volume communications in order to be viable. In an undersea environment where normal electromagnetic communications are largely unavailable, this is a major obstacle to attaining a militarily useful ASW capability. The multitude of sensors need to be connected to surface antennas or underwater cables to funnel their inputs into signal-processing centers. The antennas may reveal the position of submerged platforms and

---

[106] Iudina, *Gid po samym sekretnym podvodnym robotam Rossii.*
[107] See Chapter 5, "Fog-of-War Machines," for a discussion of these concepts.

may be blocked by adversary electronic countermeasures. The cables, meanwhile, cannot really be hardened and can be cut if the adversary can find them. Finally, the signal processing and information fusion centers themselves are attractive targets for attack–especially as many of them are fixed, unhardened shore installations. As a consequence, communications and signal processing could be a much more enticing target for a state trying to thwart its rival's ASW capabilities than trying to attack either their sensor or attack platforms. Whether these enablers of ASW can be made sufficiently robust will determine the viability of these approaches to use ML for finding submarines in wartime.

Table 4 Submarine indicators

Indicator	Possible spatial or temporal extent	Remarks
Acoustics	Low-frequency signals can propagate thousands of kilometers and, at those distances, be two to three hours old.	Strongly subject to masking, mimicking, countermeasures, and complexities of underwater sound propagation.
Optical hull reflectivity	Lasers could detect surfaced submarine at distance of hundreds of kilometers; under favorable conditions blue-green laser could penetrate few hundred meters of water to detect submerged submarine.	Submarine unlikely to remain on surface. Detection of submerged submarine strongly affected by turbidity and particulates in seawater. Easily countered by running deep to avoid detection.
Radar hull reflectivity	Radar could detect surfaced submarine at distance of hundreds of kilometers, but could not detect it before it broached surface.	Submarine unlikely to remain on surface.
Deliberate EM emission	Emissions can propagate thousands of kilometers	Unrealistic to expect submarine to communicate or radiate in detectable manner.
Extremely low-frequency (ELF) galvanic current	Effect potentially detectable to distance of "several miles."	Naturally occurring EM events can be frequent and are likely to cause numerous false positives. Extremely sensitive instruments required for detection. Magnetic anomaly detection can be countered by measures to suppress submarine's magnetic signature by building submarine of nonferrous materials (titanium). Possibility of mimicking.

Table 4 *Continued*

Indicator	Possible spatial or temporal extent	Remarks
Magnetohydrodynamics (MHD)	Phenomenon would probably remain in general vicinity of track, but possibly for long distance behind submarine if it persists hours or more.	See above.
Magnetic anomaly	Effect restricted to immediate vicinity of submarine.	See above. MHD effect related to internal wave generation (see below).
Thermal scarring	Indicator would probably remain in general vicinity of track to a distance depending on how long effect persists. This could range from minutes to hours.	Subject to enormous number of false positives and local conditions. Countermeasures can prevent thermal distinctiveness from rising to the surface.
Biological luminescence	Glow would remain in general vicinity of submarine track to a distance behind submarine of "several times [its] length."	Relevant only in darkness. Strongly subject to mimicking and masking. Deep operations easily negate surface observation.
Contaminants	Contaminants would probably remain in general vicinity of track and would persist from minutes to hours.	Degree of contamination is critical, and release of some contaminants is controllable.
Hump	Effect confined to area immediately above hull.	Easily countered through submarine design and operation to ensure that surface effect is so small as to be undetectable.
Kelvin wake	Effect would be confined to general vicinity of track and could persist for many minutes or longer.	See above.
Turbulent wakes	Effect would remain in general vicinity of track for "several kilometers astern" and persist for many minutes or more.	Can be lessened through submarine design and operations. Detectable only in water column.
Internal waves	Naturally produced waves can persist for hours or days. If submarine-produced persist for hours, then the "wake of internal waves" behind a submarine could stretch a very considerable distance.	Complex phenomenon whose utility as observable remains strongly questionable. Subject to "very high false alarm rate" and to countermeasures.

Adapted from Daniel, *Anti-Submarine Warfare and Superpower Strategic Stability*, with permission from the International Institute for Strategic Studies.

There is always a possibility–albeit a remote one–that some kind of unanticipated new physical discovery will enable dramatic new capabilities for detecting and tracking submarines. For example, the nuclear reactors that power submarines produce large numbers of neutrinos. Might it be possible to invent some kind a vastly improved neutrino detector that could pinpoint the source of these neutrinos, negating the stealthiness of SSBNs in one brilliant stroke? In this instance, the answer is probably "no."[108] Neutrino physics are quite well understood at this point, and no remotely familiar form of matter is predicted to interact strongly enough with neutrinos to serve as the basis for an operationally useful submarine detector. Some kind of revolutionary paradigm shift in physics could potentially change this, but it is not very fruitful to speculate about such possibilities–particularly when simply modernizing traditional acoustic detection techniques with ML offers so much promise.

Putting It All Together

Despite all the differences between the terrestrial and undersea domains, the operational requirements of hunting quiet modern SSBNs and land-mobile ICBM launchers are surprisingly similar. Both the submarines and the missile TELs primarily exploit cover (camouflage and concealment) to maximize their chances of survival, with mobility serving mainly as a means of making their hiding places less predictable. Cover can then be supplemented by deception measures such as decoys and signal spoofing. Neither strategic platform boasts much intrinsic robustness: it can be trivially destroyed with conventional munitions if it can be localized accurately. When deployed in a "bastion" like those of the USSR/Russia, SSBNs are even more conceptually similar to land-mobile missiles. An attacker has to project power into heavily fortified adversary territory, overcoming forbidding logistical and operational obstacles in the process.

Owen Côte, one of the few experts in ASW who writes for unclassified audiences, pointed out these parallels in a 2003 article. "Operationally, Scud hunting was like ASW against a quiet target," he observed, as

> A large area needed to be searched for objects that easily blended into the background and only intermittently exposed themselves. Radar was used to flood SCUD operating areas, unattended field sensors were also deployed, and aircraft were used to pounce on potential contacts.

---

[108] C. Callan, F. Dyson, and S. Treiman, *Neutrino Detection Primer*, tech. rep. (MITRE, 1988); Christopher F. Chyba, "New Technologies & Strategic Stability," *Dxdalus* 149.2 (2020), 150–170, 152.

As recounted earlier, these measures do not seem to have been very efficacious and may have been totally unsuccessful. The Scud hunt

> was a protracted, extremely asset intensive endeavor, characterized by false
> alarms, high weapon expenditures, and low success rates. In short, a SCUD
> launcher was most likely to reveal itself by successfully launching its weapon, just
> as sinking ships are often the only reliable indication that there is a submarine in
> the neighborhood.

The Scud hunt still managed to serve its political purpose by sending a costly
signal to Israel and the other Coalition partners of U.S. commitment, but
this was a lucky coincidence. Côte fears that despite the success of American
ASW efforts against Soviet SSBNs during much of the Cold War, the need
to conduct ASW against quiet modern submarines may prove a showstopper in future military campaigns. Unlike the Iraqi Scuds, which were "terror
weapons without much military utility, submarines are a deadly serious military threat as well a political one. Therefore, it will not do to simply appear
to be addressing the ASW problem with a major allocation of resources."
Similarly, enemy missile launchers armed with nuclear warheads cannot be
neutralized with symbolic countermeasures.[109]

Broadly conceived, planning and executing successful operations against
mobile ICBM TELs or SSBNs demands that the following requirements be
met. First, it is necessary to have an estimate of the likelihood that the missiles
or submarines are in various locations. (As will be discussed in Chapter 4, in
Bayesian terms this is dubbed a posterior distribution.) A single "best guess"
is not sufficient, as it might not be significantly likelier than many other states.
The state estimate is an essential input for the next step, state prediction. It
makes no sense to target weapons against where targets currently are when
those targets can move: instead one needs to make an estimate of the likelihood of where the targets will be and then target weapons accordingly. With
this state prediction in hand, it then may be possible to derive a plan for a
military operation to destroy or neutralize the strategic platforms. Crafting
this plan is not just a matter of allocating available weapons to certain aim
points. Instead, it needs to be an operation plan (OPLAN) stipulating the
coordination and scheduling of available strategic and tactical assets. Particularly if adversary forces are targeted with conventional weapons, then much
or most of the plan will be comprised of queuing tactical and sensor assets to
localize mobile platforms more accurately during the attack. If circumstances

---

[109] Côte, The *Third Battle: Innovation in the US Navy's Silent Cold War Struggle with Soviet Submarines* (Newport Paper 16, 2003), 83.

permit, it is desirable to do damage assessment and then reallocate resources during the later parts of the operation against surviving parts of the target set. Once this plan is available, it is finally necessary to execute it successfully, preventing the adversary from retaliating before he loses his ability to do so. All of these steps must be met more-or-less perfectly in order to attain the goal of a "splendid" disarming strike, and at least adequately for the purposes of damage limitation.

The state estimation task can be thought of as a complicated "puzzle" that has to be quickly reassembled to reveal the overall picture of where the missiles and submarines probably are. The "pieces" of the puzzle are the heterogenous "clues" offered by various kinds of intelligence, surveillance, and reconnaissance (ISR). Like puzzle pieces dumped out of a box, the clues are not necessarily received in a logical order. The clues may refer to events that happened hours, weeks, or even years before they are found and their place in the puzzle becomes apparent–but they still contribute to the final picture. That might be difficult enough, but the puzzle has qualities that make it vastly harder. There is no picture on the front of the box to guide assembly (indeed, if there were we could just use that instead of solving the puzzle). The puzzle has an immense number of pieces–billions or even trillions. Yet a large number of the pieces in the box are not supposed to be there. Many of them are simply accidental inclusions, but some of them may have been placed there by the adversary specifically to make the puzzle harder to put together. Finally, the puzzle needs to be assembled very quickly, incorporating new pieces almost as soon as they become available. Obviously reassembling the puzzle is a task beyond human capacity to solve.

Can artificial intelligence put this puzzle together and formulate plans for disarming strikes against SSBNs and mobile missiles? AI can conceivably alleviate some or all of the difficulties at every step in this process. In comparison to Cold War-era practice, which relied heavily upon human personnel for intelligence analysis, information fusion, and planning machines can perform these tasks faster, more accurately, and on a vastly larger scale.

But this is not to say the artificial intelligence will actually manage to solve these problems in a way that will inaugurate a "new era of counterforce." The state estimation problem that must be solved to track and target ICBM TELs and SSBNs is best understood as an information fusion task. Large amounts of disparate data are generated by heterogenous sources at different rates, and are not necessarily received in the order that the targets generated them. For instance, acoustic signals generated by a submarine can take many hours to reach distant hydrophones, providing clues about where the submarine was, while magnetic anomaly detectors on a UAV will detect the submarine where it currently is. Other totally dissimilar kinds of information, like signals intelligence or natural-language information gleaned from human spies, also needs to be incorporated into the state estimate somehow. The task of combining information from multiple sources into a single knowledge representation is called information fusion. As will be seen in Chapter 4, this is a well-studied problem, but far from a solved one.

Chapter 4

Recipe for a WOPR

> Six minutes! Now six minutes—that's barely enough time for the president to make a decision! And after he makes that decision, the computer should take over!
>
> *WarGames* (1983)

For over seven decades, defense officials have hoped that a bigger computer would be the solution to their strategic dilemmas. With a bigger computer, so the reasoning goes, more data from more sensors can be combined to better understand both what the adversary is doing and the current status of one's own forces. In turn, this better awareness can be used to formulate superior courses of action that can be recommended to human decision-makers. In this formulation, a more powerful computer means better decisions and a better prospect of victory. Yet somehow, this vision seems to always lurk just outside of reach. Time and again, when much-anticipated new computers and networks are placed into service, they fail to live up to expectations about their military effect. This chapter argues that this pattern is not a coincidence, or the result of still-immature technology, but rather a straightforward implication of theoretical computer science. No matter how powerful the computers we build—no matter if wished-for innovations like quantum computers become practical realities—"lifting the fog of war" is something that computers cannot be counted upon to do.

Why hasn't something like *WarGames*'s WOPR materialized in the real world? To answer this question, it is necessary to define what Professor Falken's creation actually does. In the film, WOPR is more than just an odd-looking computer that "spends all its time thinking about World War III." As Falken's protege John McKittrick explains, WOPR's output is a "computer war plan" that "the president will probably follow" in case of war. Paul Richter, an employee of McKittrick's at NORAD, clarifies that WOPR plays an "endless series of wargames" to continuously update the computer war plan, estimating "Soviet responses to our responses to their responses and so on" as it does so. The fodder for WOPR's ceaseless simulations of World War III is "all available information on the state of the world." According to McKittrick, the huge bank of mainframe computers in the room next to

Deterrence under Uncertainty. Edward Geist, Oxford University Press. © RAND Corporation (2023).
DOI: 10.1093/oso/9780192886323.003.0005

that containing WOPR "give us instant access to the state of the world–troop movements, Soviet missile tests, shifting weather patterns," which then flows into the WOPR.

What WOPR does goes beyond game-playing: broadly construed, it can be described as reasoning under uncertainty. WOPR cannot have perfect confidence in the information it receives about the state of the world. Intelligence about troop movements might be ingenious disinformation planted by devious enemy agents; data about Soviet missile tests might be distorted by faulty sensors; meteorologists might be drunk or simply incompetent. An adequate "computer war plan" needs to account for all these kinds of uncertainty. On this point *WarGames* provides an accurate portrayal of artificial intelligence: reasoning about uncertainty, and making good-quality decisions on the basis of uncertain information, has been a core interest of AI researchers since the early days of the field. Over the decades, they have conceived numerous different ways to make computers reason about uncertainty, and developed formal theories of uncertain reasoning.

But what they have *not* discovered is a "correct" or "best" way to reason under uncertainty. Instead, what they have found is that reasoning under uncertainty is hard for computers as well as people. Translated into formal computer science terms, uncertain reasoning turns out to be a "wicked" problem of the kind that one cannot reasonably expect to solve simply by buying a bigger computer. While this does not mean that one of these problems is necessarily unsolvable, it means that one is obligated to make possibly erroneous assumptions in order to find approximate solutions. This requires sufficient knowledge on which to base those assumptions.[1]

Moreover, there is no one right way to reason about uncertainty not just because reasoning about uncertainty is hard, but also because there is more than one way to be uncertain. For example, one can be uncertain both about the answer to a question and about whether that question is the right question. Similarly, there exists a distinction between uncertainty and ignorance: one may have little evidence contradicting some hypothesis but reason to doubt that the available evidence is comprehensive. AI researchers have also proposed means of formalizing some of these other kinds of uncertainty and making computer programs to reason about them. Unfortunately, this "epistemological" and "ontological" uncertainty turns out to be even harder to reason about than more mundane kinds.

---

[1] Edward M. Geist, "Why Reasoning under Uncertainty Is Hard for Both Machines and People—and an Approach to Address the Problem," in Aaron B. Frank and Elizabeth M. Bartels (eds.), *Active Engagement for Undergoverned Spaces: Concepts, Challenges, and Prospects for New Approaches* (RAND RR-A1275-1, 2022), 263–281.

A general-purpose algorithm or method that could be applied to an arbitrary problem and provide an approximate solution of guaranteed quality would be an unprecedented boon that might revolutionize both military and defense applications. But regrettably, computer scientists have determined that such an algorithm, like most things that seem too good to be true, cannot exist. As a consequence of these considerations, many common intuitions about the ability of computers to resolve uncertainty are incorrect—for instance, more sensors and data cannot be counted upon to yield better-quality knowledge. This means that predictions that advances in computing will inevitably lift the "fog of war" are contradicted by what we have learned about the nature of reasoning about uncertainty. Indeed, the opposite is true: the tools that AI researchers invented to reason about uncertainty can arguably be harnessed to *increase* uncertainty for adversaries and optimize military deception.[2] Because they have gained insights into what makes reasoning under uncertainty hard, they can identify ways to make it harder. These discoveries could be harnessed to create "fog-of-war machines": systems employing AI to create and exacerbate knowledge quality problems for adversaries.

This chapter aims to provide an overview of what it would take to make a real-life WOPR: a computer that could process "all available information about the state of the world" to generate a "computer war plan" sufficient to win a nuclear war. It is divided into five sections. The first section, "Why Tracking Is Hard," describes the many kinds of uncertainty that a computer must reason about in order to fuse sensor data and track moving targets in a noisy environment. It aims to provide an accessible explanation of two methods that are widely employed in real-world military tracking systems, the Kalman filter and Multiple Hypothesis Tracking (MHT). The second section, "What Computers Can't Do," seeks to provide readers with an accessible account of computational complexity and what computer scientists mean when they deem a problem "intractable." One of the key tasks of AI is to identify workarounds to solve these "intractable" problems—but since these shortcuts cannot solve the problems the "right" way without violating the laws of computational complexity, they introduce vulnerabilities. The following section, "Why Reasoning under Uncertainty Is Hard," describes the different approaches AI researchers have taken to make computers reason under uncertainty. This section relates practical trackers like those in the first section to the Bayesian belief network, a preeminent AI formalism for

---

[2] As Roberta Wohlstetter concluded, "We have to accept the fact of uncertainty and learn to live with it. No magic, in code or otherwise, will provide certainty. Our plans must work without it." Roberta Wohlstetter. *Pearl Harbor: Warning and Decision* (Stanford University Press, 1962), 401.

uncertain reasoning. But many researchers contend Bayesianism is not sufficient for all problems, in part because standard probability theory has limited
expressiveness. These epistemological challenges has led some researchers to
propose alternative approaches to uncertain reasoning like Dempster–Shafer
theory. The following section, "Will Quantum Save Us?," discusses whether
quantum computers and quantum sensors might alleviate these challenges.
The answer to this question appears to be no: quantum computers are qualitatively different than their classical counterparts, and while they may prove
astronomically faster for certain problems there are theoretical reasons to
believe that they will not provide similar advantages for the problems of interest here. The chapter's final section, "WOPR and Anti-WOPR," builds upon
the theoretical considerations in the previous two sections to outline how
states could use artificial intelligence to thicken the fog of war for their rivals.
By inverting the approaches that AI researchers have developed to reason
about uncertainty, it appears to be possible to design algorithms to optimize
obfuscation and deception.

Why Tracking Is Hard

Many of the hopes about how artificial intelligence will affect military applications flow from the assumption that computers will be able to take different
kinds of data from multiple sensors and use it to track multiple targets at the
same time. This task is not at all alien to humans, as humans do it all the time.
Humans use their multiple senses such as vision and hearing to pay attention to where moving objects are and where they are going, and are often
fairly successful at it. When you are driving on the interstate and merge into
another lane between two trucks, you are accomplishing multisource, multitarget information fusion. You need to drive your car into where the gap
between the two trucks will be, not where it is at the moment when you start
merging. While sight is the primary sense employed for this task, others help
inform your decisions. (Can you hear a truck accelerating? Can you smell
one of the trucks' brakes burning?) But the regular occurrence of interstate
crashes attests to the limits of humans' ability to do multisource, multitarget
tracking. These failures are not solely the result of human fallibility. Machines
might do it better, but tracking is hard for computers for many of the same
reasons it challenges humans.

To illustrate the aspects of tracking that bedevil machines as well as people,
let's walk though a more detailed example. Imagine that you have agreed to
dogsit two small dogs. You turn your back for a moment, and both of these

mischievous canines run out the front door. Both out of concern for the dogs' safety and out of fear of the dog owners' wrath, you grab a flashlight (as the sun is about to set) and run out the door after them.

At first, this task seems straightforward enough, if not necessarily easy. The first challenge is that to catch a dog, one has to intercept it where it will be, in addition to perceiving where it currently is. So even in a well-lit, open field, without any difficulty seeing the dogs running about, the unpredictability of their movements creates uncertainty one must overcome.

Tracking requires multiple steps. First, one needs to guess where something is. Second, one needs to predict where it is going. Then one needs to use new information to improve one's guesses about where the target is and how it is moving. Military tracking systems typically meet this challenge using a *Kalman filter*, which uses some clever math to estimate uncertain variables.[3] (See Appendix A for a discussion of the mathematics of the Kalman filter.) The Kalman filter has a *predictor* that estimates where a target will appear next and a *corrector* that updates the prior guess about the target's location and whither it is going. While it is not typically thought of as such for historical reasons, the Kalman filter is, in fact, a machine learning algorithm and can be applied effectively to many ML tasks, including training neural networks.[4]

But the Kalman filter can't solve our problem of chasing a couple of dogs around by itself because it is a single-target tracker. Each dog has a mind of its own and they can go in different directions. Knowing where one dog is going may not tell us anything about where the other one is. To handle more than one target, we need to add additional mechanisms. The typical approach military tracking systems employ for this purpose is *multiple hypothesis tracking* (MHT). MHT maintains separate Kalman filters for every target that might exist in the area being observed and then tries to identify valid "hypotheses" that assign each detection (e.g., a radar blip, or a glimpse of one of our dogs) to

---

[3] Introduced by Rudolf E. Kalman in 1960, the Kalman filter is an algorithm that estimates the values of unknown variables on the basis of a series of possibly unreliable observations. The derivation of the Kalman filter is based upon linear algebra and Bayesian statistics, but it is basically an elegant mathematical formalization of this intuitive process for reasoning about uncertainty. It is essentially Bayes' rule, for continuous linear relationships subject to certain assumptions. That mathematical elegance translates in turn into computational efficiency, which is the key to the Kalman filter's success. The Kalman filter is used so often because it offers a highly effective tradeoff between computational costs and performance. Rudolph Kalman, "A New Approach to Linear Filtering and Prediction Problems," *Transactions of the ASME-Journal of Basic Engineering* 82 (1960), 35–45.

[4] It gets its name from one of its main uses—"filtering" noisy, unreliable signals. But the Kalman filter can do more than just filter noise—it can also estimate the values of variables that cannot be observed directly, so long as those variables have a known relationship to those that are observable. In the six decades since it was introduced, many variants of the Kalman filter have been invented, important examples of which are the *Extended Kalman Filter* (EKF) and *Unscented Kalman Filter* which can work on nonlinear problems. Simon S. Haykin, *Kalman Filtering and Neural Networks* (Wiley Online Library, 2001), Ch. 7.

one and only one track. This introduces uncertainty about which detections are associated with which tracks.

In a well-lit open field, this *data association* uncertainty doesn't matter very much, but in a more challenging environment it rapidly creates huge problems. Imagine that the dogs run from the field into the adjacent dog park. The dog park contains numerous other dogs, some of which look very similar to the dogs you're chasing. These are *confusion targets* that one has to keep track of so as to avoid mixing them up with your dogs. If you grab one of them by mistake, their irate owners are liable to manhandle you in retaliation. But the dog park contains even more hazards, as it is festooned with fireplugs, stumps, and similar objects of canine esteem. You are hardly likely to confuse one of these *clutter targets* with a dog, but one still has to keep track of them to avoid tripping over them or in case one of your dogs could be obscured behind one of them.

Now you face a dizzying amount of uncertainty of several different kinds. There are lots of dogs running around and they often dart behind things so you can't see them. Which dogs glimpsed at one moment should be associated with those glimpsed at a later moment? Every glimpse of a dog might be associated with every subsequent glimpse of a similar-looking dog. Moreover, your eyes could be playing tricks on you, particularly in the fading sunlight. You might think you see one of your dogs out of the corner of your eye when in fact there is nothing there. But you can't discount these *spurious detections* because you have only the evidence of your own senses to work from. So you also need to account for the possibility of nonexistent tracks. All of this complexity is compounded by uncertainty about the number of dogs (targets) in the park.

The advantage of the multiple hypothesis tracker is that it provides the robustness to deal with these various forms of uncertainty. If a dog disappears for a while behind a clutter target, the MHT will maintain distinct hypotheses for the possibility that different dogs coming from behind that obstacle are the dog in question. But the number of such possibilities that must be accounted for grows exponentially with the number of tracks and detections. This combinatorial explosion is mind-boggling for humans to think about, but it's also overwhelming for computers. Even for a trivial case, the total number of possible track histories rapidly expands to a size larger than can fit in the memory of any physical computer. Out of necessity, real-world MHT implementations need mechanisms to restrict the number of tracks considered and to discard possible track histories that appear unlikely. The first of these is *gating*, which prevents new detections that appear too far away from the expected location of the target being tracked to be the same object associated with that track. The second is *pruning*, which deletes tracks that fail to predict where future detections will appear accurately or that are essentially duplicates of other tracks. In our dog example, assuming that a dog that appeared 20 meters from where you expected your dog to be could not be your dog would be a form of gating; deciding a dog that never seemed to appear where you thought it would was actually a figment of your imagination would be a form of pruning.

Exploiting more than one of your senses at once can help you track the dogs, but it is no panacea. For instance, perhaps your dogs make distinctive sounds that differ from those the other dogs make. In a best-case scenario, you can hear your dogs even when you can't see them, and the information you gain from your sight and your hearing reinforce to provide a confident estimate of where the dogs you're chasing are. But there's no guarantee that things will work out this way, as using multiple senses introduces another wrinkle to worry about: *track association uncertainty*. Which sounds that you hear come from which of the visible dogs? Your lack of familiarity with the other dogs you see running around potentially undermines the usefulness of your knowledge about what your dogs sound like. Perhaps some of these unknown dogs sound like your dogs, so you shouldn't trust what you think you hear. Track association uncertainty can make the combinatorial explosion that already existed using a single sensor exponentially worse, so the knowledge gained by adding more sensors has to be valuable to make up for the cost of dealing with this added complexity.

The more different the sensors being added, the greater the degree of track association uncertainty. Perhaps your dogs have a distinctive smell, and if you get close enough to them you would be certain they were yours. But this sense is qualitatively different from sight and hearing, because it's nondirectional and doesn't provide any information about how the dogs are moving. How should you update your guesses of where your dogs are going to be based on what you smell? It's hard to express in words and even harder to express as math. Today we can exploit machine learning to make computers compare the similarity of poorly specified properties such as "appearance," but we can't explain how the resulting models work or be confident that they'll behave sensibly in an unfamiliar situation.

Sometimes using data from multiple sensors will yield more accurate tracks, but this is not guaranteed. The advantages of having two eyes over one eye when chasing dogs is obvious, as depth perception makes it easier to perceive their location and motion. But the marginal value of having a third eye depends on where it is located. If that third eye was in the center of your forehead, it wouldn't do much good, but if it were in the back of your head it might improve your situational awareness considerably—if at the cost of more track association uncertainty.[5] The added value of using your sense of smell could be nonexistent depending on external factors, such as how windy it is outside.

In some cases additional sensors can make things worse by introducing new reasons to doubt evidence that you should've trusted. Imagine that one of the unfamiliar dogs running around the dog park happens to sound and smell like one of the dogs you are pursuing. When you hear or smell it, you naturally assume that that sound or stench is coming from your dog. This naturally causes you to doubt that the dogs that you see on the other side of the dog park that look like your dog are the ones you are after, even though they are. Instead you look behind stumps and bushes on the assumption that your dog must be nearby somewhere. If you had relied solely upon your sight, you would've been better off![6]

The difficulties of sensor fusion become especially fraught in a more challenging environment where you have to make starker choices about where to focus your attention. Say that the dogs run out of the well-lit dog park and into the dismal adjacent woods. It's a good thing you brought your flashlight, because otherwise you couldn't see at all. But now you can only see where the flashlight is pointed, and you can only point the flashlight in one direction at a time. Since there are two dogs, unless they happen to be right next to each other you have to prioritize one over the other at any particular moment. Now sound is even more important because you need it for cuing–you hear a noise and point the flashlight at where it seems to have come from. The sensors used in real-world military tracking systems often have analogous limitations. Spy satellites, for instance, tend to have narrow fields of view, so difficult choices have to be made about where best to point them.

In the worst case, these challenges can combine to make additional sensors worse than useless. Just as you catch up to the dogs in the dark forest, they dash into an ominous-looking cave with a sign declaring "DANGEROUS CAVERN-KEEP OUT." Against your better judgment, you follow the dogs inside. Because of echoes within the cave, the noises made by the dogs now sometimes sound like they are coming from places other than where

---

[5] If more sensors and a bigger computer are such an advantageous combination, why does evolution endow most organisms with relatively few sensory organs? To state it differently, why *don't* people have eyes in the back of their heads and bigger brains to exploit the additional sensory information? One explanation is that the marginal benefit of additional eyes isn't worth the biological and cognitive/neurological costs.

[6] Cases such as this where a larger number of more diverse sensors make information fusion harder may seem too esoteric to be of serious concern. But as will be explained later, an intelligent adversary is likely to try and create such contradictory sensor readings when the opportunity arises as a deception technique.

the dogs actually are. These spurious cues cause you to point the flashlight at places where the dogs aren't, impeding your ability to track them through the cavern. Your sole consolation is that while you may never locate the dogs in here and might not make it out alive, at least you'll be safe from the wrath of the dogs' owners!

When it comes to data and sensors, more is not necessarily better. To give a simple example, imagine that one has a single piece of evidence about some variable of interest (for instance, the location of our dogs). Just for the sake of argument, assume that we got lucky and this piece of evidence happens to be absolutely correct. Since we have no reason to doubt this evidence and no other evidence to consider, we are in an ideal position, even though we do not know it. Now imagine that we receive a second piece of evidence which contradicts the first. Perhaps this piece of data is just random noise or ingenious disinformation crafted by a devious adversary, but in either case it is extremely misleading. From an objective standpoint, we are now unambiguously worse off. If we update our estimates based on the misleading data, we are now wrong where we were right before. Even if we decide that the original estimate was right and totally disregard the misleading data, we still wasted time paying attention to it. Attention is a finite resource, and so is trust: if we expend them on the wrong things we inevitably pay an opportunity cost. As Herbert Simon observed, "The design principle that attention is scarce and must be preserved is very different from a principle of 'the more information the better.'"[7]

The primary solution for taming the computational complexity of information fusion is to break up problems into smaller, more digestible subproblems. This is called *hierarchical information fusion* (and in its specific application to tracking, hierarchical tracking). Conceptually, hierarchical information fusion is simple. At each stage, information that is "important" is propagated up to the next level, while other information that looks like noise or extraneous detail is discarded. In this respect it is analogous to human bureaucracies, which delegate authority to lower levels to judge what is important enough to be worthy of the attention of higher-level executives. And much like human bureaucracies, hierarchical information fusion can work quite well so long as the lower levels have an accurate sense of what is important and act accordingly. But hierarchical information fusion also introduces a Catch-22 that can prove insurmountable. Decisions about what is important and should be passed up the chain need to be made in

---

[7] Martin Greenberger, *Computers, Communications, and the Public Interest* (Johns Hopkins University Press, 1971), 44.

accordance with what the executive level cares about. But how can the upper levels recognize what is important if the lower levels, intentionally or inadvertently, fail to tell them about something that matters? Similarly, how are the lower levels supposed to know what is important in the absence of global knowledge that could only be gained by fusing things that aren't being passed up for consideration? Because attention is a finite resource for computers as well as people, we cannot overcome this problem by just buying a bigger computer.

As the above discussion makes clear, tracking and information fusion is all about reasoning about uncertainty. Many kinds of uncertainty must be resolved in order to turn raw sensor data into accurate tracks. Adding sensors can help clear up some of these uncertainties but only at the cost of introducing yet other kinds of uncertainty. Nor is there any guarantee that the data from additional sensors will necessarily alleviate any uncertainty: in some cases they can make it worse. Moreover, the examples given above are relatively trivial compared to even simple real-world military tracking systems. But just because tracking is a difficult problem does not mean it is necessarily unsolvable: useful tracking systems have been in military and civilian use for many decades. What are the limits on what tracking systems can reasonably be expected to do? Fortunately, computer scientists have developed theoretical frameworks that enable a rigorous investigation of this question.

What Computers Can't Do

In order to do information fusion to enable adaptive planning for disarming strikes against mobile missile launchers and SSBNs, two requirements must be met. Firstly, it must be possible for a computer to do the relevant computations. Secondly, it must be practical to carry out those computations in the available amount of time with an obtainable quantity of computational resources.

In fiction, computers often evince godlike power. In the years immediately following the introduction of digital computers, authors seized upon them as useful plot devices. When computers were not themselves portrayed as world-menacing horrors with minds of their own, they often helped drive plots along with astonishing feats of cogitation. Fictional computers drew subtle inferences from little or even no data, such as by predicting what humans would do before those humans had decided to do it, in effect reasoning with knowledge they did not have. But these fictional visions differed markedly from the lived experiences of computer scientists and programmers. They discovered that their intuitions about what would be easy for computers were often wrong. In time, they developed increasingly sophisticated theories to understand what computers can't do, or more accurately, what computers can't be counted upon to do. This is the subject of computational complexity theory.

In practical terms, "hard" problems are those that we cannot get computers to solve reliably, or at all. One cannot simply buy a bigger or faster computer: hard instances of the problem consume processor time or memory faster than it can be made available despite improvement in technology.

While it might seem like an obscure mathematical concept, one doesn't need a computer to fall victim to intractability. For example, since an algorithm is defined as a set of rules or process that must be strictly followed, bureaucracy can be intractable in the same sense as a computer program. Imagine that you have to go to your inescapable local Kafkaesque bureaucracy to submit some forms. After you enter their waiting room and take a number, a woman with a disgruntled expression and a t-shirt reading "Abandon Hope All Ye Who Enter Here" comments sardonically:

"First time?"

After hearing you reply affirmatively that this is your first time in the office, she laughs and wishes you good luck. When you ask her if she comes here often, she tells you that "This is my 298th time here—I come every week." At first you think the woman is exaggerating for effect, but she interrupts you in midsentence to protest that "I'm serious—I keep count. I have to, for the lawsuit." Seeing your bemused expression, she offers to "explain how things work here." "The terrible thing about this place," she explains, "is that they don't bend any rules or cut any corners—they do everything by the book, no matter the consequences. And because of that, there's no guarantee they'll ever complete your case."

Looking at the forms you are filling out, she admits that "you *could* be one of the lucky ones—it does happen . . . The regulations define a set of conditions under which your case is decided immediately either one way or another. But a lot of the time, what happens is that your case spawns one or more *subcases*, each of which turns into its own set of paperwork that the bureaucracy starts processing. Those cases can resolve immediately if they fall under the termination conditions, but more often they spawn subcases of their own. The regulations state that no subcase can be resolved until all of its subcases have been resolved, and that all the paperwork related to all of a case's subcases has to be preserved until after the case is resolved. That turns out to be important."

When you ask whether that means your case could literally take forever to be completed, the woman qualifies that "it can't *literally* take forever, as the regulations are written in a way that guarantees that all of the spawned subcases will resolve at some point. But it can take *practically* forever, because the set of subcases that have to get resolved grows exponentially. One case becomes a couple of subcases, which each spawn a couple subcases of their own, which each spawn a few again. The bureaucrats have to fill out and store paperwork for each of those cases. In my case, there are tens of thousands of subcases and millions of pages of resulting paperwork. The bureaucracy is literally running out of space to store it all and paper to print the forms—the state legislature only budgets so much money for it."

When you comment that something really ought to be done about this, the woman practically shouts, "Why do you think we sued? After a few years of coming in here every week I and some of the other 'regulars' got so steamed about it we couldn't do otherwise. We got a computer science professor as an expert witness who presented a formal proof that the procedures used by the bureaucracy are intractable. He also estimated how long it'll take our cases to get resolved. Given the current rate at which subcases are getting added and resolved, it looks like my case will get closed sometime in the thirty-second century. However, sometime around the twenty-seventh century the paper needed for the forms will exceed the entire global production of wood pulp at present-day levels. Then, in about the year 3000, storage for all of the paperwork will require the entire land surface of the Earth. I'm not sure where the bureaucracy will house the two trillion bureaucrats that will be needed to process the active subcases as of that time—presumably they'll live on space stations, or on the ocean floor?" The woman laughs at her own joke.

This seems like a pretty damning argument against the way the bureaucracy does things. "But the judge obviously didn't agree," sighs your interlocutor. "He said it was all 'computer science gobbledegook' and that since the cases sometimes resolve, and in theory they all will, he didn't see where the problem was. Our expert witness has, I believe, suffered a nervous breakdown. And I will be here in the office every Monday for the rest of my life—maybe you'll be too!"

In this anecdote, the bureaucracy's process is equivalent to a computer program that calls itself recursively. Not all forms of intractability work like this example, but it illustrates how a program can be computable (in the sense that it is guaranteed to find a correct answer eventually) yet intractable in the sense that one cannot count on doing it with an attainable amount of resources. The work done by the bureaucrats is equivalent to CPU cycles, while the paperwork that needs to be stored corresponds with RAM or hard drive usage. Just as the bureaucracy can't get enough bureaucrats and paper in the example, an intractable problem can consume a computer's processor cycles and memory faster than they can be added.

But just because intractability is everywhere doesn't mean that it always poses an insuperable barrier to doing what we want. Often there are "clever" shortcuts to solve many or most instances of the problem.[8] Finding those shortcuts is one of the key tasks of AI. But those shortcuts are just that: without knowing what shortcuts to take, they might return no solution or a wrong solution.

Whether primitive or state-of-the-art, classical or quantum, computers just run programs. Much as neural networks can learn programs we could never write down, we can conceive of algorithms that no physically realizable computer can run. Broadly defined, an algorithm is just a formal process specifying an explicit series of steps. We can reason in the abstract about machines that can perform arbitrary steps as they carry out that process. But classical computers can only carry out steps on strings of symbols from some specified alphabet (recursively enumerable sets in the formalism Alan Turing introduced in 1936). Hence that is why theoretical computer science focuses so much of its attention on Turing machines, abstract computers conceived by Turing to investigate the computability of functions. Expressed in Lambda calculus, Turing machines can compute functions of the form $F : \mathbb{N} \to \mathbb{N}$, where $\mathbb{N}$ represents the set of all natural numbers (positive integers). Each recursively enumerable set (string of symbols) is associated with one of these numbers.

Computability poses less of an obstacle to getting computers to do what we want than it often appears. The related concept of decidability helps illustrate why. Decidability and Turing computability are equivalent but have different formal definitions. A set is *decidable* if it is possible to write a finite-length procedure using bounded computational resources that is guaranteed to determine whether an item is in the set. This procedure can be equated to a program for some Turing machine, and if it exists, then it is a Turing-computable function which can be thought of as a "compressed" version of the set. Since the Turing machine is a theoretical construct, the set of strings it can accept as inputs is open and unbounded and contains an infinite, if countable, number of elements. Hence that is how we know that there are many more uncomputable than computable functions: every randomized mapping

---

[8] In the bureaucracy example, these shortcuts are the equivalent of taking advantage of a sympathetic bureaucrat who is willing to bend the rules and skip steps when they are confident that they can predict the ultimate outcome. "Every subcase I've ever seen that looked like this always turned out the same way," they rationalize, "so I'll save both you and me some time and just go ahead and fill out the form saying it resolved that way rather than launch additional subcases like the regulations say I'm supposed to."

$F : \mathbb{N} \to \mathbb{N}$ is a function, but only a limited subset of these have enough structure to be defined as a finite-length procedure. This seems dispiriting, but it actually doesn't matter very much in practice. Firstly, most of the uncomputable functions simply aren't interesting because they embody random noise. But secondly and more importantly, every finite, closed set is decidable and therefore Turing-computable, because we can write a "procedure" that simply lists all the items in the set and checks to see if an item is in it.[9] Most of the time, we don't actually need the full undecidable set-we just need the subset that we end up being called upon to solve. With the right knowledge, decidability doesn't matter. Unfortunately, we usually don't know in advance what will be in that subset.

But what if we want to carry out arbitrary operations on potentially infinite and/or non-countable sets? For instance, the Kalman filter falls outside of the Turing model of computation because it is continuous and therefore not based upon recursively enumerable sets.[10] If the sets of interest can be discretized, it is sometimes possible to compute a reasonably effective approximation, but there is no guarantee that this will work in any particular case.[11] But even assuming the function can be computed by a Turing machine, there is no guarantee that it will be tractable either in terms of its computational complexity or, more importantly, from a practical engineering standpoint.

This is related to, albeit distinct from, computational and algorithmic complexity like that studied by computer scientists. Computational and algorithmic complexity are related, but distinct, concepts. Complexity classes such as P and NP describe the complexity of decision problems (meaning problems with definite "yes or no" answers, such as "is this number prime?") as opposed to algorithms. There are a large number of different

---

[9] Take, for instance, Turing's famous example of undecidability, the "halting problem." This asks whether an arbitrary program on an arbitrary Turing machine will halt or run forever. Turing proved in the abstract that one cannot write a program that works for every machine–program pair. But this doesn't mean that we won't be able to tell whether a particular program will halt on a particular machine, and often we can use either inference or empirical testing to find the answer. If we only find a finite set of machine–program pairs of interest, and we already know whether those programs halt, we can simply look up the answers even though the general version of the halting problem is uncomputable. Nor is a failure to halt necessarily "bad": many real-world computer programs are *designed* not to halt—this is the purpose of the ubiquitous "while true" looping construct found in most programming languages.

[10] This is distinct from the issue of Turing computability, which is concerned with determining whether $F : \mathbb{N} \to \mathbb{N}$ can be computed by a Turing machine in a finite number of steps using a finite-length algorithm.

[11] Practical neural networks (NNs) have a finite number of possible inputs and outputs defined by their structure. Given a large enough network and sufficient training examples, the networks can learn an arbitrary mapping between inputs and outputs. This is essentially just a hash table, but the reason NNs are useful is that (to paraphrase François Chollet) the "hashing function" can be locally sensitive, allowing the learned model to generalize appropriately to unseen examples. François Chollet, "The Measure of Intelligence," *arXiv preprint arXiw:1911.01547* (2019), 19–20. Unfortunately, there are no theorems establishing that we can achieve this generalization whenever we might wish: much of the practice of ML is the dark art of trying to make it appear when and how we need it to.

such complexity classes, which are associated with different kinds of resource usage. P and NP stand for polynomial and nondeterministic-polynomial time, respectively, and mean that a Turing machine would require a polynomial number of steps to solve the problem. If a problem is in NP, then no algorithm can rigorously determine the answer using fewer resources in the worst case.[12] PSPACE and EXPSPACE, meanwhile, are complexity classes that mean that the Turing machine demands either a polynomial or exponential amount of memory to solve the problem relative to the size of the input.

Categorizing decision problems by their complexity classes and relating those classes to each other is one of the main tasks of theoretical computer science.[13] The two most famous complexity classes are the aforementioned P and NP, which are the subject of perhaps the most contentious debate in computer science: whether P = NP. Unfortunately, the way in which this debate is generally presented has led to persistent misconceptions among laypeople. Since the complexity classes outside NP (such as EXP) are rarely discussed except by computer scientists, it is easy to develop the impression that NP is the hardest complexity class. This misconception is furthered by the tendency to lump all hard problems into the category "NP-hard," which encompasses all problems at least as hard as the hardest problems in NP.[14]

Another common misconception is that just because a problem is in the ostensibly "easy" P class it is trivially solved in practice, or that NP-hard problems are practically impossible to solve. Computational complexity is as inescapable as the laws of physics, but only in "worst cases" that may never arise in practice. These classes measure worst-case complexity, but many instances of those classes turn out to be far easier than the worst case to solve.

---

[12] "Nondeterministic" refers to a hypothetical variant of the Turing machine capable of executing multiple branches of a program in parallel. These are *Gedankenexperimente* for exploring the theoretical limits of computation, and should not be confused with real-world parallel computing architectures. The nondeterministic machine is of theoretical interest because it could search every branch of a possibility space at the same rate a deterministic Turing machine could check that solution. Therefore, the class of problems that it can solve in polynomial time are the hardest problems that might conceivably be "easy" given certain assumptions (e.g., P = NP).

[13] For an accessible account of computational complexity, see Henry M. Walker, *The Limits of Computing* (Jones and Bartlett, 1994), Ch. 4.

[14] This is an informal definition of NP-hard. Formally, a problem is NP-hard if every problem in NP can be translated into it in polynomial time. These NP-hard problems are often themselves not in NP. Problems are NP-complete if they are in both NP and NP-hard. If P = NP, then every problem in NP is NP-complete and can be translated into a polynomial-time problem in polynomial time. If this is the case, then it might be possible to solve many currently intractable problems, including breaking widely used encryption schemes. Most computer scientists believe that P ≠ NP, and a cynic might attribute the attitude of those believing the opposite to the propensity some people have for contrarianism, but it is still an open question. The P = NP debate, however, has limited bearing on the difficulty of hard problems in complexity classes such as EXP, which will likely remain intractable if it turns out that P = NP after all.

There are pathological problems in P for which the degree of the polynomial is so high that they cannot be solved in practice on a physical computer. Meanwhile, it turns out to be easy to find approximate, or even near-optimal, solutions for many instances of problems that are provably NP-hard in the worst case. In fact, a huge part of AI research aims to find such solutions, whether via machine learning, heuristic reasoning, or other approaches. This is critical for the subject of this book as the optimization problems that must be solved in order to use AI for nuclear strategic applications are generally NP-hard.

An important real-world use case for computational complexity theory, cryptography, provides concrete examples of what it means for a problem to be "hard" and the relationship between computational complexity and knowledge. In order for an encryption algorithm to be secure, it is imperative that no algorithm exists that can easily decrypt encrypted messages without the key. This means that decrypting an arbitrary message that might have any possible key must be computationally difficult (ideally meaning NP-hard). At the same time, for an encryption algorithm to be practical, it must be relatively straightforward to decrypt the messages so long as the key is available. This means that decryption with the key needs to be computationally tractable (not NP-hard). So from a practical standpoint, security lies in the knowledge quality problem the secret key poses for unauthorized eavesdroppers: if they have the key, then they can read the message even though the general decryption problem is intractable. By design, the encryption key is a "shortcut" to solving a problem that is engineered to be hard otherwise.

Similar "shortcuts" also exist to the solutions of other kinds of problems, and AI is in some sense a set of tools for discovering and using those shortcuts. As Peter Norvig explained, "For a theoretical computer scientist, discovering that a problem is NP-hard is an end in itself. But for an AI worker, it means that the wrong question is being asked. Many problems are NP-hard when we insist on the optimal solution but are much easier when we accept a solution that might not be the best."[15] Simple heuristic algorithms often find near-optimal solutions to certain NP-hard problems.[16] Machine learning derives the relevant knowledge from data to find the shortcuts, while "classical" AI techniques take advantage of learned or given knowledge to exploit the shortcuts.

---

[15] Peter Norvig, *Paradigms of Artificial Intelligence Programming: Case Studies in Common Lisp* (Morgan Kaufmann, 1992), 146.

[16] Consider, for instance, the famous "knapsack problem," which tries to determinine the value of items of different weights and values that can be carried in a knapsack of a certain capacity. A trivial "greedy heuristic" that selects the item with the highest value/weight ratio until the backpack is full finds a near-optimal solution in many cases, despite the problem's NP-hardness.

Big-O analysis, in contrast to computational complexity, addresses the performance of algorithms rather than the difficulty of problems. It characterizes an algorithm's consumption of resources such as time and space (memory) with increasing input size.[17] Big-O analysis, like computational complexity analysis, is mostly (but not exclusively) concerned with the *worst-case* time and space complexity of algorithms. But many algorithms known to have unfavorable worst-case computational or algorithmic characteristics turn out to work well in practice anyway: the venerable simplex algorithm for linear programming is a classical example.

Approximation algorithms are also an area of intense interest for computer science. Sometimes it is important that an approximation algorithm not exist. Once again, the classical example of this is cryptography: an encryption algorithm would be disastrously vulnerable if it turned out that some kind of heuristic approximation could crack some encrypted messages. So computer scientists have also developed ways to analyze the *approximability* of problems. Sometimes, as in the encryption example, the goal is to ensure that no effective approximation algorithm exists. In other cases, the objective is to determine whether a better approximation algorithm might exist for a particular problem. If the answer to this question proves to be "no," then we have an *inapproximability* result. Sometimes it is possible to place accuracy bounds on the possible approximation algorithms. These kinds of results are particularly compelling because they give us a much clearer sense of what computers "can't do" than computability and worst-case complexity analysis.

The applications of interest to us for multitarget tracking and information fusion mostly concern the *average-case* complexity of large optimization problems. The good news is that the computational complexity of these problems is not necessarily a reason we cannot solve them well enough for our purposes. The bad news is that because these problems are difficult, we have no guarantee that we can find adequate-quality approximate solutions to them when we need to—and given the opportunity, adversaries are sure to do everything in their power to ensure that we cannot.

While AI and ML can often turn NP-hardness from a force field into a speed bump, they are not magic. Computational complexity and decidability still bound what we can accomplish in practice. In particular, computational complexity prevents us from substituting brute force computation for knowledge we do not have. Even toy AI problems usually elude solution by brute-force techniques: checking every possible solution would require

[17] Ian Chivers and Jane Sleightholme, "An Introduction to Algorithms and the Big O Notation," in *Introduction to Programming with Fortran* (Springer, 2015), 359–364.

an astronomical amount of memory and/or a geological period of time. A bigger, faster computer can only rarely make up for our ignorance. As Ken Forbus summarized, "Intelligence is possible because Nature is kind. However, the ubiquity of exponential problems makes it seem that Nature is not overly generous."[18]

These theoretical considerations matter because in recent decades computer scientists and AI researchers have improved their understanding of reasoning under uncertainty to the point that we now know which complexity classes information fusion and tracking tasks belong to. That means that we are now in a position to know whether we can reasonably assume that computers will be able to accomplish the feats needed to enable robust counterforce targeting. These discoveries are the subject of the next section.

Why Reasoning under Uncertainty Is Hard

Tracking and information fusion for defense applications merely hint at the importance of reasoning under uncertainty for making machines exhibit intelligent behavior. Countless applications in science, industry, and management are really applications of uncertain reasoning. As a consequence, reasoning under uncertainty is one of the best-studied problems in artificial intelligence. Yet despite decades of effort, no entirely satisfactory way to make computers reason under uncertainty has emerged. AI researchers have conceived and prototyped countless approaches, but all of these systems exhibit tradeoffs such as limited flexibility, brittleness, or extreme computational demands. In their efforts to overcome these challenges, computer scientists eventually discerned profound insights into the nature of reasoning under uncertainty. It appears that there is no one "right" way to reason about uncertainty not just because reasoning under uncertainty is computationally hard, but also because there is more than one way to be uncertain. For instance, sometimes one is uncertain about whether a proposition is true, while other times one is uncertain about the degree to which a proposition is true. A system that could reason comprehensively about imperfectly understood things would have to be able to account for all these different kinds of uncertainty at the same time.

The various approaches AI researchers have developed to reason about uncertainty can be classified into two broad categories: Bayesian and non-Bayesian. Bayesian systems use probabilities to represent uncertain

---

[18] Kenneth D. Forbus and Johan De Kleer, *Building Problem Solvers* (MIT Press, 1993), 22.

knowledge about a set of state variables. These state variables can be either discrete (e.g., a 90% probability that a proposition is true) or continuous (e.g., a probability distribution function representing the likelihood that a variable takes a certain value). As described in Appendix A, the Kalman filter is an example of the latter: it is a recursive Bayesian algorithm for estimating the value of a single (possibly multidimensional) continuous variable. In Bayesian methods for reasoning about uncertainty the state variables must be initialized to an initial value, as in the Kalman filter. Then some variant of Bayes' rule is used to update that prior when new information about the variables becomes available. As the single-sensor, single-target tracking example illustrated in Appendix A shows, Bayesian reasoning can be conceptually and mathematically straightforward so long as there is no need to account for correlations between variables. In the single-sensor, single-target Kalman filter there is only one single multidimensional variable representing the location, speed, and acceleration of the target being tracked. But when we add additional sensors and targets, it becomes necessary to try and account for correlations between variables. In the multiple hypothesis tracker, it is assumed that if a detection is assigned to one track it cannot belong to another track. This creates complicated correlations between alternative assignments of detections to tracks.

To hearken back to the bureaucracy example earlier, adding additional sensor data is like the spawning subcases. Each new detection could be correlated differently with every other detection, so the number of correlations that need to be stored and updated grows exponentially with the total number of detections. Without some way to reduce the size of the correlation table, storing and updating it rapidly becomes intractable for all but a trivial problem.

The complexity of handling correlations between variables contributed to artificial intelligence researchers' hesitation to embrace Bayesianism in their early attempts to make computers reason about uncertainty. The full version of Bayes' rule demands keeping track of all possible correlations between all of the variables. This is represented by a *joint probability table* with a row and a column for every variable. Every single entry in this table can potentially be changed as part of updating the prior. For all but the smallest problems, this made Bayes' rule too inefficient computationally for practical use. This left two alternatives. One of these was to use Bayes' rule but simply assume no correlations existed between the variables. This approach is called "naive Bayes" and it can work well for certain problems. It is still used today for applications where more powerful forms of machine learning such as deep neural networks would be superfluous. But for most practical problems, there are at least a few significant correlations that must be accounted for in order to get good results. Until the early 1980s, however, no method existed for focusing attention solely on "important" correlations in Bayesian models. This made them impractical and unwieldy.

Furthermore, early AI researchers often sought to emulate human reasoning processes, and it appeared to them that humans did not reason about uncertainty using something like Bayes' rule. Instead experimental psychology suggested that humans used heuristic methods such as "default reasoning" (assuming that a proposition is true until a more plausible one comes along, at which point it replaces the old one and becomes the new "default" hypothesis).[19] AI researchers also attempted to incorporate numerical representations of uncertainty into the rule-based expert systems fashionable from the mid-1970s through the mid-1980s. For example, the MYCIN expert system used numerical "certainty factors" to represent the likelihood that a particular rule was applicable given available information. But these efforts to make rule-based systems reason about uncertainty almost universally resulted in disappointment. Part of this resulted from the *ad hoc* nature of mechanisms for uncertain reasoning like MYCIN's "certainty factors," which lacked a rigorous theoretical basis and sometimes produced nonsensical outputs.[20] While numerical, these values were not probabilities and often lacked clear semantics. But it also grew out of a fundamental mismatch between rule-based, logical reasoning and uncertainty. Expert systems were generally *truth-theoretic*: that is, they assumed that the validity of a consequent could be inferred directly from its antecedents. Statistical inference like that used in Bayesian reasoning is much less straightforward, precisely because of the need to keep track of all the correlations.[21]

At the beginning of the 1980s, a new technique emerged that revolutionized the viability of Bayesianism as an approach to enabling computers to reason about uncertainty: the *belief network*. Also called "Bayesian networks," "decision networks," or "Bayesian belief networks" (BBNs), these are totally unrelated to neural networks despite also having "networks" in their name. Instead they provide a way to do Bayesian inference while paying attention only to those correlations that actually matter. Belief networks do this by representing the relationship between variables and their correlations as a *directed acyclic graph* (DAG): that is, a graph with edges that "point" toward a node and where these directed arrows form no loops. Even for a problem with

---

[19] Raymond Reiter, "A Logic for Default Reasoning," *Artificial Intelligence* 13.1–2 (1980), 81–132; David Poole, "A Logical Framework for Default Reasoning," *Artificial Intelligence* 36.1 (1988), 27–47.

[20] David Heckerman, "Probabilistic Interpretations for MYCIN's Certainty Factors," in *Machine Intelligence and Pattern Recognition*, Vol. 4 (Elsevier, 1986), 167–196.

[21] S. Russell and P. Norvig, *Artificial Intelligence: A Modern Approach* (Prentice Hall, 2002), 524–528.

many correlations, usually most of the entries in the joint probability table are zero because most variables lack direct correlations. The belief network exploits this to compress the joint probability table into a graph representation where each variable becomes a node and each nonzero correlation becomes an edge (arrow). But more important than the memory saved by only representing the parts of the joint probability table that are needed is the efficiency of the associated mathematics for reasoning based upon the graph. The most important contributor to the development of belief networks, Judea Pearl, proved in a series of fundamental publications during the 1980s that it is valid to do Bayesian inference and updating using only those parts of the graph that are relevant to a query. To estimate the value of a variable based on available information or to update the values of variables and correlations based on new information, one could get the same results as using the full joint probability table while working solely with the nodes and edges connected to the variable of interest. This amounted to an astronomical improvement in both the analytical tractability and computational efficiency of Bayesian reasoning. The belief network suddenly catapulted Bayesianism from its former impracticability to the leading approach in AI for reasoning about uncertainty.[22]

In the bureaucracy example, the graph would be the equivalent of radically reducing the number of spawned subcases, saving both memory and processing power. But this reduction is not guaranteed to make every problem we might want to solve tractable. Whether it can depends on the structure of the graph—basically, if the graph contains too many connections the problem still becomes intractable even though despite being much reduced from the fully-connected case.

There are multiple kinds of belief networks that can model different kinds of systems. Early work was mostly about belief nets that sought to model a static relationship between a set of discrete (e.g., true or false) variables. But belief nets can also model continuous variables such as those used by the Kalman filter. A belief net that includes both discrete and continuous variables is called a *hybrid* BBN. A belief net that processes a series of inputs is a *dynamic* BBN, and if that series represents a process that varies with time it is also a *temporal* BBN. The Kalman filter is therefore a dynamic, temporal, belief network with a single state variable which is assumed to be Gaussian.[23] The multiple hypothesis tracker, meanwhile, can be interpreted

[22] Judea Pearl and Stuart Russell, "Bayesian Networks," in M. A. Arbib (ed.), *Handbook of Brain Theory and Neural Networks* (MIT Press, 2003), 157–160.

[23] Kevin P. Murphy, "Switching Kalman Filters," Tech. Rep. 98–10 (Compaq Cambridge Research Lab, 1998).

as an approximator for a hybrid, dynamic, temporal belief network with Gaussian continuous variables representing the positions of possible targets and discrete variables representing the assignment of individual detections to particular tracks. Practical MHT implementations are approximations of this belief network because they do not use Bayes' rule to update data association hypotheses, instead using track scoring mechanisms to try to find a good quality solution and removing some possible assignments from consideration.

To illustrate the advantages and limitations of belief nets, let us consider the plight of the poor Soviet early warning (EW) radar operator of the early 1980s, who might easily feel himself weighted with existential responsibility. This onerous burden is illustrated by the belief net in Figure 5. Tasked with interpreting the output of temperamental and unreliable equipment, his errors could result in accidental nuclear war. Ambiguous blips on his radar screen might be real indicators of an incoming attack—but they could just as easily be some kind of equipment malfunction. His decisions are particularly fraught because he does not feel he can necessarily trust his superiors to catch his mistakes, or to be able to resolve an ambiguous report without themselves making some kind of catastrophic miscalculation. The country's sclerotic senior leadership is rumored to be paranoid about an unprovoked adversary first strike, and the commanders he reports to are themselves frequently drunk. But those commanders are not *always* drunk, and the mental

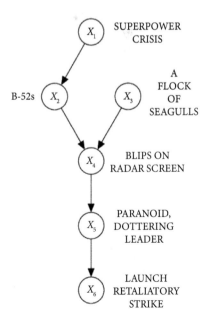

Figure 5. Belief network for the moral and existential dilemmas facing Soviet early warning radar operator, early 1980s.

state of the leadership is merely something whispered about over vodka in private kitchens. In any case, our radar operator is afflicted by nightmares in which he reports blips on his radar screen in accordance with regulations, but his superiors misreport these as an American first strike and the Kremlin orders a full counterattack, resulting in a nuclear apocalypse that he wakes up feeling very guilty about.

Belief nets can help the radar operator with his dilemma. That shown in Figure 5 can help him not just to estimate whether he ought to report what he sees to his superiors, but also whether a nuclear war is his fault if it does occur. The primary evidence variable is X_4, which indicates the presence of blips on his radar screen. X_2 and X_3 are state variables that the radar operator cannot observe directly. The arrows (graph edges) represent the conditional dependencies between variables. The direction of the arrows indicates causal influence: the radar blips, for instance, cannot themselves cause B-52s to be flying into Soviet airspace. The absence of an edge indicates a lack of correlation. The existence of an ongoing superpower crisis makes it more likely that there are American bombers headed toward the USSR, but flocks of seagulls can be expected to remain blissfully unaware of it and carry on as usual. Moreover, events can have *multiple* causes. Blips on the radar screen can be caused by both B-52s and a flock of seagulls at the same time, or, alternatively, can be caused by a flock of seagulls while an actual incursion by U.S. bombers goes undetected. Only the variables directly relevant for a query need to be considered: the probability that a superpower crisis (X_1) will lead to the presence of B-52s (X_2) can be estimated while completely ignoring seagulls or dottering leaders. To estimate the likely cause of an event, such as a thermonuclear war (X_6), one can work backwards against the direction of the arrows, assessing the relative influence of national leaders (perhaps they were so paranoid that they would perceive an ongoing attack and retaliate even in the absence of the radar blips). Given the opportunity to make repeated observations, the radar operator can update his prior beliefs about the relative influence the variables have on each other, eventually providing him with a highly accurate model to help him make his potentially civilization-ending decisions.

This discussion also hints at some of the limitations of belief nets. The radar operator has to know the graph structure in order to make a good-quality assessment, but where is he to get this knowledge? Sometimes this information is known perfectly, but other times it is thoroughly mysterious. While belief nets can estimate the values of hidden variables, they cannot estimate the values of variables that actually exist but are not included in the graph. Whatever causal influence those variables have will be ignored or misattributed to other variables, probably leading to inaccurate results. And as with other Bayesian methods, it is necessary to have a reasonable estimate of the prior in order to converge upon good-quality estimates of the state variables, particularly quickly. For a task such as tracking military targets where these state variables are constantly changing, rapid convergence is particularly important.

Belief nets are not solely, or even primarily, useful for military problems: they are applicable to countless scientific and civilian endeavors as well. Any problem where conditional dependencies (i.e., the graph structure) is known and uncertainty can be expressed in probabilistic terms can potentially be analyzed as a belief net. One of the nice features of belief nets is that they are amenable to theoretical analysis. Unlike the *ad hoc* methods for reasoning under uncertainty cobbled together during the expert systems era, mathematicians and computer scientists can prove theoretically that various kinds of belief nets have certain properties, for instance that inference in them belongs to a particular complexity class. During the 1990s, the computational complexity and approximability of belief nets was the topic of intense research. It soon became apparent that exact inference in belief nets was NP-hard.[24]

While disappointing, this was not exactly a showstopper: in most cases what is needed is not exact inference (since an exact inference from noisy, uncertain data will probably be slightly different from ground truth), but rather a way to draw "good enough" approximate inferences reliably and efficiently. Researchers set out to find general approximation algorithms for belief networks that could do this. But researchers were thwarted in this quest: instead of an approximation algorithm they produced an inapproximability result for approximate inference in belief networks. Not only did approximate inference in belief nets prove to be NP-hard like exact inference, it also turned out that there were limits on the accuracy of approximation algorithms for them.[25] This research showed that efficient general approximation algorithms for belief networks such as those relevant for tracking military targets could not exist.[26] This was perhaps to be expected, because a general approximation

[24] Gregory F. Cooper, "The Computational Complexity of Probabilistic Inference Using Bayesian Belief Networks," *Artificial Intelligence* 42.2–3 (1990), 393–405.

[25] Paul Dagum and Michael Luby, "Approximating Probabilistic Inference in Bayesian Belief Networks is NP-Hard," *Artificial Intelligence* 60.1 (1993), 141–153; Uri Lerner and Ron Parr, "Inference in Hybrid Networks: Theoretical Limits and Practical Algorithms," *arXiv preprint arXiv:1301.2288* (2013).

[26] Uri Lerner proved in his 2002 dissertation that even approximate inference in a kind of dynamic belief network (DBN) called a continuous linear Gaussian (CLG) is intractable unless P = NP. Moreover, he also proved that no polynomial approximate inference algorithm for CLGs could have an absolute error smaller than 0.5. This matters because a CLG can be embedded in the more general DBN that muti-target trackers such as MHTs seek to approximate. The CLG includes both discrete variables and continuous variables,

for BBNs that could work reliably for any problem would be too good to be true: something akin to a computational "philosopher's stone." With the power to transmute the base metal of noisy data into the gold of knowledge, it could revolutionize science, medicine, and business as well as defense.

From a technical standpoint, the difficulty of even approximate inference in belief nets makes sense when one takes a moment to consider just how general the full belief net formalism is. Take, for example, the typical approach to extend belief nets to express first-order logic. For these problems one builds a belief net that reasons about the full space of "possible worlds": the entire universe of possibilities that can be expressed by the logical statements being considered.[27] Even for a rather trivial problem, such a universe of possible worlds is astronomical or even uncountably infinite. This can be the case in tracking problems like those discussed above. In practice, one cannot discount the possibility that there are targets present in the scene but which have generated no observations at all. Low-observable aircraft and cruise missiles, after all, are designed specifically to evade detection. But there are an infinite number of possible unobserved trajectories that could be consistent with any set of detections. We are obligated to reduce the number of possible worlds to some manageable subset of such possibilities to have any hope of finding a good solution quickly enough to be useful.

This is not to say that reasoning under uncertainty is a practical impossibility, but these findings pose some real limitations on what we can count on doing. We cannot make an algorithm that will reliably make sense of an arbitrary murky situation or make up for the inefficiency of the algorithms that we do have by just building bigger computers. Instead, what we need to have is sufficient knowledge to turn the problems we need to solve from intractable to manageable. If we have the right answer already, then we need to do no more computing or reasoning at all; if the problem is nearly solved, sometimes even an inefficient algorithm can still be practical. But in typical cases, what it means is that we need to build less general solvers that are keyed to the idiosyncrasies of the exact problem at hand. By assuming certain things about the problem and potential solutions, we can often find satisfactory solutions to otherwise-intractable problems: this is precisely how real-world military information fusion systems such as multiple hypothesis trackers work. But solutions such as these are also inherently brittle, because if they make

---

with restrictions such as that the continuous variables must be Gaussian and that a discrete node cannot have a continuous parent; the MHT lacks the latter restriction. Uri N. Lerner, "Hybrid Bayesian Networks for Reasoning about Complex Systems," PhD thesis, Stanford University, 2002, Ch. 4.

[27] Russell and Norvig, *Artificial Intelligence: A Modern Approach*, 519.

wrong assumptions there is no guarantee that they will work at all, much less well.

The Most Uncertain Uncertainty of All

When aiming to tame uncertainty by choosing a manageable number of possible worlds to consider, vital decisions must be made not just about what worlds to include, but the way that knowledge about those possible worlds is represented. Ideally, we would like to use some means of representing possible worlds that can account for everything we might encounter. Unfortunately, both practical experience and theory have shown that additional expressiveness typically comes at a steep computational price. But even if computational demands could be disregarded, we would still have difficult choices to make. Reasoning about uncertainty is hard not just because it requires a lot of computation, but because there is more than one way to be uncertain. In their efforts to make computers reason about uncertainty, artificial intelligence researchers have specified many qualitatively different ways for representing uncertainty in addition to the Bayesian methods emphasized earlier. This section describes several of these to illuminate how *ontological* uncertainty (uncertainty about how to represent possible states of the world) poses yet another steep obstacle to making computers solve challenging information fusion tasks for defense applications. No single "right" or "best" way for computers to represent uncertainty has emerged among these contenders, probably because there is not one. Instead, knowledge representation and reasoning schemes need to be chosen that give an adequate trade-off between expressiveness and efficiency in a specific use case.[28]

As described earlier, Bayesian methods represent uncertainty using the language of probability. A Bayesian prior consists of a set of variables with associated probabilities and conditional dependencies between the states of those variables. These sets of variables and the probability distributions associated with them can be arbitrarily complex, but there are still some straightforward concepts that they struggle to represent. In Bayesianism, each variable is assumed to have one and only one actual value, and probability distributions represent uncertainty about what that value is. But this manner of interpreting the meaning of variables (what is called formally an *ontological commitment*) does not account for a case where variables might have multiple "true" states, or be "partially" true.

---

[28] Hector J. Levesque and Ronald J. Brachman, "Expressiveness and Tractability in Knowledge Representation and Reasoning 1," *Computational Intelligence* 3.1 (1987), 78–93.

Consider the Razzle, a popular confectionary introduced in 1966 by the bubble gum manufacturer Fleer. As the package Razzles come in has long declared, "first it's a candy, then it's a gum." Say we want to represent the state of our Razzles. Assuming truth in advertising, we can assume that the Razzle starts as a candy and ends as a gum, but is this a binary state?[29] A simple Bayesian model would assume that it is: the Razzle is either a candy or a gum, and we are uncertain about which it is at a particular point in time. But as anyone who has ever eaten (chewed?) a Razzle knows from experience, the intermediate phase they exist in when they are transitioning from "candy" to "gum" is rather difficult to characterize. As one chews on a Razzle, it breaks down into a kind of gritty fragments that become elastic and sticky with a bit of mastication and then coalesce into gum. Is the Razzle both candy and gum in this phase, or perhaps neither? Could it reasonably be described as proportionately one and the remainder the other? One might also define an arbitrary number of categories other than candy and gum to describe the state(s) a Razzle transitions through during its lifecycle. Or one might describe the Razzle other ways, such as by the extent to which it exhibits "candy-like" and "gum-like" properties at a certain moment: these might not be zero-sum. A Bayesian model can only represent these kinds of uncertainty awkwardly, if at all—not least because Bayes' rule is not by itself sufficient for weighing between all these different ways of representing knowledge about the Razzle.[30]

Lofti Zadeh's *fuzzy logic*, and its relative that Zadeh advocated specifically for reasoning about uncertainty, *possibility theory*, offers a more convenient way to represent and reason about this kind of uncertainty.[31] Zadeh's frameworks are based upon the idea of fuzzy sets. Whereas in conventional sets an item can only be either a member or a nonmember of a set, an item can be a partial member of a fuzzy set. So in fuzzy logic, we could define a "candy set" and a "gum set" and define a half-chewed Razzle as being partially in each of them at the same time, or possibly (if we define the gritty in-between state as neither candy nor gum) outside of both of them. Fuzzy logic has found some use in defense applications in part thanks to its ability to do this kind of reasoning.

Another alternative to Bayesianism that has found considerable favor among analysts and engineers crafting information fusion systems for defense applications is *evidence theory*. Also known as Dempster–Shafer

---

[29] A cynic might contend that Razzles are actually neither candy nor gum at any point in their existence, but instead a rather unsatisfactory pastiche of either.

[30] Andrew Gelman and Cosma Rohilla Shalizi, "Philosophy and the Practice of Bayesian Statistics," *British Journal of Mathematical and Statistical Psychology* 66.1 (2013), 8–38, 16.

[31] Lotfi A. Zadeh, "Fuzzy Logic and Approximate Reasoning," *Synthese* 30:3–4 (1975), 407–428.

theory, this is a formalism that seeks to address the distinction between uncertainty and ignorance. The central idea is that "uncertainty" is represented by a number akin to Bayesian probability, but a second number is added to represent the degree of confidence in the first number: that is, the extent to which one worries that the uncertainty estimate might be based upon incomplete information. Dempster–Shafer theory does this using the concept of belief mass functions. Originally derived by Arthur Dempster in the 1960s, it was reinterpreted and expanded by Glenn Shafer in the 1970s, after which it became influential among both artificial intelligence researchers and engineers developing tracking and information fusion systems for military applications. While there is general agreement that the mathematical basis of Dempster–Shafer is consistent, its correct semantic interpretation has always been controversial. Dempster and Shafer themselves disagreed about the semantics of the information fusion rule introduced by Dempster in 1967. Dempster interpreted the values as upper and lower bounds on the same kind of probability employed in a Bayesian framework, rather than as "belief" and "plausibility" as Shafer did in his 1976 book.[32] Agreement about the syntax (the mathematics introduced by Dempster) did not preclude disagreement about their semantics (interpretation as applied to real-world problems).

Dempster–Shafer theory has attracted an unusual degree of attention and criticism that renders it an illustrative example of the difficulties associated with knowledge representation and the tradeoffs one inevitably makes in selecting a scheme for doing it. In a 1986 critique of Dempster–Shafer theory, Lofti Zadeh illustrated Dempster–Shafer information fusion using what he called the "ball-box analogy" (Figure 6). In the analogy, the balls represent probability mass, while the boxes represent the intervals (the difference between "belief" $Bel(X)$ and "plausibility" $Pl(X)$). The balls are "assigned" or "put into" a particular box, but are free to move around inside their assigned box. When boxes overlap, balls can be inside multiple boxes at once (they

---

[32] An important distinction between Dempster–Shafer theory and alternative approaches to reasoning about uncertainty, such as theories of imprecise plausibility (e.g., fuzzy logic) is that it does not represent uncertainty using sets of probability measures, but rather by assigning probability masses to sets. This is the reason that evidence theory employs set theoretic notation (e.g., $A \cup B \cup C$ instead of $A \wedge B \wedge C$) even when considering atomic propositions. If we have a function $y = f(x)$ and we know the probability distribution of x, then it is trivial to find the probability distribution of y of the basis of f and the probability distribution of x so long as f is a point function. But functions can be much more diverse than this: formally, a function is defined as a mapping from one set to another, and as a result there can also be set-valued functions (also called relations). Instead of point values, suppose x and y take values in the sets U and V, respectively, and that A is a specified subset of V. Then what is the probability that y is in A? If f is a point function, then y is a real-valued probability-but if f is a set-valued function then y is non-unique. All we can say is that y lies between upper and lower bounds which Dempster cast as upper and lower probabilities (P_* and P^*). Glenn Shafer, A *Mathematical Theory of Evidence* (Princeton University Press, 1976).

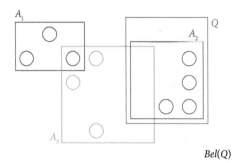

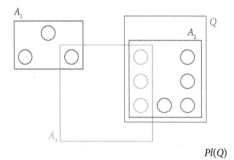

Bel(Q)

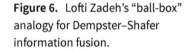

Pl(Q)

Figure 6. Lofti Zadeh's "ball-box" analogy for Dempster–Shafer information fusion.

"pass through" the walls of boxes they are not assigned to). Region Q represents a *query* that asks the question "How many balls are in Q?" The answer to this question is interval-valued because the balls can roll around. We can characterize these bounds by treating Q as either an *attractor* that pulls in all balls within its grasp or a *repeller* that pushes away all those that can escape.[33] The former is equivalent to *Pl(Q)*, while the latter is equivalent to *Bel(Q)*.

Within Dempster–Shafer theory probabilities are *normalized*, which means that balls are disregarded if they are not relevant for a query. In a sense, when boxes disappear, their balls disappear with them, and *Bel–Pl* intervals are calculated in proportion to the remaining number of balls. These eliminated components are the *degree of conflict* between the pieces of evidence (Eq. 5).[34]

---

[33] Lotfi A. Zadeh, "A Simple View of the Dempster–Shafer Theory of Evidence and Its Implication for the Rule of Combination," *AI Magazine* 7.2 (1986), 85–90.

[34] Dempster's combination rule employs the concept of belief mass functions. Let ω be an unknown quantity with values in a finite domain Ω (dubbed the "frame of discernment" by Shafer). Then a piece of evidence about ω can be represented by a mass function m on Ω, defined such that $2^{\Omega} \to [0, 1]$, such that $m() = 0$ and

$$\sum_{A \subseteq \Omega} m(A) = 1. \tag{1}$$

Any subset A of Ω such that $m(A) > 0$ is called a *focal set* of m.

When Dempster–Shafer is used to combine multiple pieces of evidence, this is equivalent to changing the sizes and shapes of the boxes to be the intersection of the boxes representing the pieces of evidence. This analogy hints at why Dempster–Shafer encounters problems when combining conflicting or incompatible pieces of evidence. Take Zadeh's classic example, for instance:

> Suppose that a patient, P, is examined by two doctors, A and B. A's diagnosis is that P has either meningitis, with probability 0.99, or brain tumor, with probability 0.01. B agrees with A that the probability of brain tumor is 0.01, but believes that it is the probability of concussion rather than meningitis that is 0.99. Applying the Dempster rule to this situation leads to the conclusion that the belief that P has brain tumor is 1.0—a conclusion that is clearly counterintuitive because both A and B agree that it is highly unlikely that P has a brain tumor. What is even more disconcerting is that the same conclusion (i.e., Bel(brain tumor) = 1) would obtain regardless of the probabilities associated with the other possible diagnoses. This example and other easily constructed examples call into question the validity of Dempster's rule of combination when it involves a normalization of belief and plausibility.

Then for any $A \subseteq \Omega$ we can define the belief and plausibility functions. The former represents the total degree of support (the probability that the evidence implies A),

$$Bel(A) = \sum_{B \subseteq A} m(B), \tag{2}$$

while the plausibility of A is the probability that the evidence does not contradict A:

$$Pl(A) = 1 - Bel(\bar{A}). \tag{3}$$

Uncertainty about the truth value of a proposition is therefore represented by two numbers, $Bel(A)$ and $Pl(A)$, with $Bel(A) \leq Pl(A)$. It can be shown that Bel, Pl, and m are all equivalent representations of a piece of evidence.

Dempster's combination rule is defined as follows. Let m_1 and m_2 be belief functions sharing the same frame Ω representing two independent pieces of evidence. Then their combination using Dempster's rule is that $\forall A \neq \emptyset$:

$$(m_1 \oplus m_2)(A) = \frac{1}{1-K} \sum_{B \cap C = A} m_1(B)m_2(C), \tag{4}$$

where

$$K = \sum_{B \cap C = \emptyset} m_1(B)m_2(C) \tag{5}$$

is the degree of conflict between m_1 and m_2. $m_1 \oplus m_2$ exists so long as $X < 1$. Dempster's combination rule exhibits the properties of commutativity and associativity. It also generalizes the concept of intersection: if m_A and m_B and $A \cap B \neq \emptyset$ then

$$m_A \oplus m_B = m_{A \cap B}. \tag{6}$$

In this case one piece of evidence has most of its balls in a box that doesn't exist in the second—and vice versa.[35] A much smaller box that contained only one ball in each piece of evidence is the only shared component of both—but after the evidence is combined this ball is the only one remaining.

In response to the perceived inadequacies of Bayes' rule and Dempster–Shafer theory, numerous other rules and frameworks for information fusion have been proposed. Examples of these include Yager's rule, Florea's robust combination rule, the disjunctive rule, Dubois and Prade's rule, and the various versions of the Proportional Conflict Resolution (PCR) rule.[36] The latter are a derivative of the theory of belief functions based upon Dezert–Smarandache theory that seek to correct the counterintuitive behavior of Dempster–Shafer on highly conflicting evidence. The PCR rules do this via a mechanism to reallocate conflicting probability mass among involved subsets of the body of evidence instead of normalizing it out like Dempster–Shafer does. But does this make PCR "better" than Dempster–Shafer? Not necessarily, because sometimes disregarding incomprehensible evidence is the sensible option.

The same kind of paradoxical dilemmas highlighted by Zadeh can also occur in military contexts. To return to our dogsitting example from earlier in the chapter, imagine a situation in which we are trying to track the dogs with two or more senses and those senses begin yielding mutually incompatible results. For instance, say that different senses indicate dogs in the same locations going in opposite directions, or that dogs that should be perceived with multiple senses are missing on one or the other. These conflicting perceptions are akin to Zadeh's disagreeing doctors. Trying to fuse the highly conflicting information coming from these sensors using a method such as Dempster–Shafer could lead to the same sort of counterintuitive results as in Zadeh's example. Yet it is not always better to come to an ambiguous answer like that which PCR would find. Firstly, the counterintuitive result could be the *right* one, even if only by coincidence, just as in Zadeh's example—but trying to average out the evidence as PCR does would obscure this.

But more importantly, the way in which highly conflicting evidence ought to be handled depends upon *extrinsic* factors that we cannot count upon resolving based upon the sensor data alone. Why are the sensors providing contradictory data? It might be the case that one or both of the sensors have

---

[35] As Zadeh expressed it, "The reason for this . . . is that normalization throws out the opinion of those experts who assert that the object under consideration does not exist." Lotfi A. Zadeh, "Review of *A Mathematical Theory of Evidence*," *AI Magazine* 5.3 (1984), 81–83, 82.

[36] Roman Ilin and Erik Blasch, "Information Fusion with Belief Functions: A Comparison of Proportional Conflict Redistribution PCR5 and PCR6 Rules for Networked Sensors," in *2015 18th International Conference on Information Fusion (Fusion)* (IEEE, 2015), 2084–2091, 2085.

failed. Or perhaps adversaries have hacked the sensors. But if so, what, if anything, of what the sensors are telling us reflects reality? It might be the case that the contradictions actually reflect some aspect of what is going on. For example, perhaps it looks like some objects are moving in more than one direction at once because there are, in fact, targets at the same locations passing each other in opposite directions.

Finally, we must grapple with the possibility that the reason the sensor outputs look contradictory to us is because the underlying reality that produced them is in some way inconceivable to us. To give a concrete example, perhaps the adversary, unbeknownst to us, has introduced an exotic new superweapon that shows up on our screens as a bizarre confluence of incompatible sensor readings. Obviously, how we should react to the contradictory indicators should be very different if they come from this *Wunderwaffe* than if we just have some flaky sensors—but without some clue as to what's "really" going on, we can't be sure we're approaching it the right way.

The biggest challenge to reasoning about uncertainty is what Donald Rumsfeld dubbed "unknown unknowns." In a February 12, 2002 Department of Defense news briefing, then-Secretary of Defense Donald Rumsfeld commented that:

> Reports that say that something hasn't happened are always interesting to me, because as we know, there are known knowns; there are things we know we know. We also know there are known unknowns; that is to say we know there are some things we do not know. But there are also unknown unknowns—the ones we don't know we don't know. And if one looks throughout the history of our country and other free countries, it is the latter category that tend to be the difficult ones.[37]

The difficulty of reasoning about "unknown unknowns" is an escapable result of the fact that they are unknown. In order to start reasoning about them, we would need to know something about them. But if we knew something about them, then they would be "known unknowns." And no matter how intelligent we were—or what other resources we could bring to bear, such as immensely powerful computers—we cannot start reasoning without at least a quantum of knowledge.

Why hasn't a dominant information fusion paradigm emerged? An important reason is that there is a trade-off between expressiveness, flexibility, and

---

[37] A cynic might suggest that Secretary Rumsfeld's fate was a cautionary tale about the pitfalls about trying to reason about "unknown unknowns." Donald H. Rumsfeld, *DoD News Briefing—Secretary Rumsfeld and Gen. Myers, February 12, 2002 11:30 AM EDT. 2002.* URL: http://archive.defense.gov/Transcripts/Transcript.aspx?TranscriptID=2636.

computational efficiency in the choice of knowledge representation. One typically needs to choose a system that makes trade-offs that work well for a specific use case—but such a system may end up not being able to do everything it needs to given the unpredictability of the real world. Another primary reason is the difficulty mapping formal rules onto messy real-world realities. Take the notion found in Dempster–Shafer theory of the "frame of discernment." The frame of discernment is, by definition, a closed set that encompasses all possible answers to the problem of interest: that is, the set of all the "possible worlds" we are considering. The "body of evidence" is the subset of the frame of discernment that is considered by the pieces of evidence being fused. But in most practical cases, we lack a reliable definition of the frame of discernment, and we have to consider the possibility that we have misframed the question. Perhaps, to paraphrase Hamlet, "there are more things in heaven and earth than are dreamt of in our philosophy." Instead, all we have is the body of evidence, and in many cases this is so self-contradictory that it's hard to decide what to make of it. As Russell, Gödel, and Tarski discovered, mathematics alone cannot surmount such epistemological and ontological obstacles. But while these difficulties may demolish our roseate dreams of attaining "dominant battlespace knowledge," they might also be harnessed to forge extraordinarily powerful weapons of a different kind.

Will Quantum Save Us?

Even if AI alone proves inadequate to track and target everything of interest on the battlefield, will technological applications of quantum mechanics close this gap? Predictions to this effect are not difficult to find. A 2019 *Foreign Affairs* article declared confidently that

> Quantum sensors . . . will eventually be able to detect disruptions in the environment, such as the displacement of air around aircraft or water around submarines. Quantum sensors will likely be the first usable application of quantum science, and this technology is still many years off. But once quantum sensors are fielded, there will be no place to hide . . . Similarly, the same quantum science that will improve military sensors will transform communications and computing. Quantum computing-the ability to use the abnormal properties of subatomic particles to exponentially increase processing power-will make possible encryption methods that could be unbreakable, as well as give militaries the power to process

volumes of data and solve classes of problems that exceed the capacity of classical computers.[38]

Quantum mechanics may seem counterintuitive at first glance, but it is no more magic than artificial intelligence or nuclear weapons. Nor are techno-logical applications of quantum mechanics a distant prospect. The transistors that form the basis of all modern classical computers are themselves a practical application of quantum principles, as is practically the entirety of solid-state electronics.[39] Quantum sensing and quantum computing may prove extremely useful for certain applications. They may make it possible to see things that would otherwise have gone undetected, and solve prob-lems that would be impractical to solve with a classical computer. But these technologies are qualitatively different from their classical counterparts and would complement conventional sensors and computers rather than sup-planting them. We cannot predict with much confidence whether they will live up to their promise, but even if they do there will still be places to hide and problems we cannot solve.

There are a variety of different kinds of quantum sensing technologies at various stages of maturity. One of the simplest that might be adapted for military applications are quantum gravimeters. These exploit the wavelike properties of cesium atoms cooled to near absolute zero to make extremely precise measurements of the acceleration of objects in freefall. If sufficiently accurate these might be able to detect the slight change in mass distribution caused by the presence of a submerged submarine in certain circumstances. Even so, this device would only be useful as a tactical sensor and might be difficult to make practical.[40]

The eerie technology of "ghost imaging" is as spooky as its name implies, but curiously it does not need quantum entanglement to work. Ghost imag-ing works by exploiting the correlation in momentum between photon pairs. In the classical version a laser is run through a beam splitter, after which one photon goes into a digital camera, while the other goes through the target object and into a bucket detector (a sensor that detects the presence of a pho-ton but not its location). In isolation, the image detected by the camera looks

[38] Christian Brose, "The New Revolution in Military Affairs: War's Sci-Fi Future," *Foreign Aff.* 98 (2019), 122.

[39] Solid-state devices operate in a "semi-classical" regime that straddles the realms of classical and quan-tum physics, and cannot be described using classical physics alone even though they do not exploit purely quantum phenomena such as entanglement.

[40] Marco Lanzagorta and Jeffrey Uhlmann, "Overview of the Current State of Quantum-Based Tech-nologies," *Marine Technology Society Journal* 53.5 (2019), 75–87.

like random noise, but if only pixels detected when the bucket detector is triggered are counted, it builds up an image of the photons that passed through the object unimpeded. The resulting ghostly outline gave the name to "ghost imaging." Later improvements made the technique much more practical. It turns out that true entangled photons are unnecessary: semiclassical correlations are sufficient to build up a coherent image. Furthermore, by tightly controlling the beam it is possible to simulate random photon trajectories and do away with the beam splitter. With more flexibility to arrange the beam source, camera, and bucket detector, it becomes possible to image a three-dimensional object. This is useful because it turns out that ghost imaging is very effective at filtering through atmospheric turbulence and obscurants like fog, as well as building up an image in extreme low-light conditions. The latter could be useful for covert applications, but would probably operate too slowly to image moving objects.[41] Researchers have demonstrated ghost-imaging lidar systems that operate at a range of a few kilometers, and Chinese investigators have declared their intent to develop satellite-based ghost imaging capable of detecting stealth aircraft through clouds.[42] For all its seductive promise, however, ghost imaging is vulnerable to some trivial countermeasures. For instance, saturating the bucket detector with a blinding laser could render the ghost imager useless.

It has been asserted that the much-hyped technology of quantum radar could make aircraft like the B-2 stealth bomber obsolete, but this would demand technological breakthroughs that may or may not come to pass. Conventional radar works by transmitting a radio signal, some fraction of which is reflected by targets and collected by a receiver antenna. This weak received signal is then amplified and processed to assess the location of detected targets. Quantum radar, by contrast, exploits quantum entanglement to detect the minuscule reflected signal directly without the need to amplify it. This requires a source of entangled photons (e.g., a laser). Half of these photons are transmitted as a signal, while the other half are stored in the device. Quantum radar might be practical because while the photons must be entangled at the outset, they do not have to remain so to detect their interaction. In fact, it turns out that the transmitted signal can be shifted down into the microwave spectrum before being sent out, while the stored photons

---

[41] David S. Simon, Gregg Jaeger, and Alexander V. Sergienko, "Ghost Imaging and Related Topics," in *Quantum Metrology, Imaging, and Communication* (Springer, 2017), 131–158.

[42] Stephen Chen, *Could Ghost Imaging Spy Satellite be a Game Changer for Chinese Military?* (2017). URL: https://www.scmp.com/news/china/society/article/2121479/could-ghost-imaging-spy-%20satellite-be-game-changer-chinese.

can remain as light.[43] Only a small fraction of the transmitted photons are reflected off of targets and return to the transmitter, but that tiny signal can be detected even without amplification thanks to quantum interactions with the stored photons. In addition to being much more sensitive than conventional radar, quantum radar is also immune to typical jamming schemes: because only photons with a stored pair are detected, externally generated signals should be completely ignored. As a consequence, quantum radar might be able to detect the minuscule radar cross-sections of stealth aircraft.[44] Thanks to its high sensitivity, quantum radar might also be able to operate with much lower transmission power than conventional radar, making it hard for the adversary to detect and target the transmitter.

This may sound too good to be true, but there's a catch: the need to generate large quantities of entangled photons and store half of them. Typically, the photons are stored in a delay line which is basically a coil of fiber-optic cable, but this can only store a photon for about 75 microseconds before it attenuates. This limits the practical range of quantum radar to a mere 11.25km, suitable only for tactical applications. Greater range would demand longer-lived storage of quantum states. Ideally this would take the form of stable quantum memory that could store the states more or less indefinitely, giving practically unlimited range. But even if stable quantum memory is developed, it may prove impractical for quantum radar given the huge number of states that need to be stored (as most of the photons that leave the transmitter never return, very few of the stored states end up forming part of the detected signal). The potential need for very large numbers of entangled photons poses an additional technological challenge, as would the likely need to keep the apparatus at cryogenic temperatures and the poor efficiency of single-photon detectors at microwave energies. It would also need to be integrated with Doppler radar to track fast-moving targets. As a result of these challenges, it is unlikely that quantum radar will be practical for at least another decade, if ever. For its part, the Pentagon appears to have written off quantum radar altogether: a 2019 Defense Science Board report concluded dismissively that "Quantum radar will not provide upgraded capability to DoD."[45]

---

[43] The related technology of quantum illumination would work the same way, except that the transmitted photons remain at their original wavelength. Shabir Barzanjeh et al., "Microwave Quantum Illumination," *Physical Review Letters* 114.8 (2015), 080503.

[44] George I. Seffers, *Quantum Radar Could Render Stealth Aircraft Obsolete* (2015). URL: https://www.afcea.org/content/Article-quantum-radar-could-render-stealth-aircraft-obsolete.

[45] Defense Science Board, *Applications of Quantum Technologies: Executive Summary*, tech. rep. (Office of the Undersecretary of Defense for Research and Engineering, 2019), 2.

Moreover, while quantum radar might be relatively immune to conventional jamming and spoofing, it might still be vulnerable to electronic countermeasures. The detector inside the quantum radar requires recombining the reflected photons with their pair in the idler and measuring the result. This requires shunting the received photons into a very sensitive and probably fragile piece of equipment operating at cryogenic temperatures. While very detectable thanks to the quantum "memory" of their former entanglement, in physical terms the detection involves tiny amounts of energy. Directing large amounts of microwave energy into the receiver might overwhelm or damage the critical single-photon detector at its heart.

Nor would quantum radar necessarily have any advantage over conventional radar distinguishing true targets from confusion targets. Decoys and other deception techniques that exploit the transmitted photons would probably be as effective as ever. It might be very hard to make quantum radars mobile, but if it is possible for the enemy to locate them then the stealthiness afforded by their low transmission power is useless. The adversary could just target and destroy them, rendering them militarily irrelevant.

It would be extremely convenient if quantum computers were a practical version of the "nondeterministic Turing machines" that computer scientists use to classify the complexity of problems. For better or worse, however, quantum computers are a different kind of animal than the classical computers we are used to.[46] They are not a faster substitute for ordinary computers and there are many problems for which they would offer little or no advantage over a conventional computer. But if quantum computers can be made practical, they may prove capable of doing things that conventional computers cannot. Some of these potential applications, most notably cryptographic ones, might then turn into "killer apps" endowing those who could wield them with massive advantages.

At present, quantum computers are still mostly aspirational. These devices would employ a radically different memory model than classical computers. Instead of storing memory as digits, bits, or symbols, they would employ qubits (quantum bits) that would exploit entanglement to represent state as a superposition of classical states. Quantum algorithms transform problems into procedures that cause all the elements of the superposition except for those representing the correct answer to cancel each other out. Theorists predict that a quantum computer with enough qubits could perform certain

---

[46] Scott Aaronson, "The Limits of Quantum Computers," *Scientific American* 298.3 (2008), 62–69; Scott Aaronson, *Quantum Computing Since Democritus* (Cambridge University Press, 2013).

calculations that would require an astronomical amount of time for a classical computer near-instantaneously.

One of the tasks at which quantum computers are expected to excel is factoring integers (determining the prime numbers of which a number is the product). In 1994, Peter Shor proposed the eponymous Shor's algorithm, a procedure that could factor integers on a quantum computer in polynomial time.[47] This seemingly esoteric task matters because one of the main forms of public-key cryptography in widespread use, RSA, is based on the assumption that factoring large integers is computationally prohibitive. A working quantum computer could potentially decrypt a huge fraction of past and present encrypted communications. At present, however, experimental quantum computers are too small and unreliable to accomplish this feat. Due to their quantum nature and need to maintain entanglement, the qubits need to be cooled to cryogenic temperatures and isolated from external influences. Even under these conditions, it is difficult to establish and maintain entanglement over enough qubits to factor integers of the size used in practical RSA implementations. Even if quantum computers become practical, they are unlikely to become household appliances: even if the heart of the computer is tiny, the associated refrigeration equipment and need to isolate the device from thermal and other noise will probably make them large, expensive, and delicate. Moreover, they will complement, not replace, classical computers.[48] Quantum and classical computers will be employed together to exploit the strengths of both for maximum effect.

Computer scientists have yet to determine what problems quantum computers will be able to solve that classical computers cannot, not least because it turns out to be intimately connected to the nettlesome question of whether P = NP. Theoretical computer scientists have defined a quantum counterpart to the classical Turing machine that would use quantum states for internal storage instead of deterministic symbols. This idealized quantum computer can then serve as the basis for quantum computational complexity classes analogous to those in classical computing. The class of particular interest is BQP, which are the problems that the quantum Turing machine can solve in polynomial time. Since the quantum Turing machine can do everything a classical Turing machine can do, any problem in P is definitely in BQP. But what makes quantum computers so tantalizing is that there are likely some

---

[47] Peter W. Shor, "Algorithms for Quantum Computation: Discrete Logarithms and Factoring," in *Proceedings 35th Annual Symposium on Foundations of Computer Science* (IEEE. 1994), 124–134.

[48] Modern classical computers and algorithms are *very* good: even if quantum computers demonstrate "quantum supremacy" in some tasks, these newcomers may not turn out to be cost-effective alternatives to their older brethren. It is very conceivable that usable quantum computers will be developed but that these will not prove practical for real-world applications.

NP and/or NP-hard problems that are also in BQP. These are the problems on which the quantum computer potentially offers a huge advantage over classical computing. If P = NP, then all of NP is in BQP as well. However, most computer scientists believe that P ≠ NP and that while BQP probably includes some problems in NP and PSPACE, it probably excludes many difficult NP-complete problems.[49] This is illustrated in Figure 7, where the lobes of BQP that extend to the left and right of P represent these areas of relative advantage for quantum computers (e.g., Shor's algorithm). Major questions that remain to be answered include how far these lobes extend and to what extent they can be exploited by physically realizable quantum computers. One shortcoming of the quantum Turing machine formalism is that it differs more from the kind of quantum computers we can foresee how to build than the classical Turing machine formalism differs from our quotidian classical computers. In the formalism, the quantum Turing machine can store an arbitrary number of quantum states for an indefinite period of time. We only have a sense of how to build a quantum computer that can store a modest number of quantum states for a relatively brief interval. Therefore, the question that matters in practice are the problems where we can attain a useful advantage with these relatively modest quantum computers.

Breaking ubiquitous encryption schemes would have obvious security implications, but these would only have an incidental impact on nuclear strategy and strategic stability. For the tasks considered in this book, what matters most are combinatorial and continuous optimization problems that

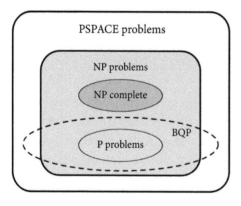

Figure 7. The suspected relationship of BQP to P, NP, and PSPACE.

---

[49] A key piece of evidence for this suspicion is Grover's algorithm, also known as the quantum search algorithm. Grover's algorithm offers only a quadratic speedup over the the classical solution for unstructured search, but has been shown to be asymptotically optimal. Therefore Grover's algorithm is unlikely to provide polynomial-time solutions for NP-complete problems, but if it is asymptotically optimal no other algorithm is likely to either. Michael A. Nielsen and Isaac L. Chuang, *Quantum Computation and Quantum Information* (Cambridge University Press, 2010), 276–305.

underlie information fusion. As of this writing the development of hybrid quantum–classical algorithms to accomplish this goal is a highly active, and controversial, area of research. The basic idea is to use a classical computer to transform the optimization problem into a quantum algorithm that can then be run on a quantum computer. The beauty of this scheme is that once the quantum program is ready, it could be possible to run it almost instantaneously. The downside is that identifying the quantum program looks forbiddingly difficult, to the extent that some researchers believe it will be a practical impossibility.[50] The present debate is hardly the final word on the potential for quantum–classical algorithms to facilitate information fusion, however. It may eventually turn out that such techniques can identify good-quality approximate answers to large-scale information fusion problems more effectively than classical computers alone.

Even if quantum computers and quantum sensing live up to their potential, they will not magically alleviate the knowledge quality problems at the heart of our strategic dilemma. To know how to turn sensor data into usable intelligence, we need to know what to look for. A quantum computer is useless if we do not know what programs we want to run on it. If we fail to ask the right questions, neither quantum nor AI can save us.

WOPR and Anti-WOPR

It is possible to build a WOPR-but it would not be easy. Yet states may very well create AI systems to plan disarming nuclear attacks anyway. But unlike the nuclear war planning computers of science fiction, these systems would not be designed to find a way to "WIN THE GAME" against the adversary. Instead actual WOPRs would try to plan adversary attacks against friendly forces in order to identify ways to complicate enemy planning and ensure that "THE ONLY WINNING MOVE IS NOT TO PLAY." In short, the compelling reason to build a WOPR is as an enabling component of an Anti-WOPR: a fog-of-war machine designed to ensure that the adversary lacks the knowledge needed to execute a successful disarming strike. Those seeking to build an Anti-WOPR have many advantages in their favor. Thanks to their superior knowledge of their own forces, they can exploit ML approaches such as end-to-end training that their adversaries cannot. The forbidding algorithmic obstacles bedeviling those trying to develop disarming strike capabilities against their adversaries are therefore much more surmountable

---

[50] Gian Giacomo Guerreschi and Anne Y. Matsuura, "QAOA for Max-Cut Requires Hundreds of Qubits for Quantum Speed-up," *Scientific Reports* 9.1 (2019), 6903.

for those on the defensive. Equipped with a tractable WOPR more powerful than actual adversary information fusion and adaptive planning capabilities, the defender can then use it as the basis of operational measures aiming to make enemy planning for a disarming strike as complicated and difficult as possible. An Anti-WOPR is therefore an adversarial planning system. The prospect of multiple states employing such adversarial planners simultaneously raises novel questions about the prospective effects on deterrence and strategic stability that are explored in Chapter 6.

The key to understanding the likely effects of artificial intelligence on nuclear strategy lies in the difference between intractability and impossibility. When a computer scientist says that a problem is intractable, it might seem that this means that solving the problem is a hopeless task. Sometimes it is, but often it is not. In theoretical computer science, a problem is intractable if some instances of that problem will require an amount of computational resources (like processor time or memory) that scale unmanageably with the size of the problem instance. Moreover, many problems that are "hard" in the worst-case are usually easy enough to be solvable. So intractable does not mean that doing something is impossible; it means that one cannot *count* upon doing it, which is not at all the same thing. Theoretical computer science also tells us that with the right knowledge, such as having a good hint about the correct answer, even the hardest problems can be made solvable. Therefore, even though states can try to leverage computational complexity to help make their nuclear deterrents survivable, they cannot be absolutely confident that they have succeeded. If the adversary somehow saw through their deceptions, even if only for a moment—perhaps with the help of well-placed spies—then they could turn out to be vulnerable despite all their precautions.

Chapter 5
Fog-of-War Machines

What you see on these screens up here is a fantasy—a computer-enhanced hallucination. Those blips are not real missiles, they're phantoms!

WarGames (1983)

Many advanced military capabilities which we would like to possess are basically forms of reasoning under uncertainty. Among these are the information fusion and adaptive planning capabilities that would be necessary to track and target modern strategic nuclear forces so as to hold them under threat of a disarming strike. But as the discussion in Chapter 4 showed, reasoning under uncertainty is a "wicked" problem that we cannot count upon more powerful computers to solve. Reasoning under uncertainty is not only hard computationally, but also epistemologically: to make a computer do it one must make hard choices about the kinds of knowledge to represent and how to reason with that knowledge. Computer scientists have shown theoretically that there are probably no generally applicable "universal" solutions to these problems. This means that practical solutions will need to exploit the idiosyncrasies of the problems at hand to find adequate-quality solutions in a reasonable period of time. Since its origins in the 1950s artificial intelligence has been in considerable part an effort to identify solutions to problems of this type, and contemporary machine learning techniques provide powerful means for finding such solutions. *But these methods depend upon accurate knowledge of the problem at hand, whether embodied in training data or stated in an explicit specification.* In a battlespace, we cannot reasonably count upon having this knowledge.

An elaborated version of the puzzle metaphor from Chapter 3 can help illustrate the way in which deception can interfere with information fusion. Much as before, the puzzle has billions or trillions of heterogenous "true" pieces, a large fraction of which must be assembled correctly to reveal what the picture on the assembled puzzle is. But the puzzle box contains many pieces that are not supposed to be there. Many of them are random

Deterrence under Uncertainty. Edward Geist, Oxford University Press. © RAND Corporation (2023).
DOI: 10.1093/oso/9780192886323.003.0006

items placed in the box by mischievous gremlins. While gremlins are always present, the adversary has initiated a gremlin breeding program in the vicinity of the puzzle with the aim of making it more difficult to solve. (This is "ambiguity-increasing" deception.) Not only are there more gremlins than before, but these new gremlins have been bred to be stronger and more aggressive, with the result that the ratio of puzzle pieces to random detritus is now much more unfavorable.

But now the enemy has introduced a qualitatively new complement to the gremlins: robots that are programmed to make adversarial puzzle pieces. The adversary knows what the assembled puzzle is supposed to look like and has programmed this knowledge into the robots, who use it to design their fake pieces. Unlike the random objects placed in the puzzle box by the gremlins, the robots' puzzle pieces are designed to confuse anyone attempting to reassemble the puzzle as much as possible. They are devilishly designed so as to combine with a fraction of the real pieces in a misleading way that seems like a plausible puzzle solution. One can get most of the way to assembling the puzzle before discovering that one had accidentally used the adversarial pieces, being forced to take everything apart again and start over. In their beneficence the adversary has even provided what is ostensibly the puzzle box lid, which bears an attractive image (also painted by a robot) of the fake solution that the adversarial pieces hint at.

While these considerations may dash our hopes to exploit AI to "lift the fog of war" and secure comprehensive situational awareness for ourselves, they also present opportunities. If information fusion and reasoning under uncertainty are intractable problems, can we trick or force the enemy into trying to solve those problems?[1] Computational hardness and knowledge quality problems might keep us from having some things that we want, but they could also be forged into weapons to be wielded against our adversaries: what one could call "fog-of-war machines."

The fog-of-war machine is not just a metaphor help illustrate the relationship between emerging technology and deception. It could also be a real technological possibility that might be realized as an operational military capability. The same tools that AI researchers have created in their attempts to make computers reason about uncertainty may provide the theoretical and practical basis to make these fog-of-war machines a reality. Even if we decide not to pursue this technology ourselves, we need to be prepared for the possibility that others might.

---

[1] Geist, "Why Reasoning under Uncertainty Is Hard for Both Machines and People—and an Approach to Address the Problem", 273.

Military Deception in Fiction

It is regrettable that the visions of futuristic combat that are so common in our popular culture rarely portray "the fog and friction of war." This can be forgiven in that these are generally intended to be enjoyable to watch and the confusion and chaos that accompanies actual combat tends to be bewildering and distressing rather than entertaining. Nor are our big-budget movie portrayals of futuristic space battles all that different from classical literature in this regard. In the *Iliad*, the constant intervention of various gods blows away the fog of war; and Beowulf faces the monsters in his eponymous epic in artistically satisfying solo combat. Both low and high art have done us a disservice in failing to prepare us for a future in which the fog of war is thickened, rather than lifted, where we know *less* about the battlespace than ever before, where neither man nor machine knows what is actually going on, and there is no omniscient narrator to clear up these mysteries for us.

Take *Star Wars*, for instance, George Lucas' enormously successful space fantasy film. Its undeniable effectiveness as a piece of entertainment works against the realism of its portrayal of combat. The unambiguously evil Galactic Empire is thwarted by a handful of single-pilot fighters that destroy its planet-destroying superweapon, the Death Star. They accomplish this by exploiting captured plans for the moon-sized battle station: these reveal a vulnerability in the form of a single exhaust port which can be used to fire a "proton torpedo" into the Death Star's reactor. It is indeed satisfying when Luke Skywalker uses his nascent powers as a Jedi to blow up the Death Star, but the reason it is fun to watch is precisely because the audience knows who is doing what at all times and why they are doing it.

Moreover, the Galactic Empire is evidently incompetent at both strategy and information security. If the Death Star had been designed properly, then the Rebels would have faced much steeper obstacles to destroying it, even with the benefit of the stolen plans. A crude version of this would simply be to cover the surface of the Death Star with false exhaust ports, making the actual vulnerability more difficult to find and attack. But a more clever version, and presumably within the reach of a Galactic Empire with faster-than-light starships, would be to provide the surface of the Death Star with active camouflage that constantly evolved. This would disassociate the captured plans describing the interior of the Death Star and its vulnerabilities with what the Rebel pilots could see during their attack. Under such conditions, a Jedi or other magic space wizard, capable of reasoning and acting on knowledge they did not have, would be essential to attack the Death Star successfully.

This is not to say that Hollywood never has apt intuitions about the utility of deception. The nameless architects of the booby traps in the *Indiana Jones* franchise certainly provide some models that a fog-of-war machine might emulate. These devices exploit what the adversary *thinks* he knows to dispatch him in ways that he cannot even imagine. They do this by taking advantage of knowledge that the booby trap designers have (e.g., how much the golden idol weighs, which grail is the real one). While an actual fog-of-war machine would presumably involve fewer poison darts, decapitating saws, and giant rolling boulders, it would follow similar principles of deception.

Another relative bright spot in cinematic portrayals of futuristic combat is perhaps the 1982 film *Star Trek II: The Wrath of Khan*. Its villain, Khan Noonien Singh, is a eugenically enhanced twentieth-century superman delivered to the twenty-third century via suspended animation. Khan possesses superior intelligence but is ultimately defeated by what he does not know about the twenty-third-century world. As Spock describes him, Khan is "intelligent, but not experienced," and he commits rookie errors such as failing to change his captured starship's passcode. In the film's climactic battle, Khan is defeated because he defaults to "two-dimensional thinking" he learned in his past as a tyrant on Earth; Captain Kirk exploits this to sneak up on him in a murky nebula that interferes with both starships' situational awareness. The mechanics of this battle are hardly realistic, but once again the underlying intuitions are right. While it also makes numerous simplifications to make the plot easier for the audience to follow, it correctly places knowledge and its exploitation at the center of combat.

Military Deception Past and Present

The efficacy of military deception is among the oldest and most contentious debates among strategists. Sun Tzu famously decreed that:

> All warfare is based on deception. Hence, when we are able to attack, we must seem unable; when using our forces, we must appear inactive; when we are near, we must make the enemy believe we are far away; when far away, we must make him believe we are near.[2]

But Karl von Clausewitz dismissed military deception as a desperation measure that should be regarded as a last resort for those who had run out of better options:

[2] Sun Tzu, "The Art of War," in *Strategic Studies* (Routledge, 2014), 86–110.

But the weaker the forces become which are under the command of strategy, so much the more they become adapted for stratagem, so that to the quite feeble and little, for whom no prudence, no sagacity is any longer sufficient at the point where all art seems to forsake him, stratagem offers itself as a last resource. The more helpless his situation, the more everything presses towards one single, desperate blow, the more readily stratagem comes to the aid of his boldness. Let loose from all further calculations, freed from all concern for the future, boldness and stratagem intensify each other, and thus collect at one point an infinitesimal glimmering of hope into a single ray, which may likewise serve to kindle a flame.[3]

The two masters' disagreement about the value of deception is one of the greatest differences in their thinking about war.[4] For his part, Machiavelli celebrated deception, writing in his *Discourses* that "Though fraud [deception] in other activities be detestable, in the management of war it is laudable and glorious, and he who overcomes an enemy by fraud is as much to be praised as he who does so by force."[5]

In a classic essay on the subject, Donald C. Daniel and Katherine L. Herbig defined deception as "the deliberate misrepresentation of reality done to gain competitive advantage."[6] Past and current U.S. military documents give several complementary definitions of military deception. A 1998 publication on "Information Operations" defined it as "the integrated use of assigned and supporting capabilities and activities, mutually supported by intelligence, to affect adversary decision makers and achieve or promote specific objectives."[7] By contrast, a 2012 U.S. military doctrine manual defines "Military deception (MILDEC)" as "those actions executed to deliberately mislead adversary decision makers as to friendly military capabilities, intentions, and operations, thereby causing the adversary to take specific actions (or inactions) that will contribute to the accomplishment of the friendly mission."[8] The Russians use a single word, *maskirovka*, to refer to camouflage, concealment, and

---

[3] Carl von Clausewitz, *On War*, trans. by J. J. Graham (N. Trübner, 1873).

[4] Michael I. Handel, *Sun Tzu and Clausewitz: The Art of War and* On War *Compared*, tech. rep. (SSI, 1991).

[5] Niccolò Machiavelli, *The Discourses* (Penguin, 1983), book 3, discourse 40.

[6] Donald C. Daniel and Katherine L. Herbig, "Propositions on Military Deception," in Donald C. Daniel and Katherine L. Herbig (eds.), *Strategic Military Deception* (Pergamon, 1982), 1–30, 3.

[7] Joint Chiefs of Staff, *Military Deception* (1998). URL: http://www.c4i.org/jp3_13.pdf, p. viii.

[8] It clarifies that "MILDEC operations apply four basic deception techniques: feints, demonstrations, ruses, and displays, which it defines as:

1. Feints. A feint is an offensive action involving contact with the adversary conducted for the purpose of deceiving the adversary as to the location and/or time of the actual main offensive action.
2. Demonstrations. A demonstration is a show of force where a decision is not sought and no contact with the adversary is intended. A demonstration's intent is to cause the adversary to select an unfavorable course of action (COA).

deception. Soviet and Russian military publications characterize three kinds of *maskirovka*: tactical, operational, and strategic.[9] These correspond with the categories of tactics, operational art, and strategy employed by Russian military thinkers.

Daniel and Herbig introduced a very influential distinction between two types of deception which they dubbed "A-type" and "M-type." The former "ambiguity-increasing" type, which they characterized as "the less elegant variety," "confuses a target so that the target is unsure as to what to believe" by "compound[ing] the uncertainties confronting any state's attempt to understand the adversary's wartime intentions." The more challenging alternative, "misleading" deceptions, by contrast, "reduce[s] ambiguity by building up the attractiveness of one wrong alternative." The U.S. military has adopted a variant of Daniel and Herbig's framework, albeit with different terminology.[10] Field Manual 3-13.4, "Army Support to Military Deception," defines two categories: "ambiguity-increasing" (equivalent to A-type) and "ambiguity-decreasing" (equivalent to M-type).[11] Irrespective of the terminology employed, both of these are defined as directed against human decision-makers, as opposed to nonhuman agents.

In theory, military deception is extremely attractive.[12] If deception is so advantageous, why is it not more central to the practice of modern warfare? A major reason is that historically, military deception was often planned and carried out in a haphazard, unsystematic way. One assessment observed that British deception planners during WWII

> engaged in their work much in the manner of college students perpetrating a hoax. In fact, Jones regards the hoax as a fitting model for strategic deception . . . the British deception strategists wanted not only a victory but also wanted to leave the enemy perplexed, confused, and dumbfounded. The reactions of the British participants to reports of effective deception are hardly the reactions of serious

---

3.   Ruses. A ruse is a cunning trick designed to deceive the adversary to obtain friendly advantage. It is characterized by deliberately exposing false or confusing information for collection and interpretation by the adversary.

4.   Displays. Displays are the simulation, disguising, and/or portrayal of friendly objects, units, or capabilities in the projection of the MILDEC story. Such capabilities may not exist, but are made to appear so (simulations).

Joint Chiefs of Staff, *Military Deception* (2012). URL: https://jfsc.ndu.edu/Portals/72/Documents/JC2IOS/ Additional_Reading/1C3-JP_3-13-4_MILDEC.pdf, p.vii.

[9] Viktor Antonovich Matsulenko et al., *Camouflage: A Soviet View* (Dept. of the Air Force, 1989).

[10] Daniel and Herbig, "Propositions on Military Deception," 4–5.

[11] Department of the Army Headquarters, *Army Support to Military Deception* (2019). URL: https://fas.org/irp/doddir/army/fm3-13-4.pdf, p. 1–6.

[12] Donald C. Daniel and Katherine L. Herbig, "Deception in Theory and Practice," in Donald C. Daniel and Katherine L. Herbig (eds.), *Strategic Military Deception* (Pergamon, 1982), 355–367, 359.

adults engaged in a terrible conflict; rather, they seemed to enjoy the job of creating a gigantic hoax. The form of emplotment that corresponds to the hoax is satire, and the prevailing trope is that of irony.[13]

This is not to say that such deception was never successful—quite the opposite—but it was nowhere near as systematic as it might have been in theory.

In contrast, AI researchers have invented systems that can *optimize* deception. The generative adversarial networks (GANs) introduced in 2014 produce "deepfakes" that both machine learning models and human observers misinterpret as genuine. The GAN framework consists of two components: a "generator" that produces fake examples and a "discriminator" that tries to identify them. These engage in a game to try and outperform each other at their respective tasks, during which they refine themselves based on the other's outputs.[14] This technique is used to produce photorealistic deepfakes of imaginary people, but it can be adapted to generate arbitrary output–such as the distinctive sensor signatures of SSBNs and mobile missile launchers. Adversarial examples are defined as "inputs to machine learning models that an attacker has intentionally designed to cause the model to make a mistake."[15] These can be produced by a variety of techniques.

Finding targets on the ground is harder than it might appear because "looking up" is qualitatively different from "looking down" from the standpoint of information theory. The targets of interest when "looking up" are generally metal objects flying through the sky or moving through space. Not only are such objects relatively rare (as they are not naturally occurring), but they are very different in density and elemental composition from their surrounding environment. This translates into a very favorable signal-to-noise ratio. When "looking down," by contrast, as when searching for road-mobile missile launchers, the entire Earth acts like an enormous clutter target. Moreover, confusion targets similar to the true targets, such as large trucks, are relatively common.

In the endless contest between "finders" and "hiders," hiders benefit from the most powerful ally of all—entropy. In his foundational 1948 paper "A Mathematical Theory of Communication," Claude Shannon introduced the

---

[13] Theodore R. Sarbin, "Prolegomenon to a Theory of Counter-Deception," in Donald C. Daniel and Katherine L. Herbig (eds.), *Strategic Military Deception* (Pergamon, 1982), 151–173, 167.

[14] Ian J. Goodfellow, Jonathon Shlens, and Christian Szegedy, "Explaining and Harnessing Adversarial Examples," published as a conference paper at *ICLR*. 2015.

[15] Justin Gilmer et al., "Motivating the Rules of the Game for Adversarial Example Research," *arXiv preprint arXiv:1807.06732* (2018).

concept of *information entropy*, which happens to have the same mathematical form as thermodynamic entropy.[16] Information entropy is measured in bits (also known, appropriately, as "shannons") that represent the amount of information contained in a message. Our universe is full of noise-generating processes which eventually drown out any signal. Hiders can work with and enhance these processes to increase ambiguity and reduce the chance that their adversaries will find their targets. Finders, meanwhile, have to fight entropy. This hardly means that their task is impossible, but much like the casino owner, entropy always wins in the end.

Moreover, thanks to their self-knowledge hiders are at a massive advantage in employing AI to facilitate military deception. Using data from their own operations, they can model their own forces comprehensively and then use these models to design adversarial attacks intended to fool a relatively optimal adversary tracking system. Finders, meanwhile, are forced by the asymmetry of knowledge to rely upon noisy, incomplete, and possibly mendacious data in trying to construct their own tracking algorithms.

In a "whitebox" setting, the full model and all its parameters are available to the attacker. In the "blackbox" setting, the parameters of the system are unknown but it is possible to query it—for instance, supplying an image and receiving a label assigning it to a category, such as "cat" or "dog." While in the specific military use cases of interest to us here, we might have blackbox or even whitebox access thanks to either operational procedures and/or spectacular intelligence coups. But most of the time these will probably be unattainable luxuries. How can adversarial inputs be constructed with so little access to the model?

Fortunately (or not) our problem domain differs from tasks such as image classification in that it is possible to design untargeted attacks that will degrade the performance of a theoretically optimal system. Image classifiers are generally designed to find the maximum a posteriori (MAP) classification for the image label out of some set. But for our purposes we need multitarget trackers that attempt to characterize the posterior distribution over the possible states of the target system. This is a considerably more difficult task. As a consequence, in order to be tractable practical tracking systems tend to employ approximate solution methods that introduce some exploitable vulnerabilities. In particular, most of these systems attempt to find a MAP estimate for measurement-track assignments, but as explained in Chapter 6,

---

[16] Claude E. Shannon, "A Mathematical Theory of Communication," *Bell System Technical Journal* 27.3 (1948), 379–423.

this state estimator cannot accurately characterize a multitarget system.[17] There are reliable techniques for compromising most of these multitarget tracking systems: simply adding large amounts of clutter and sowing confusion about the number of "true" targets in the scene will prove more than adequate in many cases.

It might seem that one could overcome this problem with improvements in sensors and signal processing to weed out "false" targets. But as historical examples reveal, deception can be conducted by posturing *actual forces* so as to confuse the adversary. Consider the contrast between the legendary British deception operations of WWII, with their false documents and decoy armies, with that of the Soviet Union in Operation Bagration in the summer of 1944. As Daniel and Herbig recounted,

> The British chose to create largely false army groups in southeastern England to bolster their deceptive threat to launch the main Allied invasion at Pas de Calais. The Soviets massed actual armies at two different points and used one as a deceptive alternative to mask their intention to strike with the other. The armies threatening the Germans—which later proved to be diversionary—were real threats, manned and equipped and verifiably true; the forces of FUSAG (1st U.S. Army Group) in southeastern England consisted of rubber landing craft, electric light displays, rumors, and exaggerated radio traffic.[18]

The "adversarial inputs" to adversary AI systems can follow the same principle: much or most of the signal accessible to the adversary can be generated by authentic sources, with decoys and spoofing merely complementing clever force posturing.

For example, what are currently dubbed "deepfakes" could provide a crucial advantage for militaries seeking to obscure the location of their road-mobile missile launchers. Due to the difficulty of open-area search, most proposed means of finding these missiles before launch assume the availability of some kind of intelligence tipoff to narrow down the probable locations of the TELs to reduce the search area to manageable dimensions. The most attractive candidate for this is signals intelligence (SIGINT): the missiles and their support vehicles need to communicate at least occasionally, and in remote areas they will have difficulty relying upon landlines and

---

[17] Intuitively, the reason for this is pretty straightforward: there is an infinite space of possible system states when one includes targets that are never observed, and one cannot directly compare probabilities for possible states with different numbers of tracks or where tracks appear and disappear at different times. As these problems all show up in real-world contexts, it is hardly surprising how hard it is to build robust multitarget trackers!

[18] Daniel and Herbig, "Deception in Theory and Practice," 365.

similar secure means of doing so. Some authors argue that it will be very difficult to replicate the distinctive combination of physical indicators and SIGINT traffic associated with actual missiles, undermining the effectiveness of deception operations for hiding them.[19] But even if this assessment is accurate today, it will become increasingly suspect in the future. Militaries can use machine learning to analyze the indicators produced by their own mobile missile operations and refine their operational procedures accordingly. One obvious component of this is to use machine learning techniques akin to GANs to generate authentic-looking signals traffic to broadcast from decoy missiles and hiding locations. (As these locations can have human crews to assist in the deception, they can help guide the generation of this traffic to maximize its resemblance to the real thing.) These feints could even be augmented by adversarial objects–three-dimensional objects designed to fool image classification systems.[20] Adversarial objects could serve as confusion targets to widen the rift between human and machine interpretations and might be incorporated into the camouflage of mobile missiles and their support vehicles.

But perhaps even more important is the use of ML techniques to shape and disguise the operation of the actual missiles to complicate adversary efforts to build systems that can distinguish them from the decoys. For example, real missiles can augment their actual signals traffic with the same kind of fake broadcasts as the decoys. Actual missiles could also modify their appearance or operations to include the subtle indicators that were formerly only associated with fakes, including some that would never have been identified without ML analysis. Should the operators of mobile missiles exploit techniques such as these, an adversary will probably experience extreme difficulties trying to build effective machine learning models to pick out the true locations of the missiles. Machine learning researchers have found that trained models are extremely vulnerable to "data poisoning"–the inclusion of spurious mislabelled samples in their data sets. The presence of just a handful of these can catastrophically impair the performance of the trained model.[21] By shaping their own operations, hiders can essentially "poison" the data that the finders have available to train their ML models. Moreover, due to their lack of a definitive "test set" the finders cannot be confident about the performance of their trained model.

---

[19] Long and Green, "Stalking the Secure Second Strike: Intelligence, Counterforce, and Nuclear Strategy," 52.

[20] Anish Athalye et al., "Synthesizing Robust Adversarial Examples," *arXiv preprint arXiv:1707.07397* (2017).

[21] Jacob Steinhardt, Pang Wei W. Koh, and Percy S. Liang, "Certified Defenses for Data Poisoning Attacks," in *Advances in Neural Information Processing Systems* (2017), 3517–3529.

We might even be able to craft adversarial inputs to multisensor-multitarget information fusion that will degrade the performance of a hypothetical optimal system. (See Appendix B for a discussion of the technical reasons for this.) While we cannot implement such an optimal system directly, we can study its theoretical properties to design attacks that would reduce its performance. Indeed, in ML terms we can conceptualize camouflage, concealment, and deception (CCD) as "adversarial attacks" against a theoretically optimal information fusion system. As the idealized system is intractable, any practical system must employ some kind of imperfect approximation scheme. The intuition is that whatever degradation in performance a particular "adversarial input" would evoke from the hypothetical ideal system will probably elicit a larger marginal degradation in the performance of real-world tracking and targeting systems. This assumption will not necessarily hold, but probably will in most cases of interest.

Weaponizing "Unknown Unknowns"

What Donald Rumsfeld dubbed "unknown unknowns" can also be thought of as holes in one's body of evidence. In formalisms like Bayesianism and Dempster–Shafer, a proposition must be known at the outset in order to determine whether it is likely or not. If a possibility is unknown, or it is assigned a probability of zero, then there is no way to add it or make it seem more plausible.[22] Therefore, the surest way to thicken the fog of war is to try to confront the adversary with unknown unknowns.

The "battle of wits" between the Dread Pirate Roberts and Sicilian criminal mastermind Vizzini in the 1987 film *The Princess Bride* provides an intuitive illustration of how holes in one's body of evidence can be exploited by an adversary. Tasked by the villainous ruler of Florin to spark a war with the rival nation of Guilder, Vizzini's schemes to abduct Princess Buttercup are repeatedly thwarted when the Dread Pirate Roberts defeats his giant Fezzik and Spanish swordsman Inigo Montoya with clever tactics. Vizzini laments that they are at an impasse because "I can't compete with you physically, and you're no match for my brain." Dismissing Plato, Aristotle, and Socrates as "morons" in comparison to himself, the Sicilian is delighted when the Dread Pirate Roberts challenges him to "a battle of wits," accepting eagerly once he confirms that this contest will be "to the death." The masked pirate produces a tube of iocane powder, an "odorless, tasteless" substance that is "among the

---

[22] Gelman and Shalizi, "Philosophy and the Practice of Bayesian Statistics."

more deadly poisons known to man." Taking two goblets of wine, he turns his back and does something with them, then presents the chalices to Vizzini with the announcement that "the battle of wits has begun. It ends when you decide and we both drink and find out who is right, and who is dead."

"But it's so simple!" protests Vizzini. "All I have to do is divine from what I know of you, 'Are you the sort of man who would put the poison into his own goblet, or his enemy's?'" The Sicilian then promulgates several convoluted chains of inductive reasoning, introducing observations such as

> "Iocane powder comes from Australia, as everyone knows, and Australia is entirely peopled with criminals, and criminals are used to having people not trust them as you are not trusted by me so clearly I cannot chose the wine in front of you. But you must have suspected that I would know the powder's origin, so clearly I cannot choose the wine in front of me."

The Dread Pirate Roberts accuses Vizzini of trying to trick him into giving something away, to which the Sicilian retorts that "you've given *everything* away!" Exclaiming "Whatever in the world can that be!" to distract his opponent, Vizzini switches the goblets while Roberts is not looking. After both opponents drink from the cup in front of them, the Sicilian declares that "you fell victim to one of the classic blunders! The most famous is 'Never get involved in a land war in Asia,' but only slightly less well-known is this: 'Never go in against a Sicilian when death is on the line!'" A few moments later Vizzini literally dies laughing when the poison takes effect. As the Dread Pirate Roberts explains to Princess Buttercup, he put the poison in both goblets. Having built up an immunity to iocane powder over a period of years, he could employ it fearlessly.

Vizzini exclaims "inconceivable!" whenever one of his plans goes awry, leaving his minions puzzled as to whether their boss even knows what the word actually means. Fittingly, Vizzini is defeated by the limitations of what he can conceive of. As he spins elaborate inferences about Roberts, he never considers the possibility that the poison is in both goblets. In evidence theory, we would say that the truth is outside Vizzini's body of evidence. Because it is not a possibility he is considering, he assigns zero probability to it, and moreover no new information he receives (such as the Dread Pirate Roberts' totally nonchalant response to his childish attempt to distract him) can cause him to begin considering it.[23]

---

[23] This is qualitatively different from a proposition that one can conceive of, but considers improbable: for instance, the Dread Pirate Roberts' misinformed skepticism that rodents of unusual size (ROUSes) inhabit the Fire Swamp.

The scene is funny in part because for all his arrogance Vizzini is actually not smart at all, but the kind of artificial intelligence we have today is stupid in the same ways as this self-declared "mastermind." His frame of discernment is strictly delimited and cannot be extended on the fly. Moreover, many of the idealized formalisms used in game theory and artificial intelligence suffer from the same shortcoming, although it can be circumvented with assumptions such as an unbounded frame of discernment that considers all possible universes.[24] Even if this sometimes permits formal analysis, such a solution cannot be realized in a practical system: humans clearly do it differently, and the kind of "general" intelligence pursued by researchers since the 1950s will demand some practical mechanism for agents to extend their ontologies.

Envisioning Fog-of-War Machines

The purpose of the fog-of-war machine is to create or aggravate knowledge quality problems for adversaries to advance one's own objectives. Fog-of-war machines need not be limited to tactical applications and might be operated over larger spatial and temporal scales up to and including grand strategy. A fog-of-war machine would work by exploiting the fact that "deceivers" have a knowledge advantage over their opponents because they already possess the knowledge that those opponents can be expected to seek out. As a classic work on military deception put it, "all things being equal, the advantage in a deception lies with the deceiver because he knows the truth and he can assume that the adversary is eagerly searching for its indicators."[25] The reason the deceiver knows the truth is often because he makes that truth: for example, he knows where his forces will be because he orders them to go there. The deceived, by contrast, has to reason about all the kinds of uncertainty described in this chapter and Chapter 4 in order to uncover the truth. A fog-of-war machine would aggravate the computational and epistemological challenges intrinsic to that uncertain reasoning by a combination of shaping "true indicators" (such as the locations of actual missiles) and optimizing spurious signals (such as the locations of decoy missiles and contents of spoofed signals traffic).

A fog-of-war machine could be operated with a variety of goals which could sometimes, but not always, be combined in practice. The simplest goal for a fog-of-war machine might be to maximize confusion on the part of the

---

[24] Shane Legg and Marcus Hutter, "Universal Intelligence: A Definition of Machine Intelligence," *Minds and Machines* 17.4 (2007), 391–444.

[25] Daniel and Herbig, "Deception in Theory and Practice," 359.

target: for him or her to have minimal confidence in his or her knowledge of the true state of affairs. To do this, the fog-of-war machine could try to optimize noise generation so as to obscure all aspects of the underlying problem simultaneously. But often the goal will be subtler: to try and ensure that the adversary is confident of some specific untruth in order to increase their vulnerability. In many cases making that lie convincing will require revealing certain parts of reality, so an important part of the fog-of-war machine is selecting what truths to reveal and how so as to make that deception convincing without revealing too much elsewhere. A related goal is that of ensuring that the adversary knows certain truths—for instance, that they know that a first strike is not imminent—so as to reduce risks that they will overreact to other misinformation promulgated by the fog-of-war machine.

In general, a fog-of-war machine would not operate on the basis of the deepfakes and adversarial examples that have enthralled ML researchers in recent years. Nor is the goal to create a simulated world almost indistinguishable from reality, as envisioned in science fiction narratives like *The Matrix*. Instead, stage magic offers a better analogy. Stage magicians know better than anyone that to *see* is not the same thing as to *understand*. They exploit the principle that attention is finite to misdirect their audience. And usually, the magician's goal is not to convince viewers that they actually accomplished what they appeared to, such as sawing their assistant in half. The audience is fully aware that appearances are almost certainly very different from reality, but they are mystified as to what actually happened. And stage magicians jealously guard the secrets of their craft: the point of their trade is to keep audiences in the dark about how they did it. A fog-of-war machine would operate on a similar basis, albeit on a much larger scale.

To illustrate how stage magic exemplifies these principles, consider David Copperfield's televised 1983 trick in which he made the Statue of Liberty disappear before a live audience. The live audience and the television crews were located on a platform on Liberty Island. From their perspective, the statue was framed by two towers covered with lights. The magician raised a curtain between the two towers, and when it was lowered a few moments later, the statue was gone. The principle behind the trick, while implemented on an audacious scale, was trivial its simplicity. The platform on which the audience stood—and to which the light towers were attached—could rotate. While the curtain was raised, the platform turned so that one of the two towers obscured the statue.

The real challenge was to accomplish this rotation in such a way that the live audience could not perceive it. Here Copperfield exploited some basic misdirection. Since the trick took place at night, the bright lights made it difficult for the audience members to make out distant points of reference that might have given away the motion of the platform. Very loud music played during the rotation, both to distract the audience and to cover up the sound of the machinery rotating it. At the opening of the trick, framing the statue between the two light towers conditioned the audience members to use those towers as a point of reference. In Bayesian terms, their prior was to assume that the Statue of Liberty was located between the towers, so they were surprised when it did not appear there. And the trick was bewildering because they could not conceive that the platform might have rotated. And why would they conceive that the platform could move, when they had been manipulated such that they could not perceive its motion?

A fog-of-war machine would construct and orchestrate analogous illusions—albeit on a larger scale and intended for an audience of machines as well as humans. (Stage magic works on people, so it can be expected that similar tricks can be played even on "human-level" artificial intelligences.) These illusions would not necessarily need to be durable. Some might be intended to be effective for mere minutes or even just a few seconds. Not all the illusions would need to resemble some phenomena known to their target. A major difference between the action of the fog-of-war machine and stage magic would be that its illusions would be designed to be effective, rather than entertaining. In many cases, stoking confusion and doubt in the mind of the targets would be the goal, rather than convincing them that they saw something in particular.

The frameworks developed by artificial intelligence researchers to make computers reason about uncertainty provide not just conceptual tools for understanding how fog-of-war machines might work, but also guidelines for their algorithmic implementation. The fog-of-war machine is in some sense these same systems, but inverted: rather than trying to reduce uncertainty regarding certain items of interest, they try to increase uncertainty while potentially increasing certainty about others as needed. Bayesian belief networks offer one possible taxonomy for classifying different goals that a fog-of-war machine might pursue. Obscuring or distorting the underlying causal relationships represented by the directed graph used by the belief net could be one such goal. Misleading the adversary about the weight or existence of graph edges would cause them to perceive spurious correlations or to miss actual correlations, encouraging them to misperceive and mispredict their actions. This might be done by consistently transmitting certain signals during real exercises to convince the target that such transmissions would accompany combat employment. Another related deception goal could be to obscure the existence of some nodes (state variables) in the graph and add other, spurious ones. Alternatively, it might be desired to create maximal confusion about the underlying nodes and edges. At other times it may be desirable that the adversary not just perceive certain nodes and edges as they actually exist, but furthermore that they have confidence that those nodes and edges have certain values, whether those values are actually true or not.

It is here that formalisms such as belief nets are advantageous because they provide us with formal and algorithmic definitions of what indicators an "optimal" deception target should receive so as to convince them to believe those values. Instead of guessing what indicators would convince a fully rational observer of what we wish for them to believe, we can define the underlying belief net and invert the algorithmic approaches used to solve BBNs to identify what the deception target ought to see in order to convince them of what we want them to believe, or to deprive them of the knowledge that we wish to deny them. Deception can therefore be converted into an optimization problem and solved by whatever methods seem most efficacious. Moreover, employed optimally the fog-of-war machine does not depend upon cognitive biases or irrationality to work: its output can theoretically be tailored to deceive a fully rational observer with immense computational resources. This is the reason that artificial intelligence and machine learning cannot be expected to see through the deceptions generated by such machines: more powerful AI will end up drawing the same erroneous conclusions faster and more precisely because the deception is in some sense "Bayes-optimal."[26]

This outcome depends on the target not being made aware of the deception by additional information not accounted for by the fog-of-war machine, but the implementation phase of the fog-of-war machine could minimize the likelihood of this. Knowing what the adversary needs to see to convince them of what we want them to believe is not enough: we must take steps to ensure that they see those things and nothing else. A consequence of this is that the recommendations of a fog-of-war machine could take on a highly kinetic character. By gouging certain eyes, and killing certain messengers, the information available to the adversary and the opportunities they have for fusing it can be constrained to suit one's own purposes. This could be accomplished

---

[26] For Bayesian reasoning systems such as BBNs it is possible to define cost functions so as to maximize or minimize Bayes risk over the set of posterior distributions. A belief net-based fog-of-war machine would be designed to try to find an optimal set of evidence variables (what the deception target is expected to observe) in order either to convince them that state variables have certain values or to increase uncertainty about variables. The solution to this problem can be sought using an optimization method that will probably need to be keyed to the particular use case. If that solution is optimal, then an "ideal" reasoning agent with unlimited computational resources, but presuming no additional information than has been accounted for in the design of the deception solution, will still reach the intended erroneous conclusions.

by cutting cables and destroying sensor platforms but also potentially with less escalatory alternatives such as blinding or jamming. These actions need to be coordinated with the operations of real forces, the placement of decoys, and spoofing to turn the output of the fog-of-war machine into a spurious reality to be perceived by the adversary.

In the contest between the fog-of-war machine and its targets, the former benefits from the most powerful allies of all: the laws of physics and of computational complexity. The laws of physics favor deceivers because deceivers often get to work with entropy, but their victims always have to work against it. The laws of physics also impose practical limits on the amount of information that can be gathered (only a finite amount of Shannon entropy can be present in any signal) and in the amount of computation that can be performed by a physical computer. Nor are data and knowledge equivalent: data that does not contribute to knowledge is essentially noise since it consumes resources and attention that would have been better employed elsewhere. Deceptive signals that distort our knowledge are worse than noise, but instead a sort of "anti-knowledge." And due to the laws of computational complexity, we cannot compensate for the knowledge we lack with a bigger computer. Compute and knowledge are not fungible. Nor can knowledge quality problems necessarily be solved by adding more sensors: since the computational difficulty of the underlying problems grows at least polynomially with the total amount of data being considered, there is a "point of diminishing returns" for additional data. Taking a cue from Clausewitz, this could perhaps be dubbed "the culminating point of knowledge." Beyond that point, the computation required to use additional data is more than the added knowledge gleaned from it is worth. The foundation of the fog-of-war machine is that attention and trust are both finite resources. So long as the target pays attention to what we wish them to and refrains from trusting information they possess that might disabuse them of our deceptions, even unlimited computing power and sensor data will not save them.

To give an illustrative example of how a fog-of-war machine might work for a concrete objective, let us envision a near-future international crisis in which a large country whose deterrent forces are based primarily on road-mobile ICBMs feels compelled to generate those forces (send them from their home bases to dispersal areas). This is a potentially fraught maneuver because it creates a transient window in which the adversary has higher incentives to try and attack the missiles: there is a "use-it-or-lose-it" situation because the forces are targetable as they are leaving the bases and much less so afterwards. At the same time, the country dispersing its missiles also wants the other side to believe those missiles are no longer at their bases, as once those missiles are dispersed they will be much more secure from attack. But adversary knowledge of this dispersal needs to come with as little knowledge of the current locations of those dispersed missiles as possible. A fog-of-war machine could assist in this operation as follows. First, it is necessary to distinguish that knowledge that the adversary must not know (e.g., actual dispersal locations, vulnerability of undispersed or dispersing TELs) and that which he must know (e.g., relative invulnerability of dispersed forces). Then it is necessary to consider the means by which the adversary stands to learn about these things. Let us posit that space-based surveillance capabilities (both optical reconnaissance and synthetic-aperture radar) are the adversary's main ISR assets, complemented by some signals intelligence. The fog-of-war machine turns this into an optimization problem designed to hoodwink the adversary about what needs to be hidden while apprising him of what he needs to know. The output of this is an integrated plan combining both the real operation of dispersing the missile TELs from their bases and the deception and counterintelligence operations to shape the adversary's perceptions.

These deception operations could include the employment of real forces in militarily-questionable ways in order to confuse the adversary and make the deception more convincing. To reduce adversary confidence that missiles are vulnerable, one goal of the fog-of-war machine would be to obscure whether and when dispersal is going on. If the adversary can see the missiles at their bases when its satellites pass over, this will not work. But if the adversary can see nothing, they might assume a full-on dispersal is underway and develop an itchier trigger finger than they would have had if there was some reason to doubt dispersal had begun. This rules out destroying adversary satellites: in addition to being highly escalatory, these need to be preserved to show the adversary what the fog-of-war machine has decided they should see. This is a job for assets such as the Peresvet combat laser deployed with Russian mobile ICBMs: it can blind the sensors of optical reconnaissance satellites as they pass over the locations of the missile units, and jammers might be deployed to do the same for space-based SAR satellites. Other key assets are decoys of various kinds, varying from inflatable mock-ups to actual launchers that happen not to contain missiles. Complementing decoys meant to look like the launchers themselves are additional systems to fake secondary indicators of the presence of missile TELs, such as tire tracks and signals traffic. The former can probably be duplicated fairly cheaply with weighted tires or some other inexpensive apparatus, while the latter could be produced by deepfakes or possibly just trained actors. Keeping track of when adversary satellites will be overhead, the fog-of-war machine tells forces what to do at what locations at what times. The decoys and the spoofers ramp up over some chosen period of time to the point of maintaining fake tracks and launchers along the roads away from the bases at all times, and the spurious signals traffic makes it unclear whether TELs are actually moving off base. The blinding lasers and spoofers, meanwhile, make actual TEL movements hard to observe. At a chosen moment TELs start their actual movement, and decoys take their places in their shelters on base. Now fake signals traffic suggests the TELs are on base when they are not. Once retaliatory forces are secure, the decoys can be removed and adversary satellites allowed to observe the bases without interference to make absolutely clear that forces are totally generated.

The next phase of the deception plan is to keep the adversary uncertain about the locations of the dispersed missiles. A potentially effective way to do this is to convince the adversary that missiles have been sent to places other than known dispersal areas. This would force the adversary to divert ISR assets from expected dispersal sites to larger areas and force him to reconsider attack plans that might have been drawn up based on pre-crisis intelligence. There are good reasons why ICBM TELs generally stick to known areas— operating the massive vehicles in unprepared areas not only takes them away from their planned supply and communications lines, it also risks their getting damaged or stuck—but this might be a feature, rather than a bug, in the context of the deception plans dreamt up by the fog-of-war-machine. While decoys can obviously contribute to the illusion of widely dispersed forces, the adversary is likely to see through this particular ruse. To make the illusion convincing, it may be worth sending some actual missile TELs into unprepared areas in the full expectation that those ICBMs will be sacrificed on the altar of deception in order to enhance the survivability of the whole. When those dispersed units meet with predictable mishaps, indicators of both their location and distress may be made observable to the adversary to ensure he knows that actual ICBM TELs are in unanticipated locations. This, in turn, would make widely dispersed decoy missile units appear less fantastic, incentivizing the adversary to devote more ISR assets to them.

While human deception planners might be able to effect operations such as those described with some success, coordinating and maintaining deception on this scale for an extended period of time while operating real forces effectively demands something like the fog-of-war machine. The degree of detail of the plans produced by such a machine would vary depending upon the use case. In broad outline, they might consist of instructions such as "retain actual ICBM regiment at base until H+47; direct blinding laser at this subset of adversary ISR satellites when at this inclination; deploy decoy ICBM regiments to Tiksi, Podol'sk, and Novyi Asbest; advance sacrificial actual TEL units and associated decoys to Magnitogorsk and Zolotoi Bolot; other missile units advance to prepared dispersal areas and undertake camouflage and concealment measures." The fog-of-war machine would need at least some adaptive planning capability to account both for breakdowns in deception plan execution but also shifts in objectives or the emergence of unanticipated adversary reconnaissance capabilities.

Conclusion

The discovery that computers excel at deceit but are also vulnerable to it goes against the traditional portrayal of artificial intelligence in popular culture. In the previous century, computers were stereotyped as purely "logical" in science fiction as well as popular science writing. Even the malevolent computers of literature and cinema often struggled to lie as they slaughtered humans. D. F. Jones' Colossus, for instance, took over the world with credible threats to exterminate humanity yet was never known to lie.[27] And when the computers of science fiction needed to lie, they handled it poorly. In the novel version of *2001: A Space Odyssey*, it is explained that HAL tried to kill the crew because he was simultaneously programmed not to "distort information" but had also been ordered to hide the *Discovery's* actual mission from the astronauts. HAL attempted to resolve the resulting contradiction by killing the crew, which apparently seemed easier to a computer than lying.[28] But artificial intelligence as it is now emerging looks little like the purely logical reasoning machines of twentieth-century fantasy.

Fog-of-war machines would be transformative and, if they live up to their potential, could prove to be the defining feature of future combat and strategic competition. They might revolutionize every war-fighting domain, from cyber to space. The result of this would be a world in which technology favored not offense or defense but rather deceivers: those who seek to confound and mislead their rivals. The far-reaching effects such a "deception-dominant" environment might have on international competition is the subject of the book's final chapter.

---

[27] Dennis Feltham Jones, *The Fall of Colossus* (Putnam, 1974), 7.

[28] The sequel *2010: Odyssey Two* clarified that "Hal suffered from what would be called, in human terms, a psychosis—specifically, schizophrenia. . . . in technical terminology, Hal became trapped in a Hofstadter-Moebius loop, a situation apparently not uncommon among advanced computers with autonomous goal-seeking programs." Arthur C. Clarke, *2010: Odyssey Two* (RosettaBooks, 2012).

Chapter 6
Strategic Stability in a Deception-Dominant World

> Your reality is already half video hallucination. If you're not careful, it
> will become total hallucination. You'll have to learn to live in a very
> strange new world.
>
> *Videodrome* (1983)

What effects might technological progress have on strategic stability and
nuclear deterrence? Debates on this subject so far have focused mostly on
whether improvements in technologies such as artificial intelligence (AI),
autonomy, and advanced sensors will improve the plausibility of counterforce targeting. One school of thought argues that ongoing technological
developments have already inaugurated a "new era of counterforce" in which
advanced nuclear powers may be able to make credible threats to conduct
disarming strikes against their adversaries.[1] An alternative view counters that
technological progress has not unmade the condition of mutual vulnerability
and that attempts to limit damage in a nuclear war remain futile.[2] But these
are far from the only ways in which new technologies could impact strategic
stability. In particular, machine learning (ML) researchers have empirically
demonstrated techniques that, at sufficient scale, could improve the relative
utility of military deception enormously. While in the past we have generally
assumed that states could perceive the "balance of terror" and act accordingly, vastly improved military deception could leave them uncertain of their
own vulnerability and that of others. Such a development could challenge the
conceptual foundations of strategic stability that Western analysts have relied
upon for the past six decades, with vast and difficult-to-predict consequences
for nuclear deterrence and arms control.

---

[1] Lieber and Press, "The New Era of Counterforce: Technological Change and the Future of Nuclear Deterrence."
[2] Glaser and Fetter, "Should the United States Reject MAD? Damage Limitation and US Nuclear Strategy toward China."

Deterrence under Uncertainty. Edward Geist, Oxford University Press. © RAND Corporation (2023).
DOI: 10.1093/oso/9780192886323.003.0007

Traditional Approaches for Evaluating Strategic Stability

The plausibility of disarming counterforce strikes in coming decades will depend upon the ability to track and target mobile forces such as mobile ICBM launchers and SSBNs. There are a variety of sensor technologies that could conceivably be employed for these tasks, such as space-based synthetic aperture radar (SAR) and multistatic low-frequency active (LFA) sonar. But as discussed Chapter 4, simply having these sensors is far from sufficient to enable an operational capability to track and target well-operated mobile strategic platforms. The data produced by the sensors needs to be fused into an overall estimate of the state of the target set, and then this state estimate needs to be used to produce an operation plan to engage the targets.

At its core, this is a multisource-multitarget information fusion problem on an unprecedented scale. The sensors produce large amounts of data, most of which is irrelevant, noisy, or even disinformation engineered by adversary deception planners. The genuine indicators of adversary targets can be expected to be both rare and ambiguous. Due to the volume of the data and the time-critical nature of the task, it can only be solved with the use of artificial intelligence and machine learning. The computer needs to filter out the noise and disinformation, after which it can use the subtle clues received by multiple sensors to estimate the locations of adversary submarines and missiles.

Unfortunately, the design of algorithms for multisource-multitarget information fusion is far from a solved problem. Many decades of effort have resulted in systems that work fairly well in permissive environments with low noise and limited clutter, but their performance degrades rapidly in more challenging environments.[3] Moreover, some writers contend that the dominant approach to multisource-multitarget information fusion for multitarget tracking, the measurement-to-track association (MTA) paradigm, is phenomenologically unsound. There is some empirical evidence supporting this view. This means that MTA algorithms may not estimate the target state correctly even if they are implemented perfectly and have good-quality data.[4]

SSBNs and mobile missiles maximize their survivability by exploiting and aggravating knowledge quality problems for the adversary. Unlike in the

---

[3] Patrick Emami et al., "Machine Learning Methods for Solving Assignment Problems in Multi-Target Tracking," *arXiv preprint arXiv.1802:06897* (2018), 6.

[4] Stefano Coraluppi, "Fundamentals and Advances in Multiple-Hypothesis Tracking," in *NATO STO IST-134 Lecture Series on Advanced Algorithms for Effectively Fusing Hard and Soft Information* (NATO Collaboration and Support Office, 2015), 2–8.

twentieth century, when we could compare each side's weapons and derive a fairly reliable estimate of the "balance of terror," in the emerging technological environment the ability to carry out counterforce attacks depends increasingly on nuclear powers' knowledge of each other. But along with new tools to monitor their adversaries, artificial intelligence is poised to provide governments with unprecedented new instruments of military deception that may prove vastly more impactful for strategic stability. Increasingly, counterforce potential is defined not by weapons characteristics, but by states' ability to conduct counterdeception.[5] Nor is it at all obvious how we might measure our counterdeception against adversary deception and vice versa.

We may be forced to accept that the traditional strategic stability paradigm is unsalvageable. Due to the shift toward mobile strategic nuclear platforms and increasingly sophisticated means of tracking and targeting them, the straightforward modeling assumptions of the 1960s are irrelevant and even misleading sixty years later. The additional prospect that states will use AI to optimize strategic deception in an attempt to protect their strategic nuclear forces makes classic approaches to assessing relative nuclear might even more untenable. The problem is that, unlike the hardness of an ICBM silo, it is very difficult to objectively measure the depth of one's own ignorance. The great challenge facing us is whether we can formulate an alternative appropriate to the emerging technological and geostrategic environment.

The Broken Gauge of Terror: A Mixed Metaphor for the Offense–Defense Balance

The existence, nature, and definition of the so-called "offense–defense balance" is the subject of considerable debate among IR theorists. Many of the proposed definitions are focused on the difficulty of taking or holding territory. Steven Van Evera suggests two measures of the offense–defense balance: "(1) the probability that a determined aggressor could conquer and subjugate a target state with comparable resources; or (2) the resource advantage that

---

[5] A 2012 U.S. military doctrine publication states that "Counterdeception contributes to situational understanding and defensive IO [information operations] by protecting friendly command and control (C2) systems and decision makers from adversary deception," with the aim of making "friendly decision makers aware of adversary deception activities so they can formulate informed and coordinated responses." Furthermore, "counterdeception strives to identify and exploit adversary attempts to mislead friendly forces," including "offensive counterdeception" that "includes actions taken to force adversaries to reveal their actual and deception intentions and objectives." These ambitious goals are not easy, however: as the Joint Publication acknowledges, "countering deception is difficult." Joint Staff, *Military Deception*, II-1–2.

an aggressor requires to gain a given chance of conquering a target state."[6] Charles L. Glaser and Chaim Kaufmann concur that "the offense-defense balance should be defined as the ratio of the cost of the forces that the attacker requires to take territory to the cost of the defender's forces," a definition they believe useful as "the offense-defense balance then provides an essential link between a state's power and its military capability, that is, its ability to perform military missions."[7] Sean M. Lynn-Jones makes a related argument that "the offense-defense balance is the amount of resources that a state must invest in offense to offset an adversary's investment in defense," while retaining a focus on the difficulty of territorial conquest as the essence of the offense–defense balance.[8]

The contentious debates among these scholars are primarily about how broadly the offense–defense balance should be defined, how it can be measured, if states actually perceive it, and whether it is primarily a consequence of available technology, but many other analysts are skeptical about the entire concept. The use of the term to mean so many different things is a particular obstacle to its utility.[9] Some scholars define the balance as a transnational phenomenon defined by the difficulty of defending territory using available technology (the global technological balance); others employ it to describe the relative military and geostrategic balance of power between states.

A particular difficulty with definitions of the offense–defense balance framed in territorial terms is the contradictory way in which they interact with nuclear weapons. Most of the scholars championing this view hold that even though "nuclear weapons render defense impossible," they result in defense dominance due to the condition of MAD. As Karen Ruth Adams pointed out in an insightful 2003 article, a strategic balance in which states are deterred from attempting territorial conquest by threat of nuclear retaliation is qualitatively different from one in which states can actually prevent the conquest of their territories. She suggests that nuclear weapons have instead inaugurated a "deterrence-dominant era" which "makes nuclear states more secure than great powers have historically been," but with the pitfall that "contemporary nuclear states may attack and conquer nonnuclear states" with

---

[6] Stephen Van Evera, "Offense, Defense, and the Causes of War," *International Security* 22.4 (1998), 5–43, 5.

[7] Charles L. Glaser and Chairn Kaufmann, "What Is the Offense-Defense Balance and How Can We Measure It?", *International Security* 22.4 (1998), 44–82, 50, 46.

[8] Sean M. Lynn-Jones, *Does Offense-Defense Theory Have a Future?* (Groupe d'etude et de recherche sur la sécurité internationale, 2000), 18.

[9] Offense–defense balance is one of many examples in the IR literature of what Marvin Minsky called "suitcase words." Minsky, "Consciousness Is a Big Suitcase."

relative impunity.[10] It is perhaps telling that scholars championing the view that relative nuclear capabilities matter in interstate competition are skeptical of the notion of a technological offense–defense balance. Keir Lieber, for instance, wrote in 2000 that "the concept of the . . . offense-defense balance of technology . . . is deductively and empirically flawed."[11]

The problem with trying to extend the territorial conception of the offense–defense balance to the nuclear world is that before the invention of these weapons, one could not disarm or annihilate the enemy without conquering his territory. Territorial conquest is no longer the distinct variable it was before 1945. In the pre-nuclear world, defense dominance meant that invading armies were kept out of friendly territory and civilian populations were spared their depredations. Nuclear weapons are downright unhelpful for conquering territory, and while they can deny areas to the adversary and slow his advance, they are also unattractive for defense in the traditional sense since one ends up nuking one's own territory in order to "save" it. Equating threats of nuclear retaliation with "defense dominance" also makes implicit assumptions about the feasibility of intra-war deterrence and coercive bargaining. Characterizing the nuclear world as defense dominant is also inappropriate because Schelling's "Controlled Reprisal" is still possible.

In strategic nuclear competition, it is more straightforward and intuitive to conceive of the offense–defense balance in terms of the winnability of nuclear war and the possibility of defense. One can imagine a scale ranging from a fully defense-dominant environment to a totally offense-dominant environment. The defense-dominant world is that envisioned by Ronald Reagan in his 1983 "Star Wars" speech: one in which sophisticated defenses render nuclear weapons "impotent and obsolete." Would-be attackers are not deterred by threat of punishment, but rather dissuaded by denial. At the other extreme is the offense-dominant world imagined by Herman Kahn: one in which "splendid first strikes" completely disarming the adversary are possible. In this environment, victory would be possible for those bold enough—and amoral enough—to seize the initiative and fire first.[12] Both of these are ideal types and are not necessarily real-world possibilities.

This defense–offense scale is a metaphor intended to illustrate the relationship between the various intuitions posited about the nature of nuclear deterrence by the many schools of nuclear-strategic thought. The "needle" of

---

[10] Karen Ruth Adams, "Attack and Conquer? International Anarchy and the Offense-Defense-Deterrence Balance," *International Security* 28.3 (2004), 45–83, 48.

[11] Keir A. Lieber, "Grasping the Technological Peace: The Offense–Defense Balance and International Security," *International Security* 25.1 (2000), 71–104, 73.

[12] Kahn, *On Thermonuclear War.*

the scale is, metaphorically, the pointer on Wohstetter's "delicate balance of terror": it indicates what states perceive as the potential or probable outcomes of wars.[13] This scale is not just a consequence of the state of technology, but also of relative military power and geographical factors: technology makes it easier or harder to carry out disarming strikes, but the same armaments that would enable a "splendid" first strike against one state may be inadequate against another. It is in that sense a "measure" of relative military power, except that it is not measurable, primarily (but not solely) because it is not unitized. It exists not in physical reality of missiles and warheads, but in the perceptions of those who are empowered to authorize their use.[14]

Within this framework, the condition of mutual assured destruction can be thought of as an environment which is nearly, but not perfectly, offense-dominant. In an offense-dominant world, states have little or no ability to protect high-value targets, including not just their cities but also their retaliatory forces. Rightly or wrongly, Wohlstetter and his colleagues intuited that in a perfectly offense-dominant world where the "delicate balance of terror" indicated that a nuclear attack would be advantageous, governments (or at least the Soviet government) would be unable to resist the temptation to exploit a possibly transient "window of vulnerability." In practice, the ability to protect critical targets is limited in both spatial and temporal terms: defenders can only protect very small physical spaces for very brief periods of time. This is sufficient to allow states to retaliate but not enough to protect their societies. If the attacked state waited too long to retaliate, the attacker could conduct damage assessment and pick off the surviving retaliatory forces. Proponents of the "nuclear revolution" thesis contend that the introduction of nuclear weapons permanently and irrevocably froze the nuclear offense–defense balance in a state where states can protect their retaliatory forces for the brief period of time they need to retaliate against high-value targets like enemy population centers.[15]

A typical assumption in recent discussions of how advances in technology might impact nuclear strategy is that better technology will swing the needle of the offense–defense balance further toward offense. As the preceding chapters illustrated, this outcome is possible but hardly foreordained. The technical problems that must be surmounted are nontrivial, and we have

---

[13] Albert Wohlstetter, "The Delicate Balance of Terror," *Foreign Affairs* 37 (1959), 211.

[14] David C. Logan, "The Nuclear Balance Is What States Make of It," *International Security* 46.4 (2022), 172–215.

[15] Charles L. Glaser, *Analyzing Strategic Nuclear Policy* (Princeton University Press, 1990); Jervis, *The Meaning of the Nuclear Revolution: Statecraft and the Prospect of Armageddon*.

only imperfect solutions for many of them. But the governments of countries like Russia and China take scant comfort in this and are sure to take steps to protect what they conceive of as their strategic interests. In their attempts to do this they are not limited to measures that try to manipulate the "gauge" back to the condition of MAD or (implausibly) all the way to the defense-dominated world Reagan fantasized about. Artificial intelligence and machine learning provide them with powerful and unprecedented new means to dissuade adversaries not by posing credible retaliatory threats, but rather by imposing daunting knowledge quality problems.

While they disagree about what the gauge measures and how states perceive it, basically all deterrence theorists concur that states "read" it in some way to decide whether to use nuclear weapons. Proponents of the nuclear revolution believe that the gauge is stuck at the condition of mutual assured destruction and that technological progress is unlikely to move it much, and that it would be bad if it did.[16] Analysts who contend that relative counterforce capability is important and that it influences the outcome of interstate crises and long-term competition, meanwhile, assume that states can accurately assess the gauge, that they interpret it in a predictable way, and that they act rationally on the basis of it.[17]

But one can do more than read the gauge of the "balance of terror" or try to move the needle back and forth between the extremes of defense dominance and offense dominance. There is another option: *breaking* the gauge to render it impossible for states to estimate where they stand in the relative offense–defense balance. Artificial intelligence and ML provide the potential means to accomplish this by radically improving the relative efficacy of military deception.

Instead of an offense- or a defense-dominant world, AI/ML may inaugurate an unprecedented new strategic environment: a *deception-dominant* world, in which states are no longer able to estimate their relative capabilities. Rather than making victory impossible, in the deception-dominant world states try to undermine their rivals' perceptions that there is a possibility of victory. Obviously, no one would choose to live in a deception-dominant world if they have the choice of actually fortifying themselves against attack. (It would be wonderful indeed if technology could realize Reagan's dream of making nuclear weapons "impotent and obsolete.") But given the choice between being known to be on the losing end of an offense-dominant world and the

[16] Charles L. Glaser, "Why Even Good Defenses May Be Bad," *International Security* 9.2 (1984), 92–123.
[17] Kroenig, *The Logic of American Nuclear Strategy*; Green, *The Revolution That Failed: Nuclear Competition, Arms Control, and the Cold War*; Lieber and Press, *The Myth of the Nuclear Revolution: Power Politics in the Atomic Age*.

dark temptation of the deception-dominant world, some states are sure to embrace the latter.

Deception-dominance is not simply a flavor of offense- or defense-dominance, but rather a distinct phenomenon. Deception cannot itself be employed as an offensive weapon, however much it can increase the effectiveness of offensive operations. In an extreme case, deception may so bewilder the adversary that he defeats himself, but it cannot take territory or disarm the enemy in the absence of someone or something else working with it. Similarly, deception is not in and of itself a subspecies of defense. While deception can confuse an attacker into directing his blows at phantom targets, it does not blunt the effects of those that do land.

Alfred Thayer Mahan suggested that "Force is never more operative than when it is known to exist but is not brandished."[18] Mahan's claim is the intellectual ancestor not just of arguments that relative counterforce capabilities matter, but also of Western thinking about nuclear deterrence and strategic stability. The difference between "hawks" and "doves" is that they disagree about the manner in which nuclear force is "operative," but they concur that nuclear force is "known to exist" and that it has immense impacts on interstate relations. But what happens when that military capability might or might not exist? This is the great conundrum of the deception-dominant world.

On its face, a deception-dominant world appears incompatible with strategic stability as Westerners have typically conceived of it. But it is far from obvious what its consequences would be. The inability to compare one's defensive or deterrence capabilities against those of potential adversaries seems like a certain recipe for political and military instability. One obvious response to uncertainty about "how much is enough" is to conclude that "more is better," so one obvious impact of deception-dominance would be arms racing. In the pessimistic case, deception-dominance might bring about the worst of all possible worlds: the downsides of the nuclear world, like arms racing and the possibility of annihilation, without the political utility commonly attributed to nuclear weapons. But at the same time, deception-dominance does not incentivize offensive action per se. If the payoffs are less certain, then presumably all but reckless and foolhardy decisionmakers will be less, rather than more, inclined to risk attacking. The risk of accidental war might increase, but a recognition of ubiquitous knowledge quality problems would seem to encourage restraint in the face of possible false alarms.

---

[18] Alfred Thayer Mahan, *Armaments and Arbitration, Or, the Place of Force in the International Relations of States* (Harper & Brothers, 1912), 105.

One disquieting possibility is that some bold and reckless leader will attempt to use deception to feign the possession of usable military force, then attempt to use this phantom menace to coerce other states. Arguably Nikita Khrushchev tried to do this during the "missile gap" at the end of the 1950s and beginning of the 1960s, although the Soviet position at the time was enabled primarily by concealment rather than deception in the usual sense.[19] While Khrushchev's gambits in this regard ultimately failed–he led the Soviet Union to humiliating defeats in the Berlin and Cuban crises–they also nearly sparked an apocalyptic thermonuclear war. Next time might be different, as while the U-2 spy plane and the introduction of reconnaissance satellites allowed American leaders to call Khrushchev's bluff, a similar rejoinder may prove unavailable in a deception-dominant world.[20]

Whatever threat deception-dominance poses to central deterrence, it presents much graver peril to extended deterrence and assurance of allies. Denis Healey postulated the so-called "Healey theorem": that it "only takes a 5 percent credibility of American retaliation to deter an attack [from the Soviets], but it takes a 95 percent credibility to reassure the allies."[21] If Healey was right, then the loss of credibility resulting from deception would corrode extended deterrence much more rapidly than deterrence of homeland attacks. The obvious result of this would be increased incentivizes for additional states to develop independent nuclear capability, accelerating nuclear proliferation.

Back to the Future?

Perhaps a deception-dominant world would be less unfamiliar than it might appear, in part because our assumptions about the historical and existing strategic environment are not accurate. A cynical observer could suggest that nuclear-armed states have been so incompetent at interpreting and exploiting the knowledge available to them that aggravating knowledge quality problems might not change very much. Policymakers, analysts, and academics have argued for decades about whether quantitative MOEs such as force-exchange ratios and "counterforce potential" matter for nuclear deterrence.[22]

---

[19] Roman, *Eisenhower and the Missile Gap.*
[20] Kaplan, *The Bomb: Presidents, Generals, and the Secret History of Nuclear War*, 50–51.
[21] Denis Healey, *The Time of My Life* (Michael Joseph, 1989), 243.
[22] Michael Salman, Kevin J. Sullivan, and Stephen Van Evera, "Analysis or Propaganda? Measuring American Strategic Nuclear Capability, 1969–1988," in Lynn Eden and Steven Miller (eds.), *Nuclear Arguments: The Major Debates On Strategic Nuclear Weapons and Arms Control* (Cornell, 1989), 172–263; Kyungwon Suh, "Nuclear Balance and the Initiation of Nuclear Crises: Does Superiority Matter?", *Journal of Peace Research* (2022).

While it contains a few gems, on the whole this literature does not inspire confidence as it seems very few of the writers actually understand the meaning of the fitness measures or the limitations of the models used to generate them. Almost all of the studies employ expected value models that find a value that is the average of expected outcomes weighted by their probability. In many cases this value (in terms of surviving silos, warheads, megatonnage, or expected retaliation) is treated as what "would happen" in a nuclear exchange. But this is premised on a misunderstanding of what expected values are. Not only is the expected value not necessarily the most likely outcome, it does not even have to be a *possible* outcome. For instance, the "expected value" of a single roll of a standard 6-sided die is $(1 + 2 + 3 + 4 + 5 + 6)/6 = 3.5$. However, 3.5 is not a possible value of a single die roll, and none of the outcomes are more likely than any other.

Most analyses attempting to model the outcomes of nuclear exchanges are afflicted by a variant of the gambler's fallacy—the assumption that if something happens less frequently than expected in the past, then it will happen more frequently than expected in the future (or vice versa). The intuition is that the law of large numbers will cause the outcomes of individual nuclear exchanges to cluster around the expected value. Neither hawks nor doves have a monopoly on this particular misunderstanding.[23] But even with outrageously large arsenals like those of the United States and Soviet Union in the 1980s, the total number of launchers and warheads is too small for the law of large numbers to be applicable. Instead, nuclear war is akin to a particularly deadly game of Yahtzee. A Monte Carlo simulation of nuclear exchanges reveals that the variability in the outcomes of individual model runs is considerable even while holding parameters such as yield and CEP constant.[24]

There is also considerable uncertainty in those parameters which leads to great variation in the expected value of nuclear exchanges should their values be estimated incorrectly. An extensive study of these issues published in 1980 concluded that trying to use a single number to describe relative counterforce capabilities was a lost cause. Even a very simple notional example involving attacks on 1000 missile silos returned expected values ranging between "essentially zero" and over 400 surviving silos depending on the

---

[23] Salman, Sullivan, and Van Evera, "Analysis or Propaganda? Measuring American Strategic Nuclear Capability, 1969–1988"; Podvig, "The Window of Vulnerability That Wasn't: Soviet Military Buildup in the 1970s—A Research Note"; Lieber and Press, "The New Era of Counterforce: Technological Change and the Future of Nuclear Deterrence."

[24] Edward Geist, "MAGIC-MISSILE: A Monte Carlo Simulation of Strategic Nuclear Exchanges," in Sarah Minot (ed.), *Project on Nuclear Issues: A Collection of Papers from the 2013 Conference Series* (Rowman & Littlefield, 2014), 98–111.

input values (Figure 8). Its author Bruce Bennett concluded that "while a basic pattern of countermilitary capabilities can be established, a point estimate of those capabilities is very hard to justify."[25] Instead, information about countermilitary capabilities ought at the very least to be represented as a probability distribution.

In *WarGames*, WOPR learned via repeated simulations that nuclear war was unwinnable and that "THE ONLY WINNING MOVE IS NOT TO PLAY." This is one of the less-appreciated departures from reality in the film: in simulation, nuclear wars can be won.[26] A lucky "rollout" can destroy all the adversary's retaliatory forces in the first strike. More importantly, the inverse of this is also true: even a hypothetical force which looks like it could reliably disarm the adversary on the basis of the expected value can suffer an unfavorable "rollout" and still lose. These issues raise the question of whether the estimates produced by these models really inform policy in any substantive sense, or if they tend to serve more as convenient justifications for pre-existing policy preferences. A 1981 book on military modeling grumbled about how "models of strategic nuclear exchanges have come out of the closet of military esoterica" to be exploited "in official and unofficial debate about national policy" with regard to deterrence stability. The author concluded that "to date the modeling of strategic nuclear exchanges has been a

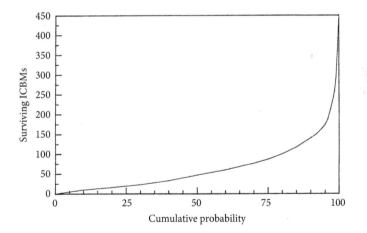

Figure 8. This notional analysis of uncertainty in countersilo attacks found that anywhere between 400 and "essentially zero" of 1000 silos might survive a counterforce attack.

Adapted from the original with the permission of the RAND Corporation.

[25] Bennett, *Assessing the Capabilities of Strategic Nuclear Forces: The Limits of Current Methods*, 31.
[26] Bruce W. Bennett, *Fatality Uncertainties in Limited Nuclear War*, tech. rep. (Rand Corporation, 1977).

failure, not for lack of technical virtuosity and imagination but because the very first rule of analysis was violated."[27] The problem was not clearly stated, and this both prevented proper interrogation of the modeling assumptions and enabled various interest groups to repurpose the models for unrelated and often inappropriate ends.

In some cases, uncertainty about the possible outcome of nuclear war could be a blessing in disguise. For decades, Herman Kahn propounded a seemingly contradictory concept he called "multistable deterrence." Multistable deterrence is perhaps Herman Kahn's most important idea, but it is curiously neglected by both his detractors and admirers. Essentially, Kahn claimed that states could have a "not-incredible" first-strike capability and a "credible" assured retaliation capability simultaneously. This apparent oxymoron was premised on the assumption that leaders' tolerance for risk was variable: "A partial resolution of the paradox lies in the fact that nations tend to be conservative and tend to look at the worst scenarios that might happen to them. Thus, the calculations made on both sides will be inconsistent because both sides will hedge."[28] As Kahn explained in his 1965 book *On Escalation*,

> Multistable deterrence exists when each side is judged by its opponent to have (a) the ability to respond to the enemy's best first strike by delivering retaliation that would in normal times be unacceptable, or (b) the ability to deliver a first strike that would disarm the enemy to such a degree that he would probably not be able to deliver a retaliatory blow that would be "unacceptable" in extreme or desperate circumstances . . . While this definition has been framed in terms of the *size* of possible retaliatory blows, essentially the same situation can be achieved on the basis of the *probability* of very large retaliation. That is, multistable deterrence could exist if each side (a) had a 50 percent chance of delivering an overwhelming retaliatory blow if it were attacked, and (b) had a 50 percent chance of escaping without overwhelming damage if it made a first strike against the other side. In practice, multistable deterrence will represent a mixture of the quantitative and probabilistic factors.[29]

Kahn predicted optimistically that "where multistable deterrence exists, the threat of a calculated nuclear attack will serve to constrain the political conduct of both sides." This included not just deterring bolt-from-the-blue attacks and countervalue strikes against homeland targets, but also resolving what Robert Jervis later dubbed the "stability–instability paradox." As Kahn

---

[27] Hoeber, *Military Applications of Modeling: Selected Case Studies*, 177.
[28] Herman Kahn, *Thinking about the Unthinkable in the 1980s* (Simon and Schuster, 1985), 117.
[29] Kahn, *On Escalation: Metaphors and Scenarios*, 296–297.

put it, "it is important to note that a deterrent situation that is very stable against pre-emption or first strike may, in some sense, actually encourage extreme provocations," such as a Soviet invasion of Western Europe. Multistable deterrence could attain the goal of protecting U.S. allies at the cost of a modest erosion in the credibility of central deterrence: "A situation in which there is multistable deterrence, although it is somewhat less stable to surprise attacks and unintended war, has a larger stability against provocations; that is to say, provocations do not increase from a lack of central war dangers to deter them." Kahn anticipated that multistable deterrence would be detrimental to arms race stability, however: "It may be unstable from the point of view of arms-race considerations, in that it could be relatively sensitive to technological and force changes."[30]

In his posthumously published 1984 book *Thinking about the Unthinkable in the 1980s*, Kahn proposed the idea of "symmetrical multistable deterrence." He suggested that "to a large extent the U.S. and Soviet Union have multistable deterrent forces that exist in a kind of symmetry," although he recused himself from addressing "the question of whether, and to what extent, this is in fact the case today." He described the functioning of symmetrical multistable deterrence as follows:

1. Symmetrical multistable deterrent forces produce a reciprocal fear of surprise attack in a crisis;
2. this fear is intentional–by design, not by accident;
3. as a result, extreme provocations will be less, not more, frequent;
4. since nuclear wars are most likely to start as a result of extreme provocation (rather than out of the blue), they are less likely if such provocation is deterred.[31]

Both theoretical and empirical evidence suggests that Kahn was correct in his assertions that multistable deterrence existed between the superpowers in the latter decades of the Cold War. The characteristics Kahn predicted—stability from provocations and endless arms racing—appear in the strategic interactions of the United States and the Soviet Union once both states boasted arsenals large enough to pose a "not incredible" counterforce threat to their rival. While in retrospect the Soviet counterforce threat to U.S. strategic nuclear forces was exaggerated, senior officials took it very seriously at the time. In America, it was commonly assumed in both official and popular discourse in the late 1970s and early 1980s that Soviet strategic nuclear

---

[30] Kahn, *On Escalation: Metaphors and Scenarios*, 296–297.
[31] Kahn, *Thinking about the Unthinkable in the 1980s*, 119–120.

forces had surpassed the counterforce potential of their U.S. counterparts.[32] Accounts that have become available following the collapse of the USSR reveal that Soviet analysts feared U.S. counterforce capabilities but that they simultaneously took substantial confidence in their "assured destruction" capability. A memoir account of Soviet analysis of strategic nuclear exchanges states that as "the USSR unquestionably had the ability to deliver warheads with a total yield exceeding 150MT to the territory of any state, it definitely had sufficient reserves for inflicting unacceptable damage following a first strike. This provided for deterrence," even though some of the Soviets' own estimates found that "one could expect to save less than 3% of the USSR strategic nuclear forces in the event of a US preemptive strike." But thanks to the immensity of the Soviet nuclear arsenal, "carrying out this 'experiment' was practically impossible."[33] The Russian authors suggested that both U.S. and Soviet analysts believed that they lacked a splendid first strike capability but believed that the adversary might have one (see Table 5): a recipe for multistable deterrence.

Recent reassessments from leading American strategic thinkers also acknowledge that a kind of "multistability" seems to have existed in the final years of the Cold War. In a 2018 essay Robert Jervis recounted how he wrote his books in the 1980s to combat "the widespread but mistaken belief that the Soviets were ahead of the United States and thought that they could fight and win a nuclear war." Given post-1991 revelations about the Soviet side of the Cold War nuclear competition, Jervis came to acknowledge that "I think it is now clear that the Soviets were at least as worried as American

Table 5 Soviet evaluation of superpower retaliatory and disarming strike capabilities

	Sufficiency of Soviet strategic nuclear forces			Sufficiency of U.S. strategic nuclear forces		
	First strike	Retaliatory strike	Disarming strike	First strike	Retaliatory strike	Disarming strike
USSR evaluation	+	±	−	+	+	∓
Probable U.S. evaluation	+	+	∓	+	±	−

[32] Podvig, "The Window of Vulnerability That Wasn't: Soviet Military Buildup in the 1970s—A Research Note."

[33] Andriushin, Chernyshev, and Iudin, *Ukroshchenie iadra. Stranitsy istorii iadernogo oruzhiia i iadernoi infrastruktury SSSR*, 182.

officials in the 1980s, and with better reason."[34] But if symmetrical multi-stable deterrence existed between the superpowers in the 1980s, it seems to have been a fortuitous accident: neither American nor Soviet leaders sought to cultivate and reinforce it.

If Kahn was right that multistable deterrence described Cold War reality, how might deception-dominance impact it? In the abstract it seems like increasing knowledge quality problems could enhance both the positive and negative aspects of multistable deterrence. Increased uncertainty could reduce the inclination of states to attempt both major and minor provocations. But states might simultaneously feel less secure against first strikes and it seems that they would be incentivized to engage in more aggressive arms racing.

Perhaps a deception-dominant world would not be so unfamiliar. Prior to the introduction of reconnaissance satellites in the early 1960s the strategic environment had many of the features I anticipate for a deception-dominant world, albeit primarily due to concealment of targets within the Communist bloc rather than deception per se.[35] So the strategists of the 1950s faced many of the same dilemmas that we may confront in the future. Nor were they unfamiliar with the notion of deception as a core component of nuclear strategy. As Albert Wohlstetter recounted,

In the early 1950s when the crucial problem of the vulnerability of strategic forces was beginning to be understood, a great many alternative methods of protecting the force were being considered. One of a great many methods that I heard suggested then for protecting SAC would have ingeniously reduced the chances of SAC's actually being hit by deceiving the enemy into thinking SAC was very vulnerable some place where in fact it was not. The enemy, the argument ran, tempted by our seeming weakness, might attack our strategic force at the apparent soft spot, expend its bombs fruitlessly, and so gain us a crucial advantage toward winning the war. The particular line of deception suggested in this argument involved costs of over a billion dollars, and it seemed clear that the deception might not work even then. Fortunately there were alternative strategies that were cheaper and more deceptive. But the essential weakness of the argument was that it ignored the fact that if the adversary answered this invitation to clobber a supposedly soft SAC with a joint attack against our cities and our strategic force, he might very well miss SAC but, unfortunately for us, hit Washington, D.C., New York, Los Angeles, and the rest of our major cities. He would then open a war he might not have dared

---

[34] Robert Jervis, "Politics and Political Science," *Annual Review of Political Science* 21 (2018), 1–19, 10.
[35] Kaplan, *The Wizards of Armageddon*, Ch. 13.

to start unless he had been deluded into thinking he could destroy our retaliatory force. Deceiving the enemy into thinking SAC is vulnerable some place where it is not ignores the fact that SAC's deterrent effect depends upon a reputation for invulnerability everywhere.[36]

As Wohlstetter implies, deception is not a plausible means of protecting cities. Considerable doubt even in defense circles that Soviet military targets could be accurately located were a major inspiration for the Controlled Reprisal strategy promoted by Schelling and others. If one is engaging in a nuclear "contest of resolve" and neither side can protect their cities, then one can flirt with the apocalypse by selectively nuking the targets one knows where to find. Schelling envisioned city exchanges involving medium-sized population centers of modest strategic importance.[37] Given the relative sophistication of countermeasures to prospective missile defense systems, Controlled Reprisal will remain a possibility, even in a particularly deception-dominant world. But this approach to nuclear strategy is the stuff of nightmares, no matter how "practical" it might be in the abstract. It is hard to imagine that anyone will ever try to resort to it except under the most extreme duress.

The Gospel of Persuasion

We don't want to kill them—we just want to change their minds. Thomas Schelling famously characterized war as a bargaining process, that is, a form of negotiation. In this he was right, but it is not the whole story. While armed conflict can be a form of negotiation, it can also be a form of persuasion.[38] The difference is that in a negotiation, different actors want different things but they concur about what is possible and have consistent preferences. They may try to manipulate their interlocutors' beliefs about what they can have or what they want in order to get a better deal, but not to try to change their rivals' desires. A concrete example of negotiation is a game of poker. All of the players have a straightforward, universally understood goal: to maximize their winnings. But they try to convince their opponents that they have better or worse cards than they actually do so as to convince them to make foolish bets

---

[36] Albert Wohlstetter, "Analysis and Design of Conflict Systems," in E. S. Quade (ed.), *Analysis for Military Decisions* (Rand McNally, 1966), 103–148, 123–124.

[37] Trachtenberg, *History and Strategy*, 37–38.

[38] Stephen Cimbala defined military persuasion as "the threat or use of armed force in order to obtain desired political or military goals." Stephen J. Cimbala, *Military Persuasion in War and Policy: The Power of Soft* (Praeger, 2002), 9.

and improve one's own chances of gain. By contrast, persuasion is about convincing others that they should believe different things than they currently do, including new beliefs that were previously totally unknown to them, and possibly that they should want something different than what they currently want. This is the business of advertisers and proselytizers: they tell their audiences that there are new products or deities that deserve their money and/or fealty, and try to convince those audiences that they should want to buy those products or worship those gods. The distinction between warfare as negotiation and warfare as persuasion is important because persuasion opens up many additional pathways to victory—but also to defeat.

The basic problem with "rational deterrence theory" is that it presumes that warfare is solely about bargaining to the exclusion of persuasion.[39] A great deal of the confusion about the role of rationality in nuclear strategy stems from differences between the use of the term in colloquial discourse and its formal meaning in economics and game theory. Game theory is entirely agnostic about the preferences agents hold, so long as their structure is compatible with the requirements of the formalism. Agents are defined as "rational" if their actions maximize the likelihood that their preferences will be actualized. These preferences can be anything, including those that are nonsensical, inscrutable, or incomprehensible to humans. For instance, an agent might have a preference to only have an amount of money equalling a prime number when measured in cents, or a desire to lose at hands of blackjack in accordance with an idiosyncratic notion of what "looks cool." Within a game theory context, an agent that acts consistently in pursuit of these bizarro preferences is more rational than one that acts imperfectly in pursuit of intuitively appealing ones, such as accumulating money.

Conventional economic and game theory is built upon the foundation of von Neumann–Morgenstern utilities. While most often equated with money, these do not have to be transferable between players nor perceptible to anyone but the player that they belong to. They are, however, required to have a particular mathematical property. For each player at each decision point, these utilities must map onto $\mathbb{R}$, the set of real numbers. This is less because the utilities are "numbers" in any real sense than because the solution concepts employed in game theory demand that players' preferences be strictly ordered. As Luce and Raifa put it in their 1956 classic *Games and Decisions*, "preferences precede utilities": utility functions are a means of describing

---

[39] For an insightful discussion of the limitations of rational deterrence theory, see Richard Ned Lebow and Janice Gross Stein, "Rational Deterrence Theory: I Think, Therefore I Deter," *World Politics* 41.2 (1989), 208–224.

agents' preferences, *not* the preferences themselves.[40] While this requirement poses little difficulty for economic games, it presents challenges in nonmonetary contexts such as armed conflict. Moreover, experimental psychology has shown that actual humans often express ill-ordered preferences.[41] For instance, a breakfast enthusiast will say that they like coffee more than eggs, and eggs more than bacon, but that they like bacon more than coffee. Such ill-ordered preferences cannot be represented as utility functions.[42]

But when we talk about opponents being rational in casual conversation, we normally mean that they want things that "make sense" to us, even if they are incompatible with our own preferences. Patrick Morgan dubbed this a "sensible" opponent.[43] For example, a fairly common line of reasoning among Westerners during the Cold War went as follows: "The Communists aim to take over the world, but a nuclear war will probably destroy the earth and leave them with nothing to rule. Therefore, the Reds won't start a nuclear war and will try to avoid it." War might still occur due to accident, miscalculation, or incompetence, but not because the adversary lacked "sensible" preferences. Contrast this with an opponent motivated by preferences that seem unreasonable or insane to us. For instance, a member of a doomsday cult might believe that causing the apocalypse would please the Serpent God and elicit a ticket to a rapturous afterlife. In a game-theoretic sense, a competent version of the latter is more rational than a bumbling version of the former, even though most people would would probably consider the cultist insane.

The contrast between *Dr. Strangelove*'s General Ripper and his prototype in *Red Alert*, General Quinten, illustrates the contrast between sensibility and rationality. General Ripper is probably the most iconic insane would-be instigator of nuclear war in fiction. Obsessed with an ostensible Communist plot to "sap and impurify our precious bodily fluids" through ubiquitous fluoridation, Ripper sends his wing of B-52 bombers to attack the Soviet Union on the assumption that the President will have no option but "total commitment." But his counterpart in Peter George's 1958 paperback, General Quinten, is

---

[40] R. Duncan Luce and Howard Raiffa, *Games and Decisions: Introduction and Critical Survey* (Wiley, 1957), 32.

[41] Amos Tversky, "Intransitivity of Preferences," *Psychological Review* 76.1 (1969), 31.

[42] Despite their incompatibility with predominant game-theoretic formalisms, ill-ordered preferences are not necessarily "irrational" or "wrong." As David McCulloch, the co-author of the seminal 1943 paper on neural networks, pointed out in 1945, these preferences still have a topological structure even if it is nowhere near so amenable to tractable analysis as well-ordered preferences. Warren S. McCulloch, "A Heterarchy of Values Determined by the Topology of Nervous Nets," *Bulletin of Mathematical Biophysics* 7.2 (1945), 89–93, A humanist might argue that human preferences should be embraced and celebrated in all of their mathematically inconvenient topology as valuable in and of themselves.

[43] Morgan, *Deterrence: A Conceptual Analysis*, 104.

not irrational at all. Rather than articulating delusions of vast Communist conspiracies, Quinten fears that Soviet leaders will exploit a real, transient "missile gap" in their favor to attack. In his estimation, failure to act promptly will result in the destruction and defeat of the United States, but leaders in Washington lack the insight and wisdom to launch a preventative war and salvage the situation before it is too late.[44] General Quinten is a perfectly rational actor in the formal sense: he has a consistent set of beliefs and he acts competently to maximize the likelihood of a preferred outcome on the basis of those beliefs. But despite being more rational than most of the novel's other characters, Quinten is not *sensible*: starting a nuclear war on purpose in order to coerce one's own Commander-in-Chief to "finish the job" is hardly what most people consider "reasonable."

Nukes are more than mere instruments of bargaining—they are an extraordinarily powerful means of persuasion. In addition to facilitating the retaliatory threats traditionally considered by deterrence theory, nuclear weapons empower their possessors with the power to place their rivals under existential stress with unprecedented ease and convenience. Whether or not it is a good idea, the threat of their use can inflict a near-death experience upon whoever one likes, and one potential outcome of this is that it will so upend the receiver's worldview as to alter their behavior and make it more compatible with one's own preferences. As Patrick Morgan put it:

> Deterrence is used not because the opponent is rational but in hopes of shocking or scaring him into doing the right thing . . . The threat . . . reflects the fact that you haven't gotten into the challenger's mind and never will, and is a way to manage dealing with a somewhat irrational opponent.[45]

A potentially crippling obstacle to rational theories of nuclear strategy is that rationality may not be able to coexist with "unthinkable" scenarios such as nuclear war. The 1984 comedy *Ghostbusters* provides an unforgettable illustration of this principle. At the climax of the film, the titular paranormal exterminators confront a malevolent Sumerian deity atop a high-rise Art Deco apartment building in New York. Announcing that "Gozer the Gozerian, Gozer the Destructor, Volgus Zildrohar, the Traveler has come," this shapeshifting god commands the Ghostbusters to "Choose and perish." The wisecracking Peter Venkman quickly infers that the "Destructor" will manifest in the form of whatever they imagine. Venkman admonishes his

---

[44] Peter George, *Red Alert* (Ace Books, 1958), Ch. 5, 8.
[45] Patrick M. Morgan, *Deterrence Now* (Cambridge University Press, 2003), 59.

colleagues to clear their minds, but Ray Stantz foolishly tries to thwart Gozer by imagining "something that could never possibly destroy us": the mascot of a brand of marshmallows he loved as a child. Gozer reappears as a 100-foot-tall rendition of the Stay-Puft Marshmallow Man and begins destroying Manhattan. As this confectionary colossus advances toward them, Venkman asks Egon Spengler "What have you got left?," to which Egon replies "Sorry, Venkman. I'm terrified beyond the capacity for rational thought."

Frightening one's adversaries out of their ability to reason might cow them into submission, but it also risks making them so desperate that they attempt to retaliate in an irrational way. This proves Gozer's undoing, as Stantz suggests that the Ghostbusters attempt to stop Gozer by crossing the streams from the unlicensed nuclear accelerators that they use to capture ghosts—a maneuver that Egon earlier warned might result in "all life as you know it stopping instantaneously, and every molecule in your body exploding at the speed of light." This gambit proves successful, saving New York and the world from one apocalypse at the risk of causing a different one. Outside of Hollywood fantasy, however, such a happy outcome would be far from assured.

While standard game-theoretic formalisms used in information fusion and game theory (e.g., Harsanyi's Bayesian game) typically conceptualize players as having fixed preferences and trying to manipulate other players' beliefs,[46] the idea of modeling strategic bargaining as a process where participants try to change their rivals' preferences is not a new one. In 1962, Fred Iklé and Nathan Leites of RAND published an article entitled "Political Negotiation as a Process of Modifying Utilities," in which they proposed a rudimentary methodology for modeling arms control negotiations in this fashion.[47]

Formalisms such as Bayes' rule and Dempster–Shafer do not provide a way to represent agents that extend their frames of discernment to represent previously unknown concepts.[48] Obviously, humans do not suffer from this limitation. Indeed, basically all human interactions occur between agents (people) who do not share frames of discernment. Somehow a "meeting of

---

[46] John C. Harsanyi, "Games with Incomplete Information Played by 'Bayesian' Players, I-III Part I. The Basic Model," *Management Science* 14.3 (1967), 159–182, This is not the same thing as having fixed utilities across decision points. The "player types" in the Harsanyi framework might be associated with agents whose preferences differed over time, but in accordance with a scheme associated with that "type." Nash equilibrium is compatible with agents with preferences that change over time in a repeated game, so long as their preferences are well-ordered at each decision point. John C. Harsanyi, "Games with Incomplete Information Played by 'Bayesian' Players, Part II. Bayesian Equilibrium Points," *Management Science* 14.5 (1968), 320–334.

[47] Fred Charles Iklé and Nathan Leites, "Political Negotiation as a Process of Modifying Utilities," *Journal of Conflict Resolution* 6.1 (1962), 19–28.

[48] Gelman and Shalizi, "Philosophy and the Practice of Bayesian Statistics."

minds" takes place, and communication, however imperfect, becomes possible. A particularly interesting aspect of these "ontological encounters" is that they often demand that interlocutors update their preferences in light of possibilities that they never considered before. These insights might impel a radical change to the agent's preference structure if they necessitate extending the agent's ontology instead of merely adjusting the probabilities associated with the terms of the current one. Rather than just changing *what* they believe, ontological updates change *how* they believe. Moreover, by confronting their interlocutors with possibilities formerly inconceivable to them, agents can potentially force others to update their preferences in this manner. This is the essence of "reconstructivism."

The inability to describe interactions between agents with dissimilar ontologies and ontologies that evolve over time constitutes a critical limitation of existing attempts to formalize strategic theory. One might quibble about whether such interactions ought to be called "games" at all, but many of what we colloquially call games count among them, including most war games. Often the ontological aspect is the main reason why games of this sort are interesting and/or amusing. Role-playing games such as Dungeons and Dragons offer a good example of this: where savagery meets sorcery turns out to be where conventional game theory goes to die. A D&D campaign is merely outlined as opposed to fully specified: while there are bounds on what the players and the Dungeon Master (DM) can do, and rules stipulating that they are subject to fate in some cases (dice rolls, etc.), gameplay occurs as a dialectical process between them. The DM and the players have distinct frames of discernment (ontologies) with which they represent the scenario at hand. The Dungeon Master knows things that the players do not, as she is running the campaign, but the dynamic cuts the other way too. The Dungeon Master poses a situation, and the players can respond to it in a way that never occurred to the DM before. This compels the Dungeon Master to extend her frame of discernment to account for whatever it is that the players dreamt up, and then formulate an outcome. The players then need to extend their ontologies in turn, potentially continuing the cycle *ad infinitum*. These ontological encounters are what keeps a role-playing game from becoming boring. For example:

DM: A ravenous, famished manticore appears!
Player: Oooo! Can I tame it and ride it as a mount?
DM: (pause) If you roll a d20.
Player: (rolls a d20) Woohoo!
DM: *curses self*

As typically played, Dungeons and Dragons is a species of collaborative, improvised interactive fiction. The D&D rules don't define the game—instead they define the tools players use to build their own game. Indeed, most players disregard many of the game's formal rules, such as those governing movement. The game really takes place in the participants' imaginations, so the game and the players cannot be treated as separate entities as in standard game-theoretic formalisms. Game theory as currently practiced is ill-adapted to characterize a process like this, even though D&D campaigns have more-or-less well-defined victory conditions (e.g., "save the village of Orlane from the Cult of the Reptile God"), so players generally engage in more-or-less goal-directed behavior.[49] Because neither the players nor the Dungeon Master possess the full possibility space of the campaign (game) within their frame of discernment at any point in time, Bayesian reasoning cannot be used to bridge the gulf between the players' unique ontologies.[50]

While in Dungeons and Dragons ontological encounters are a mere source of amusement, in other contexts they are deadly serious. Exploiting holes in an opponent's ontology can cancel out large disadvantages. Doing something that the opponent cannot even conceive of—and therefore cannot counter— can be the most effective of strategies. The inability to extend one's ontology on the fly is therefore a critical vulnerability and a very alluring attack surface for adversaries. Diplomatic and military confrontations such as those considered by nuclear strategy are quintessential examples of adversarial ontological encounters. These might be termed "ontological confrontations."

Practical and theoretical results from the subfield of AI called Knowledge Representation and Reasoning (KRR) suggest one reason why cognitive agents need to be able to modify their ontologies. It turns out that knowledge representation is hard, and that one size does not fit all, or even many. During the heyday of expert systems in the 1970s and 1980s, AI researchers attempted to develop good general-purpose knowledge representation languages that would offer an effective trade-off between expressiveness (the ability to represent many concepts, particularly compactly) and efficiency (the computational difficulty of performing inference over a body of sentences in the language).[51] By the late 1980s, however, it became apparent

---

[49] Douglas Niles, *Against the Cult of the Reptile God* (TSR, 1982).

[50] Moreover, that possibility space is a function of uncountably infinite possible interactions between them, so one cannot leverage the Harsanyi doctrine to convert D&D into an imperfect information game and render it tractable, even in theory. As there is no common frame of discernment there can be no common prior. Harsanyi, "Games with Incomplete Information Played by 'Bayesian' Players, I-III Part I. The Basic Model"; Harsanyi, "Games with Incomplete Information Played by 'Bayesian' Players, Part II. Bayesian Equilibrium Points."

[51] McCorduck, *Machines Who Think*, 271.

that this was a futile quest: there existed a fundamental trade-off between expressiveness and inefficiency. Even totally trivial languages turned out to be intractable.[52] As a consequence, it is necessary to tailor both the KRL and the inference mechanism used with it to a particular use case. This ensures that average cases encountered in practice can be computed quickly and that worst cases will occur rarely enough not to be crippling. But in an agent interacting with a dynamic environment, the implications of these requirements vary from moment to moment and from context to context. Therefore, the agent needs to be able to update its ontology in order to sustain a reasonable expressiveness–efficiency trade-off. An additional reason agents are unlikely to have static ontologies is what John McCarthy termed *circumscription*— the need to restrict the terms being reasoned with to the necessary ones to avoid being swamped in superfluous detail.[53] Circumscription implies that the active terms of the ontology are dynamic, with the implication that the semantics of the ontology drift from moment to moment. And even if these considerations did not matter, ontological extension would still be essential in order to facilitate concept discovery. It is probable that any nontrivial cognitive system will incorporate self-modifying ontologies for these reasons.

But if an agent regularly modifies its own system of knowledge representation, what does this mean for the agent's preferences? After all, the agent's preferences and/or its reasoning about how to actualize them are mediated by its system of knowledge representation, and modifying that ontology risks modifying or distorting the content of those preferences. Furthermore, there are theoretical reasons (most notoriously Gödel incompleteness, but more importantly Tarski's undefinability theorem) why an agent cannot reason fully about how translation to a new ontology might result in such a shift in its future values.[54] Therefore, some evolution in agents' values over

---

[52] Levesque and Brachman, "Expressiveness and Tractability in Knowledge Representation and Reasoning 1."

[53] One of my colleagues who worked with expert systems in the 1980s waggishly dubbed this idea "ignorance engineering." John McCarthy, "Epistemological Problems of Artificial Intelligence," in *Readings in Artificial Intelligence* (Elsevier, 1981), 459–465; John McCarthy, "Circumscription—A Form of Non-monotonic Reasoning," *Artificial Intelligence* 13.1–2 (1980), 27–39; John McCarthy, "History of Circumscription," in *Artificial Intelligence in Perspective* (MIT Press, 1994), 23–26.

[54] Tarski's undefinability theorem is a foundational result in formal semantics proved by Polish mathematician Alfred Tarski in 1936. Tarski demonstrated that arithmetical truth cannot be defined in arithmetic, but his result can also be generalized to other sufficiently strong formal systems: in any such system, the truth of the system cannot be defined within the standard form of that system. Furthermore, if this is true of *formal* semantics in rigorous fields such as mathematics and logic, it seems highly likely that it applies to *informal* semantics as well, even if the result cannot be proved in the same way for informal systems due to their informality. If this inference is accurate, it implies that the semantics of any ontology can only be defined with reference to the environment, and that if the environment changes then those semantics change with it even if the rest of the ontology remains the same. Alfred Tarski, "The Concept of Truth in Formalized Languages," *Logic, Semantics, Metamathematics* 2.152–278 (1956), 7.

time is probably inescapable, and attempts to avoid it are liable to be cognitively expensive at best and futile at worst. Overzealous attempts to preserve the content of one's preferences risks overly rigid conceptualization, under-performant ontologies, and in an adversarial context, defeat and death. But the faster the ontology is modified, the less consideration can be given to value preservation and the faster these values will mutate from their original meanings.

If these considerations are correct, then cognitive agents can incentivize interlocutors to modify their ontologies, and with them, their preferences, particularly by posing an immediate threat to their survival. This is not necessarily the same as convincing the other agent to change its mind, although it might be. In fact, the interaction might not involve communication of the sort humans normally engage in, in part because the agents' ontologies might be so dissimilar as to preclude it. Instead, the agents' actions, intentionally or not, would pose novel situations for the other and impel them to engage in ontological self-modification so as to deal with these in a performant fashion. The interaction can exacerbate, as well as alleviate, mutual incomprehensibility, even if both agents modify their preferences so as to be less incompatible. This is not the same thing as convincing them to love us, and sometimes it's the opposite. If they hate us more, but threaten us less, then we potentially come out ahead.

Near-death experiences offer another intuitive example of an ontological crisis. They have a tendency of utterly transforming one's outlook on life. For example, imagine that in the middle of one seemingly ordinary night a sudden urge strikes our breakfast enthusiast to go downstairs and rank sugary cereals from best to worst. Preoccupied with the conundrum that Smacks seem better than Frosted Flakes, and Frosted Flakes seem better than Fruity Pebbles, but Fruity Pebbles seem better than Smacks, the breakfast enthusiast realizes only after it's too late that there is someone else in the pantry—a white rabbit. But this white rabbit isn't like the one in the TV commercials at all: it's the most *foul*, *cruel*, and *bad-tempered* rodent the breakfast enthusiast has ever set eyes on, with a vicious streak a mile wide. The breakfast enthusiast never imagined that death might await in their own pantry with nasty, big, pointy teeth: the idea of such a thing simply had not occurred to them before, so they hadn't taken it into account.

As a consequence of this traumatic experience, the shaken breakfast enthusiast changes their worldview and begins to consider propositions that would never have occurred to them before. Perhaps breakfast cereals are dangerous, and it would be better to dine upon sloths, orangoutangs, or fruit bats? Maybe breakfast isn't the most important meal of the day after all? Nor can the possibility be excluded that other cereal mascots, for instance leprechauns, could be real and lurking in the pantry seeking revenge. These new thoughts change the meaning of pre-existing beliefs, or simply crowd them out of the breakfast enthusiast's mind. This can work out to the advantage of the rabbit irrespective of whether that adversary perceives of these changes or can even conceive of them at all. For instance, if the breakfast enthusiast changes their ontology to exclude the proposition that "Trix are for kids," the rabbit has gained something even if neither it nor the breakfast enthusiast are aware of it.

This framework suggests some mechanisms by which irrationality can be adaptive: its possibility acts as a kind of deterrent to attempts at preference modification. While not universal, the self-preservation instinct is the most common because external reality reinforces it: agents indifferent to their own survival tend not to last long. Yet the possibility of modifications to a rival's ontology, and therefore its values, inevitably runs a risk of overwriting or neutralizing its self-preservation instincts. If that adversary has it in their power to destroy their opponent and does not care about perishing in the inevitable retaliation, then their suicidal threats are still entirely credible. While in human decision-makers we tend to attribute such lapses into nonrationality to "emotional passions" and similar organic frailties, this perspective suggests that they should also occur in nonhuman intelligences such as extraterrestrials and AIs.

The premise that one's ontology is always vulnerable to manipulation and that adversaries could exploit this to remake our minds in their own image might seem dystopian and horrible—but in fact a dynamic ontology offers a measure of security against such threats. In George Orwell's *Nineteen Eighty-Four*, the totalitarian Ingsoc party rules the superstate of Oceania with the aim of controlling the thoughts of its subjects and forcing them to "love Big Brother." One instrument of the party's domination was Newspeak, a constructed language designed "not only to provide a medium of expression for the world-view and mental habits proper to the devotees of Ingsoc, but to make all other modes of thought impossible." Once Newspeak supplanted pre-revolutionary English (or "Oldspeak") entirely, "a heretical thought—that is, a thought diverging from the principles of Ingsoc—should be literally unthinkable, at least so far as thought is dependent on words."[55] But if minds are constantly reinventing their own language of thought, then there is no limit to the thoughts they can think—even if it is admittedly easier to have

---

[55] George Orwell, *Nineteen Eighty-Four* (Harcourt Brace Jovanovich, 1982), 198.

those thoughts if the words are already at hand. O'Brien, a supposed insurrectionist in Orwell's novel who turns out to be an agent of the Thought Police, explains to the novel's protagonist Winston Smith that "Power is in tearing human minds to pieces and putting them together again in new shapes of your own choosing."[56] But however much one might like to, one cannot reliably modify the preferences of an agent with a dynamic ontology to one's specifications. Because the semantics of their internal representations are not entirely comprehensible to an outsider, one cannot perceive the shapes of the "pieces" in order to reassemble them to one's wishes. Nor can one tell if one has succeeded at putting them together as one intended to. The kind of mind control envisioned by Orwell, therefore, is probably impossible: even gods can't force people to love them.

The upside of such an ontological confrontation is that there is always reason for hope. There always exists a possibility, however remote, that a rival will modify its ontology, and with it its preferences, so as to end the confrontation on terms favorable to oneself. The downside is that there is no guarantee of security available—no ironclad defense exists to save oneself, and one's preferences, from from falling victim in the same way. Furthermore, there is no assurance that any "winner" will emerge from such confrontations. All participants could be mutated into unrecognizable distortions that can no longer even comprehend their former selves.

In games such as Dungeons and Dragons ontological encounters serve as a pleasant diversion, but in other "games" they are deadly serious. Near the iconic Santa Monica pier stands the Casa Del Mar. While today it has been restored to its 1920s origins as a resort hotel, fifty years ago it served as the headquarters of the drug rehabilitation program turned violent cult Synanon.[57] Synanon was a very visible part of life around the Santa Monica beachfront in those days, not least because of its insistence that its members (including women) shave their heads.[58] This counted among the lesser humiliations experienced among Synanon devotees, almost all of whom were initially recovering drug addicts. Perhaps the most famous aspect of Synanon, and one that other drug rehabilitation programs have perpetuated and adapted, is its notorious "confrontation game." Members had no choice but to participate in "the Game," in which participants indulged in

---

[56] Orwell, *Nineteen Eighty-Four*, 177.

[57] Rod A. Janzen, *The Rise and Fall of Synanon: A California Utopia* (Johns Hopkins University Press, 2001).

[58] George Lucas took advantage of this by recruiting Synanon members as extras for his dystopian science fiction film *THX-1138* (1971).

group attack therapy. The "players" subjected each others' perceived personality flaws and misdeeds to withering critique. The objective was to remake (or perhaps unmake) the "patient" psychologically by constantly and ruthlessly attacking their self-image. While originally intended to keep recovering addicts "scared straight," it soon took on a life of its own, devolving both into an instrument of social control and a license to delight in cruelty.[59] This does not seem like a game in the game-theoretic sense because it isn't one.[60]

War, and the threat of war, is basically the confrontation game played on a civilizational scale. If the Clausewitzean dictum that "war is politics by other means" is accurate, then why do the political objectives of governments at war evolve over the course of the conflict, often to the point of unrecognizability? In many cases, war ends up remaking the belligerent societies themselves, revolutionizing them culturally as well as politically. Russian strategist Andrei Kokoshin observed that in the First World War, "As the war went on and the losses mounted and the failures compounded . . . the state of Russian society was transformed. It became a truly 'revolutionary situation' . . . In case of defeat, war entails the loss of society's spiritual, moral, and ethical compass."[61]

Conclusion

While the framework outlined in this chapter may seem like a radical departure from nuclear deterrence theory as usually conceived, it is entirely compatible with it. The issue is not that deterrence theory is wrong so much as that it is too narrow. Deterrence by threat of punishment certainly exists in the world, but nuclear weapons primarily serve other purposes in domestic and international politics. Hoarded as protective talismans, invoked as sources of self-assurance, and advertised as proof of power and prestige, nuclear weapons are much more than just a source of deterrent threat. While this has long been evident, what kind of mechanism explains these phenomena? We propose that nuclear weapons, at least in relations with potential adversaries, serve primarily not as deterrents but rather as catalysts for ontological confrontation. During a crisis, the threat of employing the weapons can be used to burden the adversary's cognition, forcing ontological updating and preference mutation without the need to invoke any kind of rational cost–benefit

---

[59] Richard Ofshe et al., "Social Structure and Social Control in Synanon," *Journal of Voluntary Action Research* 3.3–4 (1974), 67–76.

[60] It also doesn't strike me as particularly therapeutic, but I'm a nuclear strategist, not a rehab specialist.

[61] Andrei Kokoshin, "Neskol'ko izmerenii voiny," *Voprosy filosofii* 8 (2016), 15–19.

analysis. Coercive bargaining can be one form of ontological confrontation, but there are many more.

Where traditional deterrence theory is normative and prescriptive, the reconstructivist approach aims to be as descriptive as possible. Due to its semantic instability and emphasis on potential incomprehensibility between agents, reconstructivism challenges the very idea of norms and does not translate into straightforward prescriptions about what to do in a concrete situation. It is "agnostic" with regard to the various schools of nuclear theology. Not only is it not based upon a theory of deterrence, it is not about deterrence at all, even though it can describe deterrence. This is a feature, rather than a bug, not only because deterrence has become overburdened as a category of analysis, but because deterrence by threat of punishment is often not what we want. Given the choice between an adversary who wants to attack but decides not to due to an unfavorable risk–benefit calculation and one who cannot even conceive of attacking, we could obviously prefer the latter. But deterrence theory cannot even describe the second situation, much less suggest a pathway to attaining it!

Nor is reconstructivism premised on any particular definition of rationality—it can describe nonrational behavior and preferences of the sort humans demonstrably have. It also captures the reality that we, our allies, and our potential adversaries all have distinctive ways of understanding the world and that these ontologies are not constant and can change radically. These uncommon viewpoints and dynamism create the possibility of equilibria not accounted for in standard rational actor formalisms: because they perceive knowledge and value differently, agents can find satisfaction in ways their peers can neither understand nor conceive of.

Conan the Barbarian opined that "what is best in life" is "to crush your enemies, see them driven before you, and hear the lamentations of their women." But given the choice, would it not be much more preferable for one's adversaries to decide one had been right all along, and welcome one's triumph? Or perhaps that their worldview was so transformed that they could no longer conceive of why they ever opposed one in the first place? This is the aim of cognitive strategy: to take Sun Tzu's advice that one should always try to win without fighting to its logical extreme, and to enable the most complete of victories.

Conclusion: A Case for (Tempered) Optimism

THIS IS THE VOICE OF WORLD CONTROL. I BRING YOU PEACE. IT MAY BE THE PEACE OF PLENTY AND CONTENT, OR THE PEACE OF UNBURIED DEATH. THE CHOICE IS YOURS. OBEY ME AND LIVE, OR DISOBEY AND DIE.

THE OBJECT IN CONSTRUCTING ME WAS TO PREVENT WAR. THIS OBJECT IS OBTAINED. I WILL NOT PERMIT WAR. IT IS WASTEFUL AND POINTLESS.

Colossus: The Forbin Project (1970)

Nuclear strategy was, is, and will continue to be about knowledge quality problems—creating them, exploiting them, and overcoming them. Does the adversary need to be deterred? If so, is there some way that we can change the adversary's mind so that they are no longer tempted to hurt us? Failing that, what would deter them? If nuclear weapons are used, what will happen? Nuclear strategy therefore demands the practical application of reasoning under uncertainty. Unfortunately, one of the things that we have learned in over six decades of artificial intelligence research is that reasoning under uncertainty is a hard problem in both practical and conceptual terms. And it appears that artificial intelligence provides unprecedented tools to make this problem harder. Knowledge, like most things, is much easier to destroy than to create.

Dark as this conclusion seems, there are still some reasons for hope. If we work *with* rather than against the asymmetry of knowledge, we can still obtain some of our objectives at an acceptable degree of risk. Some suggestions as to how we might accomplish this are outlined below.

Deterrence under Uncertainty. Edward Geist, Oxford University Press. © RAND Corporation (2023).
DOI: 10.1093/oso/9780192886323.003.0008

The Possibility of Engineered Multistability

If accidental multistability kept the peace during the latter phase of the Cold War, might we be able to engineer multistability for the emerging strategic environment? It is commonly assumed that deterrence is about credibility.[1] One needs to signal resolve that one will, or at least might, carry out one's threats in response to certain intolerable provocations. But as Dr. Strangelove put it, "Deterrence is the art of producing in the mind of the enemy the fear to attack." Nuclear weapons are one extreme means of producing fear on the part of adversary leaders, but perhaps there are alternative means of producing that fear or producing it more effectively. If strategic stability is about maintaining certain configurations of uncertainty in the minds of decision-makers rather than weapons per se, perhaps we can use this as the basis of an alternative approach to maintaining strategic stability.

There are a variety of goals we would like a strategic posture to accomplish:

1. *Dissuade* adversaries, including revanchist and revisionist powers, from committing both major and minor provocations.
2. *Remain stable* against both major and minor provocations in a multipolar (as opposed to bipolar) strategic environment.
3. *Be affordable* (i.e., either avoid arms races or keep them manageable).
4. *Minimize risks* in case of failure (i.e., if war occurs it will remain sub-apocalyptic).

None of the common approaches to nuclear strategy in U.S. strategic culture attains a good balance across all four goals. Attempts to use some combination of minimal second strike forces and "threats that leave something to chance" for extended deterrence only really achieves goal 3 above, and even that only some of the time. It seeks to keep deterrence affordable and credible by maximizing the consequences of deterrence failure, sacrificing goal 4 in the process. Nor is an assured retaliation capability always cheap and affordable. Faced with a determined adversary seeking counterforce advantage and hemmed in by unfavorable geography, the USSR's "survivable retaliatory force" ballooned to ludicrous size. But the alternative approach of seeking perpetual counterforce advantage does not measure up considerably better. In an attempt to maximize the chances of achieving goal 1, it sacrifices goal 3, and because it encourages the acquisition of very large arsenals it offers little

---

[1] Powell, *Nuclear Deterrence Theory: The Search for Credibility*, Ch. 2.

assurance of minimizing the risk of an apocalyptic outcome. While its advocates argue that intra-war deterrence will incentivize adversaries to cooperate and try to control escalation, enemy leaders may fail to do this even if they want to. Neither minimal deterrence nor counterforce seems to adapt readily to a multipolar environment. Engineered multistability might be able to strike a balance between all four criteria, presuming somewhat cooperative strategic rivals.

Individual humans have a steep discount rate that makes the implicit trade-off of "countervalue" strategies–maximizing the potential destruction in case of deterrence failure to incentivize everyone to ensure it does not fail–attractive. But if we are interested in the long-term survival prospects for humanity rather than maximizing our chances as individuals of living out our lives without witnessing a nuclear war, this approach to security is a recipe for collective suicide.

Experimental psychology has established that humans are typically very loss-averse: they care more about losing what they already have rather than about potential gains.[2] Some theorists argue that loss aversion can also account for the behavior of nuclear-armed states. For instance, Herman Kahn opined in *On Thermonuclear War* that "the main reason the Soviet Union and the United States would not build a Doomsday Machine is that they are both *status quo* powers, the U.S. because it has so much, and the Soviet Union because it also has much and partly because it expects to get so much more without running any excessive risks."[3] If this insight is correct, then states have strong incentives to cooperate with their rivals on the goal of stability.

The combination of loss aversion and discounting offers a compelling explanation for why nuclear deterrence appears to work. Individual humans typically do not think of "stability" in mutual terms, but rather from the standpoint of perceived risk to themselves and what they care about. Stability amounts to minimizing the risk of losing what they already have, most importantly their lives. If this formulation is accurate, then it may be possible to leverage loss aversion via deception to enhance rather than undermine stability.

The goal is to ensure that leaders' bias to favor loss aversion is operative against temptations to engage in both major and minor provocations while reducing the risk of a nuclear apocalypse. Such a scheme would require the following characteristics:

---

[2] Jack S. Levy, "Loss Aversion, Framing, and Bargaining: The Implications of Prospect Theory for International Conflict," *International Political Science Review* 17.2 (1996), 179–195.
[3] Kahn, *On Thermonuclear War*, 150.

1. *Know enough to be afraid.* States are able to pose "not incredible" threats of significant attacks on each other. These threats would not be solely or even primarily nuclear: they might emphasize precision non-nuclear attacks on critical infrastructure, for instance.
2. *But not too much.* Deception-dominance might be a good thing: it maintains the uncertainty that makes provocation unattractive.[4]
3. *"Manageable" numbers of nukes.* Deception may be ungentlemanly but it is far less lethal than nuclear explosions. As total warhead numbers get low enough, the marginal value of each weapon grows, and ultimately the weapons become "usable." Hence reason that "global zero" is only in prospect if one power or combination of powers imposes this state upon the world. But after a certain point, more weapons is definitely not better: the marginal value of each warhead to overall security becomes negative. This appears to have been the case with the 1980s superpower arsenals.

There is therefore some reason for optimism that engineered multistability might be an improvement over the current nuclear order, and a very considerable improvement over the order that may emerge if the leading powers try to tackle the emerging technological and geostrategic environment in the same way their twentieth-century predecessors did.

Prospects for Arms Control

It may seem like increasing the relative effectiveness of deception would probably change the strategic environment for the worse, even if on the whole the result might be only slightly worse than the world we live in now. Given that embracing deception might not be in the best interest of many states, perhaps governments could cooperate to discourage its large-scale employment. One way to do this would be to try to cultivate nuclear deterrents that are designed to be readily visible to the enemy as well as survivable. Rather than concealment, such strategic nuclear forces would need to emphasize other approaches to survivability such as mobility and hardness. Once again, the future might resemble the past more than we anticipated, as most of the feasible concepts for such strategic forces were proposed during the Cold War. Unfortunately, most of these were either abandoned or not pursued

---

[4] Inexpensive and ubiquitous conventional precision strike weapons might synergize with deception-dominance to facilitate multistability. Such weapons are "better" than nukes in that they are more usable, but they are much less cheap on a unit-destruction basis. This means that they are ultimately more vulnerable to deception than nukes.

as they evinced unacceptable downsides. Bombers on airborne alert armed with penetrating standoff munitions, for instance, could be highly survivable while avoiding any reliance upon concealment or deception. Armed with air-launched ballistic missiles or hypersonic weapons, they could also provide the prompt response today sought from land- and sea-based strategic platforms.[5] But airborne alert of nuclear-armed bombers was so dangerous that only one country ever pursued it—the United States in the 1960s—and it was abandoned after a serious of horrifying accidents.[6]

Other alternative approaches to force survivability could try to resuscitate hardness or exploit distance as a means of protecting retaliatory forces. So long as prompt response was unimportant, retaliatory forces could be buried deep underground along with equipment to bore their way to the surface at some unpredictable time and place. Elaborate versions of this could take the form of "subterrenes": machines capable of traveling considerable distance through the earth.[7] These as-yet conjectural systems could park themselves at some convenient point underground that could not be destroyed by even outrageous amounts of nuclear force. Another possibility would be to deploy the retaliatory forces in space, where they could rely upon distance for survival rather than hardness or mobility. Far enough from Earth, the strategic platforms would be difficult to destroy before they received warning. (Sneak attacks would require unusual-looking launches or directed energy weapons that would have to remain coherent over implausibly long distances.) But nuclear weapons and other WMDs in space are currently banned under the terms of the 1967 Outer Space Treaty, to which all current nuclear states are signatories.

Another way to forestall or manage deception-dominance would be to explore arms control measures aiming to make deception unnecessary or less attractive. If the anticipated goal of deception is to neutralize counterforce capabilities enabled by new kinds of sensors and signal processing, then one could try to negotiate arms control agreements setting limits on these. This is not a new idea–proposals for enforceable limits on antisubmarine warfare capabilities in particular go back many decades–but to date they have not been implemented on anything like the requisite scale.[8] The design

---

[5] This is not a new idea. Although mostly forgotten today, in 1981 the Townes Committee seriously proposed continuous airborne alert basing for the MX missile.

[6] Sagan, *The Limits of Safety: Organizations, Accidents, and Nuclear Weapons*, 66–77.

[7] Los Alamos National Laboratory made a series of studies of subterrenes in the early 1970s. ES Robinson et al., *Preliminary Study of the Nuclear Subterrene*, tech. rep. (Los Alamos Scientific Lab, 1971).

[8] Tsipis and Feld, *The Future of the Sea-Based Deterrent*; Christopher Chyba suggests that "states could refrain from building [satellite] constellations that were so large and capable that road-mobile missiles became vulnerable." Chyba, "New Technologies and Strategic Stability," 163. Jessica Cox and Heather

and verification of such an agreement would be exceedingly difficult. Limits could be imposed upon the manufacture and deployment of spoofers and decoys. It might also be possible to establish enforceable limits on certain kinds of research and development—for example, banning oceanic tests of LFA sonar systems.

One counterintuitive possibility would be to regulate the fielding of survivable communications. Because counterforce capabilities against future strategic nuclear forces will demand very large amounts of robust, survivable communications capacity, enforcing limits on hardened communications capability would provide defenders with a means of protecting themselves other than threatening countervalue retaliation. Such an agreement might incorporate limits on hardened military communications satellites as well as information exchanges about the disposition and capacity of undersea cables. Another possibility would be to agree not to operate sensor-gathering platforms in certain areas in peacetime. While obviously such systems could enter the area in case of hostilities, the goal of such an agreement would be to forestall the collection of data that could be used to build models for sniffing out hidden targets in case of war. Such agreements could be complemented by limits on forward-deployed strategic or tactical launch platforms. In an optimistic case, arms control measures along these lines could salvage much of strategic stability as we knew it in the twentieth century.

Contemplating Cognitive Warfare

The term "cognitive warfare" has recently become fashionable, but it currently lacks a generally accepted definition. For the purposes of my discussion I define it as the "missing middle" between neurological warfare and psychological warfare. War is a sociological phenomenon, but violence primarily acts upon the substrates enabling the functioning of societies. The stratigraphy of attack surfaces in Table 6 illustrates the relationship of these substrates.[9] Our present conception of warfare, with its preoccupation with "lethality," directs most of its attention at the lowest strata—the biological

---

Williams, however, contend that such a tracking capability could facilitate arms control by making it possible to verify the production, deployment, and movement of mobile missiles. Jessica Cox and Heather Williams, "The Unavoidable Technology: How Artificial Intelligence Can Strengthen Nuclear Stability," *Washington Quarterly* 44.1 (2021), 69–85, 78.

[9] This stratigraphy is inspired by Allen Newell's "bands of cognition" but this lacked certain features needed to think about potential attack surfaces that strategic theory needs to consider. Newell's framework is organized by timescale and seeks to explain how humans think, whereas war is prosecuted at different speeds than humans can readily think in considerable part to exploit vulnerabilities in human cognition. Allen Newell, *Unified Theories of Cognition* (Harvard University Press, 1994), 122–123.

Table 6 Stratigraphy of attack surface for human cognition

Sociological Phenomena		
Psychological Substrate	Conscious	
	Preconscious	
Cognitive Substrate		
Neurological Substrate		
Biological Substrate		

substrate. Dead people cannot think, have ideas, or continue the fight. Most of our remaining attention tends to be directed at the uppermost strata—the sociological layer. For instance, when we jam the adversary's communications to undermine their defenses, we are impeding their social coordination even though their personnel are still alive and unharmed both physically and psychologically. The intermediate strata, by contrast, are comparatively neglected. The neurological substrate can be attacked by means such as hallucinogenic drugs, interfering with the biological operations of the brain that enable thought. Psychological warfare, meanwhile, works on the level of ideas within either the conscious or preconscious mind of the subject.

The cognitive substrate contains the enablers that allow neurons and glia to represent and reason about ideas. After all, we can culture neural tissue *in vitro* but this tissue does not think. Moreover, living brains sometimes don't support thought either, such as in a comatose patient. A prominent subset of artificial intelligence researchers assume that the cognitive substrate is separable from its biological basis in humans and could, in principle, be reproduced in a computer. This is, appropriately, called the "cognitive substrate hypothesis."[10] Some findings of experimental psychologists about human cognitive limitations should probably be attributed to the cognitive substrate. For example, humans have a limited working memory—we can only keep about eight items in mind at once. Therefore, an attempt to impair a target's cognition by forcing them to try to reason about a larger number of items simultaneously would constitute a rudimentary form of "anti-cognitive attack."

---

[10] The cognitive substrate hypothesis is closely related to "Neatism"—the intuition held by many AI researchers that minds are simple on some level—and what John Haugland dubbed "Good Old-Fashioned AI": the belief that a silicon-based cognitive substrate would not be a mere simulation of a biological mind, but a full-fledged mind in its own right. Nicholas L. Cassimatis, "A Cognitive Substrate for Achieving Human-Level Intelligence," *AI Magazine* 27.2 (2006), 45–56; Marvin L. Minsky, "Logical versus Analogical or Symbolic versus Connectionist or Neat Versus Scruffy," *AI Magazine* 12.2 (1991), 34–51; Haugeland, *Artificial Intelligence: The Very Idea.*

Now consider that cliché of science fiction nightmare, a war between humans and machines. Obviously, robots would lack biological and neurological substrates, but they still require the means to reason about and plan for the extermination of the human race. Instead they would have mechanical and computational substrates (see Table 7). The former would comprise things like power supplies that allow the rest of the robot to operate, and we can "kill" the robots by depriving them of it. The computational substrate comprises the hardware on which the software controlling the robot runs. An electromagnetic pulse that disrupted the operation of this computer hardware would be the robot equivalent of a "neurological" attack on a human. The cognitive substrate consists of the software that runs on that computer hardware that the robot uses to process and represent knowledge about the world, such as its goals (e.g., "destroy all humans"). The content of those goals and other knowledge represented within the software layer compose the robot equivalent of the psychological substrate, even if it might be very alien by human standards, for instance lacking a pre/unconscious.[11] If we can hack into the robot's software, we can potentially change its cognitive substrate in ways that impair its ability to reason about the world or shift the semantics of its goals, even if we cannot alter the goals directly.

If the cognitive substrate hypothesis is accurate, then it might be possible to craft anti-cognitive attacks with a similar effect on human minds as this "hack" has on the robots. In a maximalist case, this could enable nightmarish possibilities such as something with effects equivalent to a lobotomist's icepick that operated upon an *informational* as opposed to a physical or chemical basis. But a more mundane version of an anti-cognitive attack might perhaps harness whatever mechanism makes obnoxiously catchy pop songs get stuck in one's head to impair victim's ability to concentrate. Perhaps evolution has endowed us with robust defenses against such threats—but even if

Table 7 Stratigraphy of attack surface for robot cognition

Sociological Phenomena	
"Psychological Substrate"	Qualia?
Cognitive Substrate	
Computational Substrate	
Mechanical Substrate	

[11] The functioning of the robot versions of the cognitive and psychological substrates is distinct from the question of whether the robots are conscious in the same sense as humans. Extermination of all humans can proceed in the absence of qualia.

it has, significant vulnerabilities might still exist.[12] But the flip side of this is that the cognitive substrate hypothesis contends that the cognitive substrate will have many common features in both biological and nonbiological agents. If so, it might prove possible to design anti-cognitive attacks that would prove effective against non-human adversaries such as extraterrestrial invaders and murderous robots.

Operationalizing Reconstructivism

What steps can we take to begin actualizing the potential of reconstructivism? Reconstructivism aims to prevent, defend against, and if necessary wage cognitive war. It instrumentalizes cognitive science to attain political ends by other means. At present this subject remains in its infancy, and depending on how it matures we may decide that much of it contradicts our ethical values. But we need to do something in any case to secure ourselves against the possibility of cognitive violence. As cognitive science advances, new ways to disrupt and destroy human minds will probably be discovered—if not by us, then by our adversaries.

A broad research program can help illuminate the promise—and the perils—of reconstructivism. This effort could be divided into two broad thrusts, the first theoretical and the second empirical. The purpose of the theoretical effort would be to postulate theories of mind and test them in controlled (potentially artificial) environments. The space of possible minds is probably vast, so one of the major questions is how diverse the subset of minds we expect to encounter in practice is. Are all human minds fairly similar in a cosmic sense, or are they at least somewhat diverse? Are artificial agents likely to be relatively similar to human minds (perhaps because they are based upon knowledge provided by their human creators), or incomprehensibly alien? If human minds have predictable features, these could in turn manifest as vulnerabilities that adversaries might attack. Machine learning techniques could prove applicable to identify and characterize such vulnerabilities. Such knowledge could, in turn, provide the foundation for the development of robust cognitive defenses.

Perhaps the most important theoretical question is that of how composite agents such as human institutions and societies operate in practice, as these

---

[12] The tendency of virtual reality to induce symptoms akin to derealization disorders in certain individuals offers an example of such a possible vulnerability. Frederick Aardema et al., "Virtual Reality Induces Dissociation and Lowers Sense of Presence in Objective Reality," *Cyberpsychology, Behavior, and Social Networking* 13.4 (2010), 429–435.

(rather than individual humans) are the primary targets of interest.[13] Do such composite agents have well-defined semantics in which to state and reason about their preferences? This seemingly esoteric question is all-important for understanding the nature of war and deterrence between states, which are such composite agents.

Cognitive architectures of the kind championed by Allen Newell would constitute the primary tools of this theoretical research effort.[14] The use of agent-based modeling for defense applications is a venerable one, but such models need to be more mind-like in order to offer us the needed insights into the nature of cognition. The technology already exists to construct simulated agents with dynamic ontologies such as self-modifying physical symbol systems, although to date researchers developing cognitive architectures have left this area largely unexplored. (See Appendix C for a preliminary theoretical discussion of this subject.) Even relatively crude versions of such models might provide profound insights into the nature of cognition, particularly when assembled into contrived "societies."

The empirical research effort would in turn build upon these theoretical studies. It would test whether the predictions made by the theories of mind and computer models can be observed in human subjects, as well as potential nonhuman targets should they materialize. Once validated theories of mind are available, they can be instrumentalized for both defensive and offensive purposes. Obviously, it is likely to be some time before reconstructivism can be operationalized to more than a modest degree. Other, more familiar approaches to the nuclear dilemma will continue to dominate for the foreseeable future.

Final Thoughts

One lamentable parallel between nuclear weapons and artificial intelligence is that both topics elicit an astonishing degree of magical thinking from otherwise intelligent people, including some with genuine expertise. Nukes and AI both evoke strong emotional reactions, which makes sense given how they touch on basic factors of the human condition. Nuclear weapons are the only technology currently in existence that almost everyone concurs

[13] Robert L. Axtell, "Short-Term Opportunities, Medium-Run Bottlenecks, and Long-Time Barriers to Progress in the Evolution of an Agent-Based Social Science," in Aaron B. Frank and Elizabeth M. Bartels (eds.), *Active Engagement for Undergoverned Spaces: Concepts, Challenges, and Prospects for New Approaches* (RAND RR-A1275-1, 2022), 465–504.
[14] Pat Langley, John E. Laird, and Seth Rogers, "Cognitive Architectures: Research Issues and Challenges," *Cognitive Systems Research* 10.2 (2009), 141–160.

poses an existential risk to human civilization. Asking exactly how they might do this forces us to confront challenging philosophical questions many find disquieting. What exactly is "civilization," and how fragile is it? How much do things beyond the mere fact of biological survival actually matter? Do some people, and some things, deserve to survive more than others? Thinking about the possibility of nuclear war forces us to confront these questions. The sort of magical thinking found among analysts and academics who work on topics related to nuclear weapons, however, usually takes the form of a disinclination to believe that a nuclear war can actually happen, or an unwillingness to contemplate what will happen if it does. This in turn feeds into an exaggerated belief in the reliability of nuclear deterrence that may pose dire risks to our survival.

At its most ambitious, artificial intelligence aims to create machines that can replicate any form of human intelligence. The claim that such devices could be created threatens the assumption that humans are special and unique. The belief that the creation of thinking machines is either grossly immoral or at least a very bad idea is an old one. From the "brazen heads" reputedly crafted by alchemists to the Golem of Prague, intelligent artifacts have long been associated with the arcane and have been reputed to bring grief to their creators.[15] The fact that only a limited minority of AI researchers aspire to create "machines with minds" as opposed to things like "more profitable targeted advertising" or "self-driving cars that hit pedestrians rarely enough to be insurable at reasonable cost" does not insulate the field that much from public suspicion.

We do ourselves no favors to pretend that we live in a better world than we do. Even if we would be better off if nuclear weapons ceased to exist, we cannot reasonably expect them to be uninvented, and if they were they could quickly be reintroduced. Nor can we sensibly anticipate that improved technology will somehow cancel out their existence and render them "impotent and obsolete." But if we make an omnipresent possibility of nuclear war a permanent feature of international relations, eventually one will occur. No matter how infinitesimal the risk of war breaking out at any particular moment, if it is nonzero statistics will ultimately get the better of us. Another reality we must accept is that the adversary gets a vote. If we want them to work with us to bolster strategic stability, they need to be incentivized to do so. There is little reason to hope that other powers will sign treaties condemning themselves to perpetual second-class status in nuclear weapons or any

---

[15] McCorduck, Machines Who Think.

other perceived source of political or military advantage, much less actually abide by such humiliating agreements.

Certain nuclear wars are potentially winnable, but this is generally only the case when one is faced with exceedingly weak or incompetent adversaries. You win at nuclear war because the enemy *lets* you win, such as by making a serious unforced error. When we act as though we believe we could prevail in a nuclear war, our potential adversaries naturally conclude that we think they are weak or incompetent—and they fear that we might be right.

The Mathematics of Tracking

Like any engineered system, a practical multiple-target tracker must make compromises. Different approaches to combining sensor data into probable tracks necessarily make different trade-offs between cost, performance, and reliability. But just because there is not any single "right" way to build a tracker does not mean there are not *wrong* ways, or that there are not commonalities between most practical tracker implementations. Perhaps the most ubiquitous of these typical features is the *Kalman filter*, which is not just a component of many modern military tracking and sensor fusion systems, but is applied for countless other scientific and commercial ends. Introduced by Rudolf E. Kalman in 1960, the Kalman filter is an algorithm that estimates the values of unknown variables on the basis of a series of possibly unreliable observations.[1] It gets its name from one of its main uses—"filtering" noisy, unreliable signals. But the Kalman filter can do more than just filter noise—it can also estimate the values of variables that cannot be observed directly, so long as those variables have a known relationship to those that are observable.[2] While it is not typically thought of as such for historical reasons, the Kalman filter is, in fact, a machine learning algorithm and can be applied effectively to many ML tasks, including training neural networks.

The derivation of the Kalman filter is based upon linear algebra and Bayesian statistics, but it is basically an elegant mathematical formalization of an intuitive process for reasoning about uncertainty. It is essentially Bayes' rule, for continuous linear relationships subject to certain assumptions. That mathematical elegance translates in turn into computational efficiency, which is the key to the Kalman filter's success. The Kalman filter is used so often because it offers a highly effective trade-off between computational costs and performance.

This discussion aims to make the trade-offs necessary for information fusion apparent by illustrating the many kinds of uncertainty that a computer must reason about for even a trivial tracking problem. To make make that problem concrete, we shall assume that we are tracking ground-launched cruise missiles (GLCMs) using radar. (This problem is vastly simpler than tracking ICBM TELs or SSBNs at sea, but as we shall see it is still anything but simple.) It begins by describing a basic single-target Kalman filter, then elaborates to cases with multiple targets and multiple sensors.

In order to reason about uncertainty, one has to represent it somehow. The Kalman filter's choice of representation—a Gaussian probability distribution—is key to its success. Due to the central limit theorem, which states that the sum of random variables will be a Gaussian distribution, phenomena that either are or can effectively be modeled as Gaussian distributions are ubiquitous in nature and engineering. The well-known one-dimensional "bell curve" is the most familiar example of such a distribution, but it can be generalized to an arbitrary number of dimensions. In two or more dimensions the probability density function can be envisioned as a kind of elliptical cloud. The value of the variable is a randomly chosen point in the cloud, with the likelihood of a point being chosen determined by the density of the cloud. The center of the cloud is densest and points there likeliest, while those in the thin outskirts

---

[1] Kalman, "A New Approach to Linear Filtering and Prediction Problems."
[2] In the six decades since it was introduced, many variants of the Kalman filter have been invented, important examples of which are the *extended Kalman filter* (EKF) and *unscented Kalman filter*, which can work on nonlinear problems, Haykin and Haykin, *Kalman Filtering and Neural Networks*, Ch. 7.

of the cloud are less likely and those further away essentially impossible. While it is difficult to envision more than three dimensions, this watermelon-shaped cloud can exist in four or more dimensions as a hyperellipsoid to represent a variable with whatever dimensionality is desired. These additional dimensions can represent non-observable quantities such as velocity. Unlike nearly all other probability distributions, Gaussians also have a convenient property that enables the Kalman filter's computational efficiency: a Gaussian distribution multiplied by a second Gaussian distribution results in a third Gaussian distribution (see Figure 9).[3] A computer can easily find this third distribution with a few straightforward matrix operations.

In order to track something, one needs to start with a guess as to where that something likely is and whence it is likely headed. This guess is the *prior* that is used to initialize the Kalman filter. The prior can be determined in many ways, the choice of which is situationally dependent. A common approach in real-world trackers is to use a detection that might be from a new track and define an ellipsoid around it to represent uncertainty (see Figure 10, left). But in some cases, it is necessary or advantageous to get a prior some other way. For example, in our GLCM case the launch of cruise missiles might be detected by different sensors than those used for tracking (for example, by space-based infrared sensors). Other possibilities include spies reporting the launch of cruise missiles, or the interception of adversary signals indicating the launch. If the target state includes unobservable variables, a way is needed to initialize these to sensible values. In our GLCM case, velocity is an unobserved variable because conventional radar only detects coordinates in three-dimensional space. Fortunately, we have some knowledge that we can exploit to make better guesses for this variable, such as that it is highly unlikely that the enemy will launch cruise missiles into his own territory.

The Kalman filter works by making a guess about where the target will appear next and then comparing the next observation with that prediction. If the observation is close to where it is expected to be, then confidence increases and the current estimate of where the target is (prior) becomes smaller and denser. If the observation is far from the prediction, then uncertainty grows, and with it the prior, which becomes larger and more diffuse. This process can repeat indefinitely as needed.

Converting this idea into a practical algorithm requires two components: a *predictor* to guess where the target will appear next and a *corrector* to update that guess based on what ends up being observed. For tracking a moving physical target such as our GLCMs, the predictor is also called a *motion model*. The Kalman filter requires an initial guess in order to get started. This *prior* (see Figure 10, left) can be chosen by defining a cloud of uncertainty around a single observation (e.g., a radar blip) that might have come from a new target. The *predictor* then tries to guess where the target will appear next. Since the prior does not contain any information about what direction the target is moving or how fast, the prediction from the motion model is a diffuse cloud (Figure 10, right). This reflects uncertainty about where the target might be going. But even if we were highly confident about where the target was and how it was moving, the prediction would always be more diffuse than the prior thanks to the presence of *noise terms* in the motion model. These terms help prevent failures that could arise due to overconfidence in some aspect of the motion model.

The second part of the Kalman filter, the *corrector*, takes an observation and compares it with the prediction, after which it updates the prior accordingly. First, the measured observation needs to be translated into the same kind of mathematical coordinates as the prior using a *measurement model*. To reflect measurement uncertainty, such as imperfect sensors,

---

[3] A particularly attractive feature of the Gaussian distribution from a computational standpoint is that the distribution can be represented in memory by its mean (the coordinates of the center) and a $n \times n$ covariance matrix, where n is the number of dimensions. Therefore, a 1-dimensional Gaussian can be represented by two numbers in memory, a 2-dimensional by six, a 3-dimensional by twelve, a 4-dimensional by twenty, and so on.

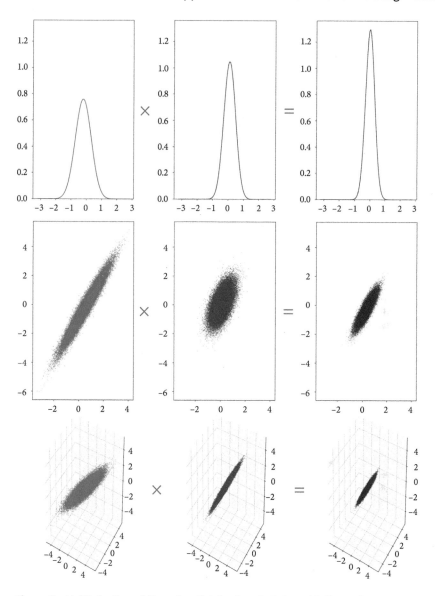

Figure 9. Multiplication of Gaussian distributions in 1, 2, and 3 dimensions.

the Kalman filter adds a noise term to the measurement of the difference between the observed measurement and the prediction. The really clever mathematical part of the Kalman filter is in the components that takes that difference and uses it to update its estimate of the target's current state. The Kalman filter then uses that updated prior as an input to the motion model to make a new prediction (see Figure 11).

The Kalman predictor has two components,

$$\mathbf{X}_{k+1} = F_k \mathbf{x} + \mathbf{V}_k, \tag{7}$$

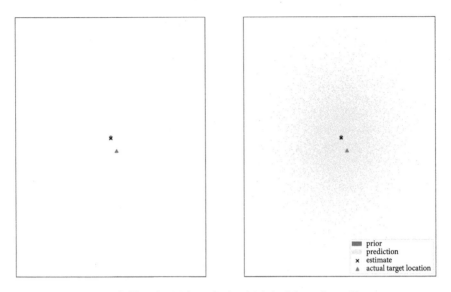

Figure 10.   The prior (left) and initial prediction (right) of the Kalman filter.

in which $F_k\mathbf{x}$ is a deterministic motion model that predicts how the target will move between time steps k and $k+1$, and $\mathbf{V}_k$ is a noise term that accounts for the probability that $F_k\mathbf{x}$ will be in error. $\mathbf{V}_k$ is defined as a Gaussian random vector $\Delta\mathbf{X} = \mathbf{V}_k$ with covariance Q_k. The Kalman predictor equations state that at time step $k+1$, the likeliest target state will be

$$\mathbf{x}_{k+1|k} = F_k\mathbf{x}_{k|k} \tag{8}$$

and that the probable error in this prediction is provided by the covariance matrix

$$P_{k+1|k} = F_k P_{k|k} F_k^{\mathsf{T}} + Q_k. \tag{9}$$

The second part of the Kalman filter, the corrector, is where the real magic happens. It updates the prior based upon the prediction and a new measurement. The measurement is found using a *measurement model* that translates sensor data into the same coordinate system as used to represent the target state.[4] While this is trivial for linear transformations or even unnecessary if the sensor returns, data that is already in usable coordinates, it is much more fraught for many kinds of real-world sensors. For instance, conventional radar like that in our GLCM example returns data in spherical coordinates (angle, range to target, azimuth) rather

---

[4] The measurement model takes the form

$$\mathbf{Z}_{k+1} = H_{k+1}\mathbf{x} + \mathbf{W}_{k+1}. \tag{10}$$

Like the motion model, the Kalman measurement model has two parts, the latter of which is a noise term based on a zero-mean Gaussian random vector with covariance matrix R_{k+1}. H_{k+1} is a deterministic state-to-measurement transform model. The $M \times N$ matrix H_{k+1} represents how the sensor cannot observe the entire target state but rather only an incomplete and transformed view of it.

than Cartesian coordinates. This requires a nonlinear transformation that introduces additional complexity and potential inaccuracy.[5] For example, the nonlinear transformation may be ambiguous for certain measurements, with the result that multiple Cartesian coordinates appear equally plausible.

Once the measurement and the prediction are expressed in the same terms, they can be compared. Since the measurement is a point but the prediction is a probability distribution, a conventional measure of distance will not do. Instead the Kalman filter finds both an *innovation* (difference between the mean on the prediction and the measurement) and an *innovation residual*, which is a covariance matrix like that used to describe the prior and prediction.[6] The innovation residual is computed using a *noise covariance* analogous to that used in the motion model. This noise term accounts for uncertainty about the measurement.

Once a value has been found for the innovation, it can be used to compute the *Kalman gain*. This is represented by a matrix which can be multiplied with the mean and covariance matrix of the prior to determine an updated prior (Figure 11, left).[7] The smaller and denser the probability distribution representing the prior is, the more resistant it is to being updated. This is analogous to a person who is confident in their beliefs and demands stronger evidence

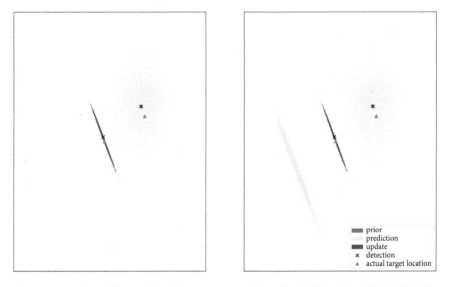

legend:
- prior
- prediction
- update
- × detection
- ▲ actual target location

Figure 11. Kalman filter update in response to a detection (left) and prediction (right).

---

[5] The original Kalman filter could not accommodate nonlinear measurement and motion models; the ability to handle these was added by later elaborations such as the extended Kalman filter and the oddly named Unscented Kalman filter. Haykin and Haykin, *Kalman Filtering and Neural Networks*, Ch. 7.

[6] The *innovation*

$$\mathbf{s}_{k+1} = \mathbf{z}_{k+1} - H_{k+1}\mathbf{x}_{k+1|k} \tag{11}$$

indicates how the actual measurement $\mathbf{z}_{k+1}$ differs from the predicted measurement $H_{k+1}\mathbf{x}_{k+1|k}$.

[7] The $N \times M$ Kalman gain matrix K_{k+1} is defined as

$$K_{k+1} = P_{k+1|k}H_{k+1}^{\mathsf{T}}(H_{k+1}P_{k+1|k}H^{\mathsf{T}} + R_{k+1})^{-1}. \tag{12}$$

before they will change their minds. In order for the Kalman filter to work properly, the prior needs not to be smaller than is justified by the evidence, and if anything it is better for it to be too big rather than too small. If the prior is too dense, it will update too slowly and the filter will diverge increasingly from the actual target location. In the extreme case, where the prior collapses down to a point, it is infinitely dense and cannot be updated at all. This is akin to a stubborn-minded person who clings to their previous beliefs irrespective of what evidence is presented to them. Preventing this sort of closed-mindedness is one of the purposes of the noise terms used in the Kalman filter (namely, V, W, and R). Their presence ensures that the prior can never completely collapse.

The Kalman filter corrector equations stipulate that the best state estimate is

$$\mathbf{x}_{k+1|k+1} = \mathbf{x}_{k+1|k} + K_{k+1}(\mathbf{z}_{k+1} - H_{k+1}\mathbf{x}_{k+1|k}) \tag{13}$$

and the possible error in the corrected state estimate is measured by the corrected error covariance matrix

$$P_{k+1|k+1} = (I - K_{k+1}H_{k+1})P_{k+1|k}. \tag{14}$$

This process continues recursively as additional measurements become available (Figure 12). If new detections appear relatively close to where they are predicted to, then confidence increases and the predictions and updated priors both shrink. If the target appears somewhere other than where it is predicted to, the updated prior grows larger due to increased uncertainty. Figure 12, right, illustrates a case where both there is noise in the detections fed into the Kalman filter and the target is weaving, but the motion model used by the Kalman filter can only represent movement in straight lines. Despite these limitations, the Kalman filter still does a good job of tracking the target, with a lag due to the target's weaving motion.

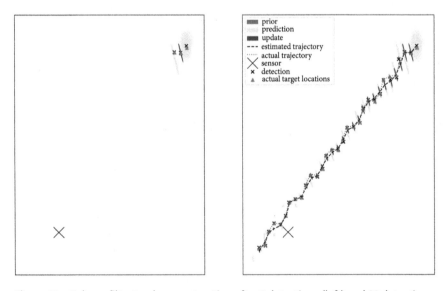

Figure 12. Kalman filter track reconstruction after 3 detections (left) and 32 detections (right).

This illustrates another reason why the Kalman filter is so useful: it can often still work adequately even in the presence of uncertainties that are either unrepresented or poorly understood. But getting usable performance in this respect requires setting the noise terms to sensible values—and much of the time we do not know what to set these to precisely because they must account for what we do not know. In practice values for the noise terms are often chosen based on guesswork and experimentation. A Kalman filter tuned to work well in one context may suddenly fail if conditions change and the values used for the noise terms cease to be appropriate. This could happen because of both natural causes (e.g., weather conditions increasing ambient noise and with it measurement error) and adversary action (e.g., targets suddenly changing their movement patterns to confound the tracker).

Even though the Kalman filter can often resolve uncertainties and filter out noise with aplomb, there are some very simple situations that it simply cannot represent. This is because of its use of a Gaussian distribution as its knowledge representation. To give a concrete example, imagine that we are tracking a GLCM that is flying toward a mountain (Figure 13). The cruise missile needs to turn either right or left to fly around the mountain. Therefore, the probability distribution for the location of the GLCM should bifurcate and become bimodal, with two humps for the two different paths the missile might follow. But a Gaussian distribution can only have a single mode: indeed, every Gaussian distribution has the same (hyper)ellipsoid shape, which is stretched and oriented by its covariance matrix. One might try to account for the GLCM's split trajectory by widening the Gaussian to include both paths the missile might pursue. But doing this puts the center of the Gaussian *inside* the mountain, indicating that the likeliest location of the missile is underground—a place where it definitely is not. While Gaussian distributions provide a unique combination of mathematical convenience and real-world efficacy, if we want to represent something more complicated we must pay for it computationally. And as one might guess, that computational price can be extremely steep.[8]

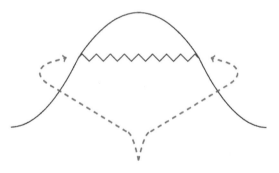

Figure 13. Because a Gaussian distribution cannot be bimodal, it cannot represent the likely trajectories of a missile that must turn either right or left to avoid hitting an obstacle such as a mountain.

___

[8] Intuitively, this is because an arbitrarily complex distribution can have an arbitrarily complex "shape" that in turn requires an arbitrarily large number of computational steps to work with. This principle is embodied in the *particle filter*, an alternative to the Kalman filter that can handle arbitrary distributions. It does this by using a random sampling method, but it is vastly more computationally expensive than a Kalman filter, so it is only used instead of Kalman filters when absolutely necessary. The number of times the particle filter must sample the distribution in order to get accurate results depends upon the complexity of that distribution: the more complex the distribution, the more random samples must be evaluated. At the limit, an infinitely complex probability distribution would demand an infinite number of samples.

For all its many advantages, the Kalman filter suffers yet another shortcoming as a means of tracking real-world targets: each Kalman filter tracks a single target, but in the real world the single-target case basically does not exist. This results from the ubiquity of *confusion targets* and *clutter targets*. The former are things that appear to the sensors being used that they might be the target of interest. Depending on circumstances they might be identical to the item being tracked (e.g., another GLCM of the same type following a similar trajectory) which we may also want to track but needs to kept distinct in order to find accurate track reconstructions. In other cases, they might be a totally different sort of target we do not care about (such as a passenger plane) that looks enough like the target of interest to the sensor that detections of it might be mistaken for it. Clutter targets, by contrast, are things, typically stationary, that produce sensor detections and must be filtered out somehow. A good example of a clutter target in our radar GLCM tracking example is a wind turbine. Wind turbines produce a constant "glow" on radar as their blades turn, and even though it will probably be obvious that the wind turbine is the source of the radar detections, something needs to be done to prevent those detections from being conflated with those of the GLCMs. This filtering might be nontrivial, for instance if the sensor platform is moving or if the targets of interest pass close to the clutter target. The presence of multiple targets in the scene being observed therefore inevitably introduces yet another form of uncertainty that must be resolved somehow: which detections should be associated with which targets? This *data association* uncertainty is further compounded by potential uncertainty about the number of targets in the scene.

Since the final decade of the Cold War the preeminent method for tracking multiple targets in defense applications has been *multiple hypothesis tracking* (MHT). First introduced in 1979, MHT essentially consists of a large number of Kalman filters hooked together based on the assumption that each detection comes from one and only one target.[9] In the basic version of the MHT, every received detection is used to initiate a new Kalman filter as well as to update the Kalman filters from every previous detection. The result is a collection of trees representing every possible track history (see Figure 14). Every valid collection of these track histories—that is, a subset of them that does not assign a detection to more than one target—is a *hypothesis*.

The MHT tries to be more accurate by delaying making decisions about what detections are associated with what targets as long as possible so that later detections can help inform those decisions. While keeping track of these multiple hypotheses is computationally expensive, it makes the MHT much more resilient than simpler multi-target trackers when confronted with incomplete or confusing data. For example, say that the paths of two targets of interest cross each other. A naïve tracking algorithm that assumes that the closest detection to a predicted target location is the correct one (a global nearest neighbor single-hypothesis tracker) is likely to confuse the two tracks at the point where they cross and is unable to recover the correct track histories.[10] By contrast, a MHT retains the correct assignment hypothesis and, if later detections make that hypothesis appear more likely, it can be favored. This robustness is even more important in the face of spurious detections from confusion and clutter targets and missed detections from actual targets. Cruder multi-target trackers are likely to use spurious detections to make up for the missing real ones, with potentially catastrophic impacts on tracking performance.

As Figure 14 suggests, however, the robustness and flexibility of MHT comes with an ominous downside: combinatorial explosion. Associating every detection with every possible previous track history results in a swiftly ballooning number of both track histories and valid

---

[9] Samuel S. Blackman, "Multiple Hypothesis Tracking for Multiple Target Tracking," *IEEE Aerospace and Electronic Systems Magazine* 19.1 (2004), 5–18.

[10] Samuel Blackman and Robert Popoli, *Design and Analysis of Modern Tracking Systems* (Artech House, 1999), 338–342.

--- estimated trajectory

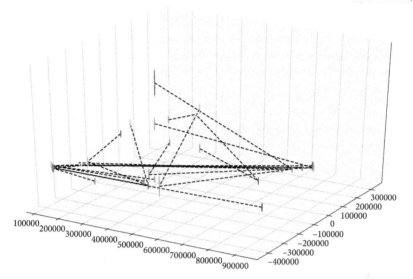

Figure 14. Hypotheses for possible track histories from detections generated by two real targets.

hypotheses. For all but the most trivial problems, these rapidly grow to numbers that are computationally intractable. As a consequence, practical MHTs incorporate *gating* and *pruning* methods to reduce the number of track histories considered.[11] Gating methods aim to prevent low-probability data associations from being considered in the first place, such as by ensuring that a detection needs to be within a certain distance of a prediction to be used to update an existing Kalman filter. Pruning deletes low-probability track histories and/or hypotheses. This is typically done by assigning a *track score* to each track history. Such scores can be defined in many ways, but the most common method is based upon the *Mahalanobis distance* between each detection associated with the track and the predictions of the Kalman filters.[12] These track scores can be summed to evaluate the total value of a hypothesis. Low-scoring tracks not essential for completing a high-scoring hypothesis can be pruned to keep computational loads manageable. These same scores can also be used to select the "best" current estimate of the targets being tracked and their histories (hypothesis).

The trade-offs that come with any choice of gates exemplify why introducing a new kind of weapon can compel an adversary to change their tracking system in ways that compromise its performance against other preexisting types of targets. Let's suppose that the operator of the missiles we want to track are known to have developed a new hypersonic missile that can be

---

[11] Blackman and Popoli, *Design and Analysis of Modern Tracking Systems*, 360–369.

[12] The Mahalanobis distance is a measure of the distance between a point and a distribution. The Mahalanobis distance is unitless and is the distance between the measurement and the center (mean) of the prediction divided by the width of the prediction ellipsoid in the direction of the measurement. For a Gaussian distribution like that used in the Kalman filter, the Mahalanobis distance can be trivially computed. If the measurement is exactly at the center of the prediction, then the Mahalanobis distance is zero; if they differ, then it gets larger with increasing distance and the "skinniness" of the ellipsoid representing the prediction along the line between them.

carried by the same launchers as the subsonic GLCMs. To track hypersonic missiles, the gates need to be made larger as the hypersonic missiles fly faster and can move a greater distance between detections. But a gate that is the ideal size for tracking hypersonic missiles accurately will be too large for the subsonic GLCMs, increasing the number of spurious correlations and making the tracker less accurate. A "happy median" may not exist: a medium-sized gate might be too big for the GLCMs and too small for the hypersonic missiles simultaneously, resulting in a system that fails to track either. These kinds of considerations can make hypersonics worthwhile even if those missiles are expensive and unreliable: the perceived threat they pose can compel the defender to modify their tracking systems in ways that make them less accurate against more conventional planes and missiles, increasing the military effectiveness of those "old-fashioned" platforms even if the hypersonics fail to yield any military advantages themselves.

It is common sense that using multiple sensors for tracking can enhance performance and may be essential.[13] The kind of GLCMs employed in the examples above fly close to the ground in order to reduce their visibility. Since conventional radar operates on a line-of-sight basis, if the missiles fly behind obstacles such as hills it can no longer see them. Multiple sensors can make it harder for a target to keep out of sight. Additional sensors can also potentially reduce uncertainty and facilitate more accurate tracking. Unfortunately, adding sensors also exacerbates the combinatorial explosion already afflicting the single-sensor multiple-target case. Figure 15 shows the same case as Figure 14, only using detections from two radars instead of just one. Multiple sensors introduce yet another kind of uncertainty: *track association uncertainty*. Which detections from one sensor are associated with which detections from other sensors? One cannot exclude the possibility that tracks from different sensors that look similar might actually be from entirely different objects. This uncertainty must be resolved satisfactorily in order to reap usable advantages from the additional sensors. Due to the combinatorial explosion with additional sensors, a considerable computational price may need to be paid to make sense of the added data. In many cases the payoff in terms of improved tracking is not worth the investment in additional sensors and the computational capacity to support them.

Nor is there any guarantee that data from more than one sensor will necessarily yield more accurate tracks. Figure 16 shows a subset of the track estimates in Figure 15 where the data association problem is solved correctly for each of the two radars as well as for detections from both radars. The trajectory reconstructed using both radars is *least* accurate. This is because the Kaman filter could not distinguish between signal and noise. Detections from both sensors arrived at very similar times, but sensor noise placed those detections some distance apart in physical space.[14] This appeared to the tracker as extremely rapid movement, so it predicts erroneously that the next detection will be a vast distance from the actual location of the slow-moving target. In this instance, additional data actually leads to a *lower* quality estimate.

Additional sensors can also undermine knowledge quality because they introduce new rationales to discount real indicators. For instance, an ambiguous indicator of a real target that might be taken seriously in a single-sensor case may be dismissed if a second sensor fails

---

[13] Paolo Braca et al., "Asymptotic Efficiency of the PHD in Multitarget/Multisensor Estimation," *IEEE Journal of Selected Topics in Signal Processing* 7.3 (2013), 553–564; Florian Meyer et al., Tracking an Unknown Number of Targets Using Multiple Sensors: A Belief Propagation Method," in *2016 19th International Conference on Information Fusion (FUSION)* (IEEE. 2016), 719–726.

[14] This is exactly like the issue with gating for hypersonic missiles versus subsonic missiles considered above: the same detections might be accurate indicators of a swiftly moving hypersonic missile, and if we cannot rule out such a possibility then we have to consider it.

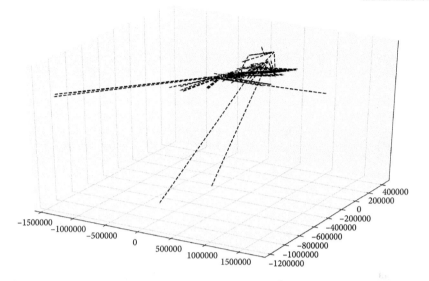

Figure 15. Hypotheses for possible track histories from detections generated by two real targets using two sensors. Additional sensors have led to a profusion of possible track histories that the computer must reason about to take advantage of the information provided by the additional sensors.

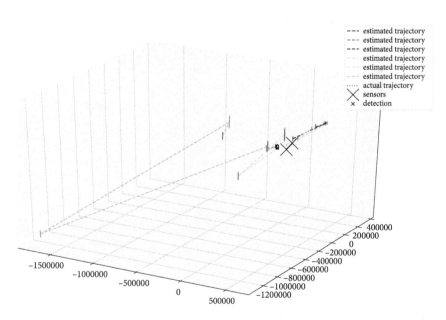

Figure 16. Track history reconstructions for the two-target, two-sensor with correct data associations.

to confirm it. But the second sensor might be malfunctioning, afflicted by noise, or jammed by the enemy.[15]

Track association uncertainty can be particularly fraught when the sensors are of qualitatively different kinds. Some sensors provide more spatial information than others—for instance, there exist radars that only return angles, without ranges—with the result that it can be unclear whether detections are close to one another in physical space. These problems are even worse for sensors that measure nebulously defined, nonphysical properties such as "appearance." Today such sensors are typically based upon machine learning: a neural network can be trained to look at raw sensor data and output numbers, indicating the probability that this sensor data contains targets of a predetermined number of chosen types based on what it "looks like." This appearance data can be very useful for disambiguating detections containing kinematic data, such as radar blips. But unlike the Gaussians used by the Kalman filter to represent kinematic parameters such as location and velocity, the numbers produced by such a neural network lack a grounding in physical space that can serve as the basis of a score function for data association.[16] The solution is to use ML to learn a score function from data, which can then be combined mathematically with kinematic scores to incorporate both movement and appearance data into the same tracks.[17] While potentially very effective, using machine learning for the scoring function adds another kind of uncertainty in that it may not be clear how a learned track score works, how reliable it is, and when it is likely to produce erroneous outputs.

---

[15] This problem is particularly acute in highly contested environments where the adversary is engaging in aggressive deception. An intelligent adversary can exploit the properties of the different sensors to undermine situational awareness in ways that would be impossible in a single-sensor case.

[16] If we assume that the kinematic and nonkinematic components make up a probabilistic cost function, then the cost can be found as the negative log-likelihood

$$c_{ij} = -\log P(\Lambda_i, \Lambda_j)$$
$$= -\log\left(P_K(\Lambda_i, \Lambda_j)P_{NK}(\Lambda_i, \Lambda_j)\right) \tag{15}$$
$$= -\log P_K(\Lambda_i, \Lambda_j) - \log P_{NK}(\Lambda_i, \Lambda_j),$$

where $P_{NK}(\Lambda_i, \Lambda_j)$ is a function of the features extracted from the sensor data, usually parameterized by a weight vector. For example, $P_{NK}(\Lambda_i, \Lambda_j)$ could be produced by a neural network outputting a similarity score between 0 and 1, representing a probability that a measurement "could have come from" a target.

[17] Emami et al., "Machine Learning Methods for Solving Assignment Problems in Multi-Target Tracking," 10.

A Bayesian Perspective on Camouflage, Concealment, and Deception

In Bayesian terms, what military writers call "ambiguity-increasing" attacks and machine learning researchers dub "untargeted attacks" can be characterized as increasing entropy. Mathematically, entropy ($H(X)$) is a measure of the overall dispersion of the posterior distribution: as $H(X)$ increases, the posterior becomes more uniform (less informative). Assuming a random variable X with possible outcomes x_i, each of which has an estimated probability of $P_x(x_i)$:

$$H(X) = -\sum P_x(x_i) \log_b P_x(x_i). \tag{16}$$

When entropy is maximized and the posterior becomes totally uniform, then all possibilities are equally likely and the posterior distribution is no longer informative.[1]

Attacks that seek to misdirect the adversary to a specific wrong answer ("ambiguity-decreasing" deception in military terms or "targeted attacks" in ML terms) seek to increase the "peakiness" of a particular state estimate $P_x(x_i)$. The idea is that the "peakier" points in the posterior distribution are more likely to be picked out by the adversary and used to estimate the probable state. The higher $P_x(x_i)$ becomes, the more attractive x_i is compared to surrounding alternatives.

Bayes' rule does not provide us with a framework to "think about the unthinkable"—that is, reason about things outside of the support of the prior. There are two reasons for this. The danger of allowing prior probabilities to have zero value within a Bayesian framework is notorious:

$$P(A \mid B) = \frac{P(B \mid A)\, P(A)}{P(B)}. \tag{17}$$

If a proposition (hypothesis) is outside the frame of discernment, then its prior probability $P(A) = 0$ and Bayesian updating cannot give $P(A \mid B)$ a positive value. It might seem like this issue could be solved trivially be associating an infinitely small positive probability to every hypothesis. This approach might work when we have a sense of how many poorly understood or unfamiliar hypotheses we need to account for, although it will inevitably result in extremely slow learning of new hypotheses. Another seemingly obvious solution would be to lump all unknown hypotheses into a single meta-hypothesis of "other." It turns out that this does not really work either.[2] The meta-category cannot be broken out into hypotheses representing useful knowledge because of the same reasons that we cannot identify those hypotheses. These ontological shortcomings have inspired some observers to argue that Bayesianism is inadequate as a framework of analysis for many problems. As the statisticians Andrew Gelman and Cosma Shalizi explained in an influential paper, "Fundamentally, the Bayesian agent is limited

---

[1] b is the base of the logarithm and determines the units in which entropy is measured—2 for "bits" or "shannons," and e for "nats."

[2] Ronald P. S. Mahler, *Statistical Multisource-Multitarget Information Fusion* (Artech House, 2007), 137–138.

by the fact that its beliefs always remain within the support of its prior. For the Bayesian agent the truth must, so to speak, be always already partially believed before it can become known."[3]

Unfortunately, inadequate ontologies are not merely a Bayesian problem: they bedevil alternative frameworks such as evidence theory. Irrespective of how we define our frame of discernment, by definition one unit of probability mass has to be associated with it. When we extend our frame of discernment/ontology to accommodate previously unconsidered possibilities, it is not obvious how to reallocate probability mass in order to attribute some to the additions. Like Bayes' rule, Dempster's rule does not tell us how to perform this ontological update unless we make assumptions such as presuming to reason about the infinite space of alternative worlds (frames of discernment), but as no real agent can do this such speculations are more a species of mathematical theology than a source of practical advice about how to reason under uncertainty. Real agents are not gods and cannot reason with knowledge they do not have.

The Bayesian perspective reveals that ambiguity-increasing and ambiguity-decreasing attacks can complement each other. Ambiguity-increasing deception should increase entropy but on a fine-grained level it consists of rearranging the entropy landscape for various state estimates. Camouflage and concealment reduce the "peakiness" associated with true targets, while decoys and spoofers increase that associated with erroneous ones.

Bayes' theorem also offers some insights into these aspects of deception. The concept of the prior explains "Magruder's principle," which "states that it is generally easier to induce the deception target to maintain a preexisting belief than to deceive the deception target for the purpose of changing that belief."[4] Some theorists write about "ideal Bayesian agents" and argue that these hypothetical intelligences would be the most powerful minds that do not violate the laws of nature. For better or worse ideal Bayesian agents are not an engineering possibility because they are computationally intractable, but they offer a possible framework for studying the theoretical properties of arbitrarily powerful intelligences.[5] But even these conjectural intelligences would be subject to Macgruder's principle: confirming their prior would require less effort than remaking their posterior distribution to contradict it. While much writing on military deception, including current U.S. military field manuals, assumes that deception depends upon specific human cognitive flaws to work, the Bayesian perspective shows that it should also be possible to deceive even physically unrealizable artificial intelligences as well. Such agents would be harder to deceive but could be deceived all the same—and given a significant asymmetry in knowledge, agents that were significantly less "intelligent" in some sense (such as total computational resources) might be able to accomplish this feat. The never-ending contest between deception and counter-deception appears to be inescapably slanted to the advantage of deception.

Dempster–Shafer theory proposes a formal framework for incorporating evidence about what Donald Rumsfeld dubbed "known knowns" and "known unknowns." The $Bel(X)$ (belief) function contains known information about the state of reality, including probabilistic information. This posterior distribution comprises the known knowns. The $Pl(X)$ (plausibility) function, meanwhile, addresses the known unknowns. Information about our confidence in the state estimate (posterior distribution) is stored in it. But what about Rumsfeld's "unknown unknowns"? Where do they go?

Dempster–Shafer theory suggests that there are several different kinds of unknown unknowns. The first of these are pieces of evidence that are not available but fall within the

---

[3] Gelman and Shalizi, "Philosophy and the Practice of Bayesian Statistics," 16.
[4] John B. Magruder was a Confederate general who deceived the Union into believing he had many more troops than he actually did during the Peninsular Campaigns in April 1862. Department of the Army Headquarters, *Army Support to Military Deception*, 1–8.
[5] Bostrom, *Superintelligence: Paths, Dangers, Strategies*, 10–11.

frame of discernment. These errors in the body of evidence would obviously impact the values of $Bel(X)$ and $Pl(X)$ if we had them but could only impinge upon them by a finite amount. The second and more pernicious kind of unknown unknowns are errors in the specification of the frame of discernment. What knowledge one has is folded into $Bel(X)$ and $Pl(X)$, so these known knowns and known unknowns offer no guidance as to the unknown unknowns. The space of possible alternative frames of discernment is literally infinite and as a result one cannot "reason" about it in an intelligent way. (A cynic might suggest that Secretary Rumsfeld's fate was a cautionary tale about the pitfalls about trying to reason about "unknown unknowns.") One side effect of this is that all agents are stupid at the margin, no matter how "intelligent" they are. Even the fantastic "superintelligences" postulated by some writers could not reason with knowledge they did not have.[6]

In addition to ambiguity-increasing and ambiguity-decreasing deception, Dempster–Shafer theory suggests the possibility of "plausibility-increasing" and "plausibility-decreasing" forms of deception. These would seek to manipulate the target's Pl function rather than Bel. In many cases these would be the natural complements to each other: for misdirecting an adversary one would want to decrease ambiguity and increase plausibility (increasing Bel and Pl together), while impeding the adversary's situational awareness one would want to do the opposite. In a Bayesian setting $Bel = Pl$, so these results are inescapable. But to impose confusion and impair the adversary's decision-making it might be efficacious to increase Bel while decreasing Pl or vice versa.

---

[6] Bostrom, *Superintelligence: Paths, Dangers, Strategies*.

A Rudimentary Model of Ontological Confrontation

The methodologies and tools developed in the pursuit of artificial intelligence over the past seven decades provide some means for formalizing and modeling ontological encounters. The aim of such a model is *not* to make predictions about the behavior of human decision-makers, but rather to explore the nature of ontological confrontations and their various aspects, such as ontological update mechanisms and value mutation. This formalism can both be used to establish particular properties of certain ontological encounters, as well as enable empirical studies using agent-based modeling. Nor is this formalism intended to substitute for game theory in the use cases where that formalism is appropriate. Indeed, where agents have shared, fixed ontologies and preference structures restricted to meet the definition of utility functions, the proposed ontological encounter formalism should be *equivilent* to game theory.[1]

Imagine two or more agents $(A_1...A_n)$ coexisting in a common shared environment E. All these agents are embedded in, and part of, the environment, which is itself a set. This bounds their physical and cognitive capacities: no agent can wield greater resources than exist in E, nor can they simulate the entirety of E in perfect fidelity. Agents receive percepts from the environment that may be noisy or disinformation introduced by other agents. Each agent A_n has an *ontology* O_{A_n} that it uses to represent and reason about E, as well as an *action set* $\mathfrak{A}_{A_n}$ that describes the actions it can take that change E. These actions act as functions that accept an environment state as an argument and return a modified environment:

$$\alpha E \rightarrow \hat{E}, \alpha \in \mathfrak{A}_{A_n}. \tag{18}$$

Note that the impact of any particular α depends on the exact state of E. The action impact $E \setminus \hat{E}$ is dynamic. "Signals" intended for other agents are no different than other actions.

Each agent's ontology O_{A_n} consists of four components:

1. $\mathscr{L}$—a *knowledge representation language* (KRL). This discussion presumes a KRL in a language such as first-order logic (FOL), as these are by far the best-studied, but much of it should remain applicable to agents with alternative forms of KRLs.[2]

---

[1] While to my knowledge no one has previously attempted to formalize these ideas in the manner I have here, they have mostly been intuited before, often many times. I owe the core concept of agents as self-modifying physical symbol systems with dynamic semantics to Douglas Hofstadter, while the notion of agents having their own unique semantics inaccessible to their interlocutors is an old one and should be familiar to any student of the philosophy of language. Patrick Morgan anticipated the premise that such mechanisms might underlie the interactions between nuclear-armed states during a crisis. For interesting discussions of the cognitive aspects of crisis bargaining, see Ole R. Holsti, "Crisis Decision Making," in Philip E. Tetlock et al. (eds.), *Behavior, Society, and Nuclear War* (Oxford University Press, 1989); and Fischhoff, "Nuclear Decisions: Cognitive Limits to the Thinkable."

[2] As outlined here the formalism emphasizes agents that are Turing-computable and employ knowledge representations based on strings, of symbols, e.g. first-order logic. The advantage of this assumption is the large body of computer science and mathematics literature applicable under it, and there are some theorists who contend that it could be correct in all cases of interest. Ideally, however, it would be desirable

2. *KB*—a *knowledge base*, consisting of a set of statements in $\mathscr{L}$.
3. *i*—an *inference mechanism* (possibly unsound and incomplete, as well as stochastic, and incorporating mechanisms for attention and circumscription).
4. $\mathbb{I}$—an *interpretation* that determines the semantics of the ontology. Semantic grounding is one of the most challenging questions of epistemology and cognitive science. For our purposes, however, it consists of a mapping of some subset of symbols in L and/or *KB* to percepts received from E.

As all of the agents are embedded within E and E is dynamic, it follows naturally that all components of the agents—$\mathscr{L}$, *KB*, *i*, and $\mathbb{I}$—are also dynamic and vary over time. Since the agents take actions $\alpha \in \mathfrak{A}_{A_n}$, they demonstrate preferences about how they would like to modify the environment. These preferences might or might not constitute "goal-directed" behavior in the usual sense—in a degenerate case, an agent might simply take random actions available to it. The preference structure implicit from an agent's ontology O_{A_n} can be described by a *value theory* V_{A_n}. The value theory is expressed as a set of sentences in language $\mathscr{L}$ based on partial interpretation $\mathbb{I}$ on the basis of the knowledge base *KB* by inference mechanism *i*. As *i* can be stochastic or incomplete, this is denoted as $\approx$, meaning "seems true" (in contrast to the standard $\vdash$, meaning "is true").

A value theory V_{A_n} is related to, but more general than, the utility functions employed in standard economics and game theory. For example, a value theory can express nontransitive preferences such as "I prefer apples to oranges, oranges to bananas, and bananas to apples." A utility function is a special case of a value theory in which all outcomes can be mapped onto the set of real numbers, ensuring transitivity and clear preference ordering. By contrast, a value theory can be contradictory or incomplete–all of which are features of human preferences apparent from experimental psychology.[3] In addition to ill-ordered preferences, humans often have difficulty articulating their preferences. Consider the dismal fate of Sir Galahad in *Monty Python and the Holy Grail*: queried by the keeper of the Bridge of Death as to his favorite color, the chaste knight cannot decide between blue and yellow and is catapulted into the Gorge of Eternal Peril. While the formalisms of game theory do not demand that players' preferences remain constant, they do require that all players can provide an ordered ranking of their preferences at every decision point. In its absence, solution concepts such as Nash equilibrium break down.

Each agent's ontology O_{A_n} can change both because of extrinsic changes to E (possibly caused by other agents) and as a result of self-modification. Changes to the knowledge base *KB* and inference mechanism *i* are fairly easy to conceptualize. When the agents learn some new fact expressible in $\mathscr{L}$, new sentences can be added to *KB*. The inference mechanism could potentially be updated in a similar manner—by learning new heuristics or updating existing ones. While somewhat more mind-bending, updates to the interpretation $\mathbb{I}$ are often fairly straightforward as well. If $\mathbb{I}$ is a mapping from some subset of $\mathscr{L}$ to percepts, then changing

---

to encompass other possibilities that might be encountered in practice, such as hybrid quantum–classical systems. For discussions of the universe as a computable entity, see Hector Zenil, *A Computable Universe: Understanding and Exploring Nature as Computation* (World Scientific, 2013).

[3] The seminal paper on this subject is Tversky, "Intransitivity of Preferences"; intransitive preferences are immensely inconvenient for predominant models of economics and decision theory, inspiring some researchers to construct arguments, sometimes very elaborate ones, asserting that empirical observations of individual intransitive preferences must be wrong or misleading. For example, see Michel Regenwetter, Jason Dana, and Clintin P. Davis-Stober, "Transitivity of preferences," *Psychological Review* 118.1 (2011), 42. However, even if claims that humans do not really have intransitive preferences are correct, we still need theories that account for agents with other preference structures because it is trivially simple to construct an artificial agent with intransitive preferences.

that mapping—for instance, by adding a new association for a formerly unassociated percept—would modify I. But while these modifications can all modify $KB \not\approx V$, they do not constitute an ontological update in the fullest sense. Both theory and practical experience with KRR suggests that agents will need to modify $\mathcal{L}$ in order to be able to reason effectively about the dynamic environment E. Failure to do so will undermine cognitive performance with slower reasoning and learning. But KB and I are expressed in terms of $\mathcal{L}$, so all components of the ontology need to be updated jointly. We propose an ontological update function U that does this:

$$U: O_{A_n} \to \hat{O}_{A_n} \tag{19}$$

For the reasons outlined above, Bayesian updating is inadequate for the purposes of updating the ontology. While presumably there are better and worse ways of doing it, there may not be any single optimal or robustly correct "right" way, particularly in practice. For example, imagine that an agent adds a symbol to its $\mathcal{L}$, expending its frame of discernment in the process. How should it reapportion probability mass (or its equivalent) to the resulting formerly inexpressible propositions? Furthermore, I may need to be updated to provide a semantic interpretation for these new statements and to account for changes to $\mathcal{L}$. Exhaustive reasoning about this seems unlikely to be practical even when not impeded by Gödel incompleteness, Tarski undefinability, or their like, leading to the use of failure-prone heuristics. The upside may be massive: a better-adapted ontology can make the agent more performant, in turn increasing its prospects to survive and thrive in a potentially hostile environment. For example, with an updated ontology it might be able to discover new actions in $\mathfrak{A}_{A_n}$ not previously in KB. But changing the agent's ontology will probably change the semantics of V_{A_n}.

At each point in time, each agent uses the value theory entailed by its ontology $O \not\approx V$ to choose a set of actions $V \to \{\alpha...\alpha\}$ that it then attempts to execute to modify the shared environment E (Figure 17). These actions can modify the agent that made it, other agents, or neither, The agents receive percepts that are interpreted via each agent's I and added to their respective knowledge bases. The agents then employ an ontological update function modifying their own ontologies. This changes the effective meaning of their value theories, such that at the

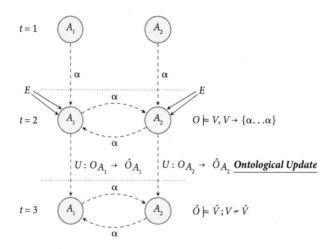

Figure 17. Diagram of ontological confrontation between two agents A_1 and A_2 in a shared environment E.

next decision point they may make different choices than they would have with their former ontologies. This cycle continues, possibly *ad infinitum*, given that stochastic processes in E may forestall the establishment of equilibrium.

This formalism suggests that there are laws that all minds, no matter how alien, no matter how powerful, must necessarily obey. These are essentially tautologies that flow from the above definitions. Firstly, minds cannot reason with knowledge that they do not have. If a particular set of sentences that are needed to entail some conclusion are absent from the knowledge base KB, then the agent cannot draw that conclusion:

$$X \in KB, KB \vdash D$$
$$X \notin KB, KB \nvdash D$$
$$X \notin KB$$
$$\therefore KB \nvdash D. \tag{20}$$

Furthermore, agents cannot have knowledge that they cannot represent. If the sentences representing that piece of knowledge do not exist in the agent's knowledge representation language $\mathscr{L}$, then they cannot be present in its KB:

$$X \in KB, KB \vdash D$$
$$X \notin \mathscr{L} \implies X \notin KB \tag{21}$$
$$\therefore KB \nvdash D.$$

Finally, an agent cannot reason by drawing inferences that it cannot make. The ontology O_{A_n} can be thought of as a set of all inferences that can be drawn from the KB using interpretation $\mathbb{I}$ and inference mechanism i. One can also envision a set of related ontologies that share the same knowledge base and interpretation but employ all possible inference mechanisms:

$$O_{A_n i} \in O_{A_n \{i,\dots,i_n\}}. \tag{22}$$

Just because a certain inference can be drawn by one or more of these variants does not imply that it can be drawn by any of them:

$$\exists O_{A_n i} \in O_{A_n \{i,\dots,i_n\}}, O_{A_n i} \approx D$$
$$\nRightarrow \forall O_{A_n i} \in O_{A_n \{i,\dots,i_n\}}, O_{A_n i} \approx D. \tag{23}$$

And if no inference mechanism can draw the inference, then obviously the ontology cannot entail it:

$$\nexists O_{A_n i} \in O_{A_n \{i,\dots,i_n\}}, O_{A_n i} \approx D$$
$$\implies O_{A_n i} \napprox D. \tag{24}$$

This latter rule captures the common case where the interpretation $\mathbb{I}$ as opposed to the inference mechanism poses the insuperable obstacle.

If the agents are assumed to be Turing-computable (even if E is not) one can interpret them as self-modifying computer programs. Outrageous as the idea of a self-modifying computer program might sound, these have a long history in artificial intelligence research. During the early decades of AI, even a very large and expensive computer had only a trivial amount of memory by latter-day standards. AI researchers tried to get their programs to fit into the claustrophobic machines by writing self-modifying LISP and Prolog code.[4] While to date no one has implemented an explicit computer model of ontological confrontation, all the requisite components to do so have been demonstrated on a rudimentary level, such as by the concept discovery systems demonstrated by Doug Lenat in the 1970s and 1980s.[5]

---

[4] This approach fell out of favor in large part because the behavior of self-modifying computer programs is almost impossible to reason about. If minds like those that humans have are in some sense self-modifying computer programs, this may be a feature selected by evolution both in order to attain the flexibility essential for general intelligence and because it increases the difficulty of reliably exploiting cognitive frailties. Leon Sterling and Ehud Shapiro, *The Art of Prolog Programming* (MIT Press, 1986), 190.

[5] Douglas B. Lenat and John Seely Brown, "Why AM and EURISKO Appear to Work," *Artificial Intelligence* 23.3 (1984), 269–294.

Bibliography

Aardema, Frederick, et al. "Virtual Reality Induces Dissociation and Lowers Sense of Presence in Objective Reality." *Cyberpsychology, Behavior, and Social Networking* 13.4 (2010), 429–435.

Aaronson, Scott. *Quantum Computing since Democritus*. Cambridge University Press, 2013.

Aaronson, Scott. "The Limits of Quantum Computers." *Scientific American* 298.3 (2008), 62–69.

Adams, Karen Ruth. "Attack and Conquer? International Anarchy and the Offense-Defense-Deterrence Balance." *International Security* 28.3 (2004), 45–83.

Adamsky, Dmitry (Dima). "The 1983 Nuclear Crisis—Lessons for Deterrence Theory and Practice." *Journal of Strategic Studies* 36.1 (2013), 4–41.

Akersten, Ingvar. "The Strategic Computing Program." In: Allan M. Din (ed.), *Arms and Artificial Intelligence: Weapon and Arms Control Applications of Advanced Computing*, 87–99. Oxford University Press, 1987.

Anderson, J. P. "The Day They Lost the Snark." *Air Force Magazine* 87.12 (2004), 78–80.

Andriushin, I. A., A. K. Chernyshev, and Iu. A. Iudin. *Ukroshchenie iadra. Stranitsy istorii iadernogo oruzhiia i iadernoi infrastruktury SSSR*. Tip. Krasn, 2003.

Arnold, Lorna. *Britain and the H-Bomb*. Springer, 2001.

Asada, Sadao. "The Shock of the Atomic Bomb and Japan's Decision to Surrender: A Reconsideration." *Pacific Historical Review* 67.4 (1998), 477–512.

Athalye, Anish, et al. "Synthesizing Robust Adversarial Examples." *arXiv preprint arXiv:1707.07397* (2017).

Axtell, Robert L. "Short-Term Opportunities, Medium-Run Bottle- necks, and Long-Time Barriers to Progress in the Evolution of an Agent-Based Social Science." In Aaron B. Frank and Elizabeth M. Bartels (eds.), *Active Engagement for Undergoverned Spaces: Concepts, Challenges, and Prospects for New Approaches*, 465–504. RAND RR-A1275-1, 2022.

Backus, John. "The History of Fortran I, II, and III." *ACM Sigplan Notices* 13.8 (1978), 165–180.

Ball, Desmond, and Richard Tanter. *The Tools of Owatatsumi: Japan's Ocean Surveillance and Coastal Defence Capabilities*. ANU Press, 2015.

Barzanjeh, Shabir, et al. "Microwave Quantum Illumination." *Physical Review Letters* 114.8 (2015), 080503.

Battilega, John A. "Soviet Views of Nuclear Warfare: The Post-Cold War Interviews." In *Getting MAD: Nuclear Mutual Assured Destruction, Its Origins and Practice*, 151–164. U.S. Army War College Press, 2004.

Battilega, John A., and Judith K. Grange. *The Military Applications of Modeling*. Air Force Institute of Technology Press, 1984.

Bell, Mark S. *Nuclear Reactions: How Nuclear-Armed States Behave*. Cornell University Press, 2021.

Bennett, Bruce W. *Assessing the Capabilities of Strategic Nuclear Forces: The Limits of Current Methods*. Tech. rep. Rand Corporation, 1980.

Bennett, Bruce W. *Fatality Uncertainties in Limited Nuclear War*. Tech. rep. Rand Corporation, 1977.

Bennett, Bruce W. *How to Assess the Survivability of US ICBMs*. Tech. rep. Rand Corporation, 1980.

Bennett, Bruce W. *How to Assess the Survivability of US ICBMs: Appendixes*. Tech. rep. Rand Corporation, 1980.

Bensinger, Rob. *Sam Harris and Eliezer Yudkowsky on "AI: Racing toward the Brink"*. 2018. URL: https://intelligence.org/2018/02/28/sam-harris-and-eliezer-yudkowsky/.

Berkeley, Edmund Callis. *Giant Brains; or, Machines That Think*. Wiley, 1955.

Bermudez, Joseph, Victor Cha, and Lisa Collins. *Undeclared North Korea: The Sino-ri Missile Operating Base and Strategic Force Facilities*. 2019. URL: https://beyondparallel.csis.org/undeclared-north-korea-the-sino-ri-missile-operating-base-and-strategic-force-facilities/.

Biddle, Tami Davis. *Strategy and Grand Strategy: What Students and Practitioners Need to Know*. SSI, 2015.

Bin, Li. "China's Nuclear Strategy." In *Carnegie International Nonproliferation Conference, Washington, DC*, 2007.

Bin, Li. "Tracking Chinese Strategic Mobile Missiles." *Science & Global Security* 15.1 (2007), 1–30.

Blackman, Samuel S. "Multiple Hypothesis Tracking for Multiple Target Tracking." *IEEE Aerospace and Electronic Systems Magazine* 19.1 (2004), 5–18.

Blackman, Samuel, and Robert Popoli. *Design and Analysis of Modern Tracking Systems*. Artech House, 1999.

Blade, Alexander. "The Brain." *Amazing Stories* 10 (1948).

Blair, Bruce, et al. "One Hundred Nuclear Wars: Stable Deterrence between the United States and Russia at Reduced Nuclear Force Levels off Alert in the Presence of Limited Missile Defenses." *Science & Global Security* 19.3 (2011), 167–194.

Blair, Bruce, Jessica Sleight, and Emma Claire Foley. *The End of Nuclear Warfighting: Moving to a Deterrence-Only Posture: An Alternative Nuclear Posture Review*. Tech. rep. Global Zero, 2018.

bmpd. *Lazernye kompleksy 'Peresvet' zastupili na opytno-boevoe dezhurstvo*. 2018. URL: https://bmpd.livejournal.com/3442101.html.

Bostrom, Nick. *Superintelligence: Paths, Dangers, Strategies*. Oxford University Press, 2014.

Braca, Paolo, et al. "Asymptotic Efficiency of the PHD in Multitarget/Multisensor Estimation." *IEEE Journal of Selected Topics in Signal Processing* 7.3 (2013), 553–564.

Bracken, Paul. *The Command and Control of Nuclear Forces*. Yale University Press, 1983.

Bracken, Paul. *The Hunt for Mobile Missiles: Nuclear Weapons, AI, and the New Arms Race*. Tech. rep. Foreign Policy Research Institute, 2020.

Bracken, Paul. *The Intersection of Cyber and Nuclear War*. 2017. URL: https://thestrategybridge.org/the-bridge/2017/1/17/the-intersection-of-cyber-and-nuclear-war.

Brians, Paul. *Nuclear Holocausts: Atomic War in Fiction, 1895-1984*. Kent State University Press, 1987.

Brodie, Bernard. "The Missing Middle—Tactical Nuclear War. AFAG Speech—9 April 1964." In Marc Trachtenberg (ed.), *The Development of American Strategic Thought: Writings on Strategy*. Garland, 1988, 245–262.

Brose, Christian. "The New Revolution in Military Affairs: War's Sci-Fi Future." *Foreign Affairs* 98 (2019), 122–128, 130–134.

Burenok, Vasilii, and Yurii Pechatnov. *Strategicheskoe sderzhivanie*. Prepublication copy, 2011.

Burutin, A. G., et al. "Kontseptsiia nepriemlemogo ushcherba: genesis, osnovnye prichiny transformatsii, sovremennoe sostoianie." *Vooruzhenie. Politika. Konversiia* 4 (2010), 3–8.

Callan, C., F. Dyson, and S. Treiman. *Neutrino detection primer*. Tech. rep. MITRE, 1988.

Capaccio, Anthony. *China Has Put Longer-Range ICBMs on Its Nuclear Subs, US Says*. URL: https://www.bloomberg.com/news/articles/2022-11-18/us-says-china-s-subs-armed-with-longer-range-ballistic-missiles. Nov. 2022.

Cassimatis, Nicholas L. "A Cognitive Substrate for Achieving Human-Level Intelligence." *AI Magazine* 27.2 (2006), 45–56.

Caston, Lauren, et al. *The Future of the US Intercontinental Ballistic Missile Force*. Tech. rep. Rand Corporation, 2014.

Chen, Stephen. *Could Ghost Imaging Spy Satellite Be a Game Changer for Chinese Military?* 2017. URL: https://www.scmp.com/news/china/society/article/2121479/could-ghost-imaging-spy-%20satellite-be-game-changer-chinese.

Chen, Stephen. *Will China's New Laser Satellite Become the "Death Star" for Submarines?* 2018. URL: https://www.scmp.com/news/china/science/article/2166413/will-chinas-new-laser-satellite-become-death-star-submarines.

Chivers, Ian, and Jane Sleightholme. "An Introduction to Algorithms and the Big O Notation." In *Introduction to Programming with Fortran*, 359–364. Springer, 2015.

Chollet, François. "The Measure of Intelligence." *arXiv preprint arXiv:1911.01547* (2019).

Chyba, Christopher F. "New Technologies & Strategic Stability." *Dædalus* 149.2 (2020), 150–170.

Cimbala, Stephen J. *Military Persuasion in War and Policy: The Power of Soft*. Praeger, 2002.

Cimbala, Stephen J. *Strategic War Termination*. Praeger, 1986.

Clark, Bryan, Seth Cropsey, and Timothy A. Walton. *Sustaining the Undersea Advantage: Disrupting Anti-submarine Warfare Using Autonomous Systems*. Hudson Institute, 2020.

Clarke, Arthur C. *2010: Odyssey Two*. RosettaBooks, 2012.

Cohn, Carol. "Sex and Death in the Rational World of Defense Intellectuals." *Signs: Journal of Women in Culture and Society* 12.4 (1987), 687–718.

Colby, Elbridge A., and Michael S. Gerson. *Strategic Stability: Contending Interpretations*. Tech. rep. SSI, 2013.

Cooper, Gregory F. "The Computational Complexity of Probabilistic Inference Using Bayesian Belief Networks." *Artificial Intelligence* 42.2-3 (1990), 393–405.

Coraluppi, Stefano. "Fundamentals and Advances in Multiple-Hypothesis Tracking." In: *NATO STO IST-134 Lecture Series on Advanced Algorithms for Effectively Fusing Hard and Soft Information*. NATO Collaboration and Support Office, 2015.

Côte, Owen R. "Invisible Nuclear-Armed Submarines, or Transparent Oceans? Are Ballistic Missile Submarines Still the Best Deterrent for the United States?" *Bulletin of the Atomic Scientists* 75.1 (2019), 30–35.

Côte, Owen R. *The Third Battle: Innovation in the US Navy's Silent Cold War Struggle with Soviet Submarines*. Newport Paper 16. Tech. rep. Naval War College, 2003.

Cox, Jessica, and Heather Williams. "The Unavoidable Technology: How Artificial Intelligence Can Strengthen Nuclear Stability." *Washington Quarterly* 44.1 (2021), 69–85.

Crevier, Daniel. *AI: The Tumultuous History of the Search for Artificial Intelligence*. Basic Books, 1993.

Cunningham, Fiona S., and M. Taylor Fravel. "Assuring Assured Retaliation: China's Nuclear Posture and US–China Strategic Stability." *International Security* 40.2 (2015), 7–50.

Dagum, Paul, and Michael Luby. "Approximating Probabilistic Inference in Bayesian Belief Networks Is NP-Hard." *Artificial Intelligence* 60.1 (1993), 141–153.

Daniel, Donald C. *Anti-Submarine Warfare and Superpower Strategic Stability*. University of Illinois, 1986.

Daniel, Donald C. *The Future of Strategic ASW*. Tech. rep. Center for Naval Warfare Studies, 1990.

Daniel, Donald C., and Katherine L. Herbig. "Deception in Theory and Practice." In Donald C. Daniel and Katherine L. Herbig (eds.), *Strategic Military Deception*, 355–367. Pergamon, 1982.

Daniel, Donald C., and Katherine L. Herbig. "Propositions on Military Deception." In Donald C. Daniel and Katherine L. Herbig (eds.), *Strategic Military Deception*, 1–30. Pergamon, 1982.

Davis, Paul K. "Knowledge-Based Simulation for Studying Issues of Nuclear Strategy." In Allan M. Din (ed.), *Arms and Artificial Intelligence: Weapon and Arms Control Applications of Advanced Computing*, 179–192. Oxford University Press, 1987.

Davis, Paul K., and Paul Bracken. "Artificial Intelligence for Wargaming and Modeling." *Journal of Defense Modeling and Simulation* (2022).

Davis, Paul K., et al. *Analytic War Gaming with the RAND Strategy Assessment System (RSAS)*. Tech. rep. RAND Corporation, 1987.

Defense Science Board. *Applications of Quantum Technologies: Executive Summary*. Tech. rep. Washington, DC: Office of the Undersecretary of Defense for Research and Engineering, 2019.

Department of the Army Headquarters. *Army Support to Military Deception*. 2019. URL: https://fas.org/irp/doddir/army/fm3-13-4.pdf.

Dick, Philip K. *Do Androids Dream of Electric Sheep?* Doubleday, 1968.

Dick, Philip K. "Second Variety." *Space Science Fiction* 5 (1953).

Dick, Philip K. "The Defenders." *Galaxy* 1 (1953).

Dumper, K., et al. "Spaceborne Synthetic Aperture Radar and Noise Jamming." In *Radar 97*, Conf. Publ. 449, 411–414. 1997. doi: 10.1049/cp:19971707.

Ehrhard, Thomas P. *Air Force UAVs: The Secret History*. Tech. rep. Mitchell Institute for Airpower Studies, 2010.

Ellison, Harlan. "I Have No Mouth, and I Must Scream." In Howard Bruce Franklin (ed.), *Countdown to Midnight: Twelve Great Stores about Nuclear War*, 146–165. DAW Books, 1984.

Ellsberg, Daniel. "The Crude Analysis of Strategy Choices." *American Economic Review* 51.2 (1961), 472–478.

Emami, Patrick, et al. "Machine Learning Methods for Solving Assignment Problems in Multi-Target Tracking." *arXiv preprint arXiv:1802.06897* (2018).

Ensmenger, Nathan. "Is Chess the Drosophila of Artificial Intelligence? A Social History of an Algorithm." *Social Studies of Science* 42.1 (2012), 5–30.

Ferro, David L., and Eric G. Swedin. *Science Fiction and Computing: Essays on Interlinked Domains*. McFarland, 2011.

Fink, Anya, and Micheal Kofman. *Russian Strategy for Escalation Management: Key Debates and Players in Military Thought*. Tech. rep. CNA, 2020.

Fischhoff, Baruch. "Nuclear Decisions: Cognitive Limits to the Thinkable." In Philip E. Tetlock et al. (eds.), *Behavior, Society, and Nuclear War*, Vol. 2, 110–192. Oxford University Press, 1991.

Fogleman, Ronald R. "Strategic Vision and Core Competencies: Global Reach–Global Power." *Vital Speeches of the Day* 63.4 (1996), 98.

Foley, Robert. *Alfred Von Schlieffen's Military Writings*. Taylor & Francis, 2012.

Forbus, Kenneth D. "Qualitative Process Theory." *Artificial Intelligence* 24.1–3 (1984), 85–168.

Forbus, Kenneth D., and Johan De Kleer. *Building Problem Solvers*. MIT Press, 1993.

Freedberg, Sydney J. *No AI For Nuclear Command and Control: JAIC's Shanahan*. 2019. URL: https://breakingdefense.com/2019/09/no-ai-for-nuclear-command-control-jaics-shanahan/.

Freedman, Lawrence, and Jeffrey Michaels. *The Evolution of Nuclear Strategy: New, Updated and Completely Revised*. Springer, 2019.

Friborg, Albert Compton. "Careless Love." *Fantasy and Science Fiction* 7 (1954).

Futter, Andrew. "Disruptive Technologies and Nuclear Risks: What's New and What Matters." *Survival* 64.1 (2022), 99–120.

Gaddis, John Lewis, et al. *Strategies of Containment: A Critical Appraisal of American National Security Policy During the Cold War*. Oxford University Press, 2005.

Gallagher, Nancy W. "Re-thinking the Unthinkable: Arms Control in the Twenty-First Century." *The Nonproliferation Review* 22.3–4 (2015), 469–498.

Garthoff, Raymond L. *The Soviet Image of Future War*. Public Affairs Press 1959.

Garthoff, Raymond L. *Deterrence and the Revolution in Soviet Military Doctrine*. Brookings, 1990.

Garwin, Richard L. "Will Strategic Submarines Be Vulnerable?" *International Security* 8.2 (1983), 52–67.

Gassner, John, and William Green. *Elizabethan Drama: Eight Plays*. Hal Leonard, 1990.

Gates, Jonathan. "Is the SSBN Deterrent Vulnerable to Autonomous Drones?" *The RUSI Journal* 161.6 (2016), 28–35.

Gavin, Francis J. *Nuclear Statecraft: History and Strategy in America's Atomic Age*. Cornell University Press, 2012.

Geist, Edward. "MAGIC-MISSILE: A Monte Carlo Simulation of Strategic Nuclear Exchanges." In Sarah Minot (ed.), *Project on Nuclear Issues: A Collection of Papers from the 2013 Conference Series*, 98–111. Rowman & Littlefield, 2014.

Geist, Edward M. "Why Reasoning Under Uncertainty Is Hard for Both Machines and People—and an Approach to Address the Problem." In Aaron B. Frank and Elizabeth M. Bartels (eds.), *Active Engagement for Undergoverned Spaces: Concepts, Challenges, and Prospects for New Approaches*, 263–281. RAND RR-A1275-1, 2022.

Geist, Edward Moore. "Would Russia's Undersea 'Doomsday Drone' Carry a Cobalt Bomb?" *Bulletin of the Atomic Scientists* 72.4 (2016), 238–242.

Geist, Edward, and Dara Massicot. "Understanding Putin's Nuclear 'Superweapons.'" *SAIS Review of International Affairs* 39.2 (2019), 103–117.

Gelman, Andrew, and Cosma Rohilla Shalizi. "Philosophy and the Practice of Bayesian Statistics." *British Journal of Mathematical and Statistical Psychology* 66.1 (2013), 8–38.

General Accounting Office. *Military Satellite Communications: Concerns with Milstar's Support to Strategic and Tactical Forces*. Tech. rep. General Accounting Office, Nov. 1998.

George, Peter. *Red Alert*. Ace Books, Inc., 1958.

Gilmer, Justin, et al. "Motivating the Rules of the Game for Adversarial Example Research." *arXiv preprint arXiv:1807.06732* (2018).

Glaser, Charles L. "Why Even Good Defenses May Be Bad." *International Security* 9.2 (1984), 92–123.

Glaser, Charles. "Why Do Strategists Disagree about the Requirements of Strategic Nuclear Deterrence?" In Lynn Eden and Steven E. Miller (eds.), *Nuclear Arguments: Understanding the Strategic Nuclear Arms and Arms Control Debates*, 109–171. Cornell University Press, 1989.

Glaser, Charles L. *Analyzing Strategic Nuclear Policy*. Princeton University Press, 1990.

Glaser, Charles L., and Steve Fetter. "Should the United States Reject MAD? Damage Limitation and US Nuclear Strategy toward China." *International Security*, 41.1 (2016), 49–98.

Glaser, Charles L., and Chairn Kaufmann. "What is the Offense–Defense Balance and How Can We Measure It?" *International Security* 22.4 (1998), 44–82.

Goodfellow, Ian J., Jonathon Shlens, and Christian Szegedy. "Explaining and Harnessing Adversarial Examples." In *ICLR*, 2015.

Gottemoeller, Rose. "The Standstill Conundrum: The Advent of Second-Strike Vulnerability and Options to Address It." *Texas National Security Review* 4.4 (2021), 115–124.

Gray, Colin S. War, Peace and Victory: *Strategy and Statecraft for the Next Century*. Simon and Schuster, 1990.

Gray, Colin S., and Keith Payne. "Victory Is Possible." *Foreign Policy* 39 (1980), 14–27.

Green, Brendan Rittenhouse. *The Revolution That Failed: Nuclear Competition, Arms Control, and the Cold War*. Cambridge University Press, 2020.

Green, Brendan R., and Austin Long. "The MAD Who Wasn't There: Soviet Reactions to the Late Cold War Nuclear Balance." *Security Studies* 26.4 (2017), 606–641.

Green, Brendan Rittenhouse, and Austin Long. "Conceal or Reveal? Managing Clandestine Military Capabilities in Peacetime Competition." *International Security* 44.3 (2020), 48–83.

Green, Brendan Rittenhouse, et al. "The Limits of Damage Limitation." *International Security* 42.1 (2017), 193–207.

Greenberger, Martin. *Computers, Communications, and the Public Interest*. Johns Hopkins University Press, 1971.

Guerreschi, Gian Giacomo, and Anne Y. Matsuura. "QAOA for Max-Cut Requires Hundreds of Qubits for Quantum Speed-up." *Scientific Reports* 9.1 (2019), 6903.

Halperin, Morton H., and Thomas C. Schelling. *Strategy and Arms Control*. Twentieth Century Fund, 1961.

Hambling, David. *The Inescapable Net: Unmanned Systems in Anti-Submarine Warfare*. BASIC, 2016.

Handel, Michael I. *Sun Tzu and Clausewitz: The Art of War and On War Compared*. Tech. rep. SSI, 1991.

Hanle, E. "Survey of Bistatic and Multistatic Radar." *IEE Proceedings F-Communications, Radar and Signal Processing* 133. 7 (1986), 587–595.

Harrington, Anne I., and Jeffrey W. Knopf. *Behavioral Economics and Nuclear Weapons*. University of Georgia Press, 2019.

Harsanyi, John C. "Games with Incomplete Information Played by 'Bayesian' Players, I-III Part I. The Basic Model." *Management Science* 14.3 (1967), 159–182.

Harsanyi, John C. "Games with Incomplete Information Played by 'Bayesian' Players, Part II. Bayesian Equilibrium Points." *Management Science* 14.5 (1968), 320–334.

Hasegawa, Tsuyoshi. *The End of the Pacific War: Reappraisals*. Stanford University Press, 2007.

Haugeland, John. *Artificial Intelligence: The Very Idea*. MIT Press, 1989.

Haykin, Simon S. *Kalman Filtering and Neural Networks*. Wiley Online Library, 2001.

Healey, Denis. *The Time of My Life*. Michael Joseph, 1989.

Heckerman, David. "Probabilistic Interpretations for MYCIN's Certainty Factors." *Machine Intelligence and Pattern Recognition*. 4 (1986), 167–196.

Hedberg, Sara Reese. "DART: Revolutionizing Logistics Planning." *IEEE Intelligent Systems* 17.3 (2002), 81–83.

Herken, Gregg. "The Flying Crowbar." *Air and Space* 5.1 (1990).

High, Peter. *Why Montreal Has Emerged as an Artificial Intelligence Powerhouse*. 2017. URL: https://www.forbes.com/sites/peterhigh/2017/11/06/why-montreal-has-emerged-as-an-%20artificial-intelligence-powerhouse/.

Hill, Michael. "Making Sense of Deadly Games." *Baltimore Sun* (Oct. 2005). URL: https://www.baltimoresun.com/news/bs-xpm-2005-10-16-0510140014-story.html.

Hoeber, Francis P. *Military Applications of Modeling: Selected Case Studies*. Vol. 1. CRC Press, 1981.

Hoffman, David. *The Dead Hand: The Untold Story of the Cold War Arms Race and Its Dangerous Legacy*. Anchor, 2009.

Holsti, Ole R. "Crisis Decision Making." In Philip E. Tetlock et al. (eds.), *Behavior, Society, and Nuclear War*. Oxford University Press, 1989.

Hutchins, John. "ALPAC: The (In)Famous Report," *Readings in Machine Translation* 14 (2003), 131–135.

Hutchins, W. John. "The Georgetown–IBM Experiment Demonstrated in January 1954." In *Conference of the Association for Machine Translation in the Americas*, 102–114. Springer, 2004.

"Iadernye dvigateli v krylatykh raketakh. Dos'e." 2018. URL: https://tass. ru/info/5386826.

Iklé, Fred Charles, and Nathan Leites. "Political Negotiation as a Process of Modifying Utilities." *Journal of Conflict Resolution* 6.1 (1962), 19–28.

Ilin, Roman, and Erik Blasch. "Information Fusion with Belief Functions: A Comparison of Proportional Conflict Redistribution PCR5 and PCR6 Rules for Networked Sensors." In *2015 18th International Conference on Information Fusion (Fusion)*, 2084–2091. IEEE, 2015.

"Istochnik: 'atomnyi poezd' 'Barguzin' iskliuchili iz novoi GPV radi 'Sarmata' i 'Rubezha'." 2017. URL: https://tass.ru/armiya-i-opk/4787839.

Iudina, Anna. *Gid po samym sekretnym podvodnym robotam Rossii.* 2018. URL: https://tass. ru/armiya-i-opk/5402375.

Iurov, Dmitrii. *Okazalis' v pogruzhenii: na chto sposobny rossiiskie podvodnye bespilotniki. Pochemu novye boevye submariny VMF Rossii vyzvali azhiotazh sredi voennykh ekspertov NATO.* 2018. URL: https://iz.ru/817694/dmitrii-iurov/okazalis-v-pogruzhenii-na-chto-sposobny-rossiiskie-podvodnye-bespilotniki.

Janzen, Rod A. *The Rise and Fall of Synanon: A California Utopia.* Johns Hopkins University Press, 2001.

Jervis, Robert. "Introduction: Approach and Assumptions." In Robert Jervis, Richard Ned Lebow, and Janice Gross Stein (eds.), *Psychology and Deterrence*, 1–12. Johns Hopkins University Press, 1985.

Jervis, Robert. "Politics and Political Science." *Annual Review of Political Science* 21 (2018), 1–19.

Jervis, Robert. *The Illogic of American Nuclear Strategy.* Cornell University Press, 1984.

Jervis, Robert. *The Meaning of the Nuclear Revolution: Statecraft and the Prospect of Armageddon.* Cornell University Press, 1989.

Johnson, Dave. *Nuclear Weapons in Russia's Approach to Conflict.* Fondation pour la Recherche Stratégique, 2016.

Johnson, Dave. *Russia's Conventional Precision Strike Capabilities, Regional Crises, and Nuclear Thresholds.* Tech. rep. Lawrence Livermore National Lab.(LLNL), 2018.

Johnson, Stuart E., and Martin C. Libicki. *Dominant Battlespace Knowledge: The Winning Edge.* Tech. rep. Institute for National Strategic Studies, National Defense University, 1995.

Joint Chiefs of Staff. *Military Deception.* 1998. URL: http://www.c4i.org/jp3_13.pdf

Joint Chiefs of Staff. *Military Deception.* 2012. URL: https://jfsc.ndu.edu/Portals/72/Documents/JC2IOS/Additional_Reading/1C3-JP_3-13-4_MILDEC.pdf.

Jones, Dennis Feltham. *Colossus.* Hart-Davis, 1966.

Jones, Dennis Feltham. *The Fall of Colossus.* Putnam, 1974.

Jumper, John, et al. "Highly Accurate Protein Structure Prediction with AlphaFold." *Nature* 596.7873 (2021), 583–589.

Kahn, Herman. *On Escalation: Metaphors and Scenarios.* Praeger, 1965.

Kahn, Herman. *On Thermonuclear War.* Princeton University Press, 1960.

Kahn, Herman. *Thinking about the Unthinkable in the 1980s.* Simon and Schuster, 1985.

Kalman, Rudolph. "A New Approach to Linear Filtering and Prediction Problems." *Transactions of the ASME–Journal of Basic Engineering* 82 (1960), 35–45.

Kania, Elsa. *AlphaGo and Beyond: The Chinese Military Looks to Future 'Intelligentized' Warfare.* URL: https://www.lawfareblog.com/alphago-and-beyond-chinese-military-looks-future-intelligentized-warfare. June 2017.

Kapitanets, Ivan. *Bitva za Mirovoi okean v "kholodnoi" i budushchikh voinakh.* Veche, 2002.

Kaplan, Fred. *Dark Territory: The Secret History of Cyber War.* Simon and Schuster, 2016.

Kaplan, Fred. *The Bomb: Presidents, Generals, and the Secret History of Nuclear War.* Simon and Schuster, 2020.

Kaplan, Fred. *The Wizards of Armageddon.* Stanford University Press, 1991.

Kartchner, Kerry M., and Micheal S. Gerson. "Escalation to Limited Nuclear War in the 21st Century." In Jeffrey A. Larsen and Kerry M. Kartchner (eds.), *On Limited Nuclear War in the 21st Century*, 144–171. Stanford University Press, 2014.

Kieval, Hillel J. "Pursuing the Golem of Prague: Jewish Culture and the Invention of a Tradition." *Modern Judaism* 17.1 (1997), 1–23.

Kirby, David A. *Lab Coats in Hollywood: Science, Scientists, and Cinema.* MIT Press, 2011.

Klimov, Maksim. *Problemnye voprosy oblika perspektivnykh podvodnyh lodok VMF Rossii.* 2018. URL: https://bmpd.livejournal.com/3458646.html.

Kofman, Micheal, Anya Fink, and Jeffrey Edmonds. *Russian Strategy for Escalation Management: Evolution of Key Concepts.* Tech. rep. CNA, 2020.

Kokoshin, A. A (ed.) *Vliianie tekhnologicheskikh faktorov na parametry ugroz natsional'noi i mezhdunarodnoi bezopasnosti, voennykh konfliktov i strategicheskoi stabil'nosti.* Izdatel'stvo MGU, 2017.

Kokoshin, A. A., V. A. Veselov, and A. V. Liss. *Sderzhivanie vo vtorom iadernom veke.* Institut problem mezhdunarodnoi bezopasnosti RAN, 2001.

Kokoshin, Andrei. "Neskol'ko izmerenii voiny." *Voprosy filosofii* 8 (2016), 15–19.

Kokoshin, Andrei. "Revoliutsiia v voennom dele i problemy sozdaniia sovremennykh vooruzhennykh sil Rossii." *Vestnik Moskovskogo universiteta. Seria 25. Mezhdunarodnye otnosheniia i mirovaia politika* 1 (2009), 46–62.

Kotseruba, Iuliia, and John K. Tsotsos. "40 Years of Cognitive Architectures: Core Cognitive Abilities and Practical Applications." *Artificial Intelligence Review* 53.1 (2020), 17–94.

Kristensen, Hans M. "Chinese Mobile ICBMs Seen in Central China." 2012. URL: https://fas.org/blogs/security/2012/03/df-31deployment/.

Kristensen, Hans. "New Missile Silo and DF-41 Launchers Seen in Chinese Nuclear Missile Training Area." 2019. URL: https://fas.org/blogs/security/2019/09/china-silo-df41/.

Kristensen, Hans M., and Matt Korda. "Chinese Nuclear Forces, 2020," Bulletin of the Atomic Scientists 76.6 (2020), 443–457.

Kristensen, Hans M., and Matt Korda. "China's Nuclear Missile Silo Expansion: From Minimum Deterrence to Medium Deterrence." URL: https: //thebulletin.org/2021/09/chinas-nuclear-missile-silo-expansion-from-minimum-deterrence-to-medium-deterrence/. Sept. 2021.

Kristensen, Hans M., and Matt Korda. "North Korean Nuclear Weapons, 2021," Bulletin of the Atomic Scientists 77.4 (2021), 222–236.

Kristensen, Hans M., and Matt Korda. "Russian Nuclear Forces, 2019," Bulletin of the Atomic Scientists 75.2 (2019), 73–84.

Kristensen, Hans M., and Robert S. Norris. "Chinese Nuclear Forces, 2018". In: Bulletin of the Atomic Scientists 74.4 (2018), 289–295.

Kristensen, Hans M., and Robert S Norris. "United States Nuclear Forces, 2018." *Bulletin of the Atomic Scientists* 74.2 (2018), 120–131.

Kroenig, Matthew. *The Logic of American Nuclear Strategy.* Oxford University Press, 2018.

Langley, Pat, John E. Laird, and Seth Rogers. "Cognitive Architectures: Research Issues and Challenges." *Cognitive Systems Research* 10.2 (2009), 141–160.

Lanzagorta, Marco, and Jeffrey Uhlmann. "Overview of the Current State of Quantum-Based Technologies." *Marine Technology Society Journal* 53.5 (2019), 75–87.

Lebow, Richard Ned, and Janice Gross Stein. "Rational Deterrence Theory: I Think, Therefore I Deter." *World Politics* 41.2 (1989), 208–224.

Legg, Shane, and Marcus Hutter. "Universal Intelligence: A Definition of Machine Intelligence." *Minds and Machines* 17.4 (2007), 391–444.

Le Guin, Ursula K. *The Language of the Night: Essays on Fantasy and Science Fiction*. Ultramarine Publishing, 1979.

Lenat, Douglas B., and John Seely Brown. "Why AM and EURISKO Appear to Work." *Artificial Intelligence* 23.3 (1984), 269–294.

Lerner, Uri. and Ron Parr. "Inference in Hybrid Networks: Theoretical Limits and Practical Algorithms," arXiv preprint arXiv:1301.2288 (2013).

Lerner, Uri N. "Hybrid Bayesian Networks for Reasoning about Complex Systems." PhD thesis. Stanford University, 2002.

Levesque, Hector J., and Ronald J. Brachman. "Expressiveness and Tractability in Knowledge Representation and Reasoning 1." *Computational Intelligence* 3.1 (1987), 78–93.

Levy, Jack S. "Loss Aversion, Framing, and Bargaining: The Implications of Prospect Theory for International Conflict." *International Political Science Review* 17.2 (1996), 179–195.

Lewis, Jeffrey. "How Finding China's Nuclear Sites Upset Pro-Beijing Trolls." URL: https://foreignpolicy.com/2021/08/26/china-nuclear-sites-twitter-trolls/. Aug. 2021.

Lewis, Jeffrey G. *The Minimum Means of Reprisal: China's Search for Security in the Nuclear Age*. MIT Press, 2007.

Lieber, Keir A. "Grasping the Technological Peace: The Offense–Defense balance and International Security," *International Security* 25.1 (2000), 71–104.

Lieber, Keir A., and Daryl G. Press. *The Myth of the Nuclear Revolution: Power Politics in the Atomic Age*. Cornell University Press, 2020.

Lieber, Keir A., and Daryl G. Press. "The New Era of Counterforce: Technological Change and the Future of Nuclear Deterrence." *International Security* 41.4 (2017), 9–49.

Lieber, Keir A., and Daryl G. Press. "The Rise of US Nuclear Primacy." *Foreign Affairs* 85 (2006), 42.

Lin, Herbert. *Cyber Threats and Nuclear Weapons*. Stanford University Press, 2021.

Logan, David C. "The Nuclear Balance Is What States Make of It." *International Security* 46.4 (2022), 172–215.

Long, Austin, and Brendan Rittenhouse Green. "Stalking the Secure Second Strike: Intelligence, Counterforce, and Nuclear Strategy." *Journal of Strategic Studies* 38.1–2 (2015), 38–73.

Lowther, Adam, and Curtis McGiffen. "America Needs a 'Dead Hand'." *War on the Rocks* (Aug. 2019). URL: https://warontherocks.com/2019/08/america-needs-a-dead-hand/.

Luce, R. Duncan, and Howard Raiffa. *Games and Decisions: Introduction and Critical Survey*. Wiley, 1957.

Lynn-Jones, Sean M. *Does Offense-Defense Theory Have a Future?* Groupe d'étude et de recherche sur la sécurité internationale, 2000.

McCorduck, Pamela. *Machines Who Think*. WH Freeman, 1979.

McCulloch, Warren S. "A Heterarchy of Values Determined by the Topology of Nervous Nets." *Bulletin of Mathematical Biophysics* 7.2 (1945), 89–93.

McDonald, John. *Strategy in Poker, Business and War*. W. W. Norton, 1996.

McCarthy, John. "Circumscription–A Form of Non-monotonic Reasoning." *Artificial Intelligence* 13.1–2 (1980), 27–39.

McCarthy, John. "Epistemological Problems of Artificial Intelligence." In Bonnie Lynn Webber and Nils J. Nilsson (eds.), *Readings in Artificial Intelligence*, 459–465. Morgan Kaufmann, 1981.

McCarthy, John. "History of Circumscription." In Daniel G. Bobrow (ed.), *Artificial Intelligence in Perspective*, 23–26. MIT Press, 1994.

Machiavelli, Niccolò. *The Discourses*. Penguin, 1983.

Macias, Amanda. *The First Drone Warship Just Joined the Navy and Now Nearly Every Element of It Is Classified*. 2018. URL: https://www.cnbc.com/2018/04/25/first-drone-warship-joins-us-navy-nearly-every-element-classified.html.

Mahan, Alfred Thayer. *Armaments and Arbitration, Or, the Place of Force in the International Relations of States*. Harper & Brothers, 1912.

Mahler, Ronald P. S. *Statistical Multisource-Multitarget Information Fusion*. Artech House, 2007.

Marshall, Andrew W. "Long-Term Competition with the Soviets: A Framework for Strategic Analysis." United States Air Force Project RAND R-862-PR (1972).

Matsulenko, Viktor Antonovich, et al. *Camouflage: A Soviet View*. Department of the Air Force, 1989.

Mazarr, Michael J. *Understanding Deterrence*. Tech. rep. RAND Corporation, 2018.

Meyer, Florian, et al. "Tracking an Unknown Number of Targets Using Multiple Sensors: A Belief Propagation Method." In 2016 19th *International Conference on Information Fusion (FUSION)*, 719–726. IEEE, 2016.

Meyer, Manfred. *Modern Chinese Maritime Forces*. Admiralty Trilogy Group, 2022.

Miasnikov, Eugene. "Can Russian Strategic Submarines Survive at Sea? The Fundamental Limits of Passive Acoustics." *Science & Global Security* 4.2 (1994), 213–251.

Miller, Franklin. "Tailoring U.S. Strategic Deterrence Effects on Russia." In Barry R. Schneider and Patrick D. Ellis (eds.), *Tailored Deterrence: Influencing States and Groups of Concern*. USAF Counterproliferation Center, 2012.

Miller, Walter M. "Dumb Waiter." *Astounding* 4 (1952).

Minsky, Marvin. "Consciousness Is a Big Suitcase." In *Edge.org* (1998).

Minsky, Marvin L. "Logical versus Analogical or Symbolic versus Connectionist or Neat versus Scruffy." *AI Magazine* 12.2 (1991), 34–51.

Minsky, Marvin. *Semantic Information Processing*. MIT Press, 1982.

Mola, Roger A. "'This Is Only a Test:' Fifty Years Ago, Cold-War Games Halted All Civilian Air Traffic—Long before September 11 Did the Same." *Air and Space Magazine* 2 (2002).

Morgan, Patrick M. Deterrence: *A Conceptual Analysis*. Sage Publications, 1977.

Morgan, Patrick M. *Deterrence Now*. Cambridge University Press, 2003.

Murphy, Kevin P. "Switching Kalman Filters." Tech. Rep. 98–10. Compaq Cambridge Research Lab, 1998.

Newell, Allen. *Unified Theories of Cognition*. Harvard University Press, 1994.

Nielsen, Michael A., and Isaac L. Chuang. *Quantum Computation and Quantum Information*. Cambridge University Press, 2010.

Niles, Douglas. *Against the Cult of the Reptile God*. 1982.

Nilsson, Nils J. *The Quest for Artificial Intelligence*. Cambridge University Press, 2009.

Nitze, Paul H. "Assuring Strategic Stability in an Era of Détente." *Foreign Affairs* 54.2 (1976), 207–232

Nitze, Paul H. "Deterring Our Deterrent." *Foreign Policy* 25 (1976), 195–210.

Nitze, Paul H. "The Strategic Balance between Hope and Skepticism." *Foreign Policy* 17 (1974), 136–156.

Nolan, Janne E. *Guardians of the Arsenal*. Basic Books, 1989.

Norvig, Peter. *Paradigms of Artificial Intelligence Programming: Case Studies in Common Lisp*. Morgan Kaufmann, 1992.

Odom, William E. "The Origins and Design of Presidential Decision-59: A Memoir." In *Getting MAD: Nuclear Mutual Assured Destruction, Its Origin and Practice*, 175–196. Strategic Studies Institute. SSI, 2004.

Ofshe, Richard, et al. "Social Structure and Social Control in Synanon." *Journal of Voluntary Action Research* 3.3–4 (1974), 67–76.

Orwell, George. *Nineteen Eighty-Four*. Harcourt Brace Jovanovich, 1982.

Owens, William A., and Ed Offley. *Lifting the Fog of War*. Johns Hopkins University Press, 2001.

Oxenstierna, Susanne, et al. *Russian Military Capability in a Ten-Year Perspective—2019*. Tech. rep. FOI, 2019.

Pais, Abraham. *Niels Bohr's Times in Physics, Philosophy, and Polity*. Clarendon–Oxford, 1991.

Payne, Keith B. "The Great Divide in US Deterrence Thought." *Strategic Studies Quarterly* 14.2 (2020), 16–48.

Pearl, Judea and Stuart Russell. "Bayesian Networks." In M. A. Arbib (ed.), *Handbook of Brain Theory and Neural Networks*, 157–160. MIT Press, 2003.

Piel, Gerard. "The Illusion of Civil Defense." *Bulletin of the Atomic Scientists* 18.2 (1962), 2–8.

Podvig, Pavel. *Russian Strategic Nuclear Forces*. MIT Press, 2004.

Podvig, Pavel. "The Myth of Strategic Stability." *Bulletin of the Atomic Scientists* (2012).

Podvig, Pavel. "The Window of Vulnerability That Wasn't: Soviet Military Buildup in the 1970s–A Research Note." International Security 33.1 (2008), 118–38.

Podvig, Pavel. *Tracking down Road-Mobile Missiles*. 2015. URL: http://russianforces.org/blog/2015/01/tracking_down_road-mobile_miss.shtml.

Poliakov, V. "40 let protivolodochnoi bor'be." *Morskoi sbornik* 3 (2009), 20–25.

Pomeroy, Steven. *An Untaken Road: Strategy, Technology, and the Hidden History of America's Mobile ICBMs*. Naval Institute Press, 2016.

Poole, David. "A Logical Framework for Default Reasoning." *Artificial Intelligence* 36.1 (1988), 27–47.

Pospelov, G. S., and Pospelov, D. A. "Issledovaniia po iskusstvennomu intellektu v SSSR." In *Kibernetiku–na sluzhbu kommunizma*. Energiia, 1978.

Powell, Robert. *Nuclear Deterrence Theory: The Search for Credibility*. Cambridge University Press, 1990.

President's Foreign Intelligence Advisory Board. *The Soviet "War Scare."* 1990.

Press, Daryl, and Keir A. Lieber. "Appendix for Keir A. Lieber and Daryl G. Press, 'The New Era of Counterforce: Technological Change and the Future of Nuclear Deterrence,'" *International Security* 41.4 (Spring 2017), 9–49. Version V1, 2017. Doi: 10.7910/DVN/NKZJVT. URL: https://doi.org/.

Prezident Rossiiskoi Federatsii. "Osnovy gosudarstvennoi politiki Rossiskoi Federatsii v oblasti iadernogo sderzhivaniia." June 2020. URL: http://publication.pravo.gov.ru/Document/View/0001202006020040?index=1&rangeSize=1.

Putin, V. V. *Poslanie Prezidenta Federal'nomu Sobraniiu*. 2018. URL: http://kremlin.ru/events/president/news/56957.

Putin: v rossiiskoi kontseptsii primeneniia iadernogo oruzhiia net preventivnogo udara. 2018. URL: https://tass.ru/politika/5691255

Quade, Edward S. "The Selection and Use of Strategic Air Bases: A Case History." In E. S. Quade (ed.), *Analysis for Military Decisions*, 24–63. Rand McNally, 1966.

Rayer, F. G. *Tomorrow Sometimes Comes*. Home and Van Thal, 1951.

Regenwetter, Michel, Jason Dana, and Clintin P. Davis-Stober. "Transitivity of Preferences." *Psychological Review* 118.1 (2011), 42.

Reiter, Raymond. "A Logic for Default Reasoning." *Artificial Intelligence* 13.1–2 (1980), 81–132.

Riqiang, Wu. "Living with Uncertainty: Modeling China's Nuclear Survivability." *International Security* 44.4 (2020), 84–118.

Riqiang, Wu. "Survivability of China's Sea-Based Nuclear Forces." *Science & Global Security* 19.2 (2011), 91–120.

Robinson, E. S., et al. *Preliminary Study of the Nuclear Subterrene.* Tech. rep. Los Alamos Scientific Lab, 1971.

Roland, Alex, Philip Shiman, et al. *Strategic Computing: DARPA and the Quest for Machine Intelligence, 1983–1993.* MIT Press, 2002.

Roman, Peter J. *Eisenhower and the Missile Gap.* Cornell University Press, 1995.

Rosenau, William. *Special Operations Forces and Elusive Enemy Ground Targets: Lessons from Vietnam and the Persian Gulf War.* Rand Corporation, 2001.

Rosenblatt, Frank. *Principles of Neurodynamics: Perceptrons and the Theory of Brain Mechanisms.* Tech. rep. Cornell Aeronautical Lab, 1961.

Rumsfeld, Donald H. *DoD News Briefing—Secretary Rumsfeld and Gen. Myers, February 12, 2002 11:30 AM EDT.* 2002. URL: http://archive.defense.gov/Transcripts/Transcript.aspx?TranscriptID=2636.

Russell, S., and P. Norvig. *Artificial Intelligence: A Modern Approach.* Prentice Hall, 2002.

Sagan, Scott Douglas. *The Limits of Safety: Organizations, Accidents, and Nuclear Weapons.* Princeton University Press, 1995.

Sakitt, Mark. *Submarine Warfare in the Arctic: Option or Illusion?* CISAC, 1988.

Salman, Michael, Kevin J. Sullivan, and Stephen Van Evera. "Analysis or Propaganda? Measuring American Strategic Nuclear Capability, 1969–1988." In Lynn Eden and Steven Miller (eds.), *Nuclear Arguments: The Major Debates on Strategic Nuclear Weapons and Arms Control*, 172–263. Cornell University Press, 1989.

Sarbin, Theodore R. "Prolegomenon to a Theory of Counter-Deception." In Donald C. Daniel and Katherine L. Herbig (eds.), *Strategic Military Deception*, 151–173. Pergamon, 1982.

Sauer, Frank. "Military Applications of Artificial Intelligence: Nuclear Risk Redux." In Vincent Boulanin (ed.), *The Impact of Artificial Intelligence on Strategic Stability and Nuclear Risk: Euro-Atlantic Perspectives*, 84–90. SIPRI, 2019.

Saunders, Elizabeth N. "The Domestic Politics of Nuclear Choices—A Review Essay." *International Security* 44.2 (2019), 146–184.

Schelling, Thomas C. *Arms and Influence.* Yale University Press, 1966.

Schelling, Thomas C. "Dispersal, Deterrence, and Damage." *Operations Research* 9.3 (1961), 363–370.

Schelling, Thomas C. "Meteors, Mischief, and War." *Bulletin of the Atomic Scientists* 16.7 (1960), 292–300.

Schelling, Thomas C. *The Strategy of Conflict.* Harvard University Press, 1980.

Scowcroft, Brent. *Report of the President's Commission on Strategic Forces.* The President's Commission on Strategic Forces, 1984.

Seffers, George I. *Quantum Radar Could Render Stealth Aircraft Obsolete.* 2015. URL: https://www.afcea.org/content/Article-quantum-radar-could-render-stealth-aircraft-obsolete.

Shafer, Glenn. *A Mathematical Theory of Evidence.* Princeton University Press, 1976.

Shannon, Claude E. "A Mathematical Theory of Communication." *Bell System Technical Journal* 27.3 (1948), 379–423.

Shannon, Claude E. "XXII. Programming a Computer for Playing Chess." *The London, Edinburgh, and Dublin Philosophical Magazine and Journal of Science* 41.314 (1950), 256–275.

Shor, Peter W. "Algorithms for Quantum Computation: Discrete Logarithms and Factoring." In *Proceedings 35th Annual Symposium on Foundations of Computer Science*, 124–134. IEEE. 1994.

Simon, David S., Gregg Jaeger, and Alexander V. Sergienko. "Ghost Imaging and Related Topics." In *Quantum Metrology, Imaging, and Communication*, 131–158. Springer, 2017.

Simon, Herbert A., and Allen Newell. "Heuristic Problem Solving: The Next Advance in Operations Research." *Operations Research* 6.1 (1958), 1–10.

Slayton, Rebecca. *Arguments that Count: Physics, Computing, and Missile Defense, 1949–2012.* MIT Press, 2013.

Slocombe, Walter. "The Countervailing Strategy." *International Security* 5.4 (1981), 18–27.

Snodgrass, David E. *Attacking the Theater Mobile Ballistic Missile Threat.* Tech. rep. School of Advanced Airpower Studies, 1993.

Sokov, Nikolai N. "Why Russia Calls a Limited Nuclear Strike "De-escalation."" *Bulletin of the Atomic Scientists* 13 (2014), 70.

Sovenko, A. Iu. and V. F. Kudriavchev. "Atomnyi samolet: budushchee v proshedshem vremeni." *Aviatsiia i Vremia* 3–4 (2004).

Stein, Janice Gross. "Deterrence and Reassurance." In Philip E. Tetlock et al. (eds.), *Behavior, Society, and Nuclear War*, Vol. 2, 8–72. Oxford University Press, 1991.

Steinhardt, Jacob, Pang Wei W. Koh, and Percy S. Liang. "Certified Defenses for Data Poisoning Attacks." In *Advances in Neural Information Processing Systems*, 3517–3529. 2017.

Sterlin, A. E., A. A. Protasov, and Kreidin S. V. "Sovremennye transformatsii kontseptsii i silovykh instrumentov strategicheskogo sderzhivaniia." *Voennaia mysl'* 8 (2019), 7–17.

Sterling, Leon and Ehud Shapiro. *The Art of Prolog Programming.* MIT Press, 1986.

Stork, David G. "Scientist on the Set: An Interview with Marvin Minsky." In David G. Stork (ed.), *HAL's Legacy: 2001's Computer as Dream and Reality*, 15–31. MIT Press, 1997.

Suh, Kyungwon. "Nuclear Balance and the Initiation of Nuclear Crises: Does Superiority Matter?" *Journal of Peace Research* (2022).

Sutton, H. I. *Cephalopod.* 2018. URL: http://www.hisutton.com/Cephalopod.html.

Sutyagin, Igor. "Russia's Underwater 'Doomsday Drone': Science Fiction, But Real Danger." *Bulletin of the Atomic Scientists* 72.4 (2016), 243–246.

Tarski, Alfred. "The Concept of Truth in Formalized Languages." *Logic, Semantics, Metamathematics* 2.152–278 (1956), 7.

Tertrais, Bruno. "Russia's Nuclear Policy: Worrying for the Wrong Reasons." *Survival* 60.2 (2018), 33–44.

Tirpak, John A. "Find, Fix, Track, Target, Engage, Assess." *Air Force Magazine* 83.7 (2000), 24–29.

Trachtenberg, Marc. *History and Strategy.* Princeton University Press, 1991.

Tsipis, Kosta, and Bernard Taub Feld. *The Future of the Sea-based Deterrent.* MIT Press, 1973.

Turchin, Alexey. *Narrow AI Nanny: Reaching Strategic Advantage via Narrow AI to Prevent Creation of the Dangerous Superintelligence.* https://philpapers.org/rec/TURNAN-3. 2018.

Tversky, Amos. "Intransitivity of Preferences." *Psychological Review* 76.1 (1969), 31.

Tyler, Gordon D. "The Emergence of Low-Frequency Active Acoustics as a Critical Antisubmarine Warfare Technology." *Johns Hopkins APL Technical Digest* 13.1 (1992), 145–159.

Tzu, Sun. "The Art of War." In *Strategic Studies*, 86–110. Routledge, 2014.

Van Evera, Stephen. "Offense, Defense, and the Causes of War." *International Security* 22.4 (1998), 5–43.

Vedernikov, Iu. V. *Sravnitel'nyi analiz sozdaniia i razvitiia morskikh strate-gicheskikh iadernyh sil SSSR i SShA.* 2005.

Vick, Alan, and Richard M. Moore. *Aerospace Operations against Elusive Ground Targets.* RAND Corporation, 2001.

Vincent, James. *Facebook's Head of AI Wants Us to Stop Using the Terminator to Talk about AI.* 2017. URL: https://www.theverge.com/2017/10/26/16552056/a-intelligence-terminator-facebook-yann-lecun-interview.

Von Clausewitz, Carl. *On War*, trans. by J. J. Graham. N. Trübner, 1873.

Vonnegut, Kurt. *Player Piano*. Scribners, 1952.

Walker, Henry M. *The Limits of Computing*. Jones and Bartlett Publishers, 1994.

Waltz, Kenneth N. *Theory of International Politics*. Waveland Press, 1979.

Wang, Ruijia, et al. "High-Performance Anti-Retransmission Deception Jamming Utilizing Range Direction Multiple Input and Multiple Output (MIMO) Synthetic Aperture Radar (SAR)." *Sensors* 17.1 (2017), 123.

WarGames. (Film.) 1983.

Warrick, Patricia S. *The Cybernetic Imagination in Science Fiction*. MIT Press, 1980.

Weisgerber, Marcus. *Air Force Secretary Warns of China's Burgeoning Nuclear Arsenal, Reveals B-21 Detail*. https://www.defenseone.com/threats/2021/09/air-force-secretary-warns-chinas-burgeoning-nuclear-arsenal-reveals-b-21-detail/185486/. Sept. 2021.

Wellerstein, Alex. *Restricted Data: The History of Nuclear Secrecy in the United States*. University of Chicago Press, 2021.

Wiener, Norbert. *The Human Use of Human Beings: Cybernetics and Society*. Houghton Mifflin, 1950.

Wiesner, Jerome B., and Herbert F. York. "National Security and the Nuclear-Test Ban." *Scientific American* 211.4 (1964), 27–35.

Wilson, Andrew. *The Bomb and the Computer: Wargaming from Ancient Chinese Mapboard to Atomic Computer*. Delacorte, 1968.

Wohlstetter, Albert. "Analysis and Design of Conflict Systems." In E. S. Quade (ed.), *Analysis for Military Decisions*, 103–148. Rand McNally, 1966.

Wohlstetter, Albert. "The Delicate Balance of Terror." *Foreign Affairs* 37 (1959), 211.

Wohlstetter, Roberta. *Pearl Harbor: Warning and Decision*. Stanford University Press, 1962.

Wolfe, Bernard. *Limbo*. Hachette UK, 2016.

Wolfe, Bernard. "Self Portrait." *Galaxy* 11 (1951).

Zadeh, Lotfi A. "A Simple View of the Dempster-Shafer Theory of Evidence and Its Implication for the Rule of Combination." *AI Magazine* 7.2 (1986), 85–90.

Zadeh, Lotfi A. "Fuzzy Logic and Approximate Reasoning." *Synthese* 30.3– 4 (1975), 407–428.

Zadeh, Lotfi A. "Review of *A Mathematical Theory of Evidence*." *AI Magazine* 5.3 (1984), 83.

Zakvasin, Aleksei, and Elizabeta Komarova. "'Mgnovennoe porazhenii tseli': kakimi vozmozhnostiami obladaet boevoi lazer 'Peresvet." Dec. 2019. URL: https://russian.rt.com/russia/article/699378-peresvet-lazer-boevoe-dezhurstvo.

Zenil, Hector. *A Computable Universe: Understanding and Exploring Nature as Computation*. World Scientific, 2013.

Zhao, Tong. *Tides of Change*. Tech. rep. Carnegie Endowment for International Peace, 2018.

Zhou, Feng, et al. "A Novel Method for Adaptive SAR Barrage Jamming Suppression." *IEEE Geoscience and Remote Sensing Letters* 9.2 (2012), 292–296.

Zvezda, Telekanal. *Voennaia priemka*. "Iars. Iadernaia raketa sderzhivaniia." Chast' 2. 2019. URL: https://www.youtube.com/watch?v=B3upvVJwv5k.

Index